# JAVA

## WITH

# BORLAND C++

# JAVA

## WITH

# BORLAND C++

CHRIS H. PAPPAS / WILLIAM H. MURRAY

**AP Professional**
**AP Professional is a division of Academic Press, Inc.**

**Boston San Diego New York**
**London Sydney Tokyo Toronto**

**AP PROFESSIONAL**
An Imprint of ACADEMIC PRESS, INC.
A Division of HARCOURT BRACE & COMPANY

**ORDERS (USA and Canada):** 1-800-3131-APP or APP@ACAD.COM
**AP Professional Orders:** 6277 Sea Harbor Dr., Orlando, FL 32821-9816

**Europe/Middle East/Africa:** 0-11-44 (0) 181-300-3322
**Orders:** AP Professional 24–28 Oval Rd., London NW1 7DX

**Japan/Korea:** 03-3234-3911-5
**Orders:** Harcourt Brace Japan, Inc., Ichibancho Central Building 22-1, Ichibancho Chiyoda-Ku, Tokyo 102

**Australia:** 02-517-8999
**Orders:** Harcourt Brace & Co. Australia, Locked Bag 16, Marrickville, NSW 2204, Australia

**Other International:** (407) 345-3800
**AP Professional Orders:** 6277 Sea Harbor Dr., Orlando FL 32821-9816

**Editorial:** 1300 Boylston St., Chestnut Hill, MA 02167 (617) 232-0500

**Web**: http://www.apnet.com/approfessional

This book is printed on acid-free paper. (∞)




*United Kingdom Edition published by*
ACADEMIC PRESS LIMITED
24–28 Oval Road, London NW1 7DX



**Library of Congress Cataloging-in-Publication Data**
Pappas, Chris H., 1953-
Java with Borland C++ / Chris H. Pappas, William H. Murray.
p. cm.
ISBN 0-12-511960-7 (alk. paper)
1. Java (Computer program language) 2. Borland C++. I. Murray, William H., 1943- II. Title
QA76.73.J38P36 1996
005.2--dc20 96-27899
CIP

Printed in the United States of America
96 97 98 99 IP 9 8 7 6 5 4 3 2 1

Dedication:

*Chris H. Pappas -->* *Toni Ferro and Kathy Ferro Weiss*

*William H. Murray -->* *Dr. Frank X. Sutman, Temple University*

# Contents

# 1

# Quick Get Me Started—An Introduction to Java

If you have picked this book off the shelf, you already know the latest buzz word, *Java*, and unless you work at Sun Microsystems, Inc. (birthplace of the Java language), the only associations you currently have to the word Java percolate through a dark brown liquid that helps you meet your programming deadlines. In a way, this is the perfect metaphor for the Java Language—a tool given to programmers, designed to help you meet your programming deadlines!

## WHO INVENTED JAVA?

Knowing *who* invented a programming language is pivotal to your understanding the capabilities of that language. Successful *new* languages solve problems left unresolved by older technologies. With today's accelerated rate of software and hardware development, there are now many programming problems which older languages are incapable of solving, for example C and

C++, developed by Dennis Ritchie and Bjarne Stroustrup. These languages were originally invented to design operating systems (on the DEC PDP-11 with UNIX) and to provide the modular, portable, reusable, and easy up-to-speed implementations generated by object-oriented technologies. However, as you will soon learn, in many ways C/C++ are inappropriate for today's state-of-the-art development environment—the Internet.

Java was developed by a small programming team headed by James Gosling at Sun Microsystems, Inc. in Mountain View, California. The team's goal was to solve one problem, design a language for programming consumer products. This new language did not necessarily have to be breakneck fast at run time, but it did need to work on a diverse set of devices and require minimal hardware overhead.

For example, a microprocessor-controlled VCR does not need a Pentium or PowerPC microprocessor to calculate recording start and stop times. However, with today's burgeoning interconnections, soon you will have the capability of dialing your home phone and instructing your telephone-connected VCR to catch a late-breaking story—the latter capability requiring a rather sophisticated computer algorithm. And with cost of manufacturing, always the bottom line, manufacturers know consumers won't want to pay hundreds of dollars more for these features.

Many of today's existing computer languages fell short of this design team goal, even C and C++. The biggest problem with all currently available languages is that they all have to be compiled for a particular computer chip. Not only does the original source file need compiling to a specific platform, but with new chip designs being gestated in less than nine months, all existing software must be recompiled in order to take full advantage of new hardware advancements.

As an application developer, you may have to recompile, or worse, rewrite your source code, for another reason than hardware advancements. What if the compiler itself is updated? For example, once a C/C++ program is compiled, it is not easily adapted to use new software libraries. Often, the programs have to be rewritten and recompiled from scratch when the libraries change. This naturally would make it very difficult for a manufacturer to patch or update the program in your microprocessor-controlled lawn-mower. One of today's solutions to this scenario is Java.

As tradition has it, the name for this new language was the direct result of the development team's frustrating, afternoon-long, name-the-language, brainstorming session. James Gosling had originally called this new language Oak, reportedly named after the tree outside his office window. Unfortunately or fortunately, the name Oak was already a registered programming language. The ensuing coffee break at the local coffee shop lead to the stimulating name—Java! The official announcement of the Java technology was made in May 1995 at the SunWorld conference in San Francisco.

## Why Do YOU Need Java?

Do you want to *get* a job? Do you want to *keep* your job? Do you want to have *fun* programming for a change? Do you want to use a language that's *easy to learn*? Do you want a *state-of-the-art Internet presence*? Then YOU need Java! While Java's original design goal was for programming consumer devices, its real horsepower breaks the gate when you use it to program for the Internet. Whether you are IBM, Microsoft, Apple, a local distributor, or one of hundreds of thousands of individuals with a home page on the World Wide Web, you will quickly become addicted to the fun and useful features Java can add to your Internet presence.

## What Is HotJava?

Beginning in early 1993 the Internet went from a text-based to a graphical interface. It immediately occurred to the Java development team that a hardware-neutral language, such as Java, would be ideal for programming on the World Wide Web. Java code was the ideal solution since it would run on the many types of computers hooked into the Internet, from PCs to Macs to UNIX. This led to the development of a Web browser called *HotJava* which was the first Web browser capable of supporting

Java. In May 1995, at the SunWorld conference in San Francisco, Marc Andreessen, founder of Netscape Communications, announced that their very popular *Netscape Navigator Web browser* would support Java.

## What Are Java's Strengths?

In a nutshell—Java's major strengths are that it is a relatively fast, small, and reliable language that is hardware neutral. This means that you can write one Java source file that is compiled and shipped "as is" to any Java-supported architecture. Java is similar to C, C++, Pascal, and Modula-3. Java's small size makes it easy to learn from scratch, and especially easy for those programmers already familiar with the C and C++ languages. Java even goes one step further in that it solves, or actually prevents, many of the most nefarious sources of bugs found in C and C++ applications, namely memory leaks. Finally, not only is Java simple to use, but it is object oriented, statically typed, compiled, hardware neutral, multithreaded, garbage collected, robust, secure, extensible, and fun!

## What Are Java's Weaknesses?

Look out anytime you meet a programmer that tells you language *XYZ* is *the* defacto standard, the language that solves all your programming needs, and *the* language for today and into the next millennium. The gurus at Sun Microsystems, Inc. would almost have us believe that Java fits this description. However, no such language has ever been invented, nor, with the pace of technoevolution, will it *ever* be invented! Beware, Java is not for everyone, or every application. It will not replace *any* language used today. For the majority of readers, instead, Java will easily and richly enhance your presence on the World Wide Web. There are four major weaknesses to the Java Language:

1. Most readers will not use Java for anything other than enhancing their World Wide Web presence. While it is true that Java is capable of designing standalone applications, most readers are already well versed in

an existing language which would serve this purpose, without the effort required to master a new language like Java.

2. Java will not run on *all* microprocessors, only those microprocessors for which Sun Microsystems, Inc. has translated the Java language. As of this writing, Java will run on IBM-PCs and IBM compatibles, Macs, and UNIX machines.
3. The more complex your Java application (in the sense of multimedia, multithreaded applets), the slower its run-time performance.
4. Because it is *similar* to other languages such as C/C++, Pascal, and Modula-3, yet *different*, Java throws a curve to any programmer experienced in those other languages. This is because every Java feature does not necessarily behave the same as its other language predecessor.

## WHAT CAN I USE JAVA FOR?

What can *you* use Java for? The answer is, just about anything, from standalone Java applications to multimedia World Wide Web Java applets. For example, publishing companies are now taking a serious look at publishing systems via the Internet. The leisurely pastime of reading a magazine article, in hand, will be supplanted by the same material displayed on-line. Many companies are just beginning to discover the profit potential of on-line catalogs.

Other companies, such as National Semiconductor Corp., have found that making the real-time updates of technical information, for their more than 30,000 products, available on-line has dramatically improved sales. Finally, companies like Market Vision Corp. (security trading) didn't miss a beat in this fast-paced arena of multimedia, Internet opportunities, since they incorporated a Java applet front end that communicates directly with Market Vision's Link (up-to-the-minute stock information). This platform-independent solution provides access to any user with an Internet browser—not just Market Vision's own products.

While Java is capable of much more in an industrial setting, the majority of programmers will use Java to quickly, easily, and enjoyably add punch and pizzazz to their World Wide Web home page. The intention of this book is to show you just how easy and fun this is to accomplish.

## What's the Difference Between Applications and Applets?

In short, Java *applications* are standalone Java programs that are run by using just the Java interpreter, for example, from the command line:

```
c:javajava myclass.class
```

The first few example programs you write will fall under this category.

Java *applets*, however, are run from inside a World Wide Web browser. A reference to an applet is embedded in a Web page using a special HTML (Hyper Text Markup Language) tag. When a reader, using a Java-aware browser, loads a Web page with an applet in it, the browser downloads that applet from a Web server and executes it on the local system (the one running the browser). Because Java applets run inside the Java browser, they have access to the same capabilities that the browser has: sophisticated graphics, drawing, image processing, networking, and event handling. Java applications can also take advantage of these features, but they do not require them.

## Main Features of the Java Language

You may have heard the phrase, "something old, something new, something borrowed, something...." In a way, this describes Java. Java incorporates many of the programming fundamentals found in older, existing programming languages, such as Pascal and C. Java adds its own unique blend of new characteristics, for example, firewall protection (determining resource access privileges for Java applets), and completes its formal definition by borrowing from object-oriented design philosophy. The following section describes Java in greater detail.

## Easy to Learn

Some things never change. Take human nature for instance. While we all know that exercise is good for us, most of us have trouble sticking to a regimented exercise routine. While we all know that multitasking, object-oriented, GUI (graphical user interface) Window applications are state-of-the-art, their development demands the mastery of many new things, from OOP design philosophy to learning C++.

Many companies, relying on the human trait to resist anything new and/or difficult, have profitably come to the programmer's rescue. Take for instance Borland's Delphi or Microsoft's Visual C++. These development tools take away some of the burden of Windows application development by presenting the programmer with a point-and-click environment automatically generating the required code. From the programmer's perspective, these products actually replace the tedious Windows development phase with a product that is, well, *fun* to use! The same holds true for Java.

Java is a pleasant, easy-to-learn synthesis of many existing and successful languages, such as Pascal, Modula-3, C, and C++. For many programmers, this means that Java source code will already have a familiar look to it. From day one, Sun Microsystem, Inc.'s design goals were to keep Java small, simple, easy to write, easy to compile, easy to debug, and yes, most important, easy to learn. Keeping the language small also makes it more robust because there are fewer chances for programmers to make difficult-to-find mistakes. However, despite its size and simple design, Java still has a great deal of power and flexibility. Although Java looks similar to C and C++, most of the more complex parts of those languages have been excluded from Java, making the language simpler without sacrificing much of its bite.

Specifically, Java is missing C++'s pointers and the related topic of pointer arithmetic. Strings and arrays are real objects in Java. Memory management is automatic. To an experienced C/C++ programmer, these omissions may be difficult to get used to, but to beginners or programmers who have worked in other languages, they make the Java language far easier to master.

## Is Both Compiled and Interpreted

Who ever said, "There's nothing new under the Sun." You know that in the world of computer languages, well at least until Java, there are interpreted languages, such as BASIC, and many more languages that are compiled. You may even know, technically, that assembly language source code is *assembled*. But you have probably never heard, or conceived, of a language that is both compiled and interpreted! Welcome to Java. You *compile* a Java source file into a platform-independent binary form, officially called *bytecode*. It is this bytecode file that is then *interpreted* by a platform-specific Java run-time environment.

This two-step process allows you to develop and maintain a single source of Java code, generating the hardware-neutral compiled bytecode, which in turn runs on many platform-specific Java environments. For example, you develop a single Java application and compile it. You can then run the same application on a PC, UNIX, or Mac, as long as each has a platform-specific Java environment—one Java source file, many architectures.

Technically speaking, the compiled, binary bytecode file contains more compile-time data than is usually found in noninterpreted languages. This extra information is carried over and made available at run time, providing checks for security, robustness, and even debugging. Most important, the interpretation phase of the binary bytecode frees developers from having to worry about version mismatch problems so common to most development environments. Java uses something similar to the UNIX make tool to resolve inconsistent definitions for module interfaces, allowing developers to maintain a single source collection of Java code that easily moves to multiple targets. During interpolation, Java even allows information to be included from the run-time environment providing dynamic behavior.

## Is Hardware Neutral

One of the key features of Java programs compared with other programming languages, particularly for systems that need to work on many different platforms, is that Java is *hardware neutral*. Java is hardware neutral, or platform independent at both the source and binary levels. At the source level, Java's primitive data types have consistent sizes across all architectures. Java's standardized class libraries make it easy to write code that can be moved from machine to machine without the need to generate machine-specific versions.

Beyond source level independence is Java's hardware-neutral binary files, called bytecode, which run on multiple platforms without the need to recompile the source. You can use the compiled bytecode with the Java interpreter by itself (for Java applications), or use the bytecode interpreter incorporated into Hotjava, or any other Java-capable browser (for Java applets), like Netscape.

## Is Portable

Java's hardware neutrality is one of the big reasons why a Java program is so portable. However, another aspect of portability deals with Java's formal use of data structures or types in the language, such as integer, string, and floating point. This is possible since Java takes advantage of the IEEE standards for common data types of many computers.

For example, a Java float always complies with the IEEE 754 standard for floating-point numbers, with integers always being a 32-bit, signed two's complement value. Java's hardware-neutral bytecode also takes care of the memory mapping of low byte at low address, high byte at high address, and vice versa issues, presented by different types of architectures. For example, Intel-based PCs use low byte at low address/high byte at high address ordering, but Motorola-based PCs use the reverse.

However, not only is Java internally portable, it is also run-time environment portable. The Java compiler is written in Java itself, while the run-time environment is written in ANSI C and sports a well-defined and succinct portability interface. The POSIX standardization effort was a huge influence on Java's portability interface. The result? Implementing an abstract Java Window class object with its associated methods that will run on a PC, UNIX, or Mac computer goes straight to the bottom line because it eliminates redundant implementation, testing, and maintenance efforts altogether.

## Is Robust

The term *robust* usually refers to the degree to which an application can handle all circumstances, expected and unexpected. The more robust, the better the application is at withstanding all types of assaults. Less robust applications are typically plagued by one very annoying characteristic, they crash! The great news is that Java applications cannot cause a computer to crash. The Java system carefully checks each memory access to make sure that it is legal and won't cause any fatal errors.

Of course, things can go wrong and when they do, rather than crashing, a Java program throws an *exception*. Java language features allow for the trapping of these detected error conditions, allowing the program to recover successfully. Finally, some of Java's robustness is a direct result of a Java program's inability to change those portions of a computer's memory critical to system performance.

## Is Dynamically Linked

*Dynamic linking*, sometimes referred to as *delayed binding*, provides the utmost in programmer flexibility by not incorporating compiled subroutine code into the application's .exe file. Instead, at run time any called subroutines are brought into the processor as needed. This has many advantages, from minimizing the size of the executable to not overloading system resources with subroutines which may never be invoked. Dynamic linking also allows Java programs to adapt to changing computing environments.

Experienced object-oriented C++ programmers know that a typical program may rely heavily upon class libraries supplied by third-party vendors. Sometimes these necessary libraries ship with the operating system. Should the vendor upgrade these libraries, existing applications cannot take advantage of the code changes until the application's source code is recompiled. This takes time and money and assumes you actually have access to the original code.

Java programs circumvent this bottleneck by delaying the binding of modules. This allows programmers to take full advantage of object-oriented programming concepts, since new methods (fancy word for a function bound exclusively to a particular object), and instances (another fancy object-oriented term that simply means variable), for an existing class in a library can be added without crashing the current application.

Technically speaking, this is all possible since Java uses interfaces which specify interobject interaction, while excluding any instance variables or implementation methods. Each Java class (or object) has a run-time representation that allows programmers to query the class type. The application can then decide whether or not to dynamically link the necessary class. These run time representations also allow the run-time environment to check data structure casts at compile time as well as at run time, providing yet another layer of error detection. This feature, known as RTTI (Runtime Type Identification), is not specifically available to C++ application developers.

## Is Verified

Since there are many good programming languages, already known by most readers, available for writing standalone applications, you are most likely to use Java to enhance your World Wide Web presence. Because Java applets are downloaded to your computer and executed automatically, you may be concerned that there is the potential of infecting your machine with a virus. However, this is not the case. Java applets cannot extract information or damage your computer. (Users can set how they want Java to enforce security by selecting from one of four *firewalls*: no access, Applet Host, Firewall, and Unrestricted—these topics will be discussed thoroughly in later chapters.)

Java's security comes from its two-phase compile/interpret process. Phase one compiles the Java source code into easily verified bytecode instructions. While bytecode is very similar to other instruction sets used by computers, yet hardware neutral, it can be easily checked for potential security violations. Technically, this is possible since bytecode contains additional type information that is used to double-check that the program is legal.

Phase two security comes from the way Java interprets the bytecode. While most programming languages access functions by memory address, Java uses a totally different approach. Java methods and variables are always accessed by name. This makes it easy to determine what methods and functions are actually used. This process is called *verification*. Only after the bytecode is verified does the Java interpreter convert function names into addresses.

Even after the bytecode is verified, it must still behave itself by executing in a restricted environment. Java applets are prohibited from calling certain OS critical functions unless given specific permission to do so. This set of checks and balances prevents the applet from breaking out of the restricted environment.

## Is Object Oriented

Java is exclusively object oriented. Although C++ is also considered object oriented, C++ allows programmers to solve problems using a procedural approach. Java, however, forces the programmer to accept object orientation from the beginning, eliminating the problem of combining two dissimilar design philosophies. Of course, in maintaining the look and feel of C++, it is easy to look at Java in terms of what it does and does not have in common with C++. In many cases, Java eliminates redundancies from C to C++, and particularly any links to procedural design concepts. What Java added was automatic boundary checking, by eliminating the use of pointers and encapsulating arrays within a class structure, and automatic garbage collection, in addition to many other features that made developing a C++ application so difficult.

## Is Multithreaded

Depending on your experience with operating systems and with environments within those systems, you may not have run into the concept of threads. For example, when a program runs, it starts executing, runs its initialization code, calls subroutines (or object-oriented methods), and continues running and processing until it's done performing all required tasks. This is an example of a single-threaded program.

*Multithreading* enables several different execution threads to run at the same time, inside the same program, without interfering with each other. For example, a program may have to calculate a value using a time-consuming equation. However, the result of the equation is not needed instantaneously. A multithreaded program begins immediately to solve the equation, while simultaneously performing some other task.

Using threads in Java, you can create an applet that runs by itself without interfering with any other part of the system. Using threads, you can also have lots of applets running at once on the same page. The general rule is for an applet to use a thread for each process that is likely to continue for a long period of time, for example, an animation loop.

## Prevents Memory Leaks

Java incorporates automatic garbage collection. This built-in memory management, in addition to the built-in multithreading features of Java, makes it an ideal language to program in. Unlike C++, which allows a programmer to write code at a very low level, enabling C++ programs to access the hardware and calculate specific memory addresses and making the C++ program platform specific. Java eschewed this philosophy by ensuring that portability could be maintained by providing for all bounds checking and memory management. At the same time, Java maintained its respectable performance by adding built-in threading that could perform much of the garbage collection in a background process, simultaneously guaranteeing a robust and efficient algorithm.

## Is Client-Server Ready

At the heart of client-server applications is the distribution and sharing of information and workload. This client-server characteristic describes relationships between system objects that may be on a local or host system. In the case of the World Wide Web, this client-server relationship takes advantage of both information sharing and workload distribution. Java incorporates TCP/IP procedures in both the Java source and binary distribution code. This makes it easy for programmers to access remote information using protocols such as HTTP and FTP. Other protocols, such as gopher, news, and mailto, are well understood in the World Wide Web world but have not yet been implemented in the Java language.

### Is Fast!

Java is a lot more efficient than typical scripting languages, but currently it is about twenty times slower than C. However, for most applications, Java performance is acceptable. Even as you read this, Sun Microsystems, Inc. is working on future code generators that will make Java programs execute as fast as programs written in C and C++.

## JAVA FUTURE

With the growing acceptance of and appreciation for all that Java can do, more and more programming solutions are being coded in Java. This exponential growth is driving the continual evolution of the Java language. While you are reading this, Sun Microsystems, Inc. is furiously working on tweaking Java's performance characteristics, while third-party vendors continue inventing new uses and assumable characteristics. Two such evolving capabilities are persistence and virtual reality.

### Persistence

Persistence, as it applies to Internet-based executable code, implies that your computer can permanently host that code (usually via download to your hard drive). Internet-based executable code will be available, thanks to new features being added to the Java language. Currently, in the Sun Microsystems, Inc. and Netscape team-up, Internet-based executable code is downloaded to the browser's virtual machine for interpretation, but not to the machine itself or its local storage. This lack of persistence is one of Java's most redeeming qualities. Since Java applets have no access to the local system or any of its resources, Java applications pose no security threat to the user.

However, persistence has its good side, too. Persistent code is downloaded only once. With the majority of users now accessing the Internet over 28.8K-bps modem links, Sun Microsystems, Inc. is aware of this bandwidth bottleneck and is now working on Java persistence.

## Virtual Reality

The move toward interactive, three-dimensional World Wide Web sites took a major step forward with the official proposals for the upgrade to the "Moving Worlds" VRML specification. The specification, originally created by Silicon Graphics Inc., is being proposed for the next version of the Virtual Reality Markup Language (VRML) standard, Release 2.0., and is backed by nearly 50 vendors, including Borland International, Inc., Netscape Communications Corp., IBM, Adobe Systems Inc., and Apple Computer, Inc.

Moving Worlds would allow Web site authors to create virtual worlds that support interactivity, motions, and "behaviors." VRML 1.0 provides only an open specification for creating 3-D sites through which users can navigate. Right now, the Web is noninteractive, and behaviors add a human element to a nonhuman world. The interactive environments as a class will enable better information sharing, such as teleconferencing or shared white boards over the Internet. This new interactivity is based on Sun Microsystems, Inc.'s Java programming language, which will eventually be incorporated into the Java language, enabling users to view VRML sites, as well as add 3-D extensions to Java.

# Borland International and Java

Borland International has been known for providing one of the best, if not *the* best, programming development environments for over a decade. Borland products are known as *the* standard by which all user-friendly, programming development environments are compared. Going all the way back to the mythical miner in the hills who developed Turbo Pascal, all the way to today's state-of-the-art sophisticated Borland C++, Borland International's IDE (Integration Development Environment) is infamous.

Designed to anticipate, streamline, and automate many of the mundane tasks presented to programmers, Borland's IDE makes programming as painless as a trip to a dentist using nitrous oxide. That is why Borland International's association with Sun Microsystems, Inc. is so exciting. Not only is the Java language itself fun and easy to learn, but it has now been combined with the best development environment ever invented, Borland's IDE!

Throughout this book you will be shown just how easy the IDE makes it for you to write, compile, debug, and test your Java programs. And as an added bonus, if you are already familiar with any of Borland International's other programming development environments, such as Turbo Pascal, Turbo C, or Borland C++, well—you already know most of the IDE commands needed to develop and use Java, since they are identical.

## Hot Spots on the Internet

The following list contains http:// World Wide Web sites to help get you routed to some up-to-the-minute locations specific to Java and HotJava. To access links to companies, contests, Java events, guides, tutorials, mailing lists, utilities, user groups, and more, point to http://www.yahoo.com/Computers_and_Internet/Languages/Java/.

Want a Java reality check? The Making Sense of Java site (http://reality.sgi.com/employees/shiffman_engr/Java-QA.html) addresses some common claims and beliefs about Java and describes how accurate the claims are and where they go astray.

And, of course, be sure to check out some of the Java discussion groups. Developers of full-blown, industrial-strength Java applications (as opposed to applets) should try the STRONG-JAVA Mailing List. To subscribe, point to http://www.entmp.org/cgi-bin/lwgate/STRONG-JAVA/.

For just a little support, the Mid-Atlantic Java User Group (http://www.rssi.com/info/majug.html) or the Sacramento Java Users Group (http://www.calweb.com/~statenet/sacjug/) could be for you.

If you are concerned about security issues, try pointing your Web browser to http://www.cs.princeton.edu/~ddean/java/ for information on Java applets that can be used to attack networks behind firewalls.

## What You Need to Get Started Writing Java Code

The following configuration is recommended for the most positive experience you can have enjoying this new language:

- Pentium processor—90 MHz or better
- Windows 95
- 16 MB RAM
- 1 gig hard drive
- CD ROM drive
- 28.8 bps modem
- Internet access account (via America Online, Microsoft Network, CompuServe)
- BCWJAVA—(Borland C++ for Windows with Java)

## Java Lingo—A Dictionary of New Terms

*applet*—Java applets are dynamic, interactive programs, that can run inside a World Wide Web page. Java applets are Java programs that are downloaded over the World-Wide Web and executed by a Web browser on the reader's machine. Running Java applets requires a Java-capable browser such as HotJava (which is an example of a standalone Java application, written in Java) or Netscape 2.0. Borland C++'s Java compiler BCWJAVA ships with an AppletViewer for reader system viewing of Java applets. (Note: A single Java source file may be written to be an applet or an application—see the following definition of application.)

*application*—Java applications are more general programs written in the Java language. Java applications don't need a Web browser to run, and in fact, Java can be used to create most other types of applications written in more conventional programming languages such as Pascal, C, and C++. (Note: A single Java source file may be written to be an applet or an application—see above definition of applet.)

*bytecode*—Java source code is first compiled into a hardware-neutral form called bytecode. Bytecode is almost native machine code but not quite. The "not quite" part allows it to be hardware neutral. At run time, this bytecode is executed by a Java interpreter. So Java is both a compiled and an interpreted language.

*class*—Class is an object-oriented concept. Simply stated, a class is a higher order of record or structure. Many languages have a record or structure syntax that allows programmers to uniquely combine standard data types into new and useful, application-specific types. However, any procedures or functions working on the fields or members of a record or structure physically remain exterior to the record or structure definition. This makes it difficult to reuse these new type definitions, and their associated behaviors, because they are spread throughout your source code. Classes have a syntax that physically bundles a record or structure's data members *with* their associated function members. With this new syntax, a class behaves more like a complete miniprogram.

*firewall*—A firewall delimits which host system resources are available to a Java applet. Users can set how they want Java to enforce security by selecting from one of four *firewalls*: no access, Applet Host, Firewall, and Unrestricted.

*hardware neutral*—A Java application/applet is able to run on PowerPC, Intel, and MIPS, microprocessor-based PCs—in other words, the Java source code is hardware independent. This eliminates an application developer's need to reinvent an application for IBM-compatible, Mac, and UNIX-based machines.

*inheritance*—Many older high-level languages allow one record or structure definition to include, as one of its fields or members, a previously defined record or structure. This concept is known as nesting. Exactly the same concept is involved in inheritance, only inheritance is an object-oriented concept. Here, when one class is used to create another class, called a subclass, the subclass is said to inherit its parent's data members and function members. Java supports single-parent inheritance. Other languages such as C++ allow a subclass to inherit more than one parent's characteristics. This subtle difference isn't a problem if you have never programmed in an object-oriented language, but it does require some logical and syntactical restructuring for experienced OOPs programmers. These will be discussed in later chapters.

*instance*—Simply stated, the equivalent to creating variables in a procedure-oriented language is *instantiating* an object in object-oriented terms—same thing, new terminology. The instantiated object is referred to as the instance.

*instance variable*—Instance variables are class data members that are specific to a particular object instance.

*interface*—Many object-oriented languages allow a subclass to inherit more than one parent class's characteristics. This is not possible in Java, which allows only single-parent inheritance. However, when two separate classes need to perform some subset of common behaviors, they both define the same interface. An interface, therefore, is a syntactic way of collecting what would normally be disparate member functions.

*methods* or *member functions*—Although Java does not allow any function to be unassociated with a particular class, other high-level languages do (C++ for example). For programmers to distinguish verbally between functions not associated with a particular class and those that are associated with a particular class, there are new terms, method and member function. When a subroutine works only on a specific class, it is called a method or member function. In this context, simply using the term function tells another programmer the subroutine is standalone.

*overloading*—Subclasses are, by definition, children of some parent class's definition. Since the subclass inherits both the parent class's member data and member functions, there may come a time when the subclass will want the inherited member functions to do something different from the way they were originally written. With the proper syntax, you can override the parent class definition with an overloaded subclass member function. This process is called overloading.

*package*—All languages have some syntactic way to deal with scope or visibility issues. In other words, just where is which variable or function legally visible? Java solves the problem of visibility in one of two ways, either through the scope protection provided by the class syntax or by the use of packages. Whenever a Java class, has externally visible identifiers similar to some *other* previously defined Java class, collisions occur. The solution, logically relate all noninterfering class definitions into a package. Now, any reused, duplicate identifier names are protected within each separate package and no collisions occur.

*persistence*—Refers to a downloaded program's ability to run exclusively on the host computer. As of this writing Java applets have no persistence. However, Sun Microsystems, Inc. is updating the Java language to include this, sometimes necessary, feature.

*subclass*—A new class definition that is based on some previously defined class. The process of subclassing involves Java's object inheritance capabilities.

# 2

# Borland and Java

In this chapter you will learn the fundamental constructs of the Java language, its similarities to existing languages such as C and C++, and how its differences from these languages make Java the ideal development environment for today's programming needs. The chapter also describes how to easily install the Borland C++ Add-On for Java (BCAJ), along with a discussion of what comes with the Add-On for Java. By the time you are through with Chapter 2 you will be ready to begin knowledgeably using the Add-On for Java and writing understandable, introductory Java applications and applets.

## What Is Borland's Connection with Java?

The Borland C++ Add-On for Java (BCAJ) provides you with Java language development tools directly within Borland's C++ IDE. With BCAJ you can write, compile, debug, and view Java applications and applets from within the Borland C++ IDE. Borland International has provided Sun's complete Java Development Kit as part of this release.

## Similarity of Java to C/C++

Whether you are or are not an experienced C/C++ programmer, you will find Java's fundamental set of data types, standard operators, and logic control statements very familiar in operation to many existing high-level languages like Pascal, PL/I, and Moldula-3. Of course, of all of Java's ancestors, Java inherits most of its characteristics from C/C++. This naturally makes it easier for a C/C++ programmer to learn Java, but it also demands a little more attention for these individuals, since Java is not identical to C/C++. The following discussions help clarify Java's C/C++ similarities and differences.

## UNICODE

You have undoubtedly heard of the ASCII code, are probably aware of the EBCIDIC code, but may have never heard of UNICODE. The first two are industry agreed-upon mappings between the seven bits or eight bits in a byte and some human recognizable symbol. This relationship between binary language and human form is fine as long as you only want to code in English. However, the Internet is international. Fortunately, the computer industry has seen beyond cross-platform development (a hardware issue) to multilanguage development (a software concern) and invented the UNICODE.

The idea behind this new encryption standard was simple: come up with a new code that can represent every written language known today and any to be discovered! The only way to accomplish this Herculean task was to expand the number of bits used to map between the computer's binary language and all of the rest of the world's languages. All UNICODE characters occupy 2 bytes, or 16 bits of storage. This allows for 65,536 unique combinations of 0s and 1s, instead of just 256 (for ASCII/EBCIDIC), to which the UNICODE Standards Committee mapped every known language in the world today, leaving holes in the definition for yet undiscovered/translated symbols. Why is UNICODE important to you? Because all Java source files are written in UNICODE.

The Java compiler takes the source code written in UNICODE format and extracts individual elements known as *tokens*. These tokens can be divided into five major categories: *identifiers*, *keywords*, *literals*, *operands*, and *separators*. In addition, the compiler removes *comments* and *white spaces* (spaces, tabs, and line feeds), which are not a part of the token set. Each of these tokens is discussed in more detail in the next section.

## Comments

Every professionally written program contains meaningful documentation in the form of comments. Comments detail a program's creation date, any clarifications needed to understand the ensuing algorithm, and usually the programmer's name. A good comment neither insults the intelligence of a programmer (by stating the obvious) nor assumes too much. Of course, every program has its particular goals, such as minimum size, speed of execution, ease of maintenance, and so on, which dictate how the source code is created and documented. A good rule of thumb is to document any line of code that YOU, the author of the code, would have trouble explaining to someone else, or remembering how the code works, after not seeing the program for several weeks.

The Java compiler supports three styles of comments. The first is familiar to many languages such as Pascal and C and uses the symbol pairs /* and */. Because there are distinct opening /* and closing */ symbol pairs, this syntax allows you to easily create comments that span several lines:

```
/****************   ...  ***************/
* myfile.java                          */
* This Java file                       */
* Created:                             */
* Author:                              */
* Uses:                                */
* External Effects:                    */
****************   ...  ****************/
```

The second style of comments allowed in Java source code is similar to the syntax used in C++ programs and uses the double slash //. This style differs from the first in that there are no unique opening and closing comment symbol pairs. This style of comment, then, is necessarily terminated at the end of each line. The following comment has been rewritten taking this into consideration:

```
// **************    ...  ***************
// myfile.java                          */
// This Java file                        *
// Created:                              *
// Author:                               *
// Uses:                                 *
// External Effects:                     *
// **************    ...  ***************
```

Be careful when using this type of comment syntax, since all code to the right of the double slashes is ignored by the compiler:

```
float fTemp; // program uses Fahrenheit temperature scale
```

and remember that to make boxed comments, you must replicate the double slashes at the beginning of each comment line.

The third style of Java comment uses a rather unique syntax that begins with / and ends with */. These are special comments that are used for the *javadoc* system. Javadoc is used to generate API documentation from the code. You won't learn about javadoc in this book; you can find out more information from the documentation that came with Sun's Java Developer's Kit or from Sun's Java home page (http://java.sun.com).

## Identifiers

The term *identifier* applies to several categories of things in a program including variable (or instances in an object-oriented program) names, constant names, classes, and function (or methods in an object-oriented program) names. Every language has rules for how to construct legal identifiers. For a Java identifier to be legal it must:

1. Start with a letter* (upper-or lowercase), dollar sign, or an underscore character;
2. Continue with letters*, underscores, and the digits 0–9;

---

* *Letters are considered all the upper-and lowercase alphabet from A to Z, and all UNICODE characters with numbers above hex 00C0. This enables non-Latin characters such as Ç and ø to be used in names; however, characters such as ¶ are not included.*

3. Contain no embedded blanks;
4. Not be a reserved or keyword.

Also, like C/C++, Java is a case-sensitive language. This means that uppercase letters are seen as different from their lowercase counterparts. For example, the variable *SIZE* is seen as a different variable from one typed *size*. This case sensitivity allows you to create easily read, self-documenting source code. The following list illustrates several examples of legal identifier naming conventions:

```
String FirstName = "JoAnn";
String First_Name = "Charlie";
boolean Continue = true; // note: is a legal identifier since it starts with
                         // uppercase C not c, which would be the same
                         // as Java's reserved word continue and which would
                         // then make it an illegal identifier.
const int MAXIMUM_SIZE = 81;
```

One quick note about choosing a style for naming identifiers. There is a style known as Hungarian notation, originated by Charles Simony, at Bell Labs, Murray Hill, New Jersey. Chuck's naming convention goes like this: every identifier, no matter how it reads and whatever style you choose for them, is preceded by a mnemonic relating to the identifier's data type. For example, all Boolean variables would start with the letter b, shorts with s, integers with i, longs with l, floats with f, and so on.

The advantage of this naming convention, once you get used to it, is that you can look at any statement, *anywhere*, in a program and know each variable's data type. This has two immediate advantages. One, it saves you time by not having to track down a variable's declaring statement. Two, it lets you verify correctly written or detect incorrectly written statements in your, or someone else's, source code.

Look at the following data declarations. Each variable name begins with a reminder of its data type:

```
int iValueOne = 1, iValue2 = 2, iResult;
float fResult;
```

Now, look at the following two statements for clarity of meaning:

```
iResult = iValueOne * iValueTwo;
fResult = iValueOne * iValueTwo;
```

Now, while both statements are *legal*, certainly for any one particular application, only one is *logically* correct. But more important, notice how the Hungarian naming convention helps you immediately detect the matching (first statement), or mixed-mode operations (second statement) being performed. The alternative naming convention, seen below, speaks for itself, or better said, says nothing:

```
int ValueOne = 1, Value2 = 2, ResultA;
float ResultB;
```

Now, look at these two statements for clarity of meaning:

```
ResultA = ValueOne * ValueTwo;
ResultB = ValueOne * ValueTwo;
```

Without Hungarian notation, these two statements hide the data types of the source operands *ValueOne* and *ValueTwo*, along with the receiving variables', *ResultA* and *ResultB*, data type. Desk checks of these two statements mandate a time-consuming search for each identifier's declaring statement.

## Java Keywords

Table 2.1 lists the Java *keywords*, or reserved words, which are taught and demonstrated in the following chapters. Please note that due to the incredible popularity of the Java language, Sun Microsystems, Inc. is continually adding new features to Java. However, the following list represents the stable set of commands currently available.

## Standard Types

Since the only thing a computer understands is 0s and 1s, all computer languages define standard data types which instruct the compiler on how to map those 0s and 1s to values that mean something to us. These standard data types determine whether or not the value is character, string, or numeric, and for the last category, something about their precision. Some languages include additional data types which allow a programmer to represent logical Boolean states. The Java language has five standard data types: Boolean, character, integer, float,

**Table 2.1:** Java Keywords

| *abstract* | *do* | *implements* | *package* | *throw* |
|---|---|---|---|---|
| boolean | double | import | private | throws |
| break | else | inner | protected | transient |
| byte | extends | instanceof | public | try |
| case | final | int | rest | var |
| cast | finally | interface | return | void |
| catch | float | long | short | volatile |
| char | for | native | static | while |
| class | future | new | sure | |
| const | generic | null | switch | |
| continue | goto | operator | synchronized | |
| default | if | outer | this | |

and string. What is most important about these data types is that they are identical across all platforms, whether character (UNICODE) or numeric (IEEE floating-point format).

**Literals** Although not formally a standard data type, *literals* are frequently used with the standard data types for initialization or assignment purposes. There are three basic types of literals: numeric, character or string, and Boolean. Numeric literals can be subdivided into integral and floating point. The character literal refers to a single value of the UNICODE character set, whereas strings refer to collections of characters. To maintain compatibility with C/C++ the Boolean literal is included under numbers, since in C/C++ there was no Boolean data type; instead in C/C++ the integers 1 and 0 were used for logical true and false.

There are several integer literals, such as 5, which would fit in an **int** variable or one of type **byte** or **short**. A decimal integer literal larger than an **int** is automatically of type **long**. You can also force a smaller integer literal to a **long** data type by adding the letter 'l' or 'L' after it as in 5l or 5L. Negative integer literals are preceded by a minus sign as in -5. Any integer literal preceded by the number 0 is interpreted by the Java compiler as being an octal value in the numeric range of 00 to 07. Preceding an integer literal with a 0x, or 0X, instructs the Java compiler to view the literal in hexadecimal notation, as in 0xFFFF.

All floating-point literals contain an integer part and the decimal part. Java assigns all floating-point literals, for example 3.22198, a precision of **double** unless forced to **float** with an appended 'f' or 'F', 12.598f. Java also allows exponential notation with the letter 'e' or 'E', as in 2e8, or 10E -12.

A Boolean literal is either the keyword **true** or **false**. These keywords can be used anywhere you need a test or as the only possible values for **boolean** variables.

Java also provides string literals which represent a series of zero or more characters contained within double quotes. Java represents this type of literal in a very different way from C/C++. In C/C++, a string is an array of characters. In Java, a string literal is implemented as an object of type **String**. Here are examples of valid Java string literals:

```
"This is a complete string."
"This is a string that starts on one line and
continues on the next line."
"This is a string with a "Quote" in it!"
""    /* this is an empty string */
```

**Boolean** Java's **boolean** data type allows a programmer to declare a variable used for logical tests, such as:

```
boolean UserWantsToContinue = true; // initialized boolean declaration
.
.
.
while( UserWantsToContinue == true ) {
.
.
.
  if( inputValue == 10 )
    UserWantsToContinue = false;
.
.
.
}
```

And may only be assigned the keyword **true** or **false**. The **boolean** value is a true literal and not a representation of the integer 0 or 1 as in C/C++. These values are also *not* strings and cannot be coerced to the **String** data type.

**Character** Java uses the **char** keyword to define character variables. Character literals are distinguished in your source code by the single-quote marks surrounding them, as in 'a'. In addition, the backslash character is used to represent nonprinting or conflicting characters. All character literals can be any symbol defined in the UNICODE character set. Table 2.2 lists the control code interpretation applied to backslash-preceded symbol pairs:

Character variable declarations in Java take the following form:

```
char Gender; // unitialized character variable declaration
char DepartmentCode = 'P'; // initialized character variable declaration
```

**Integers** Java provides four standard integer data types, **byte**, **short**, **int**, and **long**. By default, all four types use signed notation, which means they can hold either positive or negative numbers. Which type you choose for your variable depends on the range of values you expect that variable to hold; if a value becomes too big for the variable's type, Java truncates it. Table 2.3 lists the four standard integer types and their signed numeric ranges.

**Table 2.2:** Control Code Interpretation

| *Interpretation* | *Representation* | *Code Pair** |
|---|---|---|
| Line continuation | <newline> | |
| New-line | NL(LF) | n |
| Horizontal tab | HT | t |
| Backspace | BS | b |
| Carriage return | CR | r |
| Form feed | FF | f |
| Backslash | | |
| Single quote | ' | ' |
| Double quote | " | " |
| Octal literal | 0ddd | ddd |
| Hexadecimal literal | 0xddd | xd or Xddd |
| Unicode literal | 0xdddd | udddd |

* *Note*: the a (bell) and v (vertical tab) control code sequences so familiar to C/C++ programmers are not supported by Java.

**Table 2.3:** Standard Integer Types

| *Standard Integer Type* | *Precision* | *Value Range* |
|---|---|---|
| **byte** | 8 bits | -128 to +127 |
| **short** | 16 bits | -32,768 to +32,767 |
| **int** | 32 bits | -2,147,483,648 to +2,147,483,647 |
| **long** | 64 bits | -9223372036854775808 to +9223372036854775807 |

The following code section illustrates several integer variable declarations and initializations:

```
byte ah_register = 0xFF;
short small_loop_control_variable = 0;
int small_jackpot;
long big_lottery_win = 50000000;
```

***Note:*** *There is no* ***unsigned*** *type specifier for integer data types in Java.*

**Floats** Java provides two floating-point precisions; **float** and **double**, used to represent decimal numbers with fractional parts such as 2.358 or 49.671. Floating-point literals can be expressed in either standard or scientific notation, for example:

```
float fValue;
double dValue;
fValue = 3.14159;
dValue = 3.14159e21;
dValue = 3.14159E21;
dValue = 1.2345e-20;
```

Variables declared to be of type **float** occupy 32 bits of storage, while variables of type **double** use 64-bit precision. Appending an 'f' or 'F' to a floating-point literal can force a **float** precision (1.298f), while appending a 'd' or 'D' can permute a **double** storage allocation (2.976D).

**String** Actually, Java does not directly support an official string data type; however, it does implement a **String** class, or object. Don't worry about the fact that **String**s are classes. Because of the very nature of classes, you don't need to worry about how to implement them—they take care of themselves.

You declare a string variable by preceding its name with the keyword **String**, as in:

```
String Full_Name; // uninitialized string variable
String Title = "A Tale of Two Cities"; // initialized string variable;
```

with each string literal creating a new instance of the class **String**.

There are actually two kinds of string objects: the **String** class is for read-only (immutable) objects. The **StringBuffer** class is for string objects you wish to modify (mutable string objects). Although strings are Java language objects, Java compiler follows the C tradition of providing a syntactic convenience that C programmers have enjoyed with C-style strings; namely, the Java compiler understands that a string of characters enclosed in double quote signs is to be instantiated as a **String** object. Thus, the declaration:

```
String HelloWorld = "Hello World!";
```

instantiates an object of the **String** class behind the scenes and initializes it with a character string containing the UNICODE character representation of "Hello World!". Java has extended the meaning of the + operator to indicate string concatenation. Thus you can write statements like:

```
System.out.println("There are " + num + " characters in the file.");
```

This code fragment concatenates the string "There are" with the result of converting the numeric value *num* to a string, and concatenates that with the string "characters in the file.". Then it prints the result of those concatenations on the standard output. Just as with array objects, **String** objects provide a **length()** accessor method to obtain the number of characters in the string.

## Placement of Variable Declarations

Where you place a variable's declaration affects where it is legally accessible within your source code. This visibility is referred to as a variable's *scope*. Java identifiers are said to have *block scope*. A *block* is defined by the two curly braces {}. The scope of a variable is from the point it was declared to the end of the block it is in. For example:

```
class MyApp {
  public static void main(String args[]) {
  main
    int iValue;
    ...
  }
  public void methodA() {
    char cValue;
    ...
  }
```

In this particular example *int iValue;* has been declared in the method **main()**. Because **main()**'s block does not include the *methodA()* block, any reference to *iValue* in *methodA()* would be an error. The same would go for *char cValue*. Since *cValue* was defined within *methodA()*'s block, accessing it in **main()** would be illegal.

***Note:*** *Java treats local redeclarations of same-named identifiers the way most older high-level languages do. This means that reusing the same identifier name inside a block, which is nested inside another block, is legal. However, any reference to the identifier within the nested block refers only to the local redefinition. For example, the following code section redefines iValue within the* ***while*** *loop's block. For this reason, the first statement, iValue++;, will take iValue's contents to 11, not 1, since only the local iValue is visible.*

However, outside the **while** loop, the local redeclaration of *iValue* goes out of scope. The second statement, *iValue++;*, now takes the first *iValule*'s contents to 1;

```
class MyApp {
  public static void main(String args[]) {
    int iValue = 0;
    boolean test = true;
    while( test ) {
      int iValue = 10;
      iValue++; // local redeclaration goes to 11 here
      ...
    }
  iValue++; // outer iValue goes to 1 here
  }
}
```

## Casting and Object Coercions

Sometimes referred to as coercion, casting is a term inherited from the C/C++ languages. *Casting* is an operation that allows a programmer to temporarily change a variable's type or precision. One of Java's security features is the restrictions it places upon run-time casting and coercion of objects and variables. These Java casting restrictions prevent the possibility of malicious system corruption. The following list details the types of casts and coercions legal in Java:

- Java programs cannot cast objects to the base types such as **Object**.
- Floating-point values can be cast to integral values.
- Integral values can be cast to floating-point precision.
- Integers cannot be cast to arrays or objects.
- Java allows instances of a class to be cast to a superclass.
- Java also allows an instance of a class to be cast to a subclass with a run-time check to ensure that it is a valid instance of the subclass or one of its subclasses. A **ClassCastException** is raised if the instance isn't a valid subclass or sub-subclass.

All other castings or coercions are illegal and cause a compile-time error.

The following example shows the syntax and use for casting:

```
int iValue;
char cValue;
iValue = (int) cValue;
```

Here, the parenthetical reference to **int** tells the compiler that you want to change the character into an integer and place it into *iValue*. On the other hand, if you need to go the other way, you write:

```
cValue = (char) iValue;
```

You must remember to take a variable's storage allocation into consideration when casting. Because both **int**s and **char**s are 32 bits, you can move from one to another without a loss of information. However, if you were to coerce a 64-bit **long** into a

32-bit **int**, you could easily truncate the value. Be careful, though, even if the two variables are the same size, as in the case of a 32-bit **int** and a 32-bit **float**, you would still lose information about the fractional numbers.

Java does not support automatic casting as do C and C++. If it did, the previous statement could be written like this:

```
cValue = iValue;
```

The following list details those casts that will not result in information loss:

| *Original Data Type:* | *Coerced To:* |
|---|---|
| **byte** to | **short, char, int, long, float, double** |
| **short** to | **int, long, float, double** |
| **char** to | **int, long, float, double** |
| **int** to | **long, float, double** |
| **long** to | **float, double** |
| **float** to | **double** |

## Logic Control

Java provides the usual set of logic control statements necessary to create meaningful algorithms. Since these control statements perform the same logical function in Java as in many programming languages, the only concern here is their syntax in Java.

**if** The **if** statement looks like:

```
if( test_expression )
  single_statement;
```

or

```
if( text_expression ) {
  statement_a;
  statement_b;
statement_n;
}
```

***Note:*** *in Java the text_expression is evaluated as a* ***boolean*** *data type, not a number as in C/C++. This means that, unlike C/C++, you cannot use an integer as a shortcut, in which 0 = false and any other* *value is true. In Java you must make some relational statement in order for the test_expression to evaluate properly. The following test_expression would not evaluate properly in Java:*

```
int iWantsToDo = 0;
if( iWantsToDo )
  something;
```

This code section would have to be rewritten to something like:

```
int iWantsToDo = 0;
if( iWantsToDo == 1 )
  something;
```

**if-else** Next in complexity is the biconditional **if-else**. Once again, the main issue here is syntax. The permutations include:

```
if( test_expression )
  single_true_statement:
else
  single_false_statement;
```

or

```
if( test_expression )
  single_true_statement:
else {
  false_statement_a:
  false_statement_b;
  false_statement_n;
}
```

or

```
if( test_expression ) {
  true_statement_a:
  true_statement_b;
  true_statement_c;
}
else
  single_false_statement;
```

or

```
if( test_expression ) {
  true_statement_a:
  true_statement_b;
```

```
  true_statement_c;
}
else {
  false_statement_a:
  false_statement_b;
  false_statement_n;
}
```

**if-else-if...** For simple subrange checks you can use the nested **if-else-if** syntax:

```
if( test_expression_a )
  do_this;
  else if ( test_expression_b )
    then_do_this;
    else if( test_expression_n )
       else_do_this;
```

**switch-case** Another alternative to nested **if-else-if** statements is the Java **switch-case** statement. A **switch-case** statement allows you to easily code multiple logic paths based on a single variable's contents. Usually the variable's contents fall into a specific, testable, subset of values. Be very careful, though; unlike many other high-level language selection statements such as Pascal's case statement, the Java **switch-case** statement has a few peculiarities. The general form of a Java **switch-case** statement follows:

```
switch( test_expression ) {
 case constant_a:
   statements_a;
   break;
 case constant_b:
   statements_b;
   break;
   .
   .
   .
 case constant_n:
   statements_n;
   break;
 default: statements; // default - optional
}
```

There is one keyword that a novice Java programmer needs to pay particular attention to, **break**. If this example had been coded in Pascal and *constant_a* equaled *test_expression*, *statements_a* would have been executed, with program execution picking up with the next statement at the end of the case statement (below the closing brace). In Java the situation is quite different.

In the preceding syntax, if the **break** statement had been removed from *constant_a*'s section of code, a match similar to the one used in the preceding paragraph would have left *statements_b* as the next statement to be executed. It is the **break** statement that causes the remaining portion of the **switch-case** statements to be skipped. Let's look at a few examples. Examine the following **if-else-if** code segment:

```
if( iOffset == SMALL_CHANGE_UP )
  iYcoordinate =   1;

else if( iOffset == SMALL_CHANGE_DOWN )
  iYcoordinate =  -1;

else if( iOffset == LARGE_CHANGE_UP )
  iYcoordinate =   10;

else
  iYcoordinate =  -10;
```

You can rewrite this code using a switch statement:

```
switch( iOffset ) {
  case  SMALL_CHANGE_UP:
    iYcoordinate =   1;
    break;
  case  SMALL_CHANGE_DOWN:
    iYcoordinate =  -1;
    break;
  case  LARGE_CHANGE_UP:
    iYcoordinate =   10;
    break;
  default:
    iYcoordinate =  -10;
}
```

In this example, the value of *iOffset* is consecutively compared to each case value looking for a match. When one is found, *iYcoordinate* is assigned the appropriate value. Then the **break** statement is executed, skipping over the remaining **cases** of the switch statements. However, if no match is found, the default assignment is performed (*iYcoordinate = -10*). Since this is the last option in the **switch-case** statement, there is no need to include a **break**. A **switch-case default** is optional. Proper placement of the **break** statement within a **switch-case** statement allows you to create a set of **cases**, all performing the same operation as in this next program:

```
class TestSwitch {
  public static void main(String args[]) {

  char a_character      = 'U';
  int NumberOfVowels    =  0 ,
      NumberOfConsonants =  0 ;

    switch( a_character ) {
      case 'a' :
      case 'A' :
      case 'e' :
      case 'E' :
      case 'i' :
      case 'I' :
      case 'o' :
      case 'O' :
      case 'u' :
      case 'U' :  NumberOfVowels++;
                    break;
      default  :  NumberOfConsonants++;
    }
   System.out.println("nNumber of vowels = " + NumberOfVowels);
  }
}
```

Notice how the **switch-case** statement enumerates several test values that all execute the same code section and the drop-through characteristic of a purposefully missing **break** statement. Several other high-level languages have their own form of selection (the case statement in Pascal and the select statement in PL/I), which allows several test values, all producing the same result, to be included on the same selection line using subranges. Java, however, requires a separate case for each. But notice, in this example, how the same effect has been created by not inserting a **break** statement until all possible vowels have been checked. Should *a_character* contain a consonant, all of the vowel case tests will be checked and skipped until the **default** statement is reached.

## Loops

Java has a few surprises when it comes to simple types of loop control statements. Actually, the loop types themselves are fairly standard in operation. What is interesting, however, is the ways in which you can alter the logic flow within a loop or exit a loop. Java includes the standard set of repetition control statements: **for** loops, **while** loops and **do-while** loops (called repeat-until loops in several other high-level languages).

The basic difference between a **for** loop and a **while** or **do-while** loop has to do with the "known" number of repetitions. Typically, **for** loops are used whenever there is a definite pre-defined required number of repetitions, and **while** and **do-while** loops are reserved for an "unknown" number of repetitions.

Java provides four methods for altering the repetitions in a loop. All loops can naturally terminate based on the expressed test condition. In Java, however, a loop can also terminate because of an anticipated error condition by using either a **break** (the other use for **break** statements, besides the **switch-case** use) or *exit()* statement. Loops can also have their logic control flow altered by a **break** statement or a **continue** statement.

## Pretest *for* Loop

The syntax for a **for** loop looks very similar to that in most high-level languages:

```
for( init_loop_control; test_expression; increment_loop_control )
```

**for** loop execution begins with the one-time-only initialization of the loop control variable, in this example, *init_loop_control*. This is done at the start of the loop, and it is never executed again. Following this, *test_expression*, which is called the loop-terminating condition, is tested. Whenever *test_expression* evaluates to TRUE, the statement or statements within the loop are executed.

If the loop was entered, then after all of the statements within the loop are executed, *increment_loop_control* is executed. However, if *test_expression* evaluates to FALSE, the statement or statements within the loop are ignored, along with *increment_loop_control*, and execution continues with the statement following the end of the loop.

To check yourself on the proper use of loop control variables, answer the following question: What is the value of the loop control variable *outside* the loop? Answer: undefined. Your program should never use the loop control variable anywhere else but *inside* the loop structure. Outside the loop, the variable's contents are volatile.

The indentation scheme applied to **for** loops with a compound block looks like:

```
for( init_loop_control; test_expression; increment_loop_control ) {
 statement_a;
 statement_b;
 statement_c;
 statement_n;
}
```

When several statements need to be executed, a pair of braces is required to tie their execution to the loop control structure. Let's examine a few examples of **for** loops. The following example sums up the first five integers. It assumes that *Total* and *ControlValue* have been predefined as integers:

```
Total = 0;
for( ControlValue = 1; ControlValue <= 5; ControlValue++ )
  Total += ControlValue;
```

After *Total* has been initialized to zero, the **for** loop is encountered. First, *ControlValue* is initialized to 1 (this is done only once); second, *ControlValue*'s value is checked against the loop-terminating condition, <= 5. Since this is TRUE, a 1 is added to *Total*. Once the statement is executed, the loop control variable (*ControlValue*) is incremented by 1. This process continues four more times until *ControlValue* is incremented to 6 and the loop terminates. In Java, as in C++, the same code segment could be written as follows. See if you can detect the subtle difference:

```
for( int ControlValue = 1; ControlValue <= 5; ControlValue++ )
  Total += ControlValue;
```

Java allows the loop control variable to be declared and initialized within the **for** loop. This brings up a very sensitive issue among structured programmers, which is the proper placement of variable declarations. In Java, you can declare variables right before the statement that actually uses them. In the preceding example, since *ControlValue* is used only to generate a *Total*, with *Total* having a larger scope than *ControlValue*, the local declaration for *ControlValue* is harmless. However, look at the following code segment:

```
int Total = 0;
for( int ControlValue = 1; ControlValue <= 5; ControlValue++ )
  Total += ControlValue;
```

This would obscure the visual "desk check" of the variable *Total* because it was not declared below the function head. For the sake of structured design and debugging, it is best to localize all variable declarations. It is the rare code segment that can justify the usefulness of moving a variable declaration to a nonstandard place, in sacrifice of easily read, easily checked, and easily modified code.

The value used to increment **for** loop control variables does not always have to be 1 or ++. The following example sums all the odd numbers up to 9:

```
OddTotal = 0;
for( OddNumber = 1; OddNumber <= 9; OddNumber += 2 );
  OddTotal += OddNumber;
```

In this example, the loop control variable *OddNumber* is initialized to 1 and is incremented by 2. Of course, **for** loops don't always have to go from a smaller value to a larger one.

## Pretest *while* Loop

**while** loops are also pretest loops, which means that the program evaluates *test_expression* before entering the statement or statements within the body of the loop. Because of this, pretest loops may be executed from zero to many times. The syntax for a Java **while** loop is:

```
while( test_expression )
  statement;
```

or for compound blocks:

```
while( test_expression ) {
  statement_a;
  statement_b;
  statement_c;
  statement_n;
}
```

Usually, **while** loop control structures are used whenever an indefinite number of repetitions is expected.

## Postest *do-while* Loop

The post test **do-while** loop is the only loop always entered at least once, with the loop condition being tested at the end of the first iteration. In contrast, **for** loops and **while** loops may execute from zero to many times, depending on the loop control variable. The syntax for a d**o-while** loop is

```
do
 statement ;
while( test_expression );
```

or for compound blocks:

```
do {
 action_a;
 action_b;
 action_c;
 action_n;
} while( test_expression );
```

Since **do-while** loops always execute at least one time, they are best used whenever there is no doubt you want the particular loop entered. For example, if your program needs to present a menu to the user, even if all the user wants to do is immediately quit the program, he or she needs to see the menu to know which key terminates the application.

## Standard Operators

All the familiar C and C++ operators apply. Because Java lacks unsigned data types, the >>> operator has been added to the language to indicate an unsigned (logical) right shift. Java also uses the + operator for string concatenation.

**Table 2.4:**

<table>
<tr><th>Operators</th><th>Associativity</th></tr>
<tr><td>() [] -> :: .</td><td>left to right</td></tr>
<tr><td>! ~ + - ++ -- & sizeof new delete</td><td>right to left</td></tr>
<tr><td>. * ->* *</td><td>left to right</td></tr>
<tr><td>* / %</td><td>left to right</td></tr>
<tr><td>+ -</td><td>left to right</td></tr>
<tr><td><< >> >>></td><td>left to right</td></tr>
<tr><td>< <= > >=</td><td>left to right</td></tr>
<tr><td>== !=</td><td>left to right</td></tr>
<tr><td>&</td><td>left to right</td></tr>
<tr><td>^</td><td>left to right</td></tr>
<tr><td>|</td><td>left to right</td></tr>
<tr><td>&&</td><td>left to right</td></tr>
<tr><td>| |</td><td>right to left</td></tr>
<tr><td>?:</td><td>left to right</td></tr>
<tr><td>= *= /= %= += -= &= ^= |= <<= >>= >>>=</td><td>right to left</td></tr>
<tr><td>,</td><td>left to right</td></tr>
</table>

Throughout the book you will be introduced to the various operators and how their precedence level affects their performance.

## Arrays

In contrast to C and C++, Java language arrays are first-class language objects. An array in Java is a real object with a run-time representation. You can declare and allocate arrays of any type, and you can allocate arrays of arrays to obtain multidimensional arrays. You declare an array of, say, *ScreenCoords* (a class you've declared elsewhere) with a declaration like this:

```
ScreenCoord  CurrentScreenCoords[];
```

This code states that *CurrentScreenCoords* is an uninitialized array of *ScreenCoords*. At this time, the only storage allocated for *CurrentScreenCoords* is a reference handle. At some future time you must allocate the amount of storage you need, as in:

```
CurrentScreenCoords = new ScreenCoord[10];
```

to allocate an array of ten references to *ScreenCoords* that are initialized to the null reference. Notice that this allocation of an array doesn't actually allocate any objects of the *ScreenCoord* class for you; you will have to also allocate the *ScreenCoord* objects, something like this:

```
int i;
for (i = 0; i < 10; i++) {
   CurrentScreenCoords[i] = new ScreenCoord();
}
```

Access to elements of *CurrentScreenCoords* can be performed via the normal C-style indexing, but all array accesses are checked to ensure that their indices are within the range of the array. An exception is generated if the index is outside the bounds of the array. To get the length of an array, use the **length()** accessor method on the array object whose length you wish to know: *CurrentScreenCoords.length()* returns the number of elements in *CurrentScreenCoords*. For instance, the code fragment:

```
howMany = CurrentScreenCoords.length();
```

would assign the value 10 to the *howMany* variable.

The C notion of a pointer to an array of memory elements is gone, and with it, the arbitrary pointer arithmetic that leads to unreliable code in C. No longer can you walk off the end of an array, possibly trashing memory and leading to the famous "delayed-crash" syndrome, where a memory-access violation today manifests itself hours or days later. Programmers can be confident that array checking in Java will lead to more robust and reliable code.

## Exceptions

If a program behaves abnormally, encounters an unexpected input, or detects an anomaly in its operation, it must react. This is called exception handling. One very nice standardized feature of Java is its exception-handling mechanism. There are two parts to the syntax for the exception mechanism: part one involves signaling an exception, while part two sets up the exception handler. To signal an exception, your program simply used the **throw** keyword, as in:

```
throw new MyExceptionMethod();
```

To set up an exception handler, your program uses the **try-catch** keywords. This statement syntax involves a **try** block, which is the code that is executed assuming no exception occurs, and then a series of **catch** blocks, which are executed if an exception has been **thrown**:

```
try {
      // try code block
  }
    catch (MyExceptionType ErrorOne)  {
            // catch statement(s) ErrorOne);
  }
    catch (MyExceptionType ErrorTwo)  {
            // catch statement(s) ErrorTwo);
  {
}
```

Exception handling will be discussed in greater detail throughout remaining chapters.

## Objects

Since many readers are undoubtedly very familiar with the procedural-oriented aspects of programming languages such as Pascal, Modula-3, and C, the initial chapters of this text use this familiarity to introduce you to Java. However, Java is an object-oriented language. In C++ and Java, then, an *object* is defined as a programming abstraction that groups data with the code that operates on that data. A *class* is a template for a set of object instances. Learning how to understand, use, and develop your own objects requires additional program fundamentals, concepts, and syntax. The discussions of these topics are delayed until Chapter 4, *Java Programming Fundamentals*, to make your learning and enjoyment of the Java language as easy as possible.

## Features of C/C++ Not in Java

The earlier part of this chapter concentrated on the principal features of Java. This section discusses features removed from

C and C++ in the evolution of Java. The first step was to eliminate redundancy from C and C++. In many ways, the C language evolved into a collection of overlapping features, providing too many ways to say the same thing, while in many cases not providing needed features. C++, in an attempt to add "classes in C," merely added more redundancy while retaining many of the inherent problems of C.

## No Typedefs, Defines, or Preprocessor

Source code written in Java is simple. There is no preprocessor, no **#define** and related capabilities, no **typedef**, and absent those features, no longer any need for header files. Instead of header files, Java language source files provide the definitions of other classes and their methods. A major problem with C and C++ is the amount of context you need to understand another programmer's code: you have to read all related header files, all related **#defines**, and all related **typedefs** before you can even begin to analyze a program.

In essence, programming with **#defines** and **typedefs** results in every programmer inventing a new programming language that's incomprehensible to anybody other than its creator, thus defeating the goals of good programming practices. In Java, you obtain the effects of **#define** by using constants. You obtain the effects of **typedef** by declaring classes—after all, a class effectively declares a new type. You don't need header files because the Java compiler compiles class definitions into a binary form that retains all the type information through to link time. By removing all this baggage, Java becomes remarkably context free. Programmers can read and understand code and, more important, modify and reuse code much faster and easier.

## No Structures or Unions

Java has no structures or unions as complex data types. You don't need structures and unions when you have classes; you can achieve the same effect simply by declaring a class with the appropriate instance variables. The code fragment below declares a class called *ScreenCoord*.

```
class ScreenCoord extends Object {
    double  X_Coord;
    double  Y_Coord;
    methods to access the instance variables
}
```

The following code fragment declares a class called Rectangle that uses objects of the *ScreenCoord* class as instance variables.

```
class Rectangle extends Object {
    ScreenCoord  LowerLeft_Coord;
    ScreenCoord  UpperRight_Coord;
    methods to access the instance variables
}
```

In C you'd define these classes as structures. In Java, you simply declare classes. You can make the instance variables as private or as **public** as you wish, depending on how much you wish to hide the details of the implementation from other objects.

## No Functions

Java has no functions. Object-oriented programming supersedes functional and procedural styles. Mixing the two styles just leads to confusion and dilutes the purity of an object-oriented language. Anything you can do with a function you can do just as well by defining a class and creating methods for that class. Consider the ScreenCoord class from above. We've added public methods to set and access the instance variables:

```
class ScreenCoord extends Object {
    double  X_Coord;
    double  Y_Coord;
    public void setX( double X_Coord ) {
         this.X_Coord = X_Coord;
    }
    public void setY( double Y_Coord ) {
        this.Y_Coord = Y_Coord;
    }
    public double X_Coord( void ) {
        return X_Coord;
    }
```

```
    public double Y_Coord( void ) {
        return X_Coord;
    }
}
```

If the *X_Coord* and *Y_Coord* instance variables are private to this class, the only way to access them is via the public methods of the class. Here's how you'd use objects of the ScreenCoord class from within, say, an object of the Rectangle class:

```
class Rectangle extends Object {
    ScreenCoord  LowerLeft_Coord;
    ScreenCoord  UpperRight_Coord;
    public void setEmptyRect( void ) {
        LowerLeft_Coord.setX( 0.0 );
        LowerLeft_Coord.setY( 0.0 );
        UpperRight_Coord.setX( 0.0 );
        UpperRight_Coord.setY( 0.0 );
    }
}
```

It's not to say that functions and procedures are inherently wrong. But given classes and methods, we're now down to only one way to express a given task. By eliminating functions, your job as a programmer is immensely simplified: you work only with classes and their methods.

## No Multiple Inheritance

Multiple inheritance—and all the problems it generates—has been discarded from Java. The desirable features of multiple inheritance are provided by interfaces—conceptually similar to Objective C protocols. An interface is not a definition of an object. Rather, it's a definition of a set of methods that one or more objects will implement. An important issue of interfaces is that they declare only methods and constants. No variables may be defined in interfaces.

## No Goto Statements

Java has no goto statement. Studies illustrated that goto is (mis) used more often than not simply "because it's there." Eliminating goto led to a simplification of the language—there are no rules about the effects of a goto into the middle of a for statement, for example. Studies on approximately 100,000 lines of C code determined that roughly 90 percent of the goto statements were used purely to obtain the effect of breaking out of nested loops. As mentioned above, multilevel break and continue remove most of the need for goto statements.

## No Operator Overloading

There are no means provided by which programmers can overload the standard arithmetic operators. Once again, the effects of operator overloading can be just as easily achieved by declaring a class, appropriate instance variables, and appropriate methods for manipulating those variables.

## No Automatic Coercions

Java prohibits C and C++ style automatic coercions. If you wish to coerce a data element of one type to a data type that would result in loss of precision, you must do so explicitly by using a cast. Consider this code fragment:

```
int  myInt;
double  myFloat = 3.14159;
myInt = myFloat;
```

The assignment of myFloat to myInt would result in a compiler error indicating a possible loss of precision and that you must use an explicit cast. Thus, you should rewrite the code fragments as:

```
int  myInt;
double  myFloat = 3.14159;
myInt = (int)myFloat;
```

## No Pointers

Most studies agree that pointers are one of the primary features that enable programmers to inject bugs into their code. Given that structures are gone and arrays and strings are objects, the need for pointers to these constructs goes away. Thus, Java has no pointers. Any task that would require arrays, structures, and pointers in C can be more easily and reliably performed by declaring objects and arrays of objects. Instead of complex pointer manipulation on array pointers, you access arrays by their arithmetic indices. The Java run-time system checks all array indexing to ensure indices are within the bounds of the array. You no longer have dangling pointers and trashing of memory because of incorrect pointers, because there are no pointers in Java.

## The Borland C++ Compiler and Java Compiler

Since using the Java language involves more than simply running programs, Borland International has chosen to provide the Java language as an optional Borland C++, user-installed add-on. This makes sense for two reasons. First, Borland knew that you would need to enter, edit, and debug Java source code, not just run Java programs. The Borland C++ IDE (Integrated Development Environment) works perfectly for these tasks and is already familiar to hundreds of thousands of programmers. Second, since Java is most similar to the C and C++ languages, nesting the Java development tools within Borland C++ makes perfect sense.

## Installing the Java Compiler

The Borland C++ installation program attempts to maximize the efficient use of your system's resources, so it does not automatically install the Java component to the IDE (Integrated Development Environment). For this reason, if you want to use Java, you must run the Setup.exe program a second time (assuming you have already installed Borland C++). Figure 2.1 shows the Setup program's initial window.

To begin the installation of Java, click on the second button marked Add-On for Java. This starts the Java installation seen in Figure 2.2.

Click on Next to begin the actual installation.

The next window you see (Figure 2.3) reminds you to close all Windows applications before continuing the Setup. Click

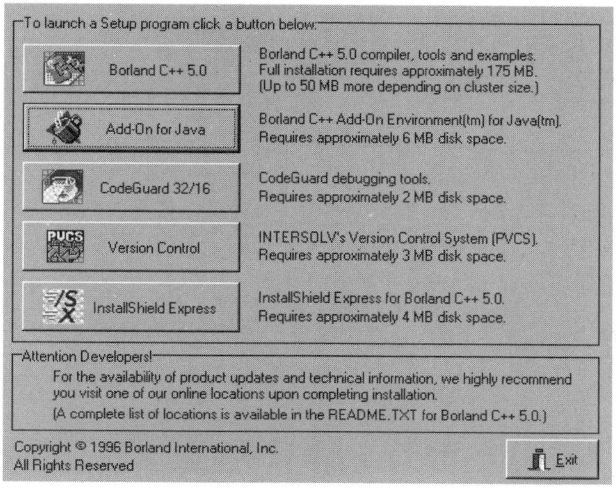


**Figure 2.1:** Initial Setup window.

on Next to continue. The "Choose Destination Location" window, seen in Figure 2.4, allows you to specify where the Java

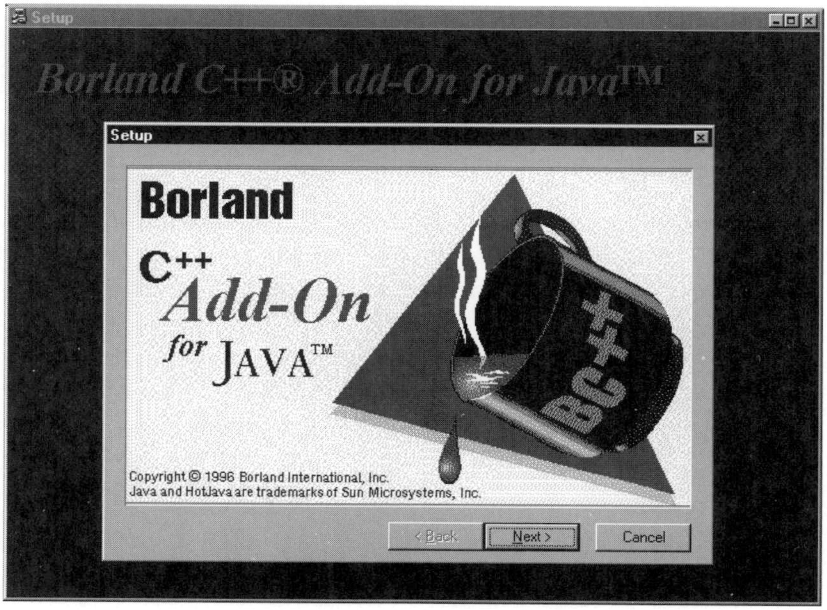


**Figure 2.2:** Java installation.

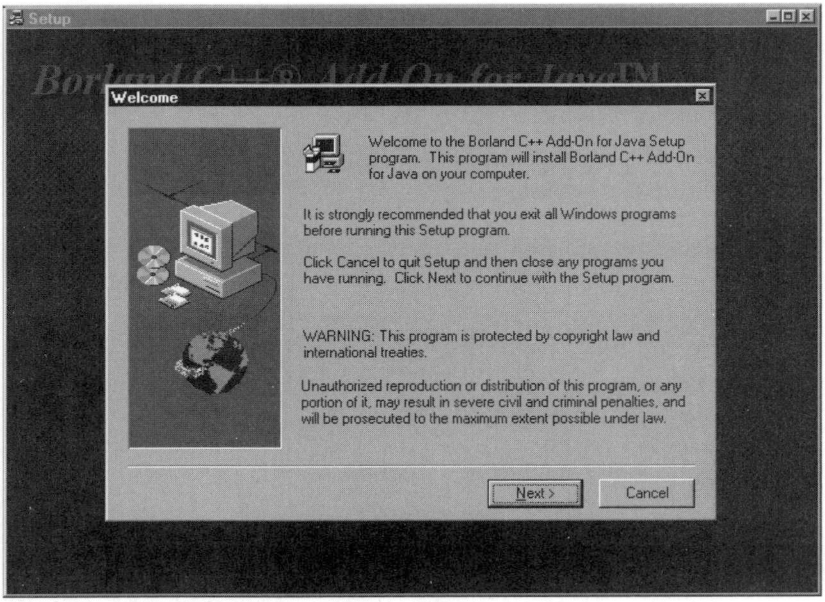


**Figure 2.3:** WARNING: message window.

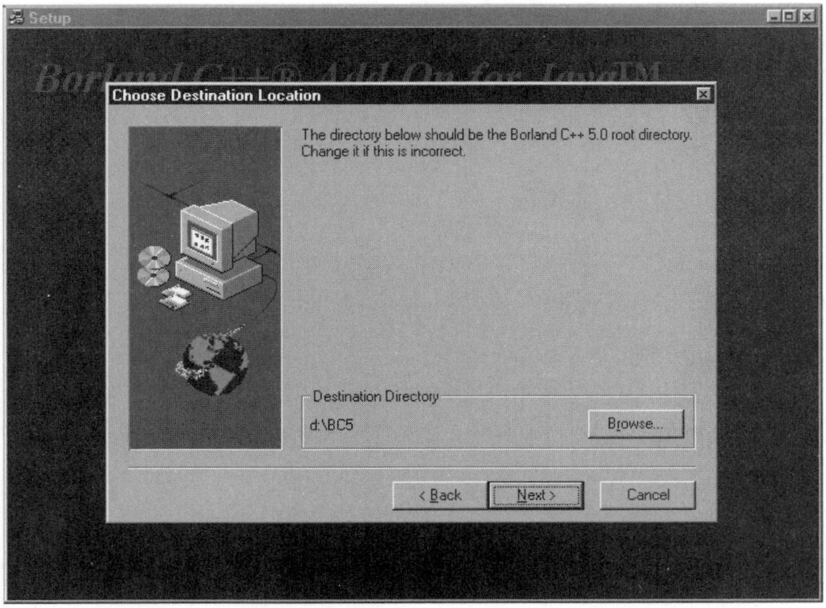


**Figure 2.4:** Selecting the drive and path for downloaded Java files.

compiler files are to be downloaded. Make sure that the "Destination Directory" matches the location of the Borland C++ compiler.

The actual Java files installation begins after setting the "Destination Directory" and clicking on the Next button, as seen in Figure 2.5.

If your install had no flagged error conditions, you will see the message window shown in Figure 2.6.

Simply click on the OK button to finish the Java installation. At this point if you were to start the IDE you would not see any visual clues indicating that the Java component was successfully added to the Borland C++ development environment. Since you still use the Borland C++ IDE to enter, edit, and save Java source files, all of these menu items remain unchanged. It isn't until you start compiling, debugging, or running a Java program that you see and use the additional Main Menu commands added by the Setup program. These will be discussed in detail in Chapter 3. Borland highly recommends that you investigate one of the following resources

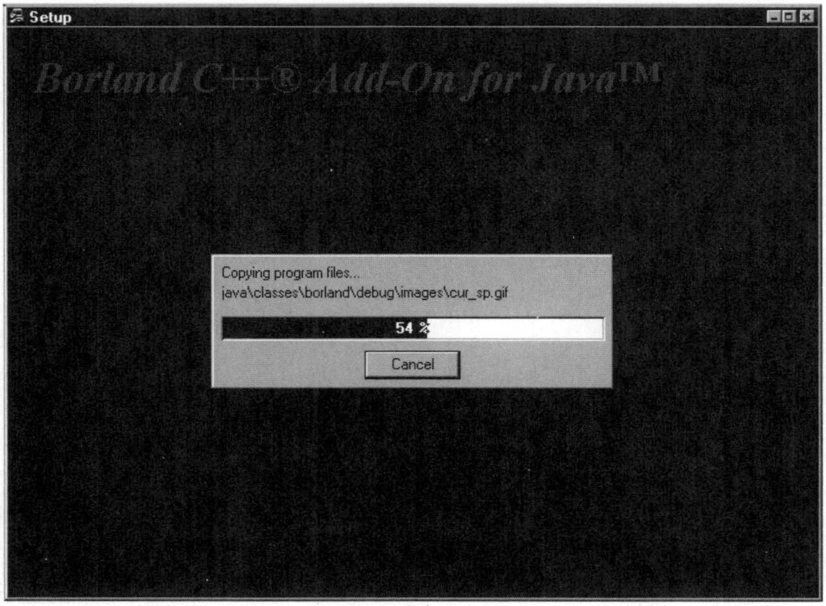


**Figure 2.5:** Copying program files window.

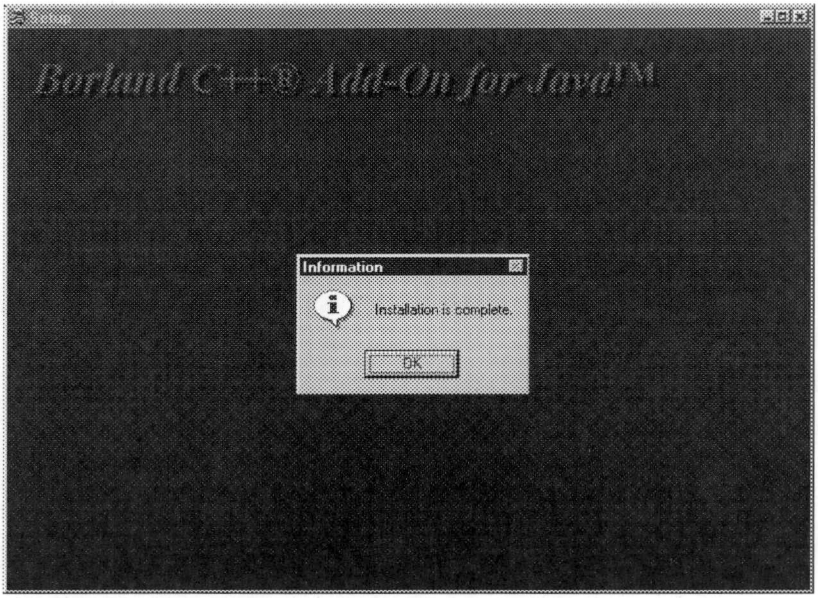


**Figure 2.6:** Installation complete message window.

as soon as you have installed your new Borland C++ 5.0 product:

| | |
|---|---|
| World WideWeb: | http://loki.borland.com/cpp/patchs.htm |
| CIS: | GO BCPP, section 3, "From Borland" |
| FTP: | ftp.borland.com |
| BBS: | (408)431-5096. 8-N-1 (I bits, No parity, 1 stop bit) |
| Listserv: | listserv@borland.com Send an e-mail message containing this text: SUBSCRIBE<space> BCPP<space> FIRST NAME<space>LASTNAME |

These locations will provide you with the most comprehensive product information, updates, and service possible with this new release of Borland C++ and its associated products. For more information on contacting Borland and support services offered by Borland, please read the file 'README.TXT' in your BC5 directory.

***Note:*** *The Java debugger requires a TCP/IP connection to run; if this is not present you will get an "UnknownHostException" when attempting to launch the Java debugger. This will often occur when an IP address is obtained automatically from a service provider and you are running off-line. It is possible to debug off-line, but you must change the Windows95 Control Panel | Network | TCP/IP properties page and specify an IP address.*

## Development Tools

Once you have installed the Add-On for Java you will have Sun's complete Java Development Kit and .HTML language references to ensure authoritative Java development. The AppAccelerator greatly speeds up the run time of Java applets and applications during your testing and debugging phases (by a factor of 2 to 10 times). The installed Java tools discussed throughout the following chapters include the:

- Java AppAccelerator
- Java AppExpert
- Java Debugger
- Java Integrated bytecode compiler
- Java project management

## JAVA LINGO

The following new terms have been discussed in this chapter and are presented here for your review:

*block*—Physically represented by brace pairs { }, which logically represent a related group of executable code statements.

*coercion*—Another term for the C/C++/Java cast operator, which refers to these languages' ability to allow a variable's type and precision to be changed temporarily.

*exception handling*—A programming language's ability to detect and then eloquently (usually through programmer-written subroutines) recover from what would normally be fatal error conditions.

*Hungarian notation*—A style of creating identifiers whereby each variable or constant name begins with an abbreviation of its data type.

*IDE*—Borland International's name for their comprehensive program development environment including: entering, editing, compiling, running, and debugging Java programs. IDE stands for Integrated Development Environment.

*identifier*—The umbrella category that collectively describes variable names, constant names, and method (or function) names.

*literals*—The term applied to the legal constant values assigned to the standard Java data types.

*UNICODE*—The new encryption standard that maps every known language in the world, and yet undefined languages, to a 16-bit value. All Java source files are created using this new universal standard.

# 3

# Java Basics

## Simple Programming Concepts

If you have never used a Borland International Program Development Environment, you are in for an exciting surprise. Borland International has spent decades designing and refining program development tools that just about write an entire program for you. This is true about their Pascal and C/C++ compilers and now the Java compiler/interpreter.

In this chapter you will learn everything you need to know about writing, compiling, interpreting, running, and debugging Java applications and applets, using Borland's Java tools. By the end of the chapter, using Borland's AppExpert, you will know how to generate a simple Java application or applet, with almost nothing more than mouse clicks!

## Writing Your First Java Application

To begin, your Borland Java compiler/interpreter is shipped to you in two versions, the command line version and the integrated IDE version. Remember that Java is a full-featured programming language capable of developing standalone programs—these are called Java applications. The first program you write will be a Java application and you will use the command line Java compiler/interpreter to compile, debug, and run, the application.

***myfirst.java* Application** To show you just how easy a process this is, using whatever text editor you choose, enter and save the following code:

```
/* myfirst.java                                   */
/* 4/4/96                                         */
/* Simple example application using WordPad to    */
/* enter the source code. The program will be     */
/* compiled with javac.exe, and then the program */
/* will be run using java.exe                     */

import java.util.Date;

class myfirst {
  public static void main(String args[]) {
    Date Today = new Date();
    System.out.println(Today);
  }
}
```

under the file name *myfirst.java*, in your *BC5/Java/bin* subdirectory. All Java source files must have a *.java* file extension. Figure 3.1 uses the Windows 95 WordPad text editor to create and save the example source file.

***Comments*** This simple Java application begins with a comment block using the /* */ comment delimiter symbol pairs. Be careful not to forget to terminate your comments.

***Note:*** *To add a Java syntax highlight button to your SpeedBar, first choose the Main Options | Environment | SpeedBar | Customize option. Slide down the Available Buttons list in the dialog box until*

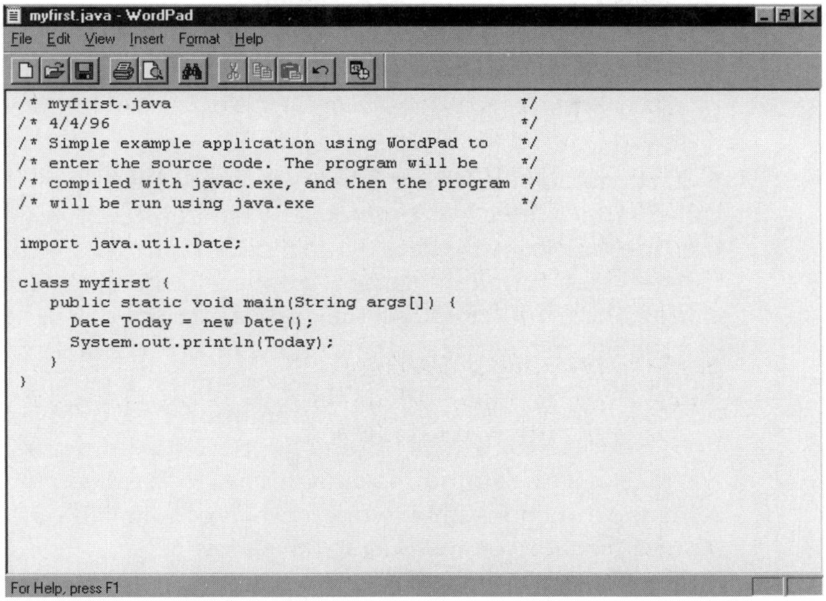


**Figure 3.1:** Using Microsoft Windows 95 WordPad to create Java source code.

*you see* Syntax Highlight Java Files *and simply click the add arrow button.*

With this option on, if you forget to close a comment block you will notice that your *entire* source file will be in a font and color used just for comments.

**The *import* Statement** The next statement in the program:

```
import java.util.Date;
```

is closest in function to Pascal's or C/C++'s **#include** statement. What is does is to pull in Java–compiler supplied class definitions.

***Note:*** *to C/C++ programmers, Java is not a two-pass compiler as C/C++ are and therefore the* ***import*** *statement is not a preprocessor statement.*

After the **import** keyword, you will notice a series of identifiers separated by periods. Many programming languages use this period . operator. In Pascal and Modula-3, this operator is used to select fields within a record. In C/C++ the operator performs the same logical function, only you would say that the operator selects *members of a structure*.

But in C/C++ the same operator is used in a more advanced syntax, namely selecting functions, only these functions are called *member functions* or *methods*. Member functions, or methods, are functions that are syntactically tied to a specific structure or class. A unique name is applied to them, instead of just calling them functions, so that programmers discussing code can distinguish between stand-alone *functions* (those written in a procedural design approach) and member functions or methods (used in object-oriented programming class or object definition). Simply stated an *object*, in object-oriented programming, is a syntactic way of bundling data declarations called *member data* with the functions that work with the member data, called *member functions* or *methods*. It's that simple.

The Java statement:

```
import java.util.Date;
```

uses the *period member operator* along with the **import** keyword to pull in Java compiler–supplied definitions for the **util.Date()** method (which from a programmer's viewpoint is closest in form to a subroutine or function). Finally, notice that all Java code statements must terminate with a semicolon.

**Your First *class*** The next statement in the application actually involves two lines of code, the first line starting with the keyword **class** and the second line containing the closing brace }:

```
class myfirst {
    .
    .
    .
}
```

To begin your understanding of a Java **class**, think of a Pascal **record** or C/C++ **struct** definition. These keywords allow a programmer to logically relate different data types into one user-defined unit. C++ and Java **class** syntax has an identical capability, only the **class** goes one step further by allowing the syntactic bundling of **class**-specific member functions. All Java programming must be done within a **class**. The Java language does not support standalone functions. Following the coded example's use of the keyword **class** is the user-defined **class** name, in this case *myfirst*. All **class** code must be surrounded with brace pairs { . . . }.

**The Required *main()* Method** The first statement within the class definition also involves two lines of code, the formal **main()** method definition and its matching closing brace }:

```
public static void main(String args[]) {
     .
     .
     .
}
```

The *compound block* (meaning more than one line of code surrounded by a brace pair { }) statement begins with the **public** keyword, which indicates that the method **main()** is globally accessible. Without going into too much detail too soon, the **static** keyword defines when the method **main()** is put into the symbol table and the persistence of the method **main()**. **void** is a keyword also used in C/C++ programming and in this syntax indicates that the method **main()** does not return any value.

Not only must all Java code be nested within a **class** definition, but all Java applications must have a method called **main()**, where program execution begins and usually terminates. The only formal argument to **main()** is *(String args[])*. The keyword **String** used in the formal argument list defines *args[]* as an array of the **String** class.

This definition allows a Java program to easily check for, and incorporate, command line arguments passed to the application. For example, the MS-DOS program *copy.exe*, when executed, expects the user to type two file names, the *file_to_copy.ext* and the *file_name_of_copy.ext*. These file names fall in the category of *command line arguments*. By putting *(String args[])* in the Java **main()** formal argument list, you give the application the ability to import and use command line arguments.

The formal argument name, *args[]* is closest to the C/C++ **main()** formal argument *argv[]*. However, there is a difference between the two languages that C/C++ programmers need to be aware of. In C/C++ the first string available in *argv[0]* is the actual name of the application, with the second string actually being the first command line argument. In our MS-DOS example, this means the first string is *copy.exe*, and the second string is *file_to_copy.ext*. In a Java application, you have no access to the program's name. This means that the first string, found at *args[0]* is the name of the first command line argument, in this case *file_to_copy.ext*.

**Instantiating Your First Object** The first statement inside the example program's **main()** method is:

```
Date Today = new Date();
```

This statement defines the member *Today* to be of type **Date** and uses the **new** keyword to dynamically allocate an instance of the method **Date()**. An *instance* of member data, or member functions, also called methods, is closest to the procedural concept of creating a variable, only instance is an object-oriented programming concept.

**Simple Output with the *println()* Method** With this accomplished the Java application now has all of the member data declarations and methods necessary to query the system's clock and fill in the data members with valid information. For this reason, the next statement:

```
System.out.println(Today);
```

can simply call the **System.out.println()** method to output *Today*'s valid member data. Easy! Now that you have some understanding of how the program works it is time to try your first compile.

## Running *javac.exe*

You'll find the Java command line compiler, named *javac.exe*. under the *BC5/Java/bin* subdirectory. To run the command line

**Figure 3.2:** Running *javac.exe* on *myfirst.java.*

compiler, switch to a DOS compatibility window and type *javac myfirst.java* as seen in Figure 3.2.

If you entered the source file without any errors, this is all you will see (Figure 3.2). However, *javac.exe* is capable of command line diagnostics. If you want the Java compiler to list error messages to the screen, you need to run it in verbose mode. To do this, simply type *javac -verbose myfirst.java*, as seen in Figure 3.3.

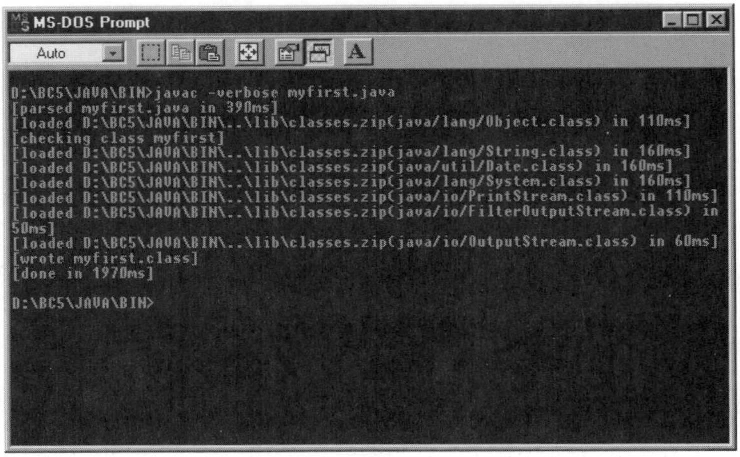


**Figure 3.3:** Running *javac.exe* in *-verbose* mode.

## Running *myfirst.class* Using *java.exe*

Regardless of whether you ran the Java compiler in standard or verbose mode, *javac.exe* took your Java source file, *myfirst.java*, and generated an executable file called *myfirst.class*. Most compilers generate executable files with an *.exe* file extension. However, a Java executable has a *.class* file extension.

To run your Java application, you use *java.exe*, which is the run-time Java interpreter. At this point you are ready to execute your first Java application by typing *java myfirst* as seen in Figure 3.4.

## Writing Your First Java Applet

The source code for your first Java applet is not that much different from its Java application counterpart. Let's take a look at the Java applet source code line by line:

```
/* mysecond.java                                  */
/* 4/4/96                                         */
/* This second example demonstrates how to write  */
/* a simple Java applet. This requires two files  */
/* first the Java source file, and second the     */
/* HTML document which will use the <APPLET>      */
/* tag to refer to the Java applet being written. */

/* The following statement is identical to the    */
```

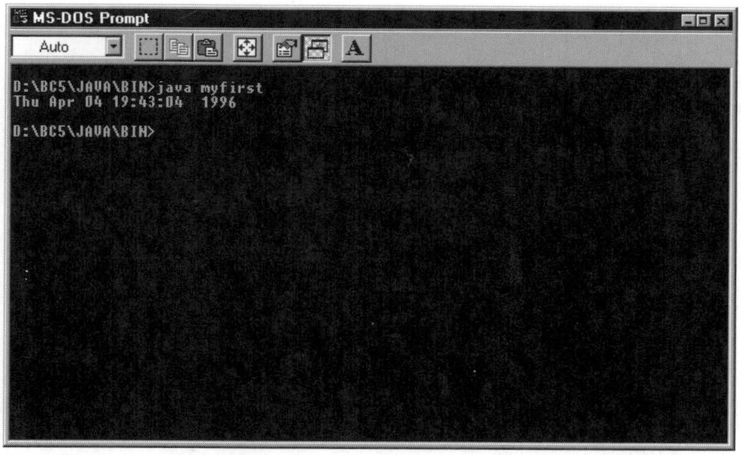


**Figure 3.4:** Running *myfirst.class*.

```
/* one used in the Java application previously    */
/* discussed.                                     */
import java.util.Date;

import java.awt.Graphics;       /* new imports    */
import java.applet.Applet;

public class mysecond extends java.applet.Applet {
 Date Today;
 String TodayAsString;

 public void paint(Graphics graphic) {
   Today = new Date();
   TodayAsString = Today.toString();
   graphic.drawString( TodayAsString, 10, 10 );
 }
}
```

Once again the program begins with a comment block. Since we want this applet to be as similar as possible to its application counterpart, it too is going to simply output today's day, date, time, and year. For this reason the program continues with the same import statement used in the Java application:

```
import java.util.Date;
```

However, the applet needs additional horsepower, which is included by the next two import statements:

```
import java.awt.Graphics;
import java.applet.Applet;
```

You already know what the **import** statement accomplishes, but let's take a closer syntactic look at what follows the keyword, namely *java.util.Date*, *java.awt.Graphics*, and *java.applet.Applet*. From previous discussions you know that the period member operator . can select either an object's data members or, in these two statements, methods. In this analogy then we would be referencing: *.Date*, *.Graphics*. and *.Applet*. At this point however, you may be wondering what the *java*, *awt*, or *applet* identifiers do.

The Java language allows you to logically relate groups of **class** definitions into a side-effect proof syntax called a *package*. The three import statements access specific methods, *.Date*,

*.Graphics*, and *.Applet*, within their respective packages, *java*, *java.awt*, and *java.applet*. Notice the Sun Microsystem style of naming these identifiers. All package names begin in lowercase, while all methods (member functions tied to a specific object **class**) begin with an uppercase letter. This is not a compiler requirement, just the developer's preference. However, since Java is a case-sensitive language, having a general idea of how compiler-supplied code is written makes it that much easier to use.

The source file continues by defining the object *mysecond*, using the **class** keyword:

```
public class mysecond extends java.applet.Applet {
     .
     .
     .
}
```

The **public** keyword acknowledges the *mysecond* **class** definition as being globally accessible and could have also been placed before the **class** keyword in the previous Java application's coded example. However, unlike the application counterpart, this **class** definition contains the keyword **extends**. ***extends*** tells the compiler that you are going to use the imported object's members (data and function types), but that the program is going to add application-specific functionality. In this case, the applet is going to define two data members:

```
Date Today;
String TodayAsString;
```

As in C/C++, when declaring data members, the member's data type comes first. Here *Today*'s data type is the class **Date**, and *TodayAsString* is of class type **String**. As in the Java application example, *Today* will be used to hold the current day, date, and year. *TodayAsString* will be used to hold the same information converted to string format for output.

The applet continues by enhancing the inherited **paint()** method defined in **java.awt.Graphics**. *Inheritance* of member functions or methods is very similar to the way a record variable, to a Pascal programmer (or to C/C++ programmers, a structure variable), inherits its formal record's declaration fields:

```
public void paint( Graphics graphic ) {
    .
    .
    .
}
```

Notice that the method's body is encapsulated within a pair of braces { }. Once again, the **public** keyword flags the compiler to this method's visibility outside the formal **class** definition. **void** means the method returns nothing—officially. *paint()* is the name of the method and the dummy argument *graphic* is of class type ***Graphics***.

Since the **paint()** method is a standard member function of the **Graphics** class, the application-specific code added to it is considered an extension of the formal **paint()** method:

```
Today = new Date();
TodayAsString = Today.toString();
graphic.drawString( TodayAsString, 10, 10 );
```

Here the member function uses the **new** keyword to dynamically allocate enough memory for an instance of the method *Date()* and then assign its memory address to *Today*. The second statement uses an inherited method, namely *toString()*, to convert *Today*'s numeric format into a string for output. Notice how easy it is to invoke an inherited object's methods (member functions) using the period member operator: *Today.toString();*. The third and final statement uses the *graphic* instance's inherited *drawString()* (formally **Graphic.drawString()** member function or method—these terms are intentionally substituted for one another so that you become comfortable with either term) to output *TodayAsString*!

## Writing Your First HTML File

Unfortunately, just rewriting the Java application's source code using applet syntax is not enough to create a Java applet. An applet, by definition, is meant to be embedded within an Internet Web page and as such needs an HTML (Hyper Text Markup Language) invocation file. After you create a class or classes that contain your applet and compile them into class files, as you would for any other Java program, you create a

Web page to hold that applet. There is a special HTML *tag* or *element* for including applets in Web pages. Java-capable browsers, like HotJava, use the information contained in that element to locate the compiled class files and execute the applet itself. In this section, you will learn how to put Java applets in a Web page and how to serve those files to the Web at large.

You include an applet on a Web page by using the HTML element **<applet>**. The following listing shows the simplest HTML file you can create to include *mysecond.class*:

```
<title>The mysecond Applet</title>
<hr>
<applet code=mysecond.class width=200 height=200>
</applet>
```

The HTML file (which is just an ASCII text file), wraps the programs title *The mysecond Applet* between the opening and closing title elements: **<title>** and **</title>**. The text between the **<title>** and **</title>** elements is displayed by browsers that do not understand the **<applet>** tag (which includes most browsers that are not Java capable). Because your Web page may be viewed in many different kinds of browsers, it is a good idea to include alternate text here so that readers of your page who don't have Java will see something other than a blank line.

You'll notice that many HTML elements have an opening and closing syntax; the closing element repeats the opening HTML element but prepends a slash symbol /. The **<hr>** represents a *horizontal rule*. This element causes the Web page to display a thin highlighted separator bar and moves the program's output pointer to the beginning of a new line.

Of particular importance to our *mysecond.java* applet is the third statement. Here the **<applet code=...>** element pulls in the compiled *mysecond.class* into the Web page. *width* and *height* are required and used to indicate the bounding box of the applet—that is, how big a box to draw for the applet on the Web page (Actually, there is more syntax required for a properly written HTML file, which is discussed later in this chapter).

Creating *mysecond.java* and the associated HTML file doesn't really look all that difficult. However, you still need to pull it all together to test it. Also, creating your third, fourth, and so on Java applets would require not only a rewrite of the Java source file but new HTML support files. A time-consuming endeavor. Fortunately, Borland has foreseen this time-wasting redundancy and included a Java-specific AppExpert right inside the IDE. In the following section you will learn just how easy it is to use this versatile Java development tool.

## Using Borland's Java AppExpert

While using the standalone *javac.exe* Java compiler and *java.exe* interpreter is straightforward, they are more cumbersome than easily useful for writing applets. For this reason, Borland has included special Java tools within the Borland C++ IDE (Integrated Development Environment), namely the Java AppExpert. Since Java applets are comprised of a minimum of two source files, the *.java* source file, along with the HTML file, the IDE uses the C++ Project Utility to pull them together.

**Starting a New Java Project** To begin writing a Java applet, start the Borland C++ IDE and click on the File | New | Project option as seen in Figure 3.5.

This will display the New Target window shown in Figure 3.6.

You begin a Java Project definition by giving the Project a path and name, for this example, *c:Applet1.ide* (notice the required *.ide* Project File extension). The IDE automatically gives the Target Name the same name, *Applet1*. At this point you are ready to select the Target Type. The default, seen highlighted in Figure 3.6, is *Application[.exe]*. However, we want to create a Java program. By sliding the Target Type slider bar down, with your mouse, you will see that the last option (not visible in Figure 3.6) is *Java[.class]*, as highlighted in Figure 3.7. Click on this option and the New Target's window options change from those seen in Figure 3.6 to those in Figure 3.7.

You complete this stage of the New Target window's settings by clicking on the *AppExpert for Java* checkbox *Launch AppEx-*

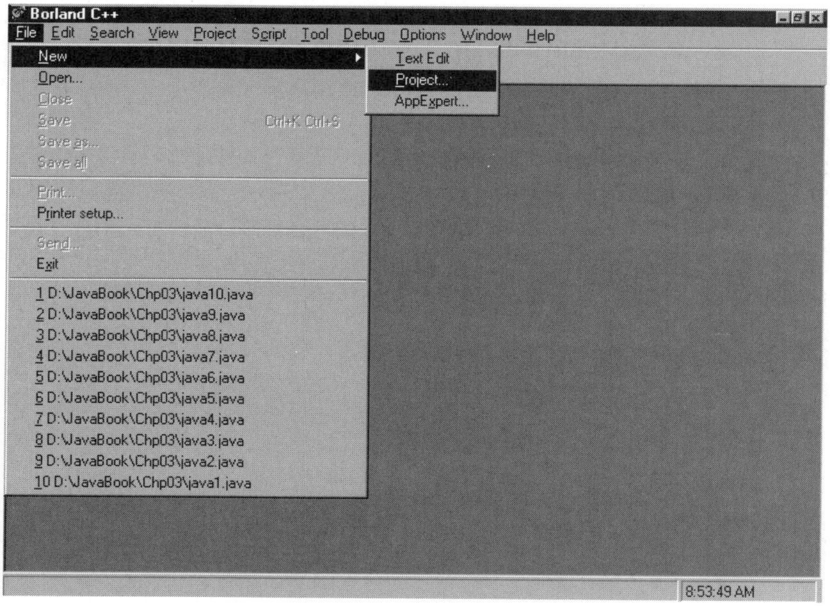


**Figure 3.5:** Starting a new Java project.

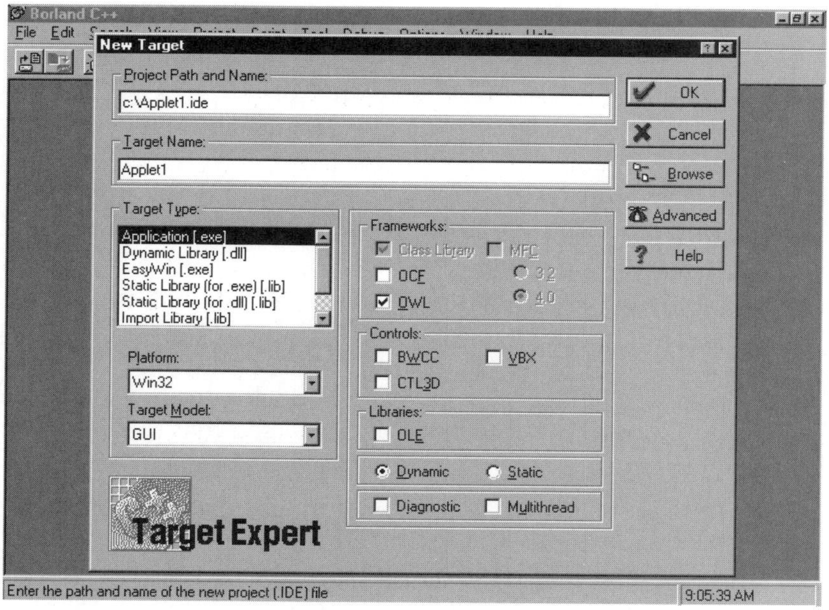


**Figure 3.6:** New Target window (default).

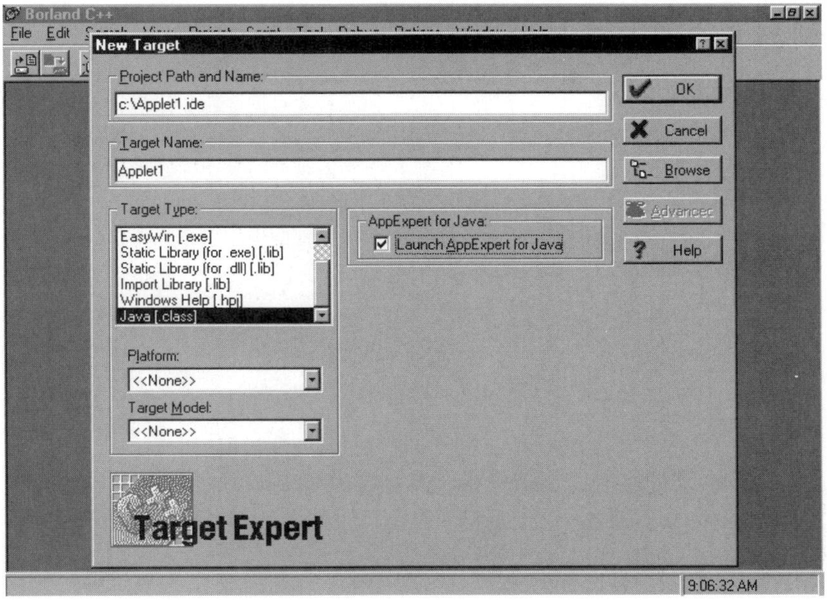


**Figure 3.7:** New Target window showing *Java[.class]* options.

*pert for Java* (seen in Figure 3.7). Acknowledge these settings by now clicking on the window's OK button.

DON'T do anything else at this point. Launching the AppExpert takes several long seconds, even for a fast Pentium processor. When what seems like a computer-long time passes you will see two things happen. First, a Project window will open, then the Borland AppExpert for Java window will superimpose itself on top of the Project window, as seen in Figure 3.8.

At the bottom of this window you will see five file folder tabs: *Admin*, *Methods*, *Derivation*, *Threads*, and *Code Preview*. The next section discusses each folder's options in detail.

The *Admin* folder allows you to add an optional copyright comment to the top of your Java source file. Figure 3.8 demonstrates the types of information you may wish to include, such as a program *Description*, *Copyright*, *Company* name, *Version* number, and *Author*. Clicking on the *Methods* tab displays the AppExpert window shown in Figure 3.9.

From previous discussions, remember that a method is really nothing more than a function tied to a specific class. The AppExpert *Methods* folder provides three options: *Stub paint*

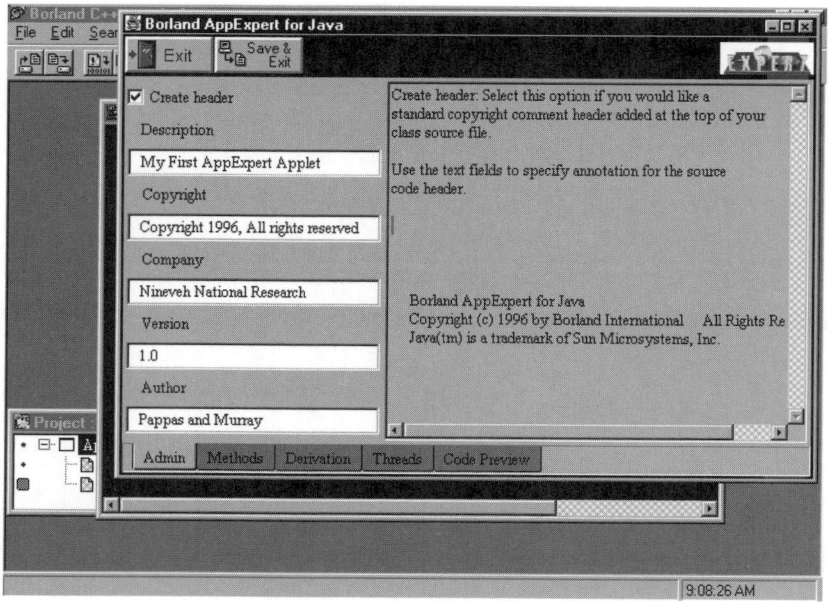


**Figure 3.8:** Borland AppExpert for Java window (*Admin* tab selected).

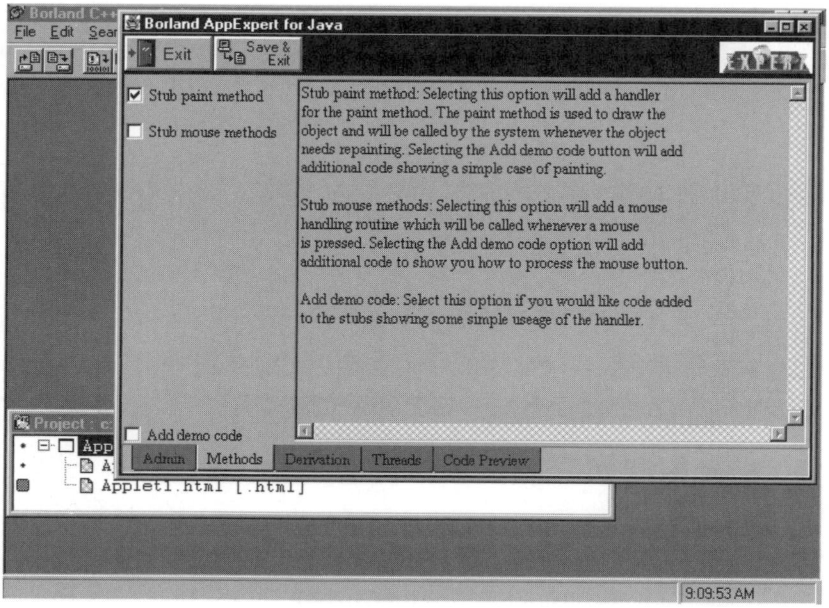


**Figure 3.9:** Borland AppExpert for Java window (*Methods* tab selected).

*method*, *Stub mouse methods*, and *Add demo code*. All of the sample programs used throughout the remaining chapters use the **paint()** *method* to draw the applet's output, so leave this option checked (the default). However, in order not to overwhelm you with pages of auto-generated code, for now, click off both the *Stub mouse methods* (this option, demonstrated in later chapters, adds a mouse interface to the applet) and *Add demo code* (adds demonstration code to the applet). With this accomplished click on the *Derivation* tab. This displays the updated window seen in Figure 3.10.

Since we want to develop an applet, leave the *Can be an applet* checkbox checked (the default). As the windowed text implies, the *Add applet stubs* option is not implemented. Leave the *Runnable* and *Add main entry point* check boxes checked. (These options are explained in greater detail in later chapters.) The *Imports* field is left blank since any imported classes will be taken care of using the Java **import** statement. Since the code we are defining is not to be placed within a package, the *Package name* field is left blank. Finally, since we want to the program to *Derive from* an applet or application, not some other

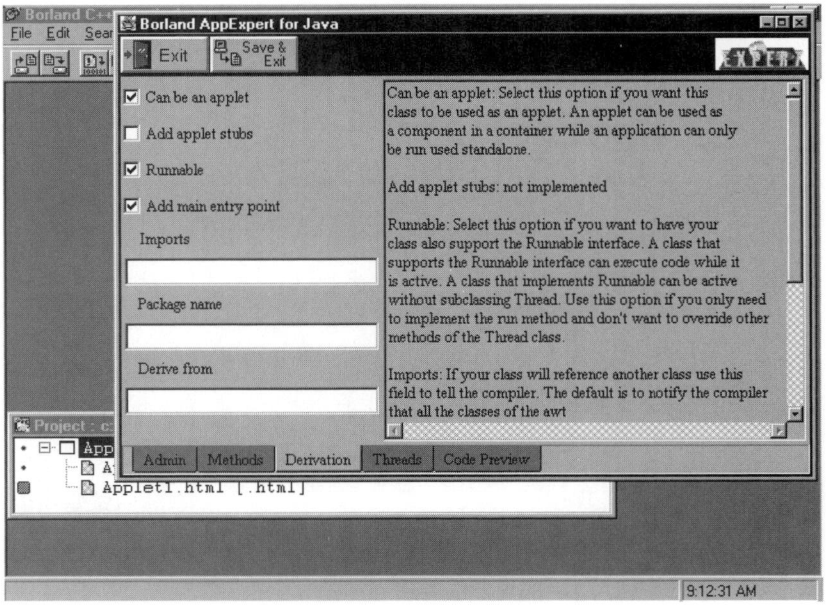


**Figure 3.10:** Borland AppExpert for Java window (*Derivation* tab selected).

class, leave this last field empty. Now click on the *Threads* tab. You will see a window similar to Figure 3.11.

Click the two *Thread* options off for now (threads allow you to write/run concurrently executing tasks). In later chapters you will learn more about threads and how to use them. For now, they aren't needed. At this point you are ready to view AppExpert's auto-generated code by clicking on the *Code Preview* tab, as seen in Figure 3.12. Whenever you are finished looking at the code, make certain you click on the *Save & Exit* button at the top of the window seen in Figure 3.12.

**Using the AppExpert's Auto-Generated Java Source File** If you were to run the code generated by AppExpert, all you would see is an empty applet window. The following discussion explains the standard elements of the auto-generated code and specifically shows how to extend the template to print today's day, time, and date.

```
//------------------------------------------------------------------------
// Applet1 My First AppExpert Applet
// Copyright 1996, All rights reserved
```

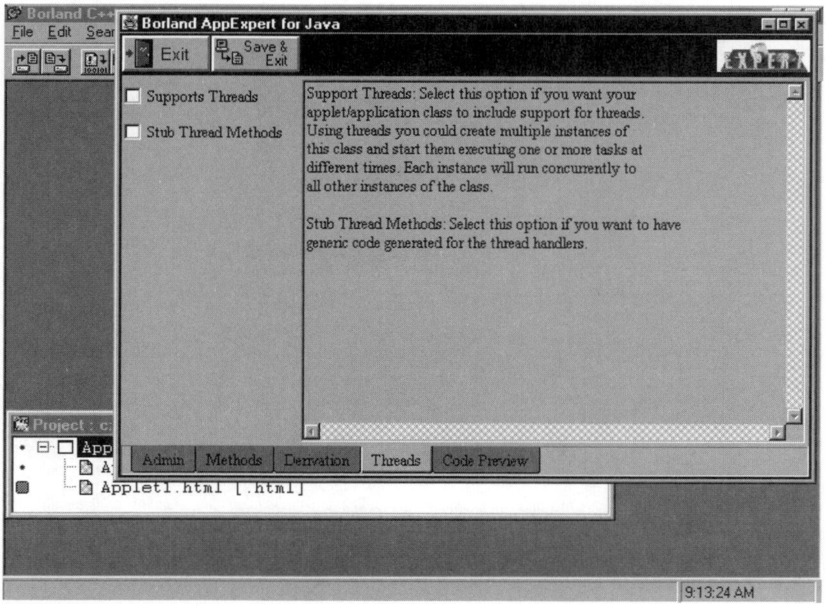


**Figure 3.11:** Borland AppExpert for Java window (*Threads* tab selected).

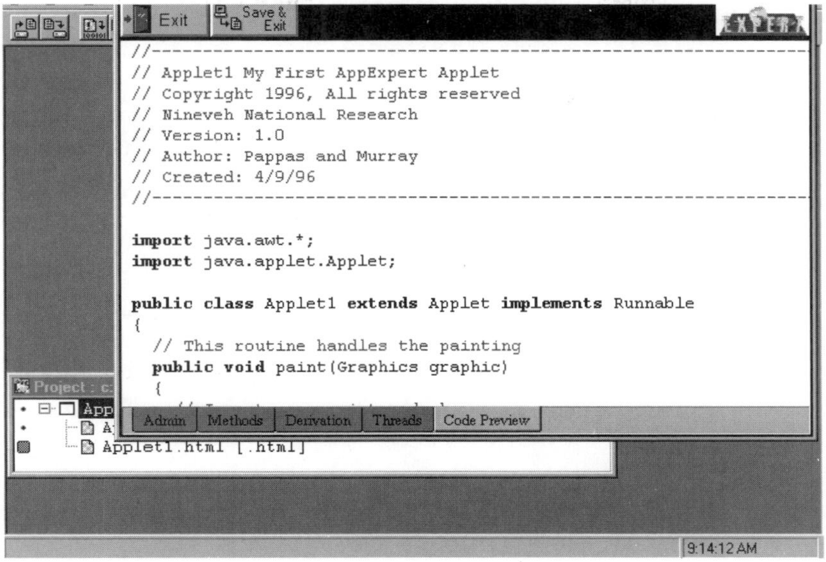


**Figure 3.12:** Borland AppExpert for Java window (*Code Preview* tab selected).

```
// Nineveh National Research
// Version: 1.0
// Author: Pappas and Murray
// Created: 4/9/96
//-------------------------------------------------------------------

import java.awt.*;
import java.applet.Applet;
import java.util.Date;

public class Applet1 extends Applet implements Runnable
{
 Date systemdate;
 String mydate;

 // This routine handles the painting
 public void paint(Graphics graphic)
 {
   systemdate = new Date();

   mydate = systemdate.toString();
   graphic.drawString(mydate, 10, 10);
 }

 // Implements Runnable Interface
```

```
  public void run()
  {
  }

  // For running standalone
  public static void main(String[] argv)
  {
    // Create the frame and launch Applet1
    Frame f = new Frame("Applet1Frame");
    f.reshape(100, 100, 200, 100);
    f.show();

    Applet1 x = new Applet1();
    f.add("Center", x);
    x.init();
    x.start();
  }

  // Constructor
  public  Applet1()
  {
  }

} // end class Applet1
```

Notice how the AppExpert has inserted the *Admin*'s folder information directly into the comment block. Below the comment you see three **import** statements:

```
import java.awt.*;
import java.applet.Applet;
import java.util.Date;
```

These three **import** statements are identical to the Java applet written earlier, without the AppExpert, except for one change, the Java applet had this statement:

```
import java.awt.Graphics;
```

while the Java AppExpert generated this statement:

```
import java.awt.*;
```

Many system commands like **dir**, **copy**, and many Windows options, such as File Manager, allow you to use what are called wild cards. *Wild cards* are symbols that the invoked utility uses for search criterion. The asterisk symbol * is one of those symbols. By changing the import extension from *.Graphics;* to *.*;*, the AppExpert has generated a more general, robust, **import** statement. Rather than just pulling in the **java.awt.Graphics** class, the statement pulls in all **java.awt.*** classes.

The next statement is generated by the AppExpert and begins the applet's **class** definition. Notice the AppExpert gives the **class** the same name as the Project file (i.e., *Applet1.ide*).

```
public class Applet1 extends Applet implements Runnable
{
    .
    .
    .
}
```

The only new feature found in this **class** definition is **implements Runnable**. A **class** that has implemented the **Runnable** interface can be run in a thread by passing the instance of the class to a new thread object (threads are discussed in the next chapter).

The next five statements were added to the auto-generated AppExpert **class** definition to enable the template to output the day, date, and time.

```
 Date systemdate;                          // added to template
String mydate;                            // added to template

// This routine handles the painting
public void paint(Graphics graphic)
{
  systemdate = new Date();                // added to template

  mydate = systemdate.toString();         // added to template
  graphic.drawString(mydate, 10, 10);     // added to template
}
```

The **run()** method, not used here, is where you can put your thread code (threads are discussed in the next chapter).

```
 // Implements Runnable Interface
public void run()
{
}
```

Surprise! Do you recognize the beginning syntax in this next portion of the auto-generated AppExpert code? Sure, it is the same **main()** declaration used at the beginning of the chapter to write a standalone Java application. You see, the AppExpert generates a source file that can be used to develop a standalone Java application, or a Java applet!

The **Frame** class implements a bordered window with the applet's title, *"Applet1Frame."* The **reshape()** method dimensions the window and the **show()** method actually displays the framed window.

```
 // For running standalone
public static void main(String[] argv)
{
  // Create the frame and launch Applet1
  Frame f = new Frame("Applet1Frame");
  f.reshape(100, 100, 200, 100);
  f.show();
```

The next four statements instantiate the object *x* of **class** type *Applet1*, use the **add()** method to *"Center,"* the applet, call the instance's (*x*) **init()** method to initialize the object, and finally invoke the **start()** method to execute the applet (Note: all of these methods are discussed in greater detail in later chapters.)

```
   Applet1 x = new Applet1();
  f.add("Center", x);
  x.init();
  x.start();
}
```

This last code section contains the **class**' constructor method stub and the closing } for the entire *Applet1* **class** definition.

```
 // Constructor
public  Applet1()
{
}

} // end class Applet1
```

A *constructor* is a special class method that is automatically invoked whenever the object is instantiated.

At this point you are ready to compile the Project.

**Compiling *Applet1.java*** To compile the *.java* source file created by AppExpert, you first click once, with the left mouse button, on the *.java* source file in the Project window, as seen in Figure 3.13.

Next, using the right mouse button, click once, again on the *.java* source file in the Project window. Figure 3.14 shows the *JavaCompile* option highlighted. To actually start the Java compiler, slide the highlight bar down to the *JavaCompile* option.

Before executing the compile, make certain that your Java source file matches the one seen in Figure 3.15.

At this point you should be able to execute a successful compile and a Translate window similar to Figure 3.16. If not, scan your IDE *Applet1.java* edit window for any typographical errors you may have made.

**Using the AppExpert's Auto-Generated HTML Source File** With the exception of the last line of code, the AppExpert's auto-generated HTML file (see Figure 3.17) is

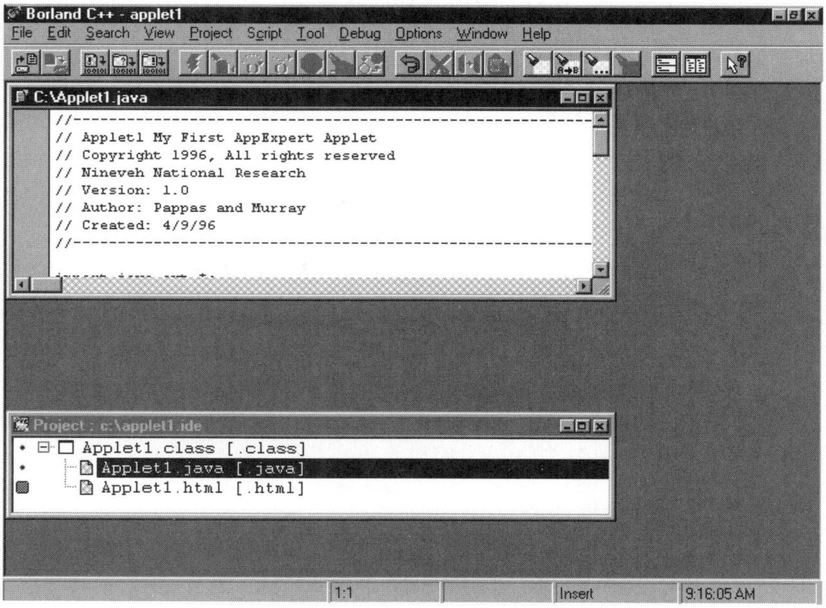


**Figure 3.13:** First step in compiling AppExpert's auto-generated source file.

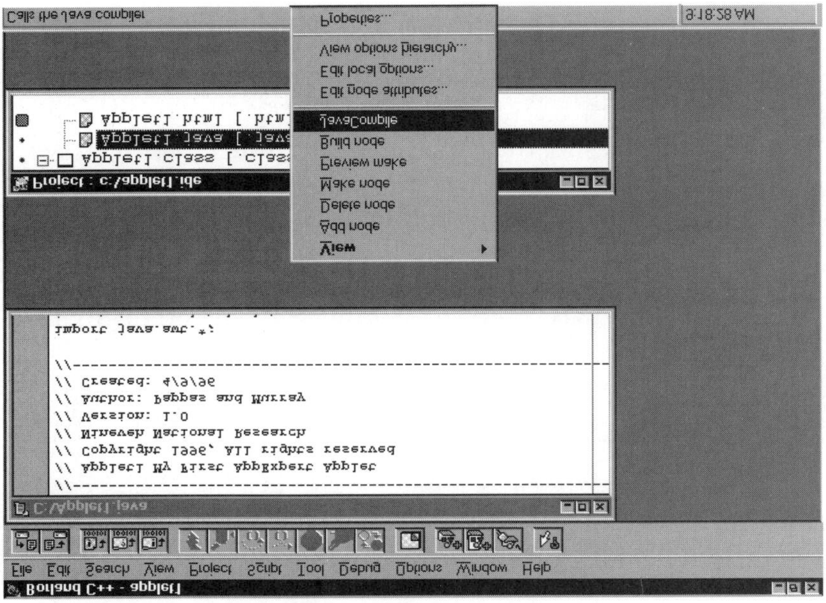


**Figure 3.14:** Selecting the *JavaCompile* option.

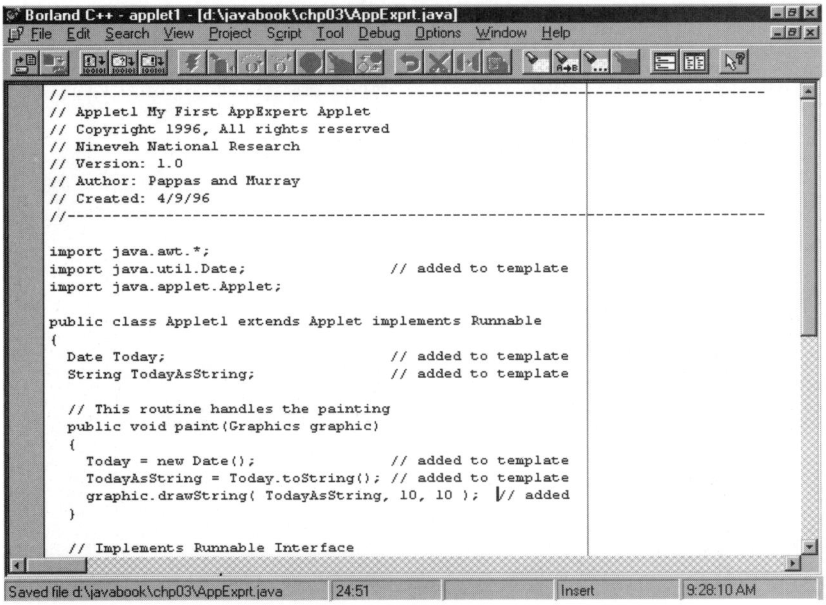

Borland C++ - applet1 - [d:\javabook\chp03\AppExprt.java]
File Edit Search View Project Script Tool Debug Options Window Help
//--------------------------------------------------------------------
// Applet1 My First AppExpert Applet
// Copyright 1996, All rights reserved
// Nineveh National Research
// Version: 1.0
// Author: Pappas and Murray
// Created: 4/9/96
//--------------------------------------------------------------------
import java.awt.*;
import java.util.Date; // added to template
import java.applet.Applet;
public class Applet1 extends Applet implements Runnable
{
Date Today; // added to template
String TodayAsString; // added to template
// This routine handles the painting
public void paint(Graphics graphic)
{
Today = new Date(); // added to template
TodayAsString = Today.toString(); // added to template
graphic.drawString( TodayAsString, 10, 10 ); // added
}
// Implements Runnable Interface
Saved file d:\javabook\chp03\AppExprt.java
24:51
Insert
9:28:10 AM


**Figure 3.15:** Edited AppExpert auto-generated code to output day, time, and date.

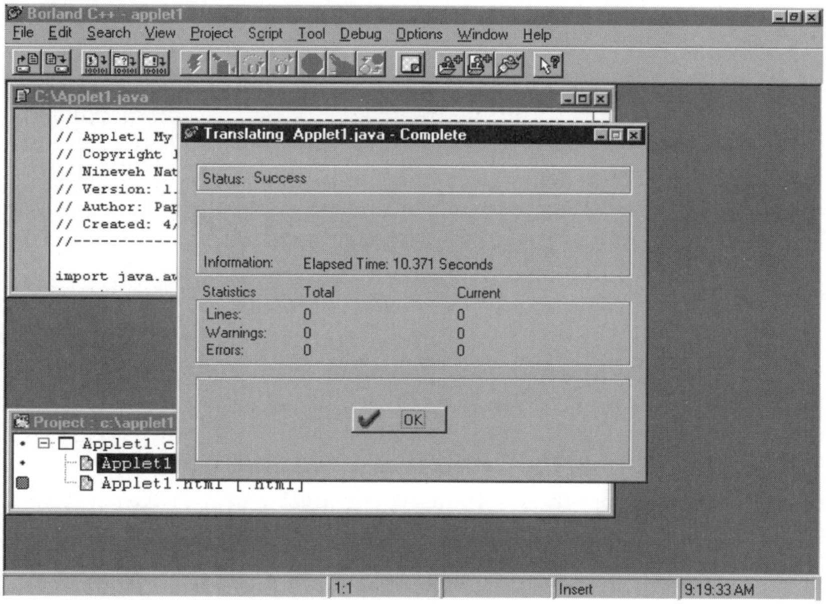


**Figure 3.16:** Completed and successful Java compile window.

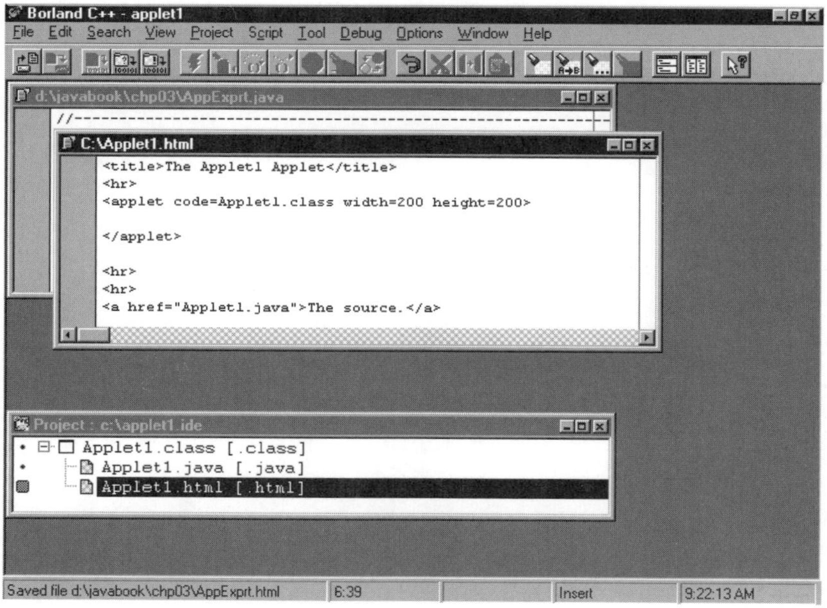


**Figure 3.17:** AppExpert's auto-generated *Applet1.html* source file.

identical to the one discussed earlier in this chapter. The new line of HTML code:

```
<a href="Applet1.java">The source.</a>
```

uses the **<a>** HTML element type to anchor, or reference, the source file link.

**Running *Applet1*** Remember that the difference between a Java application and Java applet is that the latter program format is designed to be nested within a Web page. Fortunately, the AppExpert took care of generating this for us. To run the applet simply click the left mouse button, once, on the *Applet1.html* file in the Project window, as seen in Figure 3.18.

**AppExpert's Bonus: An Applet and Application In One!** Borland's Java AppExpert automatically generates the code necessary to create not only a Java applet but a Java application as well. To run the AppExpert auto-generated code to execute a Java application, simply click the right mouse button, once, on the *Applet1.class* file in the Project window, instead of

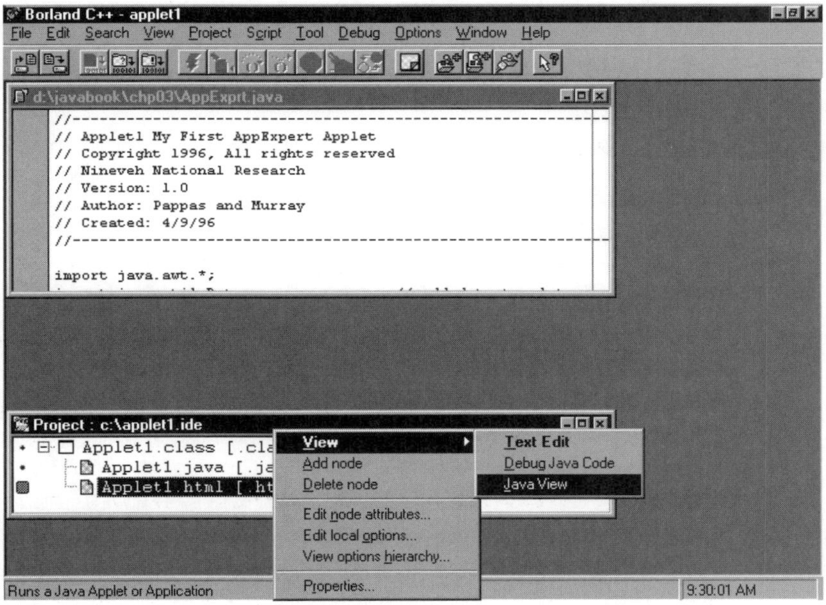


**Figure 3.18:** Using the Applet Viewer to view *Applet1.class.*

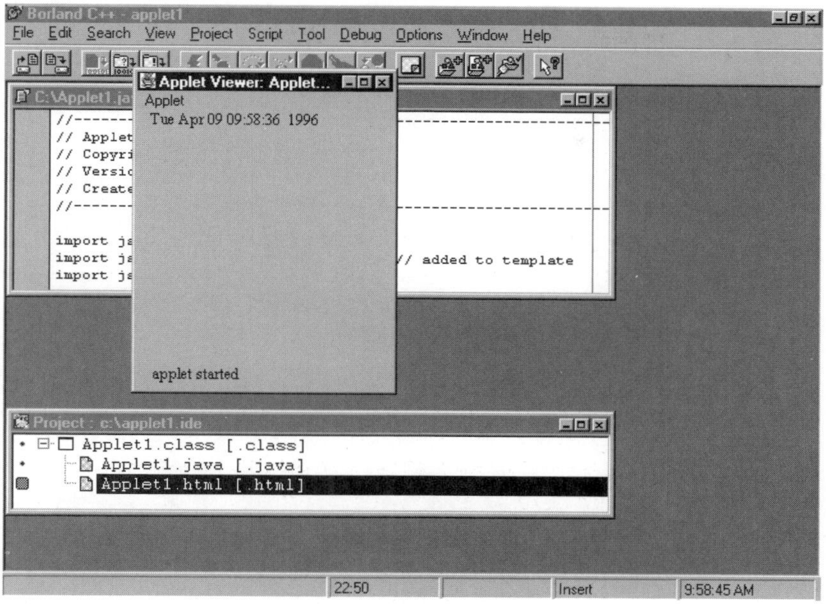


**Figure 3.19:** Running *Applet1* as a Java applet.

*Applet1.html*. Then choose the *Java View* option, as seen in Figure 3.20.

Figure 3.21 shows the resulting *Applet1* application.

## Debugging Applets

Unfortunately for most of us programmers, contrary to our programming egos, we do not always write flawless code. Once again the Borland IDE comes to the rescue with an integrated Java debugger. With the Java debugger you can set breakpoints (program execution STOP points) and view variable contents and class members. However, to access this information you must have first compiled your Java source file with the compiler's debugging information check box selected.

**Turning Debugging Information On** To have local variable information available when debugging your project, you must first compile the project and include debugging information so that a detailed symbol table is generated in your class files. You do this by selecting, in order, the IDE's

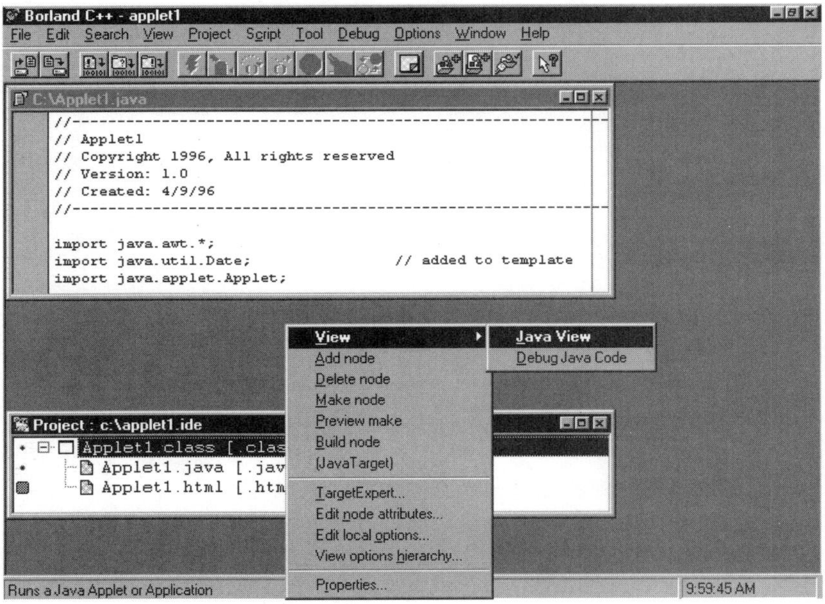


**Figure 3.20:** Running *Applet1* as a Java application.

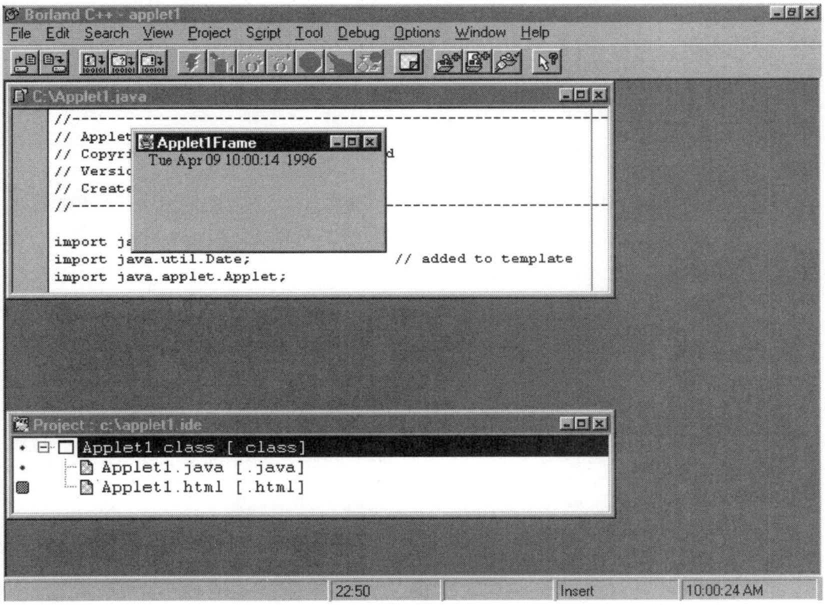


**Figure 3.21:** Viewing *Applet1* as a Java application.

main Options | Project | Java | Compiler Options | Generate Debug Information check box.

**Starting the Java Debugger** To start a Java Debug session, simply click the right mouse button, once, on the *.class* file in the Project window. For our example, this file is *Applet1.class*. When you do this you will see the Java View | Java Debug menu option, as seen in Figure 3.22.

Assuming you have turned on the debugging option in your Project's Java compiler options, when you compiled your program, the Java debugger will automatically load your program into the Borland Debugger for Java window seen in Figure 3.23. However, Figure 3.23 has had several options activated, so do not be surprised if you see a more vacant window.

Table 3.1 lists the seven major components of the Java debugger window.

The File menu contains the usual set of options, for example, opening a Java source file (the same function as the first Speed Bar icon), which is done automatically, and exiting the Java

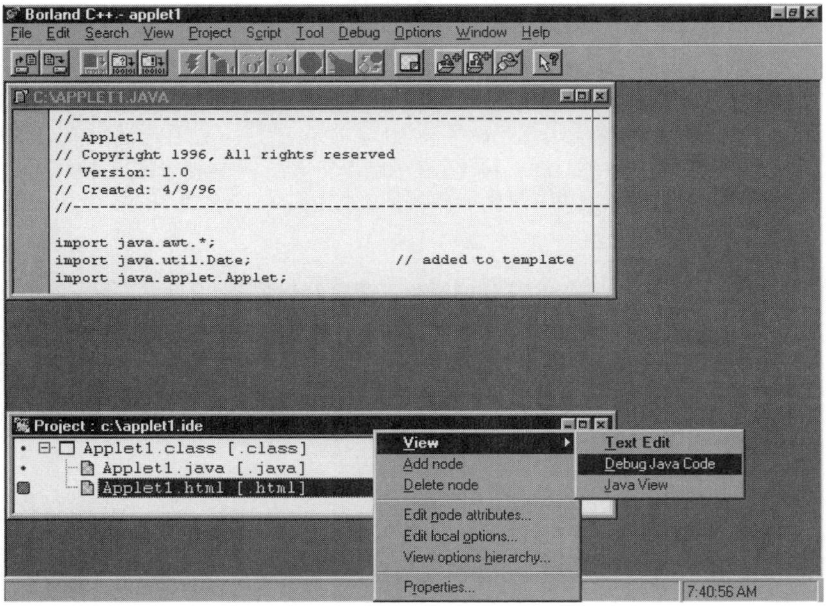


**Figure 3.21:** Starting a Debug Java Code session.

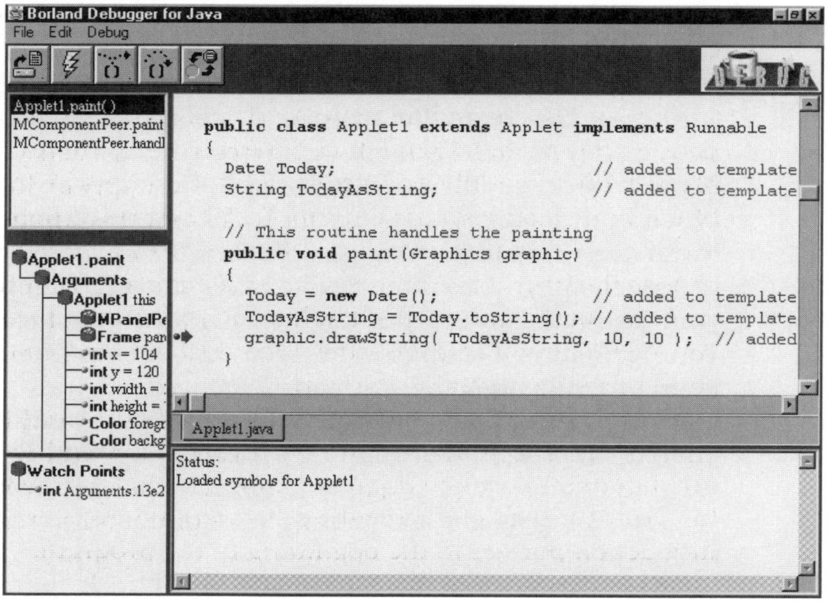


**Figure 3.22:** Set-up Borland Debugger for Java window.

Debugger. The Speed Bar buttons mimic many of the Debug menu commands described below.

The Debug | Run command executes your Java program. Step Into and Step Over instruct the Java debugger to execute your program one line at a time. The difference between the two commands is that Step Into, when executing a method call, traces *into* the method line by line, while Step Over exe-

**Table 3.1:** Java Debugger Window Components

| *Java Debugger Window Component* | *Description* |
|---|---|
| The Main menu: | File, Edit, Debug |
| The Speed Bar buttons: | (from left to right) File Open, Run, Step Into, Step Over, and Toggle Breakpoint |
| The Call Stack pane: | Upperleft frame |
| The Current Context pane: | Middleleft frame |
| The Watch pane: | Lowerleft frame |
| The Source pane: | Upperright frame |
| The Message pane: | Lowerright frame |

cutes the called method full speed. You would choose Step Over whenever you are debugging a Java method imported from a previously debugged class or program.

The Toggle Breakpoint command sets and removes an execution stop point in your Java Source pane. When you set a breakpoint you will see a small red button appear to the left of the line of source code. Figure 3.24 has a breakpoint set on the line beginning with *graphic.drawString....* When you choose the Run command, if a breakpoint is set, Run will execute the program full speed and then stop on the breakpoint. At this point you can choose to Step Into or Step Over successive code statements.

The last three Debug menu options have no Speed Bar icon equivalent. You normally use the Reset command whenever you have single stepped past a statement that you would like to check out again. Executing a program reset resets the instruction pointer to the beginning of the program.

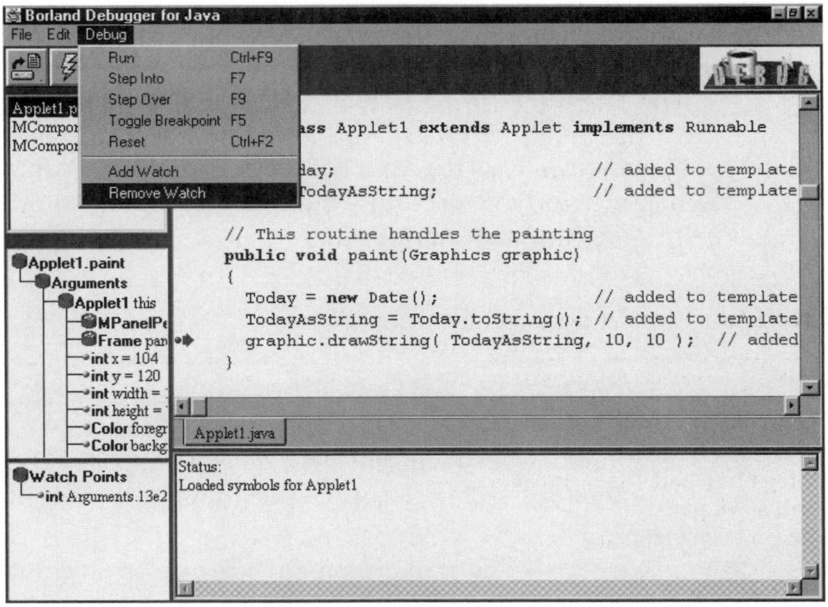


**Figure 3.23:** Debug menu commands.

Finally, executing your program line by line would be a meaningless endeavor if you could not view the contents of critical program components. The last two Debug menu commands, Add Watch and Remove Watch, allow you to place or remove a Java program component from the Watch pane. Figure 3.24 has used many of these Java debugger options.

Notice that the Call Stack pane is showing the call stack order of various Java class methods (*Applet1.paint(), MyComponentPeer.paint, MyComponentPeer.handle)*. The Current Context pane (*Applet1.paint/Arguments/Applet1*) is displaying the contents of the stack frame at the location selected in the Call stack pane (*Applet1.paint*). The Watch pane is showing ***int*** *Arguments...* contents. The Source pane is displaying *Applet1.java*, and finally the Message pane indicates that *Applet1*'s symbol table has been successfully loaded.

## Java Lingo

*class*—Java keyword used to define objects.

*compound block*—More than one executable statement syntactically bound to a controlling statement with a pair of matching braces { }, as in a formal class or member function definition.

*extends*—Tells the Java compiler that the specified class is going to have additional application-specific code added to its formal definition.

*HTML*—Hyper Text Markup Language. A file used to define Internet Web pages and specifically used with the Java language to host a Java applet.

*import*—Pulls in Java or user-supplied package and class definitions.

*java.exe*—The Java run-time interpreter. *java.exe* is used with compiled Java source files having a *.class* file extension.

*javac.exe*—The stand alone Java compiler. *javac.exe* is used with Java source files having a *.java* file extension.

*member function*—A function syntactically bound to a specific class. Also called a method.

*method*—A function syntactically bound into a specific class. Also called a member function.

# 4

# Java Programming Fundamentals

In Chapter 2, you learned about the fundamental features and syntax of the Java language. In Chapter 3, you learned more about the differences between Java applications and Java applets. You also learned how to use Borland's IDE Java tools to enter, edit, compile, debug, and run Java programs. Chapter 4 is designed to finalize your conceptual and syntactic understanding of the higher level constructs provided by the Java language.

If you are already comfortable with an object-oriented language, like Ada or C++, you will find many of the topics discussed in this chapter quite familiar. If you are new to object-oriented programming languages, Chapter 4 is particularly important. Many of the object-oriented concepts discussed in this chapter are first presented using their procedural-oriented language's underpinnings.

## Classes and Objects

To help put the concepts involved in object-oriented programming into perspective, ask yourself the following question. Did you need to go out and purchase a new computer just to execute programs designed using object-oriented technology? Of course, the answer is no. Whether the executable file you were running had procedural-design assembly language source code roots, or FORTRAN or COBOL, or Pascal or C, or object-oriented-design Ada or C++ origins, once the source file was assembled or compiled and linked into an *.exe* format, they all ran on the same computer. That's good news.

Here's the point: no matter how complex object-oriented design philosophy and syntax may appear, ultimately, when the program is compiled, all the high-brow philosophy and syntax gets translated down to machine code simple—moves, compares, jumps, shifts, adds, subtracts, multiplies, and divides! So, let's begin by demystifying objects.

First, all Java programming must be done within a class (note: in Java, there are no standalone functions). Java has the **class** keyword for this purpose. From previous chapters you know that an object is very similar to a C/C++ structure with one addition, the structure's members can be functions (called member functions, or methods). So notice that an object really does not contain any new horsepower that a Pascal record and standalone functions would provide! It's just that object-oriented languages provide a syntax that can bundle these two constructs into one side effect–proof syntax. The syntax for a Java class is:

```
class classTag {
    // member data declarations go here
    .
    // member function (methods) declarations go here
}
```

The Java keyword is **class** and the *classTag* field is where you supply a readable, self-documenting identifier as the name of the class. Notice the brace pairs { } indicating that a class definition is considered a compound block.

## Instantiating Java Class Member Data

If you are new to object-oriented programming, then you probably don't know the meaning for the word instantiating. So, let's rewrite the section title, using terms that all programmers understand: Creating Fields Within a Record. There, how's that? *Instantiation*, or *instantiating an object*, in object-oriented programming terms is very similar to *creating a variable* in procedural programming terms. Java member data instantiation has the same syntax as a standalone variable declaration:

```
class classTag {
  memberDataType memberDataName [, more_memberDataNames];
  // method definitions follow
}
```

The following code segment declares four data members, *Title*, *Age*, *HourlyWage*, and *WorkedThisWeek*, of the class *sample*:

```
class sample {
  String  Title = "The employee's paycheck is: ";
  int     Age;
  double  HourlyWage, WorkedThisWeek;
}
```

Since by definition, an object contains both data and functions that work on the data, this class definition has no functionality; all it can do is hold three types of information, **String**, **int**, and **double**.

## Methods

Methods, otherwise known as member functions, are really nothing more (syntax-wise) than functions bound specifically to a specific **class** type. The general syntax for declaring methods is:

```
class classTag {
  // member data declarations
  // method declarations
     method_ReturnType methodName( [ optionalDummyArgumentList ] ) {
         // method body
         .
         .
         // return only needed when method_ReturnType is not void
```

```
        [ return method_ReturnType_instance; ]
    }
}
```

Suppose we wanted our *sample* class to calculate an employee's weekly paycheck. The following method accomplishes this:

```
double CalculatePaycheck( ) {
    return( HourlyWage * WorkedThisWeek );
}
```

Notice that the method's body has global access to the data members *HourlyWage* and *WorkedThisWeek* and that they are not passed as actual arguments. All class data members are global to all the class' methods. However, a class' methods may define their own local variables. Normally, these variables would be visible only within the defining method. The updated *sample* class now looks like:

```
class sample {
  String  Title = "The employee's paycheck is: ";
  int     Age;
  double  HourlyWage, WorkedThisWeek;

  double CalculatePaycheck( ) {
    return( HourlyWage * WorkedThisWeek );
  }
}
```

Of course, a class that stores information and calculates some result is fairly useless unless it can output those results. This next method accomplishes this task:

```
void PrintPaycheck( ) {
  System.out.print( Title );
  System.out.println( CalculatePaycheck() );
}
```

## Constructors

If you had a good introductory, language-independent design course in your formal programming education, then you understand the need not only to declare variables but also to initialize them. In a modular design, procedural language algorithm, this is usually accomplished by a function you write.

A properly defined object also addresses this issue of member data initialization. Like its procedural counterpart, an object also uses a function to initialize the class' member data. This initialization function has a specific name. It is called a *constructor.* However, constructors have a syntax and behavior that are different from a normal class' methods.

The syntax for an object's constructor looks like this:

```
class classTag {
  // member data declarations
  // constructor method declaration
  public classTag( [ optionalDummyArgumentList ] ) {
    // constructor statement(s)
  }
}
```

There are three major differences between a class' methods and its unique constructor method. First, the constructor's identifier (name) must match the class' *classTag*. Second, constructors do not have a return type. Third, nowhere in your Java program will you ever see the constructor method called. This is because constructors are automatically invoked anytime your program instantiates the class.

The following *sample* class constructor demonstrates constructor syntax and correct logical use:

```
public sample( int AnAge, double AnHourlyWage, double HasWorkedThisWeek ){
    Age = AnAge;
    HourlyWage = AnHourlyWage;
    WorkedThisWeek = HasWorkedThisWeek;
  }
```

Notice that the name of the constructor method, *sample,* matches the class' name, *sample*. The constructor's code takes care of receiving the actual arguments passed to it, *AnAge, AnHourlyWage,* and *HasWorkedThisWeek,* and assigns these values to the class' data members. This roundabout way of initializing data members has a specific purpose, to make certain that no invalid values are ever used to initialize the object. (Note: to keep this introductory example a reasonable length, the constructor does not include all of the code necessary to perform this task.)

To make our *sample* class definition a fully functional Java application, we need to add a **main()**:

```
public static void main( String args[] ) {
    sample EmployeeOne = new sample( 23, 9.85, 40.5);
    sample EmployeeTwo = new sample( 47, 12.87, 55.0);

    EmployeeOne.PrintPaycheck();
    EmployeeTwo.PrintPaycheck();
  }
```

The method's body begins by instantiating two *sample* class objects, *EmployeeOne* and *EmployeeTwo*. Remember that when you instantiate an object, you always place its data type to the left of its identifier. For standard types like integer, you use *int objectName;* for user-defined types like *class sample*, you use *sample objectName*.

To the right of the Java assignment operator, =, you see the keyword **new**. **new** dynamically allocates enough memory to instantiate a tangible object (i.e., *EmployeeOne*) of the hypothetical blueprint type *class sample*. When the object is instantiated, its constructor method is automatically invoked. So the code to the right of **new**:

```
sample( 23, 9.85, 40.5);
sample( 47, 12.87, 55.0);
```

serves two purposes. First, it tells **new** what type of object to instantiate, and second, it passes the automatically invoked constructor any necessary initialization values. The following listing shows a complete, compilable/interpretable *sample* class:

```
import java.awt.*;

class sample {
  String  Title = "The employee's paycheck is: ";
  int     Age;
  double  HourlyWage, WorkedThisWeek;

  public sample( int AnAge, double AnHourlyWage, double HasWorkedThisWeek ){
```

```
      Age = AnAge;
      HourlyWage = AnHourlyWage;
      WorkedThisWeek = HasWorkedThisWeek;
    }

    double CalculatePaycheck() {
      return( HourlyWage * WorkedThisWeek );
    }
    void PrintPaycheck() {
      System.out.print( Title );
      System.out.println( CalculatePaycheck() );
    }
    public static void main( String args[] ) {
      sample EmployeeOne = new sample( 23, 9.85, 40.5);
      sample EmployeeTwo = new sample( 47, 12.87, 55.0);

      EmployeeOne.PrintPaycheck();
      EmployeeTwo.PrintPaycheck();
    }
  }
```

## Destructors—*finalize()*

While the subject of constructors is still fresh in your mind, let's discuss the syntax and logical use for another unique type of class method. If a constructor method serves to initialize an object, or in more detail, provide all of the code necessary to get the object up and running, then a destructor performs the logical inverse. *Destructor* methods perform object cleanup.

The syntax for many object-oriented languages' destructors also involves the class' *classTag* name preceded by a tilde ~. For our *sample* class, the constructor's name was *sample*, and in C++ the destructor method's name would be *~sample*. In Java, all class destructor methods have the same name: **finalize**. Finalizer methods are called just before the object is garbage-collected and its memory reclaimed. To create a finalizer method, include a method with the following signature in your class definition:

```
void finalize() {
  // finalize method code goes here
}
```

## OVERLOADING

When learning any new programming language, oftentimes the easy part is learning the new language's syntax. The harder part is learning the industrywide agreed upon nuances of that language. For example, programmers would not solve a problem and code the solution in assembly language, the way they would in COBOL or the way they would in an object-oriented language. This analogy holds true for overloading.

Simply stated, Java *overloading* allows you to define more than one class method, using the same method name. Here the syntax is not the problem, but rather, why would a programmer want to do that? The proper use of overloading is reserved for a piece of code that logically performs the same function but that can be started off with a different number of arguments and/or different argument types. This last statement explains why Java requires all overloaded methods to have unique formal argument lists.

Take, for example, a method written to sum arrays of three numeric values. The algorithm, or series of steps needed to perform this calculation, is identical regardless of the numeric data type (**int**, **float**, or **double**) of the array. This algorithm is a perfect candidate for overloading. Notice that the following two methods have identical sequences of events, the same number and type of statements, and that the only difference involves the variable's data types:

```
// Overloaded method to sum an array of three integers
public int SumArray( int intArray[] ) {
  int offset;
  int tempTotal = 0;

  for( offset = 0; offset < 3; offset++ )
    tempTotal += intArray[ offset ] ;

  return( tempTotal );
}
// Overloaded method to sum an array of three doubles
public double SumArray( double doubleArray[] ) {
  int offset;
  double tempTotal = 0;
```

```
  for( offset = 0; offset < 3; offset++ )
    tempTotal += doubleArray[ offset ] ;

  return( tempTotal );
}
```

## Overloading Constructors

A special case of overloading involves a class' constructor. Just as with regular methods, a class' constructor can also take a varying number and type of arguments. Since the logical use for a constructor often involves the initialization of class data members, an overloaded class constructor usually involves varying degrees of initialization.

Take, for example, a class that calculates an employee's weekly paycheck. There could be paycheck calculations based on three criteria: employees working forty hours at the standard rate, employees working more or less than forty hours at the standard rate, and employees working more or less than forty hours at a nonstandard rate. The following code segment demonstrates how you could overload the *paycheck* class constructor to represent each type of employee:

```
public class paycheck {
  int HoursWorked;
  double Rate;

// Employees working 40 hours at standard rate
  public void paycheck() {
    HoursWorked = 40;
    Rate = 8.79;
  }

// Employees working more/less than 40 hours at standard rate
  public void paycheck( int WorkedThisWeek ) {
    HoursWorked = WorkedThisWeek;
    Rate = 8.79;
  }

// Employees working more/less than 40 hours at non-standard rate
  public void paycheck( double CurrentRate ) {
    HoursWorked = 40;
    Rate = CurrentRate;
  }
```

```
  public void paycheck( int WorkedThisWeek, double CurrentRate ) {
    HoursWorked = WorkedThisWeek;
    Rate = CurrentRate;
  }
}
```

With these overloaded *paycheck* class constructors, you can now instantiate *paycheck* objects three ways:

```
paycheck standardHoursStandardRate = new paycheck();
paycheck standardHoursNonStandardRate = new paycheck(10.05);
paycheck nonStandardHoursNonStandardRate = new paycheck(55, 12.00);
```

Since each of the instantiated object's actual argument lists is unique in the number of arguments, and their data type(s), the Java compiler knows which matching overloaded constructor method to invoke.

### Operator Overloading

Many object-oriented languages provide not only method overloading but operator overloading as well. The principle here is the same, except that it applies to the language's operators. In C++, for example, you can overload the addition operator + to concatenate null-terminated strings—something it was originally incapable of doing. *Operator overloading* allows you to extend the functionality of an object-oriented language's standard set of operators. Java does *not* support operator overloading.

## INHERITANCE

The term inheritance involves the definition for a new class, based on some previously defined class. The new class is technically referred to as a subclass, while the class the subclass is based upon is known as a superclass. The subclass is then said to inherit the characteristics of its superclass.

There are many ways to refer to this inheritance relationship, with most terms having a direct logical link to family trees. So, for example, a subclass may also be referred to as a *child class*. A superclass may also be called a *parent class*. A superclass may be subclassed, and then the subclass subclassed. In this family tree structure, then, the original superclass, from which both subclasses were built, may be called a *root* or *base class*. Oftentimes in Java, a base class definition uses the keyword **abstract**, meaning the base class *must* be subclassed before it can be instantiated.

Sometimes the process of deriving subclasses is called a *derivation*. So you can say that you are *deriving* a subclass. However, since Java does not support multiple inheritance (*multiple inheritance* is where a subclass *would* inherit the characteristics of *two* parent classes), the terms parent class and child class are infrequently used. Instead, Java uses the terms superclass and subclass. *Siblings*, a term applied to derived child classes sharing the same parent class, also has a different meaning. In Java, a child class or subclass does not have *two* parents. Two subclasses, sharing the same superclass, are called siblings.

Finally, a superclass may also be referred to as a subclass' *ancestor*. A child or subclass may be referred to as a superclass' *descendant*.

## Inherited Constructors—*this*

Some constructors you write may be coded additions to an inherited constructor. Rather than duplicating identical behavior in multiple constructor methods in your class, it makes sense to be able to just call the inherited constructor from inside the body of the derived constructor. Java provides a special keyword, **this,** for this purpose. To call a parent class' constructor, you would use a statement of the form:

```
public class subClass extends superClass {
  public subClass ( type0 argumentOne, typeT argumentTwo, typeN argumentN ){
    this( argumentOne, argumentTwo, argumentN... );
  }
```

from within the derived constructor's method body.

### The Java Keyword *this*

There will be times when, defining a method, you will want to refer to the current object's instance variables, or pass the current object as an actual argument, to another method. To refer to the current object in these cases, you use the Java **this** keyword. **this** refers to the current object, and you can use it anywhere that object might appear by using the period member operator. . . For example:

```
instanceData = this.myVar;
this.myMethod( this );
```

Here the *instanceData* is the instance variable for **this** object. The class then calls the method *myMethod* and passes it the current object. The **this** object is also a legal method return type. So any method properly defined can contain within its body the final statement:

```
return this;
```

Oftentimes you are able to omit the **this** keyword since it is implied. For this reason you can refer to a class' member data and methods simply by name. So, the first two statements seen above could be rewritten as:

```
instanceData = myVar;
myMethod( this );
```

Two important notes. First, you may omit the **this** keyword only if there are no conflicting local variable name collisions. Second, methods defined as **static** cannot use **this** (see description of **static** in the following section).

## public, private, protected, static, abstract

The Java keywords **public**, **private**, and **protected** deal with the scope, or visibility, of class members (data or method). By default, class members are visible only to the class itself. This has the advantage of protecting against any external side effects, such as two classes using the same member names.

Any class member preceded by the **public** keyword is visible outside the class. Any class member marked **protected** (the default if left unspecified) is accessible only to the class itself, or any subclass derived from it. Any class member marked **pri-**

**vate** is visible only in the defining class and is *not* accessible to any subclass derived from it.

The **static** keyword is a slight bit more difficult to understand. Remember that class members may be either data or methods. The **static** modifier may be legally used for both member types. Basically, the keyword tells the Java compiler that there will ever-only-be one-of whatever is being defined, whether a data member or method. While this does not prevent any subclass from inheriting the class member, it does prevent the subclass from dynamically generating its own version.

No matter how many times a class is instantiated, if its formal description contains **static** members, all object instances share the *same* member. This can be very useful whenever all instances need to share the same piece of information or to use the same data member as an accumulator.

Notice that the previously described *sample* class has a **main()** method marked **static**. This makes sense because we would not want to create multiple instances of the method **main()** each time *sample* was instantiated. Java applications can have only one method called **main()**.

Of the five modifiers, **abstract** is the one you are least likely to use as a beginning Java programmer. The **abstract** keyword is legal only for class methods and tells the Java compiler that the associated method is so incomplete that a derived child class *must* add code to it. Indirectly then, any formal class definition, containing an **abstract** method, itself cannot be instantiated. Instead, the formal class definition, by design, was meant to be derived into a subclass.

## THREADS

The term *thread* applies to each execution path your program can take. Older high-level languages were written to execute only one thread at a time. Today, programmers and users alike demand that an application be more efficient. This efficiency is made possible by today's newer programming languages, which support the feature called multithreading.

With multithreaded tasks that can be performed in the background, a program can simultaneously download files, while waiting for network messages or updating information. For example, the HotJava Web browser allows you to browse a page and download an image vie the use of threads. You may also use threads to animate an image and play sounds.

## MULTITHREADING

A *multithreaded* Java program is capable of simultaneously running more than one execution path. The simplest example would be a Java program that concurrently prints the information in a file, while simultaneously sorting a table. Of course, unless your computer has more than one microprocessor in it, true concurrent processing is physically impossible. The illusion of concurrency is accomplished by swapping each thread in and out of the main processor, and at today's microprocessor speeds, voilá, the illusion of true multitasking.

Running a single-threaded program is fine when you have to deal with only small programs that have to do a single task, but what if you had a Web page with several applets that were all supposed to be running at the same time, or you wanted to run a calculation in the background while getting more user input? In this case, each of these tasks would have to be multithreaded. Java provides two methods of implementing multithreading. The first method involves creating a class that **extends** the **Thread** class:

```
public class myThread extends Thread {
  public void run() {
    // thread code goes here
  }
}
```

Now, to create and run an instance of your new thread class, you write two statements. The first statement creates an instance *threadOne* of the *myThread* class:

```
myThread threadOne = new myThread();
```

The second calls the object's **start()** method:

```
threadOne.start();
```

Whenever your program wants to stop a thread, it makes a call to the threaded object's **stop()** method, as in:

```
threadOne.stop();
```

Java's thread-handling capabilities are very sophisticated and even include ways to temporarily suspend and then resume a thread. The syntax is straightforward:

```
threadOne.suspend();
threadOne.resume();
```

The second approach creates a class that **implements** the **Runnable** interface. Any class can represent a thread if it implements the **Runnable** interface and defines a **run()** method, as in:

```
public class myRunnable implements Runnable {
  public void run() {
    // thread code goes here
  }
}
```

The first line of code creates a new class called *myRunnable* that **implements** the **Runnable** interface. The second statement defines the required **run()** method and would normally contain the current task's code. A class that has implemented the **Runnable** interface can be run in a thread by passing the instance of the class to a new **Thread** object, as in:

```
className classInstance = new className();
new Thread( classInstance ).start();
```

When **start()** is called, *classInstance* indirectly calls your **run()** method. Remember, you can stop the *classInstance* thread with **stop()**.

## Whether to Extend or Implement

Whether or not you should **extend** the **Thread** class or **implements** the **Runnable** class depends, to some degree, on whether you are writing a Java application or applet. A Java applet that uses the **Runnable** interface makes use of the **run()** method to house the body of a thread. In order to run with a Web browser that is Java compatible, like HotJava, an applet must be derived from the **java.applet.Applet** class. Since a class may also need to use a thread, this class cannot inherit from both the **Applet** and **Thread** classes since Java does not support multiple inheritance. For this reason, many classes choose the **Runnable** interface to implement threads.

## Finding the *currentThread()*

The following program demonstrates how you can find out which thread is currently executing by making a call to the standard method **Thread.currentThread()**:

```
class thread {
  public static void main( String args[] ) {
    Thread currentThread = Thread.currentThread();
    currentThread.setName( "My main thread" );
    System.out.println( currentThread );
  }
}
```

The output from the program looks like:

```
Thread[My main thread,5,main]
```

Here, *My main thread* represents a user-defined, self-documenting label. The *5* (the default priority) indicates the *currentThread*'s priority, which can be anywhere from 1 to 10. The *main* is the name of the group of threads that this thread belongs to.

## Thread Priorities

All Java threads are assigned a priority (from 1—**MIN_PRIORITY** to 10—**MAX_PRIORITY**, 5—**NORM_PRIORITY** is the default), which affects how the Java thread scheduler chooses when to run a thread. When threads share the same priority, they share the processor on a first-come, first-served basis. When a thread of a higher priority than any of the others comes into existence, it will get control of the processor, even if it needs to preempt a currently running thread to do so. For a thread of a lower priority then to gain control, the higher priority thread needs to go to sleep (using the **sleep()** method) or wait until notified (by calling the **wait()** method).

The problem today is that the thread scheduling is something that has not been properly specified. The current implementations have radically different behavior when it comes to scheduling. However, the good news is that the Windows 95 port seems to be the closest to what one would expect. Most of the inconsistencies arise when you have threads that are relying on a preemptive behavior, without cooperatively giving up the microprocessor.

## Extending The *Thread* Class

You begin writing your own thread by extending the **Thread** class and overriding the **Thread.run()** method. The following *sqrRoot* class does just this:

```
import java.io.*;
import java.lang.*;

class sqrRoot extends Thread {
  double findSquareRootOf = 4;
  boolean infiniteLoop = true;

  public void run() {
    while( infiniteLoop ) {
      System.out.println( Thread.currentThread().getName() );
      System.out.println( Math.sqrt( findSquareRootOf++ ) );
      try {
        Thread.sleep( 1000 );
      } catch ( InterrutedException ignored ) {
          return;
        }
    }
  }

  public void stop() {
    infiniteLoop = false;
  }

  public static void main( String args[] ) {
    char ch;
```

```
    sqrRoot ThreadONE = new sqrRoot();
    sqrRoot ThreadTWO = new sqrRoot();
    ThreadONE.start();
    ThreadTWO.start();
    try {
      while( (ch = (char)System.in.read() ) != 'n' );
      ThreadONE.stop();
      ThreadTWO.stop();
    } catch ( IOException e ) {
        System.err.println( e );
      }
  }
}
```

In this example, the class *sqrRoot* sets itself up as an infinite loop, uses the **Math.sqrt()** method to calculate the square root of a number, and then uses the **System.out.println()** method to display the result. If you were using this class and wanted to call the thread, you would create an instance of the class *sqrRoot*, the way you would any other class:

```
sqrRoot ThreadONE  = new sqrRoot();
```

To get the thread started, you simply make a call to its **start()** method:

```
ThreadONE.start();
```

Once activated, the *ThreadONE.start()* method automatically calls the object's *ThreadONE.run()* method and immediately returns to the **main()** program thread, which continues to execute. The following code segment from the *sqrRoot* class' **main()** method combines these features:

```
public static void main( String args[] ) {
// ...
    sqrRoot ThreadONE = new sqrRoot();
    sqrRoot ThreadTWO = new sqrRoot();
    ThreadONE.start();
    ThreadTWO.start();
// ...
      while( (ch = (char)System.in.read() ) != 'n' );
      ThreadONE.stop();
      ThreadTWO.stop();
// ...
```

The concurrency in execution comes from the fact that the *sqrRoot* thread is outputting squared values, while the **main()**'s **System.in.read()** method call is simultaneously polling for user input within its loop. As soon as the user presses the carriage return and inputs the required 'n' symbol, the **while** loop terminates, allowing the *ThreadONE/TWO.stop()* methods to be called.

## Implementing the *Runnable* Class

Whenever you want to create a multithreaded Java program, instead of extending the **Thread** class, you can implement the **Runnable** class. From previous discussions, you know that a class that has implemented the **Runnable** interface can be run in a thread by passing the instance of the class to a new **Thread** object, as in:

```
className classInstance = new className();
new Thread( classInstance ).start();
```

The following code segment rewrites the extended **Thread** class used in the last example, as an implemented **Runnable** class:

```
import java.io.*;
import java.lang.*;

class squareRt implements Runnable {
  double findSquareRootOf = 4;
  boolean infiniteLoop = true;

  public void run() {
    while( infiniteLoop ) {
      System.out.println( Thread.currentThread().getName() );
      System.out.println( Math.sqrt( findSquareRootOf++ ) );
      try {
        Thread.sleep( 1000 );
      } catch ( InterruptedException ignored ) {
          return;
      }
    }
  }

  public void stop() {
```

```
      infiniteLoop = false;
    }

    public static void main( String args[] ) {
      char ch;
      squareRt ThreadONE = new squareRt();
      squareRt ThreadTWO = new squareRt();
      new Thread(ThreadONE, "Thread ONE").start();
      new Thread(ThreadTWO, "Thread TWO").start();
      try {
        while( ( ch = (char)System.in.read() ) != 'n' );
        ThreadONE.stop();
        ThreadTWO.stop();
        } catch ( IOException e ) {
            System.err.println( e );
          }
    }
  }
```

## Synchronized Threads

When two or more threads need concurrent access to a shared data resource, they need to take care to access the data only one at a time. Java provides unique language-level support for such synchronization. Other multithreaded systems expose a concept called a *monitor*. A monitor is an object which is used as a mutually exclusive lock, or *mutex*. Only one thread may own a monitor at a given time.

All Java objects have their own implicit monitor associated with them. The way you enter an object's monitor is by calling a method marked with the **synchronized** keyword. The entire time a thread is inside a **synchronized** method, all other threads have to wait.

The following program contains three class definitions. The first class, called *stub*, has a single method named *call*. *call* takes a single **String** argument *stringParam*. The *call* method tries to print out the *stringParam* string after the message *Line Number 0 starting:*, and before the string *Line Number 0 done*. The tricky part has to do with the call to *Thread.sleep( 1000 );*, which pauses the currently executing thread for approximately one second.

```
  class stub {
    static int count = 1;
```

```
    void call( String stringParam ) {
      System.out.print("Line Number " + count + " starting: " );
      try {
       Thread.sleep( 1000 );
       System.out.print( stringParam );
       System.out.println(" : Line Number " + count++ + " done." );
      } catch ( Exception e ) {
          return;
       }
    }
  }

  class Driver implements Runnable {
    String currentString;
    stub astub;

    public Driver( stub thisstub, String s ) {
      astub = thisstub;
      currentString = s;
      new Thread( this ).start();
    }

    public void run() {
      astub.call( currentString );
    }
  }

  class unsynch {
    public static void main( String args[] ) {
      stub astub = new stub();
      new Driver( astub, " Which came first? " );
      new Driver( astub, " The chicken,      " );
      new Driver( astub, " or the egg?       " );
    }
  }
```

The second class, *Driver,* implements a constructor that takes a reference to an instance of the *stub* class and a **String**, which are stored in *astub* and *currentString*, respectively. The constructor also creates a **new Thread** which will call this object's **run()** method. The thread is started immediately. The **run()** method of *Driver* is also simple; it just calls the *stub* method on the *astub* instance of *stub*, passing in the *stringParam* string.

The *unsynch* class implements the **main()** method, which instantiates a single *stub* object, and three instances of *Driver*, each with a unique sentence. The same instance of *stub, astub,* is passed to each *Driver*. Look at a sample run from this program:

```
Line Number 1 starting: Line Number 1 starting: Line Number 1 starting:
Which came first?  : Line Number 1 done.
 or the egg?        : Line Number 2 done.
 The chicken,       : Line Number 3 done.
```

Obviously, the *Thread.sleep()* method in the *call* method allowed the threads to context switch and mix up the output. The solution to this problem is quite simple. By using the Java keyword **synchronized** in front of the *call* method declaration:

```
synchronized void call( String stringParam ) {
```

Now, only one instance may exist at any single moment in time allowing the sequence of: print first part of statement, delay, print second part of statement, to run uninterrupted. When the *call* method's formal declaration is changed to include the keyword **synchronized** the corrected program output looks like this:

```
Line Number 1 starting:  Which came first?  : Line Number 1 done.
Line Number 2 starting:  The chicken,       : Line Number 2 done.
Line Number 3 starting:  or the egg?        : Line Number 3 done.
```

## java.io InputStream and PrintStream

Initially, most of your Java applet input will come from your computer's keyboard with output going directly to the monitor. Input and output in Java follow the C/C++ model in which I/O support is provided by a library, not by the language itself. In Java, of course, the I/O library is a class library—the **java.io** package.

**java.io** contains two abstract (meaning they cannot be instantiated directly) classes targeted toward these needs; they are **InputStream** and **PrintStream**. Actually, the basic job of the **InputStream** class is to read bytes from whatever stream it is attached to, be it the keyboard, a disk, or the Internet. **PrintStream** output is intended for the monitor.

**java.io** classes are layered by design. At the bottom level, there are basic **InputStream** and **OutputStream** classes. Added facilities such as buffering, connecting to files, printing data types other than bytes, and so on are provided by what are called *wrapper* classes. When a Java program runs, there are three streams available by default: **System.in**, **System.out**, and **System.err**, similar to C/C++'s **stdin**, **stdout**, and **stderr**. **System.in** defaults to the keyboard, while **System.out** and **System.err** default to the display monitor (these latter two streams are **PrintStream** objects).

## Defining Your Own Stream Objects

If you do not want to use the standard **InputStream** member **System.in** and the standard **PrintStream** member **System.out,** you can set your own stream objects equal to these two **System** members. However, you should try to use the System instance variables, because they will make your code easier for other programmers to understand:

```
InputStream myInputStream = System.in;
PrintStream myOutputStream = System.out;
```

Other programmers will be familiar with the more standard **java.lang.System** protocalls. The members **System.in** and **System.out** are of type **InputStream** and **OutputStream**, respectively. Notice that the **InputStream** and **OutputStream** are not created with the Java keyword **new**.

## Keyboard Input with *System.in.read()*

One of the easiest ways for a Java program to obtain user input is with the **InputStream** method **System.in.read()**. The **read()** method automatically waits until input is available. Technically, this is called *blocking*, or waiting**.** More important, however, is how the input information is interpreted. All **InputStream** classes work with bytes, *not* characters. And since all Java programs use the new UNICODE standard, each time you input a character from the keyboard, you will not be processing the high byte of two-byte UNICODE encryption for the character. There are actually three overloaded methods with the name **read()**:

```
public abstract int read()
public int read( byte byteArray[] )
public int read(byte byteArray[], int startOffset, int howManyBytes )
```

The first overloaded **read()** method is passed no actual arguments and returns a single byte from the input stream with **int** precision. For this reason *javac.exe* typically complains by issuing an error message if you try to put the returned integer directly into a character variable due to the discrepancy in their storage allocations.

The second overloaded version of **read()** allows a Java program to input more than one byte. The method's formal argument is a *byteArray[]*. This **read()** method places the incoming bytes into this array beginning at the 0th offset (or the first element).

The last **read()** method allows you to selectively target which consecutive bytes, within the *byteArray[]*, you would like filled. The first formal argument is the *byteArray[]* buffer to be filled. The second argument, *startOffset*, tells the method where to begin storing the bytes (remember the 1st byte in *byteArray[]* is at the 0th offset!). The third argument tells the method how many bytes to input. The following program demonstrates these three overloaded **read()** methods:

```
import java.io.*;

public class read {
  static StringBuffer buildStringByteByByte = new StringBuffer();
  static int currentCharacter;

  static byte byteArray[] = new byte[ 60 ];

  public static void main( String args[] ) {

    try {
      // First overloaded read() method
      while( (currentCharacter = System.in.read()) != -1 )
        buildStringByteByByte.append( currentCharacter );
      System.out.println( buildStringByteByByte );

      // Second overloaded read( byte byteArray[] ) method
      System.in.read( byteArray );
      String aString = new String( byteArray, 0 );
      System.out.println( aString );

      // Third overloaded read( byte byteArray[],
      //                        int startOffset,
      //                        int howManyBytes )
```

```
        System.in.read( byteArray, 4, 10 );
        aString = new String( byteArray, 0 );
        System.out.println( aString );

      } catch( IOException e ) {
         System.err.println(e);
        }
  }
}
```

To understand the program, look at the following sample run:

```
abcdefg979899100101102103<ctrl-z>
aaaaaaaa
aaaaaaaa

bbbbbbbbbbcccc
aaaabbbbbbbbbb
```

The first use of **read()**,

```
// First overloaded read() method
while( (currentCharacter = System.in.read()) != -1 )
       buildStringByteByByte.append( currentCharacter );
  System.out.println( buildStringByteByByte );
```

processed the user input, *abcdefg* above, inputting one character at a time and appending it to *buildStringByteByByte*, until the user signaled end-of-file by pressing <ctrl-z>. At this point the **println()** method output the sequential ASCII values, *979899100101102103*, of each symbol.

The second use of **read()**:

```
// Second overloaded read( byte byteArray[] ) method
      System.in.read( byteArray );
      String aString = new String( byteArray, 0 );
      System.out.println( aString );
```

input the eight *as*, *aaaaaaaa*, putting them into the *byteArray*, and then used the **println()** method to output the string, *aaaaaaaa*.

The third **read()** method call:

```
// Third overloaded read( byte byteArray[],
      //                          int startOffset,
```

```
//                              int howManyBytes )
System.in.read( byteArray, 4, 10 );
aString = new String( byteArray, 0 );
System.out.println( aString );
```

input the user data *bbbbbbbbbbcccc*, into the *byteArray*, which now contains *aaaaaaaa*. However, the first *b* was overwritten to the 5th *byteArray*; element position, at an offset of *4*, and *10* consecutive characters were then grabbed and consecutively appended to *byteArray*; since the last four *c*s were after the 10 *b*s they were not appended. This time the **println()** outputs the string *aaaabbbbbbbbbb*, leaving the originally inserted *a*s alone.

## Display Output with *System.out.print()/println()*

The easiest method for performing Java program output is to use the **print()** or **println()** methods of the **PrintStream** class. The difference between **print()** and **println()** is that the latter performs a line-feed, carriage-return, after performing the required output. The following three statements:

```
System.out.print( "This is all printed " );
System.out.println( "on one line. );
System.out.println( "However, this string is on its own line." );
```

produce the following output:

```
This is all printed on one line.
However, this string is on its own line.
```

Java overloads the plus operator + so that it can concatenate **String** objects. Notice that in the following example:

```
System.out.print( "My name is: " + nameString + "." );
System.out.println("  I am " + yearsOld + " years old." );
```

each argument to the + operator is first converted to type **String** and then output. This holds true for the string variable *nameString* and the integer variable *yearsOld*. **System.out** and **System.err** are special cases of the **PrintStream** class in that they automatically flush the output buffer. For this reason, the user sees the prompts as soon as the statement is executed.

## EXCEPTIONS

Not all programming languages have the ability to "eloquently" recover from certain types of run-time error conditions. Take for example the Pascal language; if a Pascal program statement attempts a divide-by-zero, the Pascal application instantly aborts, taking you back to the command line. Not very "eloquent." Newer programming languages, such as C++, Ada, and Java, allow you to develop a program that has the ability to trap these types of fatal errors before they are dealt with by the operating system. Java code can detect errors and indicate to the run-time system what those errors were. This capability is known as *exception handling*.

Exceptions provide a clean way for a method to abort whatever it was doing and signal to the calling method that something has gone wrong. There are three Java keywords involved in writing an exception handler; they are **throw**, **try**, and **catch**. However, there are only two phases to handling an exception. The first involves signaling the exception event; for this you use the **throw** keyword.

To signal an exception event, a member function simply uses the **throw** statement with an instance of an exception class, as in:

```
throw new MyHandledException();
```

The second phase involves handling the thrown exception. Here the **try** and **catch** keywords are used together. The syntax for a **try...catch** statement looks like:

```
try {
    // code that could throw the exception goes here
              .
              .
}  catch( exceptionType exceptionName ) {
     // code to handle the thrown exception goes here
                        .
                        .
}
```

The code within the **try** block is executed. If an exception is thrown within this block, any statements below the thrown exception, within the **try** block, are ignored! Program execution continues with an attempt to catch the thrown exception by finding a **catch** block that matches the specific exception. For this reason, there may be more than one **catch** block within the **try...catch** statement, as seen here:

```
try {
     // code that could throw the exception goes here
               .
               .
}   catch( exceptionType exceptionName ) {
     // code to handle the thrown exception goes here
                         .
                         .
}  catch( exceptionType exceptionName ) {
                          .
                          .
}  catch( exceptionType exceptionName ) {
                          .
                          .
}
```

Errors and other exceptional conditions are treated as distinct from the normal flow of control in the program, which, after all, they are. When an error occurs, an exception is thrown. Exceptions climb the chain of calls until they are caught or until the program exits. The catch and throw method of exception handling offers two big advantages:

- First, the error condition can be dealt with only where it makes sense instead of dealing with it at every level between where it occurs and where it needs to be dealt with.
- Second, code can be written as if the operations in it will work.

A **try...catch** statement may contain a **finally** statement. The **finally** block is used to process statements that may be skipped within the method throwing the exception. For example, if a method is supposed to open, input, and then close a file, but throws an exception, it is possible the statement to close the file will be skipped. The **finally** statement is used in conjunction with the **try** block. Basically, it ensures that if an exception occurs, any cleanup work that is necessary is taken care of because the code in the **finally** block is guaranteed to run, even if an exception is thrown. The syntax for a **try...catch...finally** statement looks like:

```
try {
    // code that could throw the exception goes here
                .
                .
}   catch( exceptionType exceptionName ) {
    // code to handle the thrown exception goes here
                .
                .
} catch( exceptionType exceptionName ) {
                .
                .
} catch( exceptionType exceptionName ) {
                .
                .
} finally {
    // code that is ALWAYS executed no matter what!
                .
                .
}
```

Java provides a set of exceptions it raises when errors occur within a program. The default action is to print an error message to the monitor and terminate the current execution thread. This capability is provided by the Java run-time interpreter.

## Java Runtime Exceptions

Java provides a standard set of catchable exceptions designed to handle run-time errors. Table 4.1 lists the Java Error, Exception, and RuntimeException subclasses (many of these are discussed in later chapters):

## The *throw* Statement

The normal series of events for a **try...catch** statement involve first trying all of the statements in the **try** block and, if any exceptions are thrown, executing the statements in the **catch** block. However, to raise your own exception, you use the Java **throw** keyword. The argument to this operator is an instance of a subclass of the **Exception** class.

**Table 4.1:** Java Error, Exception, and Runtime Exception Subclasses

| | |
|---|---|
| Error Subclasses | **ClassCircularityError** |
| | **ClassFormatError** |
| | **Error** |
| | **IllegalAccessError** |
| | **IncompatibleClassChangeError** |
| | **InstantiationError** |
| Exception Subclasses | **ClassNotFoundException** |
| | **DataFormatException** |
| | **IllegalAccessException** |
| | **InstantiationException** |
| | **InterruptedException** |
| | **NoSuchMethodException** |
| | **RuntimeException** |
| RuntimeException Subclass | **ArithmeticException** |
| | **ArrayIndexOutOfBoundsException** |
| | **ArrayStoreException** |
| | **ClassCastException** |
| | **IllegalArgumentException** |
| | **IllegalThreadStateException** |
| | **IndexOutOfBoundsException** |
| | **NegativeArraySizeExcepton** |
| | **NullPointerException** |
| | **NumberFormatException** |
| | **SecurityException** |
| | **StringIndexOutOfBoundsException** |

The **thrown** exception aborts the method and raises the specified exception through the call stack. If there is a matching **catch** block in the caller that matches the exception, or one of its superclasses, then the exception stops there and the **catch** block handles it. However, if the caller doesn't have a matching **catch** block, the exception keeps moving through the call stack until it finds a matching **catch** block. The program terminates if no matching **catch** block is found.

To create your own exception, you first need to subclass the **exception** class, which **implements** the **Throwable** interface and provides some useful features for dealing with exceptions. Specifically, the **Exception** class provides a slot for a message and executes a stack trace. The syntax for subclassing the **Exception** class looks like:

```
class myException extends Exception {
      .
      .
      .
}
```

The advantage of subclassing the **Exception** class is that the new exception type can be caught separately from other **Throwable** exception types. In Java, the exceptions a method can **throw** are considered part of its public interface. Users of a method need to know the exceptions it might **throw** so they can be prepared to handle them. For this reason, Java requires that a method definition include a list of the exceptions it can throw. The syntax for this is straightforward:

```
public class sample {
  public static void MyException() throws thisException, anotherException {
  }
}
```

However, before writing your own exception, look at the following *inputString()* method:

```
public static String inputString() {
  int a_character;
  String buildString = "";
  boolean moreToDo = true;
  while( moreToDo ) {
    try {
      a_character = System.in.read();
      if( ( (char) a_character == 'n' ) || ( a_character == -1 ) )
        moreToDo = false;
      else
        buildString += (char)a_character;
    } catch ( IOException e ) {
        moreToDo = false;
    }
  }
  return buildString;
}
```

The *inputString()* method is designed to input a series of characters, with a call to **System.in.read()**, and build a string, character by character, until the user either presses the carriage return or generates an end-of-file. However, **System.in.read()**

can automatically throw a run-time **IOException**. The *inputString()* can handle this situation, however, since the **System.in.read()** method was placed inside a **try...catch** statement, with the **catch** block setting the **while** loop control variable *moreToDo* to **false**. The *inputString()* method is a good example of an encoded subroutine that handles its own exceptions.

However, there are times when a method should not do anything at all with an exception and, instead, pass it to the calling method. In order to tell Java this, the method throwing the unhandled exception needs to broadcast this situation with a **throws** statement in its formal header. The following code segment rewrites the *inputString()* method using this syntax:

```
public static String inputString() throws IOException {
  int a_character;
  String buildString = "";
  boolean moreToDo = true;
  while( moreToDo ) {
    a_character = System.in.read();
    if( ( (char) a_character == 'n' ) || ( a_character == -1 ) )
      moreToDo = false;
    else
      buildString += (char)a_character;
  }
  return buildString;
}
```

If you are wondering which approach is better, the general rule is for a method to deal with its own exceptions, rather than propagate them to the caller. One note, if you are writing a method that overrides a parent class' method that throws no exceptions, the overriding method must catch its own exceptions. It cannot propagate them since the parent class' method did not have a **throws** clause.

The same rules that apply to exceptions thrown by Java apply to any you may write. To throw your own exception, you have to decide what type of situation to detect and then what type of exception to throw. Take, for example, a method that is inputting bytes to a user-defined BUFFERSIZE of 512 bytes. However, end of file is encountered at only 256 bytes. Your method knows this is a fatal input error condition and decides to throw its own exception. You would write the method this way:

```
String inputString( inputFile in ) {
  // member data declarations;
  while( . . . ) {
    if( a_character == -1 ) {
      if( length < BUFFSIZE ) throw new EOFException;
    }
  . . .
}

String inputString( inputFile in ) throws EOFException {
  // member data declarations;
  while( . . . ) {
    if( a_character = = -1 ) {
      if( length < BUFFSIZE ) throw new EOFException;
    }
  . . .
}
```

Whenever a standard Java error, exception, or run-time exception just won't do, you write your own subclass of the **Exception** class. For example, the following subclass definition is interested in an input file being in UNICODE (16-bit-per-character, not ANSI ASCII 8-bit) format:

```
class notUNICODEexception extends IOException {
  public notUNICODEexception() {}
  public notUNICODEexception( String notUNICODEmsg ) {
    super( notUNICODEmsg );
  }
}
```

When writing your own exception subclass it is traditional to have both a default constructor and one that outputs an exception-specific message. The **toString()** method of the **Throwable** base class can print out this message. With your exception class defined you are ready to throw your own exception:

```
String inputUNICODEfileString( UNICODEinputFile in ) throws
notUNICODEexception {
  while( . . . ) {
    if( ...readUTF_failure ) {
      throw new notUNICODEexception();
    }
  }
}
```

## INTERFACES

*Interfaces*, like abstract methods and classes, allow a programmer to develop templates that other derived classes are expected to implement. Sometimes, interfaces are the only way around Java's lack of multiple-inheritance capabilities. Multiple inheritance defines an object-oriented language's ability to derive a subclass from two parent classes.

An interface is declared using the keyword **interface**. Similar to classes, interfaces are **private** by default. However, an interface's methods are always **public**. Interface data members are both **public** and **static**—that is, available to anyone and not permitted to be changed, renamed, or extended. The syntax for an interface looks like (note: the keywords **protected** and **private** are illegal in interface definitions):

```
public interface myInterfaceName {
  // public static member data declarations go here
  // public abstract method declarations go here
}
```

You implement the interface in a class by using the **implements** keyword, as in:

```
public class className implements interfaceName {
  // class definition
}
```

A class can also implement more than one interface by using the comma operator, as in:

```
public class className implements interfaceOne, interfaceTwo, interfaceThree {
  // class definition
}
```

### Interfaces Without Abstract Methods

One proper and simple use for Java interfaces is for shared constant declarations. Languages such as C/C++ use special syntax in files called header files for this purpose. Java does not have header files. However, a properly written interface can replace the popular C/C++ **#define** preprocessor statement. Remember that interface instance variables must be public static final implied (meaning not actually entered in the code) or explicitly documented (where the three keywords precede the instance variable's declaration). Also, interface instance variables must be initialized with constant values.

The following interface definition contains minimum and maximum screen resolution extents, default drive, and subdirectory constants:

```
public interface constant {
  public static final int     MIN_X_COORD  =    0,
                              MIN_Y_COORD  =    0,
                              MAX_X_COORD  =  639,
                              MAX_Y_COORD  =  479;

  public static final String defaultDrive = "c:",
                              defaultPath  = "encyclopediaimages";
}
```

Now any class type needing to output information can use these VGA screen resolution coordinates to make certain the displayed image is within the bounds of the current settings:

```
public class encyclopediaVideoDisplay implements constant {
  // code to display *.avi files goes here
}
public class encyclopediaBitmapDisplay implements constant {
  // code to display *.bmp files goes here
}
```

## Interfaces with Abstract Methods

You may be asking yourself what the benefit of interfaces is. By taking the time to create an interface, you can define the protocols for an abstract class without worrying about the specific implementation, leaving that until later. In addition, you can share the same interface with several classes, without worrying about how the other class is handling the methods. If you inherit the properties of the interface, other users will automatically know what the method calls are for that class.

Say, for example, you three different telephone classes, *payPhone*, *twoLineTouchTonePhone*, and *simpleHomePhone*. Each class would have its own set of member declarations. However, at some point, regardless of the phone type, you want all of them to have a *dialThePhone*() method. You could create an interface and name it *canCallOut*:

```
public interface canCallOut {
  public abstract void dialThePhone();
}
```

Now, any time you use a phone, you will know that is has a *dialThePhone()* method and what parameters it takes.

### Using Interfaces as Class Types

You can also use the *canCallOut* class as a type itself. This enables you to create member variables and methods that can hold any of the objects that implement *canCallOut*:

```
canCallOut aCall; // example member variable

void addLongDistancePrefix( canCallOut LongDistanceCall ) {
  // method code goes here
}
```

### Interface Casting

By using a class cast, you can give the previous method *addLongDistancePrefix()*, an instance of the type *payPhone*:

```
payPhone CornerOfMainAndFifth = new payPhone();
addLongDistancePrefix( (canCallOut) CornerOfMainAndFifth );
```

## PACKAGES

The main idea behind Java packages is the syntactical bundling of logically related class and interface definitions. Take for example the six packages provided by Java (see Table 4.1).

Notice how each of the classes in a package serves to perform some logically related function.

### Importing Packages

Java provides two types of syntax for accessing classes within a package. The first method uses the import keyword with the asterisk * wild card symbol:

```
import java.awt.*;
```

**Table 4.2:** Standard Java Packages

| | |
|---|---|
| java.applet | containing classes that let you create Java applets that will run in any Java-compatible browser |
| java.awt | containing classes that let you write platform-independent GUI applications |
| java.io | containing classes used to do standard input and output |
| java.lang | containing essential Java classes |
| java.net | containing classes to use network connections |
| java.util | containing utility classes such as vectors and hashtables |

Using *java.awt.** means that all of the classes in the **java.awt** package are imported or used. However, the second method allows you to use a specific class within a package without an import statement by explicitly putting the name of the package before the class. For example, the statement:

```
java.util.Date;
```

allows a program to use the **java.util.Date()** method without using the import statement. Using the import statement is a shortcut that allows you to avoid affixing the package name in front of every class in the package.

## Java Package Syntax

You begin a Java package definition by using the keyword **package**. The package name is specified as a list of identifiers separated by a period, with the initial name in the list indicating the class owner and developer. The period separator in the package name lists the level, or inheritance hierarchy, where each level usually represents a smaller, more specific grouping of classes.

The Java class library itself is organized along these lines. The top level is called **java**; the next level includes names such as **io**, **util**, and **awt**. If a package definition appears in a Java source file, it must be the first statement other than comments and white space in the compilation unit. For example, the following code segment declares the package *allSorts*. Here, each sort class is made into its own file with each individual file containing the statement *package sorts* at the beginning of the file:

```
// file name: sorts.java
package allSorts;
  public class sorts {
    // define sorts class
  }
><><><><><><><><><><><><><
// file name: bubble.java
package allSorts;
  public class bubble {
    // define bubble sort
  }
><><><><><><><><><><><><><
// file name: selection.java
package allSorts;
  public class selection {
    // define selection sort
  }
><><><><><><><><><><><><><
// file name: binaryTree.java
package allSorts;
  public binaryTree {
    // define binary tree sort
  }
><><><><><><><><><><><><><
// file name: quickSort.java
package allSorts;
  public quickSort {
    // define quick sort
  }
><><><><><><><><><><><><><
// file name: usesSorts.java
import allSorts.*;
```

All of these files would be saved in a subdirectory called *allSorts*. The first line in each file, *package allSorts;* indicates that the classes in the listing are part of the *allSorts* package. For the source files part of this package, the **package** declaration must be present at the beginning of the file, before any other statement, although it can be preceded by comments or empty lines.

When the source files are compiled, Java will create a *classname.class* file for each class in the source file and, unless directed otherwise, will store the file in the same directory as the source file. The **.class* must be located in a directory that has the same name as the package, and this directory should be a subdirectory of the directory where classes that will import the package are located.

## Java Lingo

The following new terms have been discussed in this chapter and are presented here for your review:

*ancestor*—The term used to refer to a subclass, child, or sibling class' parent, base, root, or superclass.

*base class* —The term used to refer to the highest level on a class inheritance hierarchy tree.

*child class*—The term used to refer to a parent, base, or root class' subclass.

*class*—An object-oriented concept that allows a programmer to syntactically combine data declarations, with the functions that work on those data declarations, together to form a side effect–proof object.

*constructor*—A constructor is a class member function of the same name as the class. Constructors are never directly called. Instead, they are automatically invoked whenever an instance of the class is instantiated. Constructors perform the logical task of initializing class member data.

*derivation/deriving*—The process by which a parent, base, root, or superclass is reused to create a subclass, child, or sibling class.

*descendant*—The term applied to a parent, base, root, or superclass' child, sibling, or subclass.

*destructor*—A destructor is the logical inverse of a *constructor* and usually cleans up an object before it is removed from memory. Destructors are then class methods and always have the name *finalize.*

*exceptions*—An error condition recognized by the Java run-time environment and/or program logic.

*inheritance*—In a procedural language, when one record's definition contains a nested record definition, the record is said to inherit the nested record's characteristics. In an object-oriented language, the same situation holds true for objects defined based on some previous object's definition. The new object is said to inherit the previously defined object's characteristics. However, since an object definition contains both member data and member functions, the inheritance is fully functional.

*instantiation*—In procedural programming languages, the term instantiation would be translated into *creating*. In a procedural language you create a variable. In object-oriented terms you instantiate an object. The process of creating objects is called instantiation.

*interfaces*—The work-around for Java's lack of multiple inheritance. Multiple inheritance defines a syntax whereby a child class inherits two or more parent class' characteristics. Java interfaces merely define the set of methods all formal class definitions must encode if they wish to use the interface. This allows a programmer to assume which methods will be available, no matter how many new objects are defined sharing the same interface.

*member data*—In a procedural language, member data would be called fields within a record. In object-oriented terms these fields are called member data.

*member function*—In procedural languages there is no equivalent to the term member function since procedural languages do not allow you to syntactically tie a function's definition to any particular record. In object-oriented languages, objects, by definition, may contain function declarations. In order to recognize which type of function a programmer is talking about, standalone or one tied to an object, each has its own term. Standalone object-oriented functions are just called functions. However, functions syntactically bundled with an object are called member functions or methods. Note: Java does not have standalone functions; all coding must be done in member functions.

*method*—see *member function*.

*multithreaded*—Multiple, concurrent paths of program execution.

*overloading*—The term overloading applies to an object-oriented language's ability to define more than one member function, or method, using the same name. The idea behind this syntax is to allow a programmer to replicate an algorithm that merely operates on different data types. Java does *not* support another type of overloading known as operator overloading, where a programmer can redefine a language's standard operators.

*parent class*—The term applied to the class definition from which a subclass, child, or sibling class is derived.

*root class*—The term used to refer to the highest level of a class inheritance hierarchy tree.

*siblings*—Two classes sharing the same parent, base, or root class.

*subclass*—A class definition that is based on a previously defined class.

*superclass*—The term used to refer to a subclass' base, parent, or root class.

*thread*—A single path of program execution.

*thread priority*—All Java threads are assigned a priority (from 1—**MIN_PRIORITY** to 10—**MAX_PRIORITY**; 5—**NORM_PRIORITY** is the default), which affects how the Java thread scheduler chooses when to run a thread. When threads share the same priority, they share the processor on a first-come, first-served basis. When a thread of a higher priority than any of the others comes into existence, it will get control of the processor, even if it needs to preempt a currently running thread to do so.

# 5

# Borland's Example Applets

In order to give you an instant up-and-running Java experience, Borland ships the Java Compiler/Interpreter with many exciting sample applets. Each applet demonstrates a particular Java capability. You can use the source code to study, modify, or even incorporate into one of your own applets, since they are all shipped to you copyright free.

## How to Use the Java Applets Shipped with BCWJAVA

Loading, compiling, and running the Java applets shipped with BWCJAVA are as simple as:

1. Starting the Borland IDE.
2. Choosing the Project | Open command from the Main Menu.
3. Rooting yourself over to the BC5JAVADEMO subdirectory.
4. Double-clicking on the particular folder of interest.

5. Opening the folder's **.ide* project file.
6. Compiling the **.java* source file in the automatically opened Project window.
7. And then running the applet by selecting the **.html* file in the Project window. (Note: some applets have more than one **.html* file.)

As of this writing, the BC5JAVADEMO subdirectory contained the list of folders seen in Figure 5.1.

The example applets cover every imaginable topic from simple screen output to animated screen output, simple input, complex data input, complex data output, simple to advanced keyboard interaction, mouse interaction, graphics, video, and, in case you thought the kitchen sink was left out, sound too!

In Chapters 1 through 4 you learned all of the concepts, keywords, syntax, and object-oriented design philosophies necessary to appreciate all these applets do. Since Java programming is such an enjoyable experience, an easy-to-learn language, with exciting features, take a moment at this point to sit back, relax, and experience all that Java has to offer.

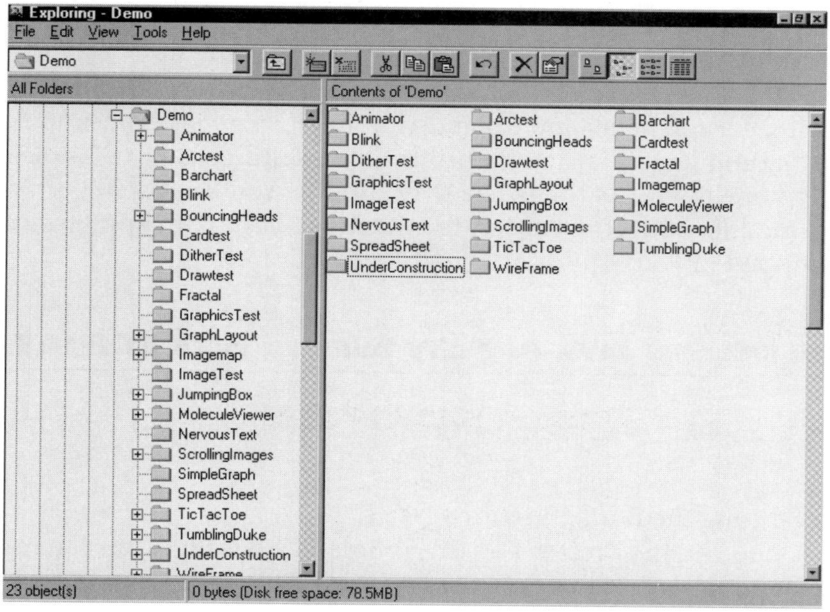


**Figure 5.1:** BC5JAVADEMO applets shipped with BCWJAVA.

This chapter does not present the applets in their alphabetical folder order but instead organizes them logically, from simplest in concept, syntax, and design to the more complex. This pedagogical order is used in each of the following chapters to teach you how to write your own Java applets.

## Put Up Your Dukes!

Here he is folks, Duke, the infamous animated Java mascot in all his various forms. You'll find Duke under the *Animation*, *TumblingDuke*, and *UnderConstruction* folders. Figure 5.2 shows Duke executing a simple animated wave (*Animator—example1.html*), and don't forget to listen.

Figure 5.3 shows duke executing a more complex animated jackhammer sequence (*UnderConstruction—example1.html*).

Figure 5.4 shows duke trying out for the Summer Olympics with a gymnastic tumble (*TumblingDuke—example1.html*).

As you run each of these applets, notice the smooth animation possible with Java applets. Figure 5.5 is also under the *Animator* folder and displays a flashing modern-art lighthouse. (*\Animator—example2.html*).

**Figure 5.2:** Java's Duke mascot waving a simple hello!

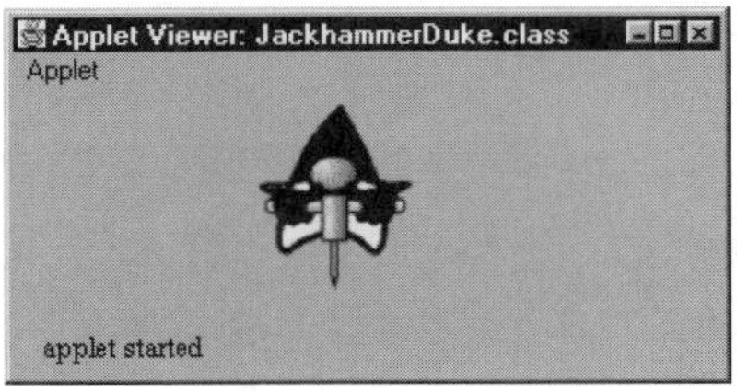


**Figure 5.3:** The jackhammer construction worker Duke.

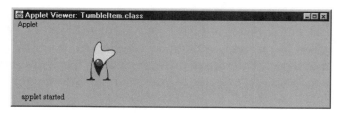


**Figure 5.4:** The gymnastic tumbling Duke.

**Figure 5.5:** Animated modern-art flashing lighthouse.

Java uses simple frame flipping to generate animation in much the same way a sequence of cartoon characters are animated by flipping images drawn in successive poses.

## ATTENTION-GRABBING JUMPING TEXT

Jazzing up a home page with some visual excitement is not just relegated to image animation. Java makes it very easy to change text color, point size, font, and, yes, to animate it! Figures 5.6 (*\NervousText—example1.html*) and 5.7 (*Blink—example1.html*) demonstrate these features. *NervousText* displays the **H o t J a v a** text jumping, squirming, up and down!

The *Blink.class* applet flashes words on and off, while changing their colors. Both applets present interesting text output options that will get your Web page popping.

**Figure 5.6:** Excited, animated, eye-catching text!

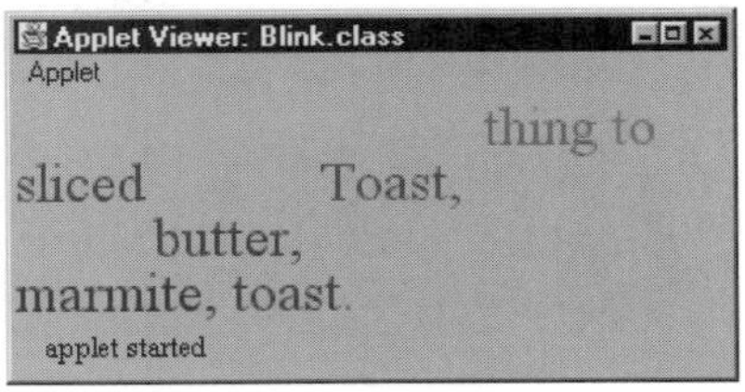


**Figure 5.7:** Visually enticing colored, flashing, text output!

## SIMPLE STATIC GRAPHICS OUTPUT

Moving on up in complexity, this next set of applets highlights Java's capabilities for simple, static, graphics output, from plotting points, seen in Figure 5.8 (*\SimpleGraph—example1.html*), to the calculation and display of an interesting fractal seen in Figure 5.9 (*Fractal—example1.html*). And finally, a graphical bar chart (*\BarChart—example1.html*) displayed in various colors and highlights (see Figure 5.10).

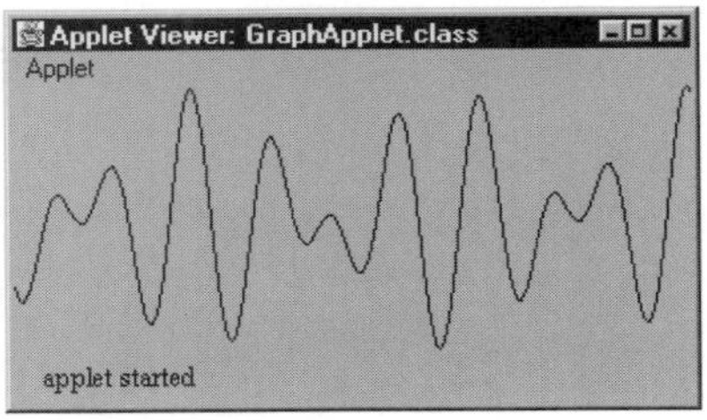


**Figure 5.8:** Simple static graphics output.

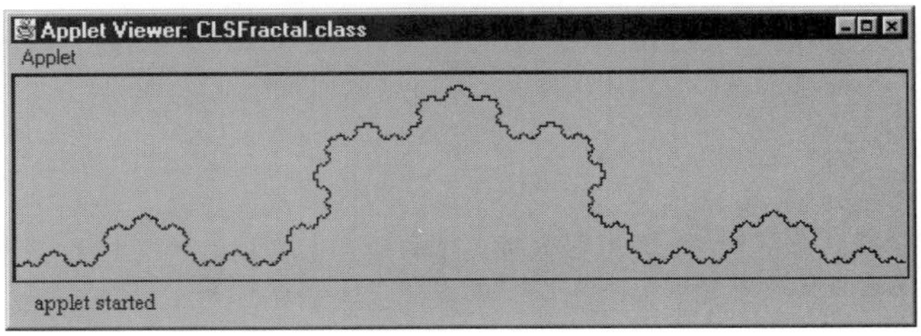


**Figure 5.9:** Graphing fractals.

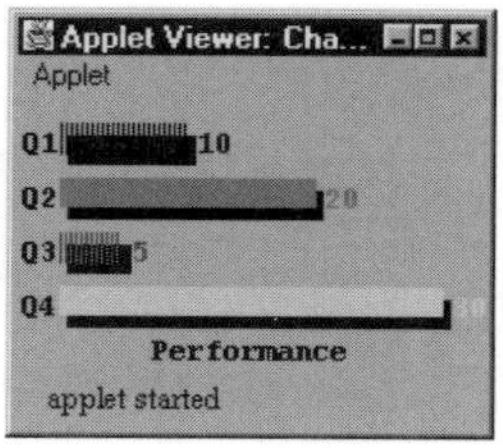


**Figure 5.10:** Colored, highlighted, bar chart applet.

You'll discover that graphical output is easy with Java's many standard graphics classes.

## INTERACTING WITH A JAVA APPLET

All of the example applets so far have simply done their thing when run. This next set of programs interacts with the user via keyboard and mouse. The first applet demonstrates how to add PageUp, PageDown, and cursor key interaction to your Java program (see Figure 5.11) (*\ImageTest—example1.html*). *ImageTest* moves the colored square left/right/up/down with each press of the cursor key, while increasing/decreasing the colored square's size with PageUp/PageDown.

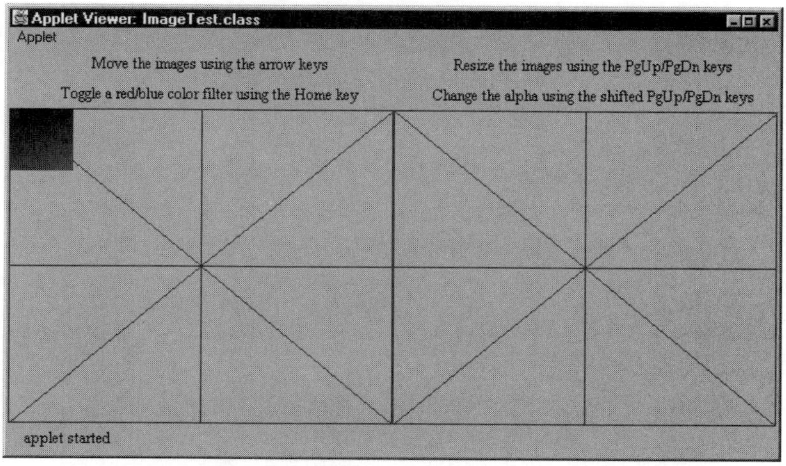


**Figure 5.11:** Adding a PageUp, PageDown, and cursor key interface to your applet.

The next sample program goes one better by recognizing not only the cursor keys but the mouse too. The spreadsheet applet allows both cursor key and mouse selection of spreadsheet cells, while performing an algorithmic computation (see Figure 5.12) (*\SpreadSheet—example1.html*).

With more and more kids logging on to the Internet, at younger and younger ages, don't forget them as a potential audience. This next applet creates a simple to use, mouse-driven, entertaining for hours, tic-tac-toe game (see Figure 5.13) (*\TicTacToe—example1.html*).

OK, no one will know that YOU had fun with that one too! When someone's looking over your shoulder, run this next applet. Figure 5.14 also demonstrates a Java keyboard/mouse-user interface with a more *professional*, *adult*, and *serious* visual interface. However, this applet goes one step further by presenting a text box entry capability for the starting and stopping angles (*\ArcTest—example1.html*). The first figure shows *ArcTest* drawing the default arc:

Figure 5.15 shows the applet drawing and filling the user-defined angle starting at 0, going to 90 degrees, and instead of

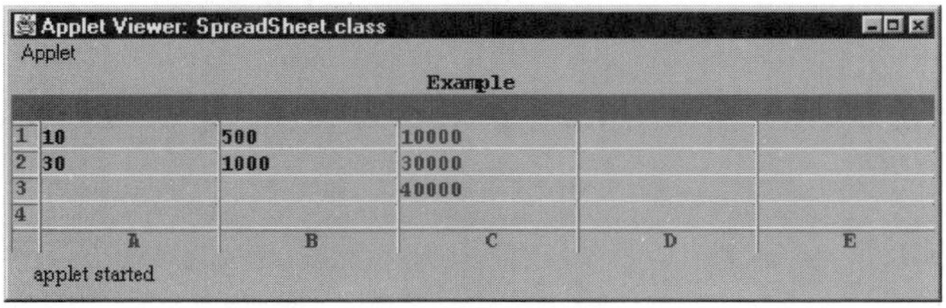


**Figure 5.12:** Java mouse/keyboard user interface applet.

**Figure 5.13:** A child's favorite—mouse-driven, colored, tic-tac-toe game.

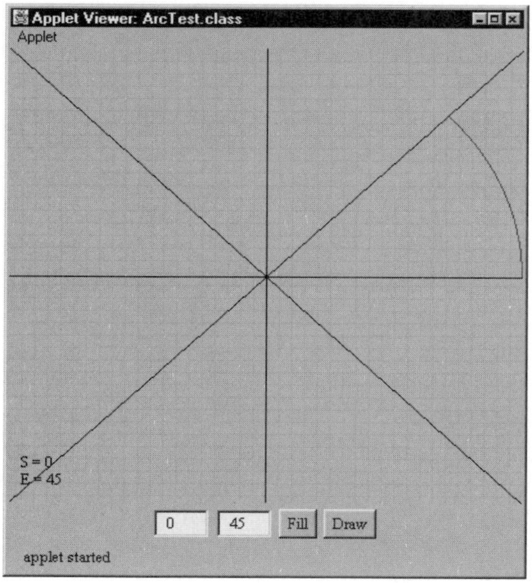


**Figure 5.14:** Initial *ArcTest—example1.html* with text box entry capability.

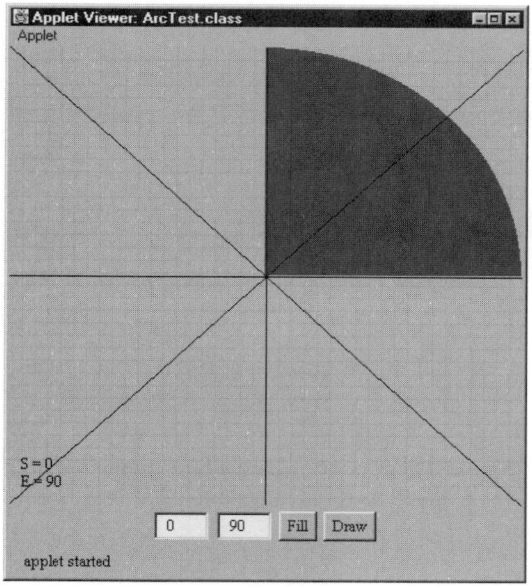


**Figure 5.15:** Using a text box and button applet interface.

just drawing the arc (using the Draw button), a filled pie slice is created after pressing the Fill button:

## ADDING A DROP DOWN LIST BOX TO JAVA APPLETS

Whenever you want to present the user with a fixed range of options, you use a drop down list box. Figures 5.16 through 5.20 allow the user to select from five graphical board layouts (by choosing the buttons marked one through five at the top of the applet window), and move to the first, next, previous, or last board layout (using the buttons at the bottom of the applet window, or by list box selection.

Figure 5.16 shows the list box in its selected position, where the object is listing the five view options (*CardTest—example1.html*). While Figure 5.16 displayed the initial applet view, Figure 5.17 shows that the user has selected view one (seen in the collapsed drop down list box). Figure 5.18 shows view two selected by pressing the next button. Selecting the last button displays board five, as seen in Figure 5.19. Figure 5.20 displays the fourth board layout after the user has clicked the mouse on the four button at the top of the applet window.

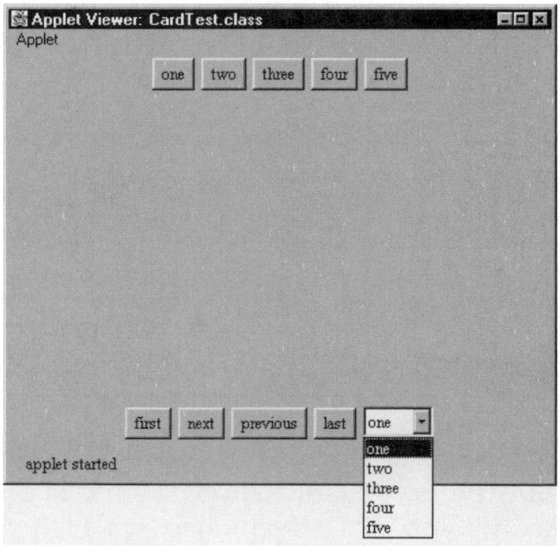


**Figure 5.16:** A Java applet with a drop down list box object.

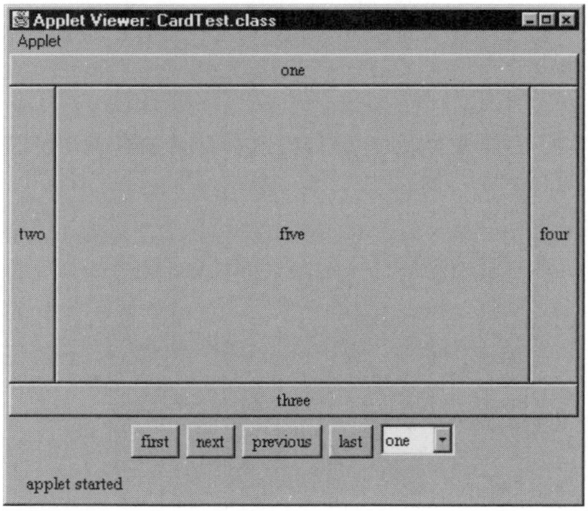


**Figure 5.17:** *CardTest* applet view one.

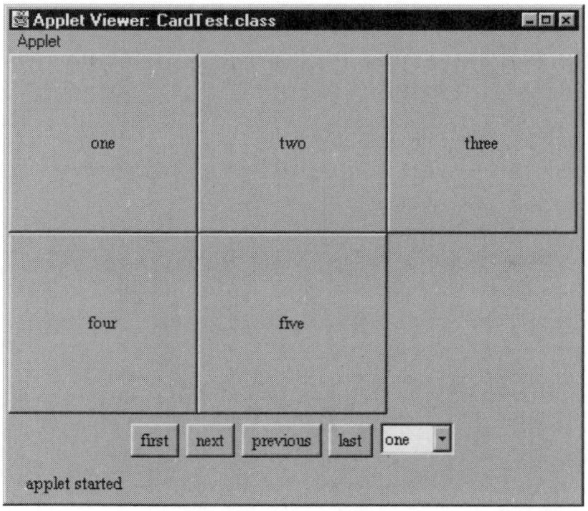


**Figure 5.18:** Viewing board two by pressing the next button.

## ALMOST ELECTRONIC PONG

If the static tic-tac-toe game gets a little boring after a while, try this next program. The *MouseTrack* applet displays a static rectangle until you move the mouse, at which point the target ran-

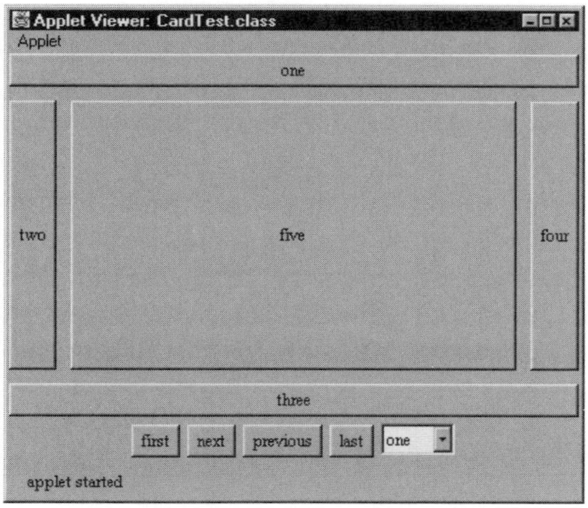


**Figure 5.19:** Selecting the last button to view board five.

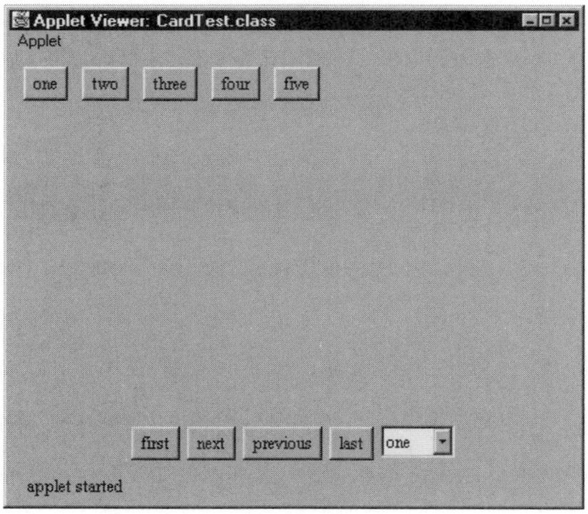


**Figure 5.20:** Using the four button to select the fourth board layout.

domly jumps (see Figure 5.21). Your goal: to move the mouse pointer fast enough to hit the target before its next leap!

This is an excellent example applet for precisely detecting when the mouse is moved, quickly calculating new screen coordinates, and registering back a successful strike.

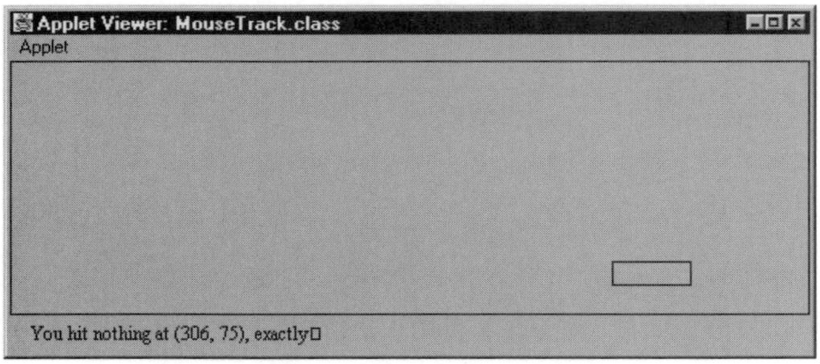


**Figure 5.21:** Hit the moving target applet.

## High-Resolution Screen Output

Java's graphical output capabilities are not simply limited to textual enhancements, lines, colors, buttons, and bar charts. A Java applet is fully capable of using the host's display resolution. Figure 5.22 does not do this feature justice since it is reproduced in black and white. However, run it on a color display, and you will be very impressed with this Java applet's graphical output saturation, intensity, and resolution (*\DitherTest—example1.html*).

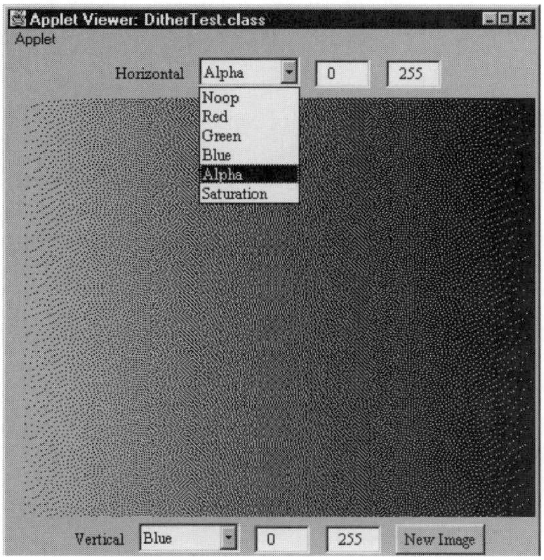


**Figure 5.22:** Java applet demonstrating high-resolution color output capabilities.

## A Java Paint Applet with Radio Buttons

Creating an interactive paint program is easy with Java by combining color, text, buttons, list boxes, mouse interaction, and Java's point and line draw capabilities. Figure 5.23 shows such a program (*DrawTest—example1.html*).

This applet introduces the concept of radio buttons. Radio buttons allow the user to select one out of several mutually exclusive options, in this case drawing color.

## Graphics Test Pattern Applet

Although the *GraphicsTest* applet is capable of five unique views, only the first is displayed next. This applet also uses many of the previously discussed Java applet capabilities, along with circle, pie slice, and fill graphics options (*GraphicsTest—example1.html*):

## Animating Video Images

The *BounceItem* applet goes the *MouseTrack* program one better by randomly selecting an output screen coordinate, not for a rectangle, but a revolving video image! Java makes it very easy

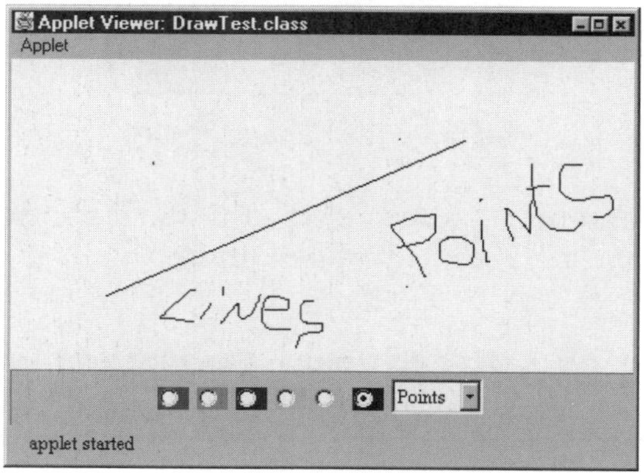


**Figure 5.23:** A Java paint program using radio buttons.

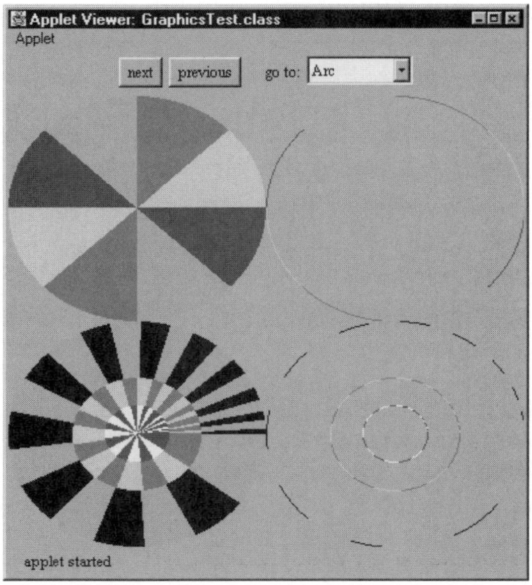


**Figure 5.24:** Graphics test pattern applet.

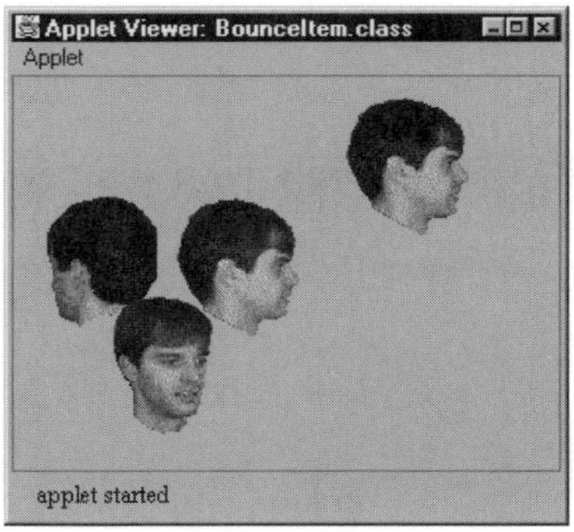


**Figure 5.25:** A bouncing rotating video image applet

to import stored video images (see Figure 5.25) (*BouncingHeads—example1.html*).

## Graphical View of a Relational Database with Check Boxes

The *GraphLayout* applet, seen in Figure 5.26, combines all of the Java applet capabilities discussed to visually output the relationship between nodes in a sample database. The Scramble and Shake buttons mix up and restart the image. However, this applet adds still another applet feature known as check boxes. By clicking on the Stress or Random check box object, the user can select or deselect relational connection types (*GraphLayout—example1.html* through *example4.html*).

The difference between radio buttons and check box items involves the number of items that can be concurrently selected. Radio button options are mutually exclusive, whereas any number of check box items may be simultaneously active.

## AN ANIMATED VIDEOGRAPHY LINE UP

OK, so everyone wants to get in on the act. This on-line streaming videotape applet continually displays a ticker tape–like message of portraits, once again demonstrating the visual animation capabilities of Java applets, along with the associated personal appeal (see Figure 5.27) (*ScrollingImages—example1.html*).

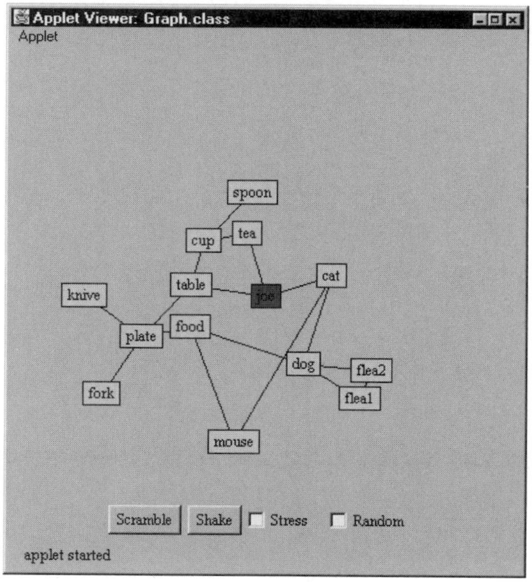


**Figure 5.26:** Java applet displaying text box options.

**Figure 5.27:** Scrolling videotape applet.

## MOLECULAR VIEWER

Figure 5.28 shows all four of the *MolecularViewer* applets running simultaneously, all using the circular solid fill graphics commands (*MolecularViewer—example1.html*).

## A THREE-DIMENSIONAL MODELING WORKSTATION APPLET

This is the absolute showstopper when it comes to articulation, screen output, resolutions, algorithmic sophistication, and advanced graphical display. The *ThreeD.class* found under the

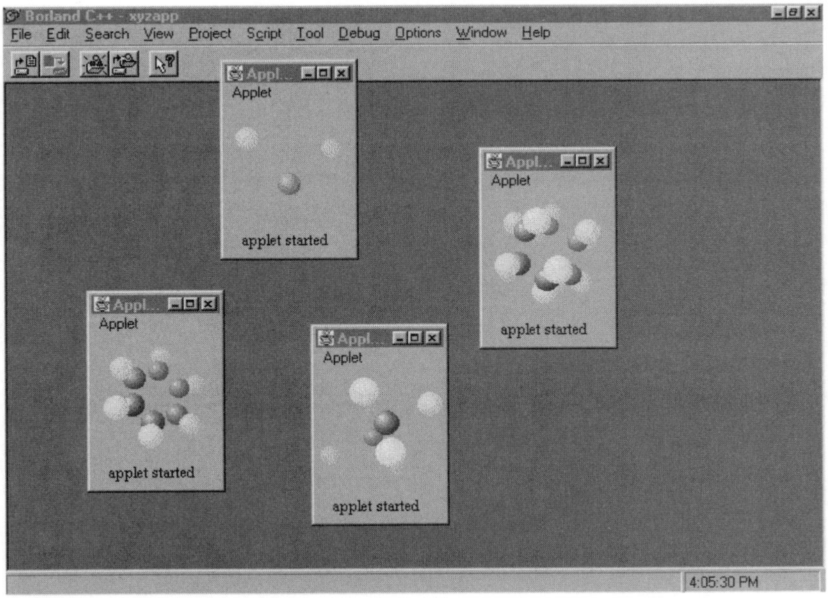


**Figure 5.28:** MolecularViewer applet.

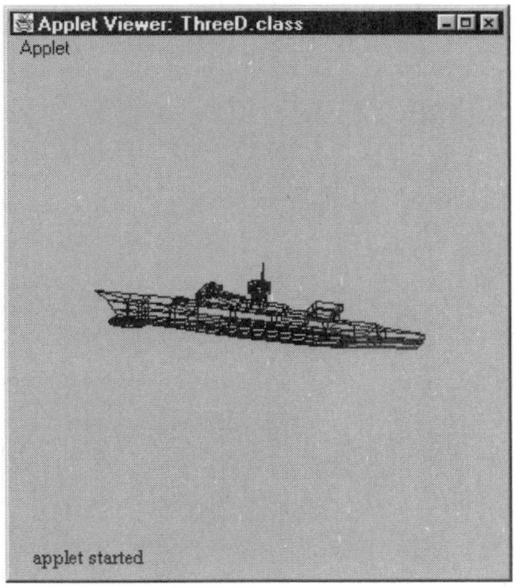


**Figure 5.29:** Initial vessel position.

*WireFrame* subdirectory outputs a very sophisticated line drawing of a military vessel (see Figure 5.29).

By clicking the mouse above, below, to the right, at angles to the initial image, the user can rotate the image on any axis. Of particular interest is Java's graphical capability of shading those portions of the wire frame closest to the user and fading as the object moves off into the distance (see Figure 5.30).

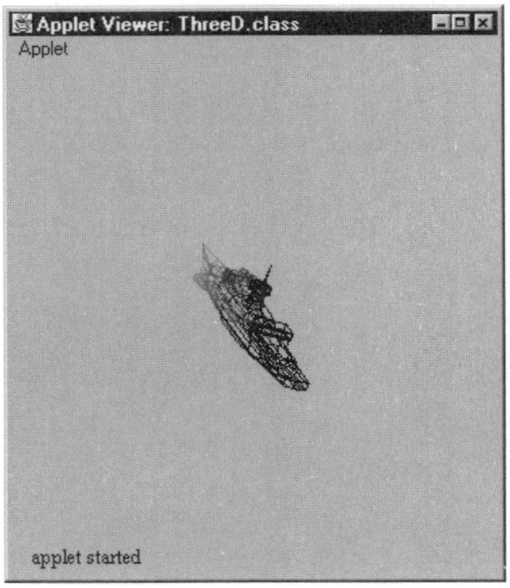


**Figure 5.30:** Rotated and scaled image showing Java's gradient shading. capability.

## Lights, Camera, Action!

Now that you have seen many of the eye-catching, user-friendly features provided by a Java applet, you are probably ready to begin learning just how to compose one of your own. If so, skip Chapter 6, which explains additional Java tools such as Java-powered browsers, for example, HotJava, and go directly to Chapter 7. You can come back to Chapter 6 after proudly developing and demonstrating your new Java prowess!

# 6

# Working with Java Tools

In Chapter 3, Java Basics, you learned how to use the Java compiler/interpreter in both standalone mode and Borland's IDE (Integrated Development Environment) sibling. This chapter goes into greater details about both. Sometimes, when you want to write and test small Java code segments, it's just easier to use the standalone Java tools. The chapter begins by reviewing and highlighting all of the standalone Java tool syntax and options.

## JAVA COMPILER—*javac.exe*

Remember, Java is both a compiled language and an interpreted language. The Java compiler translates your Java source code into language-independent bytecode. The syntax for using the Java command line compiler looks like:

```
javac [-switch] javaFileExtension.java
```

Table 6.1 lists all of the *javac.exe* Command Line Switches:

**Table 6.1:** *javac.exe* Command Line Switches

| *Switch* | *Meaning* |
|---|---|
| -classpath [directories] | Instructs the Java compiler to look in all specified *directories* for classes included in the source file. Use colons to separate multiple directory listings, as in: javabin : anotherSubMoreClasses aClass.java |
| -d [directory] | Routes the Java compiler to the specified *directory* as the first directory of a package. |
| -debug | Instructs the Java compiler to turn on debug mode stepping through the source code adding diagnostic comments. |
| -g | Instructs the Java compiler to prepare the bytecodes for debugging. |
| -nowarn | Turns off the compiler's warning messages. You should not use this option until you are very familiar with writing Java code. |
| -nowrite | This option is useful for testing your wyntax without creating an actual class file or overwriting any previously created classes, since this switch does not produce a compiled **.class* file. |
| -o | This option tells the Java compiler to translate methods into inline code. When used properly, this can speed up program execution as it eliminates the overhead associated with subroutine calls. |
| -verbose | Puts the Java compiler into verbose mode displaying all classes loaded, the time it takes to load the classes in milliseconds, and total time it takes to compile the Java source code. |

## JAVA INTERPRETER—*java.exe*

It is each computer hardware's implementation of the Java runtime environment that executes the language-independent Java-compiled bytecode. The syntax for running the Java interpreter is:

```
java [-switch] classFileExtension.class
```

Table 6.2 lists all of the *java.exe* Switches:

**Table 6.2:** *java.exe* Switches

| *Switch* | *Meaning* |
|---|---|
| -cs | This date-sensitive switch reports back whether or not the Java source file used to create the class file is newer than the class. |
| -debug | Used for remote Java file debugging, automatically generates password used by jdb [-password] switch. |
| -help | Instructs *java.exe* to output a list of all Java interpreter switches. |
| -ms [stackSize] | Selects the maximum stack size, *stackSize*, minimum setting: 1k, default: 1m. |
| -mx [heapSize] | Selects the maximum heap size, *heapSize*, minimum setting: 1k, default: 16m. |
| -noasyncgc | Switches off asynchronous garbage collection. |
| -noverify | Switches off class verification. |
| -oss [JavaStackSize] | Sets the maximum stack size for a Java process. |
| -prof | Creates the output file *java.prof* containing Java interpreter profiling information. |
| -ss [CstackSize] | Sets the maximum stack size for a C process, must be larger than 1k. |
| -v | Puts the Java interpreter into verbose mode displaying all classes loaded, the time it takes to load the classes in milliseconds, and total time it takes to compile the Java source code. |
| -verbosegc | Forces the Java interpreter to output a message for each occurrence of garbage collection. |
| -verify | Instructs the Java interpreter to verify all classes that are loaded. |
| -verifyremote | Switches on verification of any classes inherited or imported. |
| -version | Reports back which version of the Java Development Kit (JDK) was used to compile the Java source file. |

## JAVA AND C/C++—*javah.exe*

Whenever you want to interface a Java program with a C or C++ program, you need to create some additional files. One of these files is the C/C++ file, called a *header file*. Header files contain application-specific types, definitions, external references, and so on. These files are C/C++'s way of syntactically and logically relating statements of this type. The *javah.exe* utility takes your Java class definition(s) and automatically generates the required interfacing C/C++ header file. The following is a listing of *Native.h* found in your *JavaInclude* subdirectory. This is a bare-bones, minimum set of statements automatically inserted by *javah.exe*:

```
/*
 * @(#)native.h1.3 95/04/28 Arthur van Hoff
 *
 * Copyright (c) 1994 Sun Microsystems, Inc. All Rights Reserved.
 *
 * Permission to use, copy, modify, and distribute this software
 * and its documentation for NON-COMMERCIAL purposes and without
 * fee is hereby granted provided that this copyright notice
 * appears in all copies. Please refer to the file "copyright.html"
 * for further important copyright and licensing information.
 *
 * SUN MAKES NO REPRESENTATIONS OR WARRANTIES ABOUT THE SUITABILITY OF
 * THE SOFTWARE, EITHER EXPRESS OR IMPLIED, INCLUDING BUT NOT LIMITED
 * TO THE IMPLIED WARRANTIES OF MERCHANTABILITY, FITNESS FOR A
 * PARTICULAR PURPOSE, OR NON-INFRINGEMENT. SUN SHALL NOT BE LIABLE FOR
 * ANY DAMAGES SUFFERED BY LICENSEE AS A RESULT OF USING, MODIFYING OR
 * DISTRIBUTING THIS SOFTWARE OR ITS DERIVATIVES.
 */

#ifndef _NATIVE_H_
#define _NATIVE_H_

/*
 * Header file for native methods. This file should include
 * only those declarations that native methods are allowed to
 * use.
 *
 * NOTE: this currently includes too much stuff...
 */

#include "oobj.h"
#include "interpreter.h"
#include "tree.h"
#include "javaString.h"
#include "typecodes.h"

#endif
```

The syntax for using *javah.exe* is:

```
javah [-switch] myfile.ext classFileExtension.class
```

Where myfile.ext is an optional parameter for a user-defined output file name. Table 6.3 lists all of the javah.exe switches.

## Java and World Wide Web Pages—*javadoc.exe*

You use *javadoc.exe* whenever you want to automatically generate the HTML (Hyper Text Markup Language) source file needed to attach a Java applet to a Web page. The syntax for using *javadoc.exe* is:

```
javadoc [-switch] javaFileExtension.java
```

Table 6.4 lists all the HTML tags recognized by *javadoc.exe*.

## Viewing Java Applets—*appletviewer.exe*

Of course you can use the Borland IDE to run your Java applications and applets. However, once again, if you do not want to take the time to load the IDE and want a quick way to test an applet, simply run *appletviewer.exe*. The syntax for using *appletviewer.exe* is:

```
appletviewer [-debug] htmlFileExtension.html
```

appletviewer.exe has only one optional switch, *-debug*:

**Table 6.3:** *javah.exe* Switches

| *Switch* | *Meaning* |
|---|---|
| -d [directory] | Tells the utility to place the generated output in the specified *directory.* |
| -o [myfile.ext] | Allows you to specifically provide a name and extension, *myfile.ext*, for the file being generated. |
| -stubs | Redefines the role of *javah.exe* so that it generates stub files instead of header files. |
| -v | Verbose mode, printing file creation status reports while generating the header or stub output file. |
| -version | Outputs the current build version number. |

**Table 6.4:** *javadoc.exe* Recognized HTML Tags

| *Recognized HTML Tag* | *Meaning* |
|---|---|
| @see *class* | Puts a "See also" link in the HTML file containing the specified *class.javah.exe* switches |
| @see *class#method* | Places a "See also" link in the HTML file to the file containing the specified *method*. |
| @param *methodArguments* | A tag describing a method's arguments. |
| @version *version* | A tag identifying the program version. |
| @author *authorName* | Generates a tag identifying the *authorName* in the HTML file generated. |
| @return *returnValue* | Inserts a tag into the HTML file identifying the method's return value. |
| @exception *class* | Creates a link to an exception thrown by the *class* specified. |

## JAVA DEBUGGER—*jdb.exe*

In Chapter 3, you learned how to use the Java standalone debugger, *jdb.exe*. The following section lists this utility's optional switches. The syntax for using *jdb.exe* is:

```
jdb [-switch] classFileExtension.class
```

Table 6.5 lists two of the most frequently used *jdb.exe* switches.

**Table 6.5:** *jdb.exe* Switches

| *Switch* | *Meaning* |
|---|---|
| -host Remote SystemName | Allows *jdb.exe* to remotely debug the Java program on the *RemoteSystemName*. |
| -password validPassword | Used in conjunction with remote debugging, the **-password** switch sends the password assigned by the Java interpreter (when the interpreter is in **-debug** mode). |

## JAVA DISASSEMBLER—*javap.exe*

If you have a need to back up, that is, you have access to a Java **.class* file but have either lost the Java **.java* source file or just never had it, you can disassemble the bytecode back to pure Java source code. To do this you run *javap.exe*. The syntax for using *javap.exe* is:

```
javap [-switch] classFileExtension.class
```

Table 6.6 lists all the *javap.exe* switches:

## INTEGRATING *native* METHODS INTO JAVA PROGRAMS

The Java language allows a programmer to extend the system at run time with code written in C. However, this is a fairly dif-

**Table 6.6:** *javap.exe* Switches

| *Switch* | *Meaning* |
|---|---|
| -version | Displays the JDK version currently being executed by *javap.exe*. |
| -p | Prints out both private and public member variables and member functions (methods). |
| -c | Instructs *javap.exe* to disassemble the source file and display the bytecodes produced by the Java compiler. |
| -h | This option tells the disassembler to output information on the particular class in the C header file to be used by a C program that wants to use the methods in that class. |
| -classpath [directory] | Instructs the Java disassembler to look in all specified *directories* for classes included in the source file. Use colons to separate multiple directory listings, as in: javabin : anotherSubMoreClasses aClass.java |
| -verify | Outputs verification messages on all classes being loaded. |
| -v | The disassembler's, verbose mode switch, turning on more advanced, detailed information on the disassembler's progress. |

ficult procedure and not something you should need to do immediately. For this reason you can skip this topic, move on to Chapter 7, and return when your application's needs dictate.

Whenever you need to link a C/C++ program to Java you need to use a new Java keyword **native**. You use the Java keyword, **native** to declare methods. Unlike normal Java methods, which have their method bodies defined within a Java source file, **native** method bodies are implemented in the C/C++ program. The syntax for declaring a **native** method looks like:

```
public native returnType methodName( [formal argument list] );
```

where the method's prototype is preceded by the keyword **native**. The best use for extending the Java run-time system involves machine-specific code tweaked for high performance. There are basically five steps to this entire process:

1. Define your class with **native** methods.
2. Generate the required header files, **.h*, that the C program **#include**s.
3. Generate the stub functions that the Java run time will use to call your **native** methods.
4. Create a Dynamic Link Library, **.dll*, with the generated stub functions and your C functions.
5. Link the library into the Java run-time system.

Your Borland Java compiler/interpreter is shipped with a complete working project to demonstrate this somewhat unobvious scenario. You can find the example under *BC5ExamplesJavaNative*.

The file *NativeExample.java* contains the following **native** method definitions:

```
class NativeExample {
    public native void Display(String str);
    public native long Sub(long a, long b);

    static {
        System.loadLibrary("native");
    }
}
```

To link a dynamic library containing **native** methods into Java, you create a **static** initializer for the class. The **static** initializer uses the *System.loadLibrary("native");* statement for this purpose. The file *Main.java* contains the **static** initializer for the *NativeExample* class:

```
class Main {
    public static void main(String args[]) {
        NativeExample n = new NativeExample();
        n.Display("5 - 2 = " + n.Sub( 5, 2) + "n");
    }
}
```

The file *NativeExampleImpl.c* contains the **native** method bodies, as seen below:

```
#include [lang]StubPreamble.h[rang]
#include [lang]native.h[rang]
//#include "NativeExample.h"
#include [lang]stdio.h[rang]

#define BUF_LEN 1024

void NativeExample_Display(struct HNativeExample *this, Hjava_lang_String *str)
{
    char buf[BUF_LEN];
    printf(javaString2CString(str, buf, BUF_LEN));
    return;
}

int64_t NativeExample_Sub(struct HNativeExample *this, int64_t a, int64_t b) {
    return ll_sub(a, b);
}
```

While you could use the standalone *javah.exe* utility to generate the header file and stubs, Borland has made this process much easier by simply turning on the appropriate Java compiler switches. Simply click on the IDE's Main Project menu, then route yourself through to Options | Java | Compiler Options. At this point in the dialog box you will see the category: *Native method stubs*. Click on the check box marked: *Generate .c and .h files.*, it's that easy!

Actually, before you create the project's **.ide* file, you need one more file. The file *NativeExampleWrap.c* is a wrapper file around generated code that uses the -vu compiler option as a **#pragma**. This option eliminates the underscore prepended to all exported symbols:

```
#pragma option -vu
#include "NativeExample.c"
```

Some final notes. You will need to include the *bccjavai.lib* in your **.dll* instead of Java's anticipated file *javai.lib*. *bccjavai.lib* is the Borland version of the import library to the virtual machine.

Also, the Java 64-bit integer type **long** is mapped to the C **struct** *int64_t* defined in *typedefs.md.h*. In **native** methods, 64-bit quantities must be manipulated using the macros defined in *typedefs.md.h*, for example, the following Java statements:

```
long lOne, lTwo, lResult;
lOne    = 1;
lTwo    = 2;
lResult = ( lOne + lTwo ) * ( lOne - lTwo );
```

should be written in the C source file as:

```
int64_t lOne, lTwo, lResult;
lOne    = int2ll( 1 );
lTwo    = int2ll( 2 );
lResult = ll_mul( ll_add( lOne, lTwo ), ll_sub( lOne, lTwo ) );
```

Executing a project make or build generates the following **.h* and **.c* files. The first is *main.h*:

```
/* DO NOT EDIT THIS FILE - it is machine generated */
#include [lang]native.h[rang]
/* Header for class Main */

#ifndef _Included_Main
#define _Included_Main

typedef struct ClassMain {
    char PAD;/* ANSI C requires structures to have a least one member */
} ClassMain;
HandleTo(Main);

#ifdef __cplusplus
extern "C" {
#endif
#ifdef __cplusplus
}
#endif
#endif
```

Next is *NativeExample.h*:

```
/* DO NOT EDIT THIS FILE - it is machine generated */
#include [lang]native.h[rang]
/* Header for class NativeExample */

#ifndef _Included_NativeExample
#define _Included_NativeExample

typedef struct ClassNativeExample {
    char PAD;/* ANSI C requires structures to have a least one member */
} ClassNativeExample;
HandleTo(NativeExample);

#ifdef __cplusplus
extern "C" {
#endif
struct Hjava_lang_String;
__declspec(dllexport) void NativeExample_Display(struct HNativeExample *,struct
Hjava_lang_String *);
__declspec(dllexport) int64_t NativeExample_Sub(struct HNativeExample
*,int64_t,int64_t);
#ifdef __cplusplus
}
#endif
#endif
```

There's the C file *main.c*:

```
/* DO NOT EDIT THIS FILE - it is machine generated */
#include [lang]StubPreamble.h[rang]

/* Stubs for class Main */
```

And the *NativeExample.c* stub file:

```
/* DO NOT EDIT THIS FILE - it is machine generated */
#include [lang]StubPreamble.h[rang]

/* Stubs for class NativeExample */
/* SYMBOL: "NativeExample/Display(Ljava/lang/String;)V",
Java_NativeExample_Display_stub */
__declspec(dllexport) stack_item *Java_NativeExample_Display_stub(stack_item
*_P_,struct execenv *_EE_) {
    extern void NativeExample_Display(void *,void *);
    (void) NativeExample_Display(_P_[0].p,((_P_[1].p)));
    return _P_;
```

```
}
/* SYMBOL: "NativeExample/Sub(JJ)J", Java_NativeExample_Sub_stub */
__declspec(dllexport) stack_item *Java_NativeExample_Sub_stub(stack_item
*_P_,struct execenv *_EE_) {
    Java8 _t1;
    Java8 _t2;
    extern int64_t NativeExample_Sub(void *,int64_t,int64_t);
    Java8 _t0;
    SET_INT64(_t0, _P_, NativeExample_Sub(_P_[0].p,GET_INT64(_t1,
_P_+1),GET_INT64(_t3, _P_+3)));
    return _P_ + 2;
}
```

Don't be too worried if this last section seems a bit overwhelming. The Java language is so rich in built-in features that the average Java programmer will never need to extend its native horsepower. Also, Sun Microsystems, Inc. is continually gleaning, pruning, and adding state-of-the-art industry-driven features on a regular basis. So, if there is something that Java can't do today, hold on, within several months it will!

# 7

# The Java Environment

In the previous chapters you have learned how to create simple Java applets and applications. Starting with this chapter, you will learn about many of the rich features of the Java language and environment. In later chapters you will learn how to write robust Java code that will allow you to add animation, color, control, dialog box, font, graphic, menu, mouse, and sound capabilities to your projects.

No doubt, many people reading this book have also written Windows applications using the Borland C++ compiler and the standard Windows API functions. Where it is appropriate, we will try to point out important similarities and differences between the Windows API and the Java API.

## An Investigation

All programming environments including DOS, Windows, and Java have a default set of features such as background color, printing color, and drawing color. For example, if you create a simple "Hello World" C application, your text will print in a white DOS screen with a default system font. If you are developing a similar Windows application, expect to see your text printed in black with the default Windows font. Additionally, the Windows background color will be white with the window's size initially determined by the operating system. What about Java? The best way to answer that question is to develop a simple application and investigate the resulting graphical environment when the application is executed.

## A Simple Java Application

Let's build a simple application using Borland's Java tools, compiler, and AppExpert for Java. We'll use this application to investigate the default Java graphical environment that we're provided with.

**Creating a Java Application** Here are the steps you will need to follow from within the Borland C++ compiler to create a Java application similar to our example:

1. Select File | New | Project.
2. Set the Project Path, Name, Target Type, and AppExpert launch information as shown in Figure 7.1.
3. A Project description, similar to Figure 7.2, will appear on your screen. (The .html file can be eliminated since this will be a standalone application.)
4. Use the Admin button to set header file options, as shown in Figure 7.3.
5. Use the Methods button, as shown in Figure 7.4, to select *only* the Stub paint method.
6. Use the Derivation button to view the Derivation options. The AppExpert defaults are shown in Figure 7.5. No changes need to be made.
7. Use the Threads button to view thread options. Figure 7.6 shows that these options are not used for our code.
8. Use the Code Preview button to generate the application code for the Java project. The code for this project is shown in Figure 7.7.
9. Click on the second icon to save this code and return to the Project windows shown earlier in Figure 7.2.

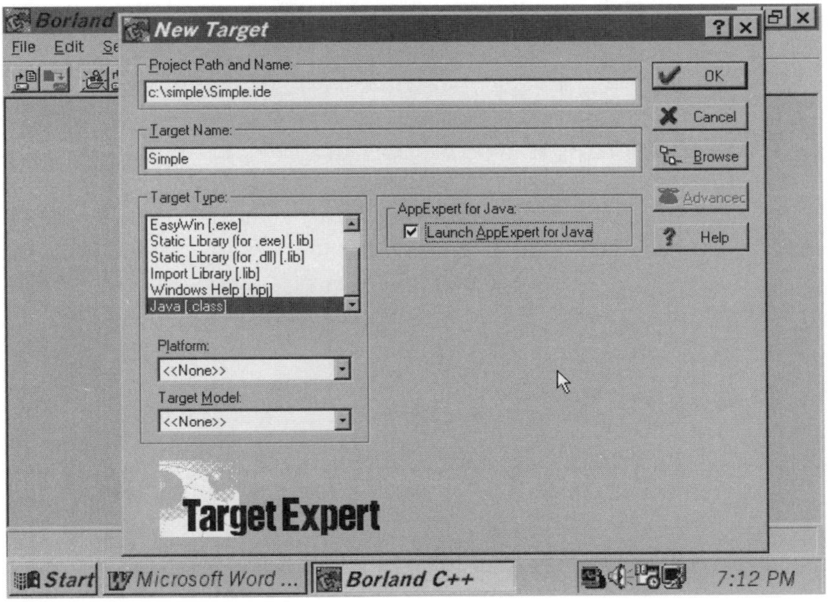


**Figure 7.1:** Use the New Target dialog box to set the name, path, and target for the new Java application.

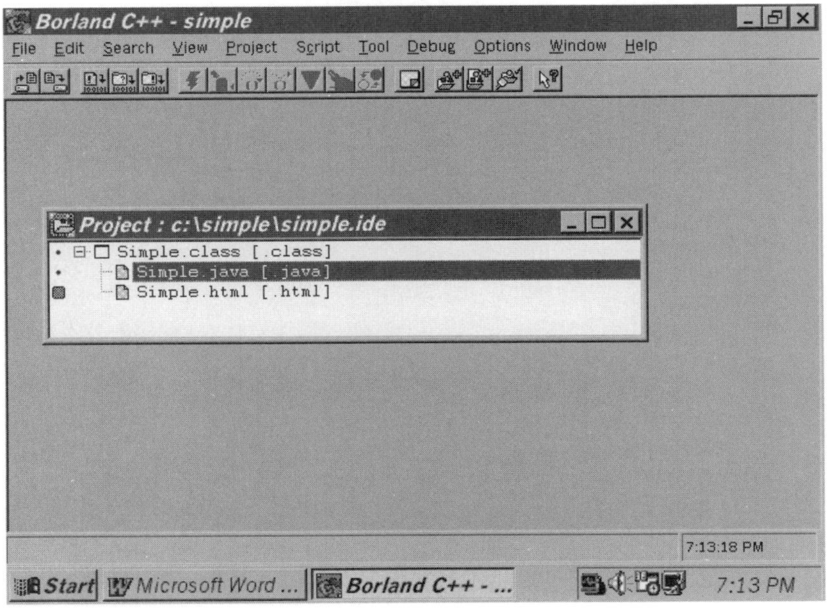


**Figure 7.2:** The Project window describes the components of the new project.

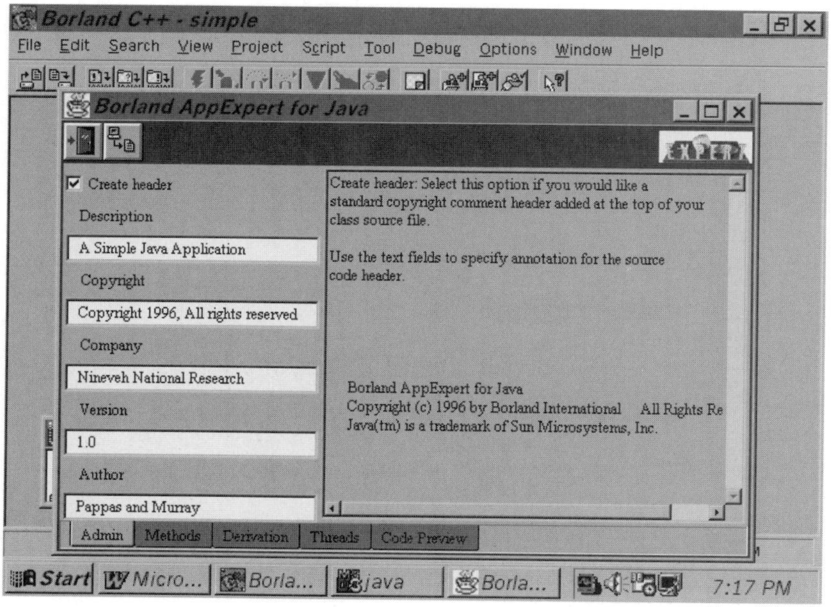


**Figure 7.3:** The AppExpert first requests information on the project's header file.

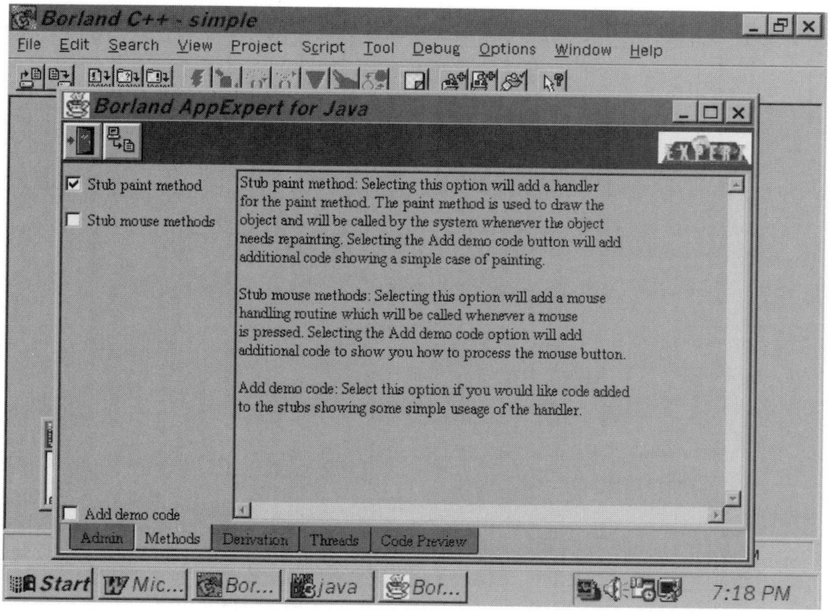


**Figure 7.4:** Use the Methods button to include a Stub paint method.

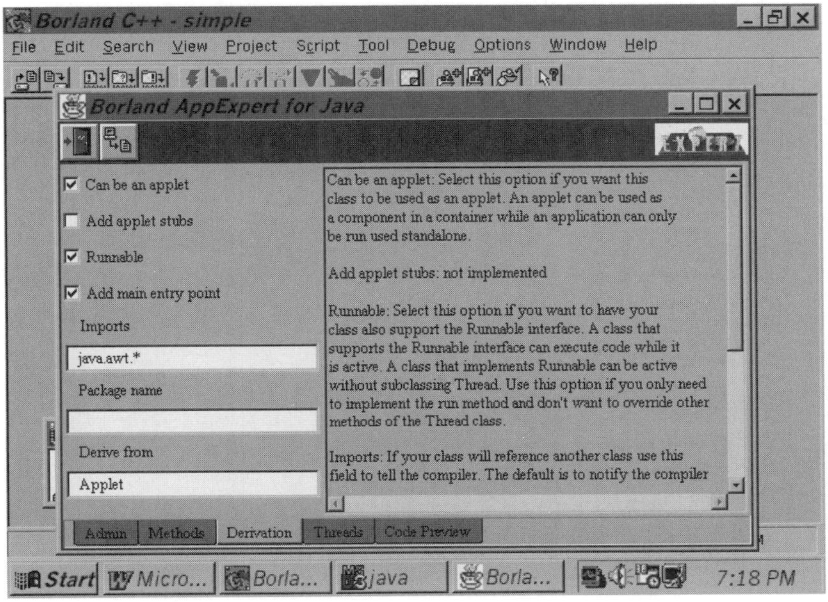


**Figure 7.5:** The Derivation button reveals the AppExpert's defaults for this project.

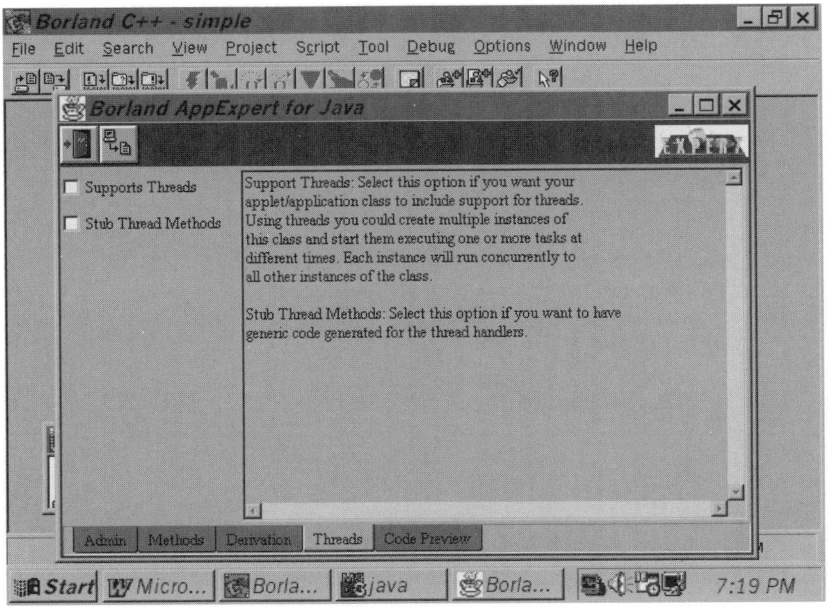


**Figure 7.6:** The Threads button is used to set thread options.

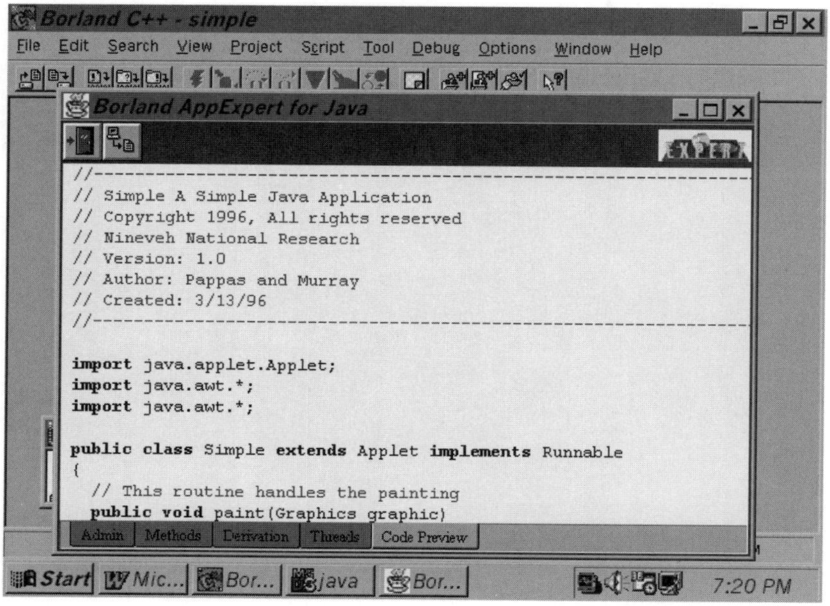


**Figure 7.7:** The Code Preview button is used to preview the AppExpert's code and eventually save it to the Simple.java file.

If you now select the Simple.java file from the project window, you will be able to modify the default code in the Borland C++ editor, as shown in Figure 7.8.

The following code listing is the modified version of the AppExpert's code. The changes to the AppExpert code are noted in a bold font.

```
//----------------------------------------------------------------
// Simple A Simple Java Application
// Copyright 1996, All rights reserved
// Nineveh National Research
// Version: 1.0
// Author: Pappas and Murray
// Created: 3/13/96
//----------------------------------------------------------------

import java.applet.Applet;
import java.awt.*;

public class Simple extends Applet implements Runnable
{
  // This routine handles the painting
```

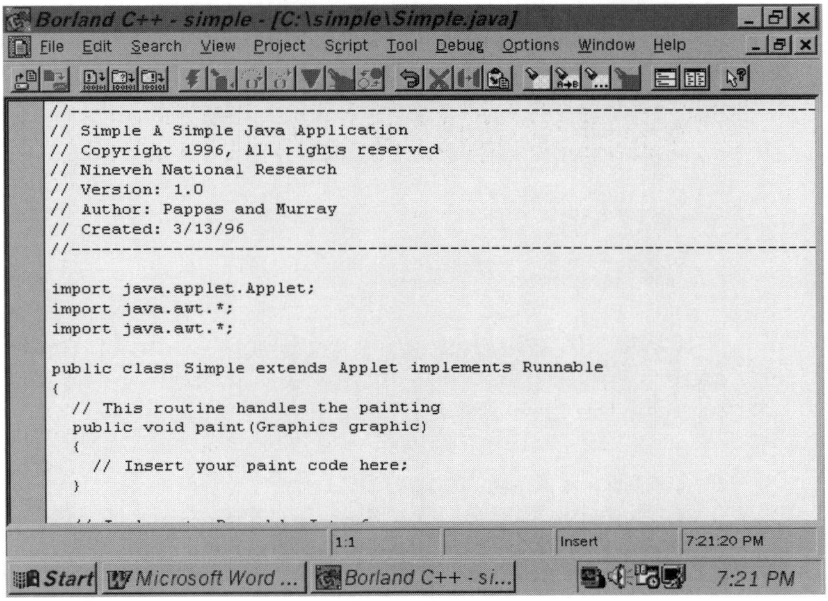


**Figure 7.8:** The code created by the AppExpert can be edited with the Borland C++ editor.

```
public void paint(Graphics graphic)
{
  graphic.drawString("Here is sample text to draw.", 10, 10);
  graphic.drawOval(20, 20, 100, 150);
  graphic.fillOval(340, 20, 100, 150);
}

// Implements Runnable Interface
public void run()
{
}

// For running standalone
public static void main(String[] argv)
{
  // Create the frame and launch Simple
  Frame f = new Frame("SimpleFrame");
  // f.reshape(100, 100, 200, 100);

  f.show();

  Simple x = new Simple();
  f.add("Center", x);
```

```
      x.init();
      x.start();
    }

    // Constructor
    public  Simple()
    {
    }

} // end class Simple
```

If you are working along with this example, modify your code to match the code in the listing. You are now ready to compile the Java application.

**Building a Java Application** Building a Java application is simple and can be done directly from the Project Window shown earlier in Figure 7.2. Use the following steps as a guide:

1. Click the right mouse button on the Simple.java file shown earlier in the Project window.
2. Choose the JavaCompile option to compile the Java application, as shown in Figure 7.9.
3. The Compile dialog box should show a successful compile operation, as you see in Figure 7.10.
4. Click on the OK button to return to the Project window.

If your compile operation was successful, you are now ready to launch the Simple Java application.

**Launching the Application** A successfully compiled Java application can be launched from the Project window. Use the following steps as a guide for launching Java applications:

1. Click the right mouse button on the Simple.class file shown earlier in the Project window.
2. Choose the Java View | View option to launch the Java application, as shown in Figure 7.11.
3. A window will open for the launched application.

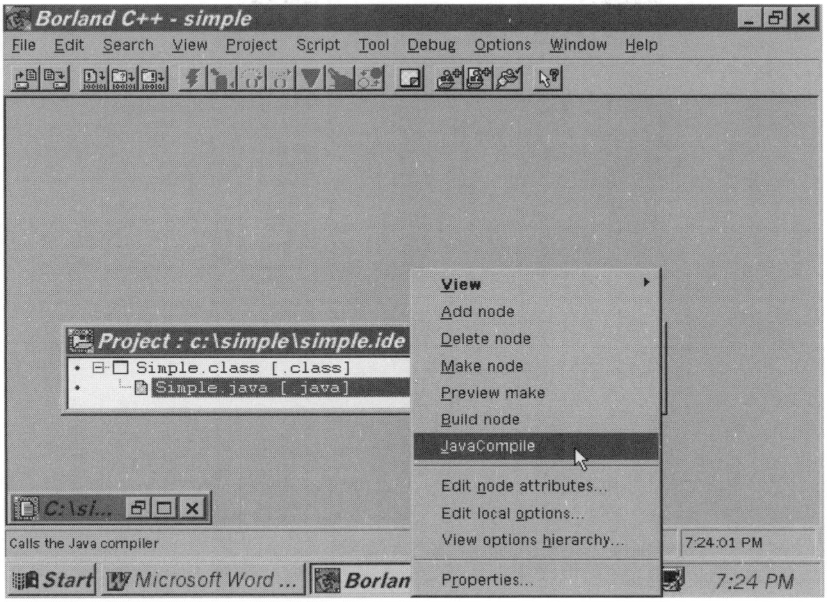


**Figure 7.9:** Select the JavaCompile option to compile the new Java project.

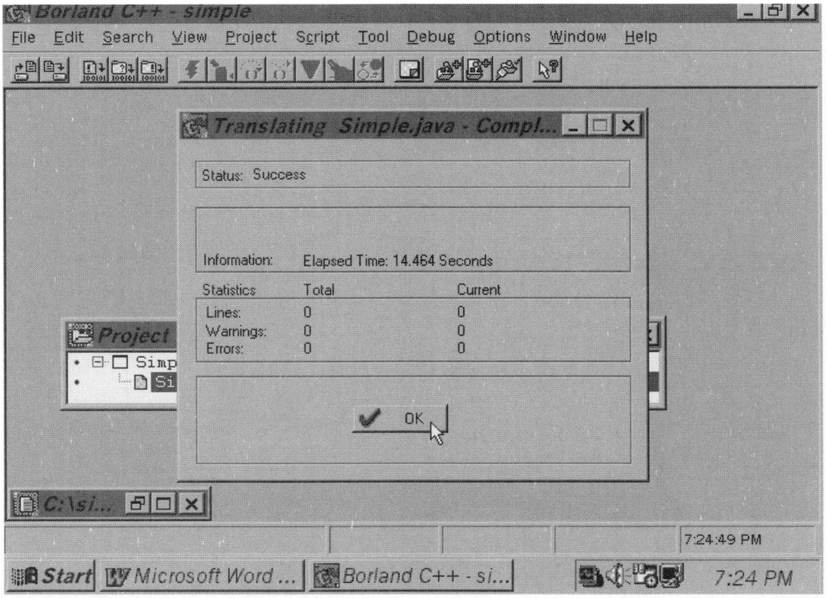


**Figure 7.10:** The Compile dialog box will show the status of your compile operation.

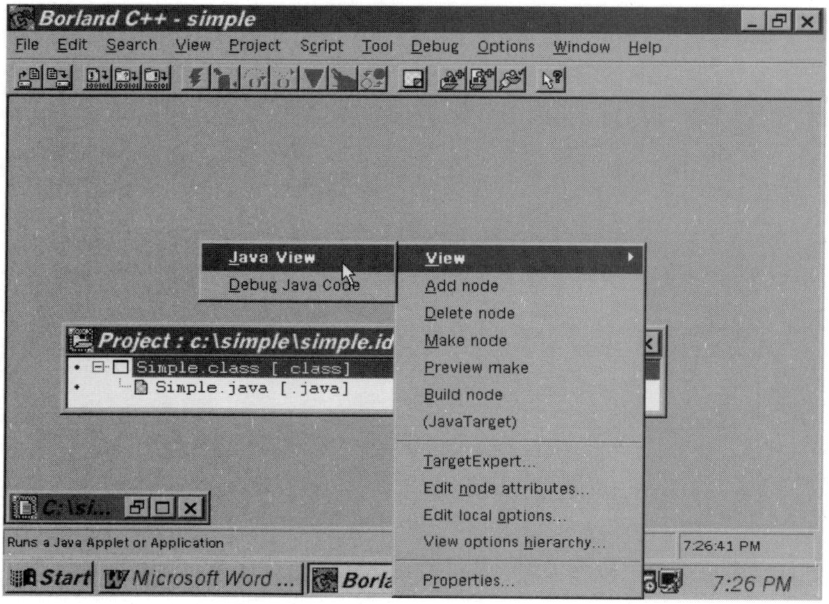


**Figure 7.11:** A Java application can be launched from the Project window.

Figure 7.12 shows the window created by the Simple.class when it is executed. It's that tiny little window pointed to by the cursor. Why is it so small? We'll tell you shortly.

Figure 7.12 does not tell us too much about our default environment, or does it? In the next section we'll investigate what we have learned from this application.

## Environment Clues Revealed

Figure 7.12 shows us that we should expect nothing more than a standard Windows title bar and system menu options from our environment. Actually, the initial window size can be forced to a specific size. The AppWizard for Java sets the initial Window size with the following portion of code:

```
f.reshape(100, 100, 200, 100);
```

You may have noticed in the complete listing, shown earlier, that this portion of code was commented out. Insert this code and the launched application will start drawing a window 100 pixels from the left side of the Borland IDE screen and 100 pix-

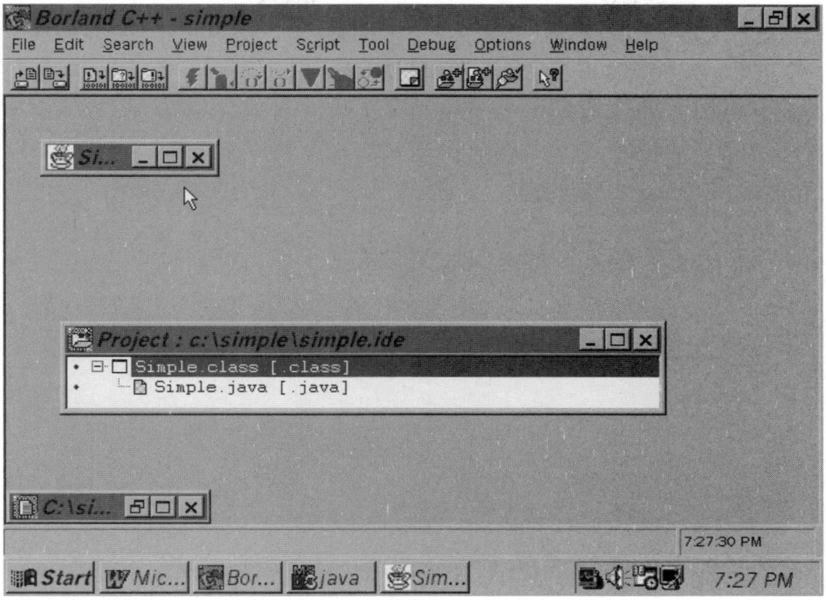


**Figure 7.12:** The Simple Java application's window.

els from the top of the Borland IDE screen. The window will be 200 pixels wide and 100 pixels high.

***Note:*** *Windows programmers will notice that the third and fourth parameters specified in the* ***reshape()*** *member function (method) call gives the actual width and height of the window. Under Windows, these parameters usually represent the window's extent. When programming with Windows API functions, the width is determined by finding the difference between the third and first parameters and the height by finding the difference between the fourth and second parameters.*

If you are operating in VGA mode and want your window to fill the entire screen you can use the following values when you call the **reshape()** member function:

```
f.reshape(0, 0, 640, 480);
```

If you click on the maximize icon, you should see a window similar to Figure 7.13.

First, notice the default background color provided by the Borland Java tools. It is a light gray color. Text is drawn in a

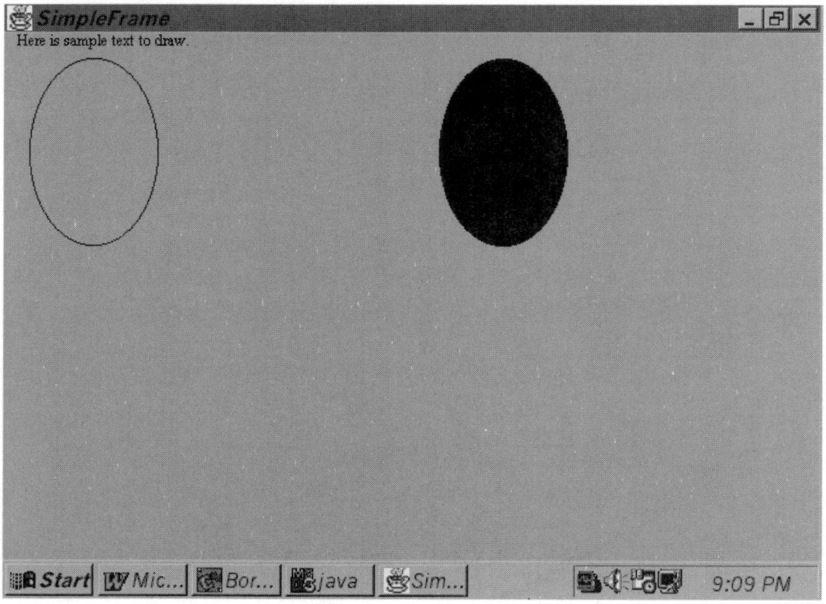


**Figure 7.13:** The Simple application's default window has been maximized to reveal even more detail about the default Java environment.

default Windows font, in black. Lines are drawn in black. Shapes that are filled are filled in black.

***Note:*** *Windows programmers are familiar with similar environment characteristics. They would say that the text color is black, the default pen color is black and the fill brush is a solid black brush.*

Java programmers do not talk of pens and brushes. We draw various graphics primitives by first setting the drawing color and then drawing the graphics shape. The point to be made here is that the default color for text, lines, and fills is black.

The code to draw the text and graphics figures is simple and straightforward.

```
graphic.drawString("Here is sample text to draw.", 10, 10);
graphic.drawOval(20, 20, 100, 150);
graphic.fillOval(340, 20, 100, 150);
```

These specific member functions will be discussed in more detail in the next chapter. For our purposes, now, we're more interested in the parameters passed to the member functions.

Apparently we knew something about the graphics coordinate system when we wrote this program. Figure 7.14 shows coordinates for a VGA screen. Notice that the origin is in the upper left corner of the window.

***Note:*** *Windows programmers know that they have six drawing modes available to them. Java is limited to one drawing mode. It is Windows MM_Text mode (the default) that is most closely associated with Java's coordinate system.*

The **drawString()** member function is used to draw the text string to the window. The coordinates specify the starting X and Y positions of the string.

The **drawOval()** and **fillOval()** member functions draw two shapes in the window. The first two parameters of each member function specify the starting point of each shape on the previously mentioned coordinate system. The second two parameters specify the actual width and height of the shape.

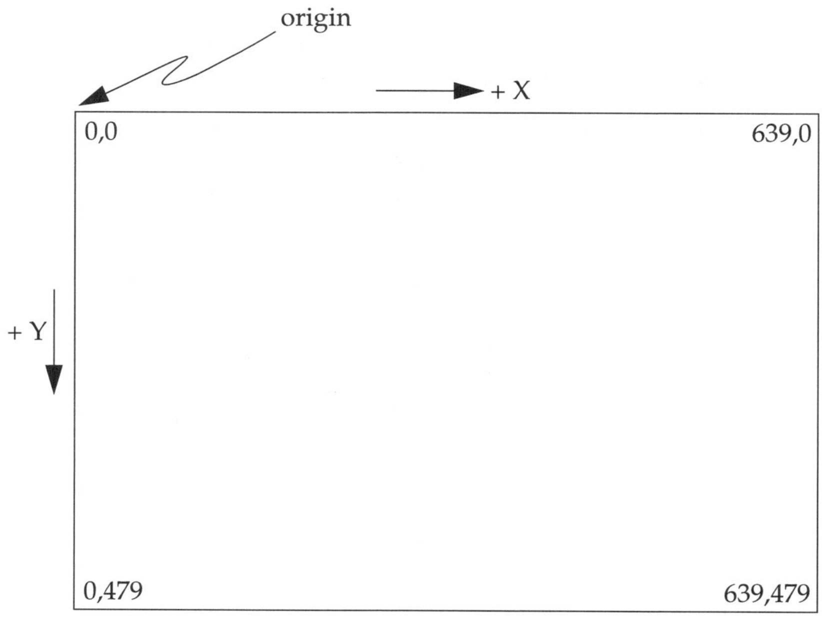


**Figure 7.14:** The graphics coordinate system with values specific to a VGA window.

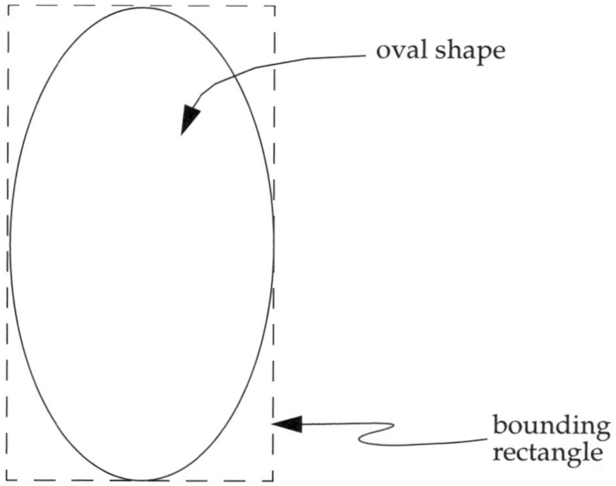


**Figure 7.15:** The sizes of graphics shapes are specified with respect to a bounding rectangle.

***Note:*** *Windows programmers will again notice that the third and fourth parameters specified in the Java member functions give the literal width and height of the graphics shape. Under Windows, these parameters usually represent the extent of the graphics shape measured from the first two parameters.*

Many graphics shapes, as you'll learn in the next chapter, are drawn as if they are contained within a *bounding* rectangle. When this is the case, the parameters specified in the Java graphics member functions are those for the bounding rectangle. Figure 7.15 shows how the shape created by the **drawOval()** member function is contained within a bounding rectangle.

The coordinate system and the graphics primitives we've use in this chapter are described in the Java Graphics class. In the next section, we'll investigate Java classes available to us.

## Java Classes

Java's many classes provide the member functions necessary for creating applications. These classes are included in your

Java code, created by the AppWizard for Java, with the following portion of code.

```
import java.awt.*;
```

If you were using only member functions in the Graphics class, that line of code could have been replaced with:

```
import java.awt.Graphics;
```

The following listing gives all of the classes available to us. Many of these classes will be discussed in later chapters.

```
ARITHMET.JAV
CHARACTE.JAV
BOOLEAN.JAV
CLASS.JAV
STRING.JAV
DOUBLE.JAV
CLASSCAS.JAV
EXCEPTIO.JAV
FLOAT.JAV
LONG.JAV
INTEGER.JAV
INTERNAL.JAV
SYSTEM.JAV
MATH.JAV
ILLEGALA.JAV
THREAD.JAV
THROWABL.JAV
RUNTIME.JAV
PROCESS.JAV
NUMBER.JAV
ARRAYSTO.JAV
NEGATIVE.JAV
STACKOVE.JAV
NULLPOIN.JAV
UNKNOWNE.JAV
OBJECT.JAV
NUMBERFO.JAV
RUNNABLE.JAV
NOSUCHME.JAV
STRINGBU.JAV
CLONEABL.JAV
COMPILER.JAV
INCOMPAT.JAV
```

```
UNSATISF.JAV
OUTOFMEM.JAV
ERROR.JAV
ABSTRACT.JAV
CLASSLOA.JAV
ARRAYIND.JAV
CLASSCIR.JAV
VIRTUALM.JAV
THREADDE.JAV
INSTANTI.JAV
CLASSFOR.JAV
NOCLASSD.JAV
LINKAGEE.JAV
SECURITY.JAV
THREADGR.JAV
RUNTIMEE.JAV
ILLEGALT.JAV
VERIFYER.JAV
CLASSNOT.JAV
STRINGIN.JAV
INDEXOUT.JAV
INTERRUP.JAV
CLONENOT.JAV
NOSUCHFI.JAV
ILLEGALM.JAV
ENUMERAT.JAV
RANDOM.JAV
HASHTABL.JAV
VECTOR.JAV
STACK.JAV
PROPERTI.JAV
EMPTYSTA.JAV
OBSERVAB.JAV
BITSET.JAV
DATE.JAV
STRINGTO.JAV
DICTIONA.JAV
NOSUCHEL.JAV
OBSERVER.JAV
DATAOUTP.JAV
FILEOUTP.JAV
BUFFERED.JAV
INPUTSTR.JAV
FILEINPU.JAV
OUTPUTST.JAV
BYTEARRA.JAV
PRINTSTR.JAV
FILTERIN.JAV
```

```
FILTEROU.JAV
PUSHBACK.JAV
FILE.JAV
RANDOMAC.JAV
FILENAME.JAV
IOEXCEPT.JAV
STREAMTO.JAV
DATAINPU.JAV
FILEDESC.JAV
LINENUMB.JAV
SEQUENCE.JAV
FILENOTF.JAV
UTFDATAF.JAV
EOFEXCEP.JAV
PIPEDOUT.JAV
PIPEDINP.JAV
SERVERSO.JAV
SOCKET.JAV
PROTOCOL.JAV
INETADDR.JAV
PLAINSOC.JAV
SOCKETIM.JAV
SOCKETEX.JAV
SOCKETIN.JAV
URL.JAV
SOCKETOU.JAV
UNKNOWNH.JAV
URLSTREA.JAV
URLCONNE.JAV
UNKNOWNS.JAV
URLENCOD.JAV
CONTENTH.JAV
MALFORME.JAV
DATAGRAM.JAV
TOOLKIT.JAV
COLOR.JAV
BUTTON.JAV
BORDERLA.JAV
COMPONEN.JAV
DIMENSIO.JAV
FONT.JAV
CONTAINE.JAV
EVENT.JAV
GRAPHICS.JAV
FRAME.JAV
POLYGON.JAV
CHECKBOX.JAV
LAYOUTMA.JAV
```

```
LIST.JAV
LABEL.JAV
SCROLLBA.JAV
CARDLAYO.JAV
MENUITEM.JAV
MENU.JAV
AWTEXCEP.JAV
TEXTAREA.JAV
TEXTFIEL.JAV
CANVAS.JAV
FONTMETR.JAV
CHOICE.JAV
PANEL.JAV
IMAGE.JAV
WINDOW.JAV
GRIDLAYO.JAV
FLOWLAYO.JAV
MENUBAR.JAV
FILEDIAL.JAV
POINT.JAV
RECTANGL.JAV
MENUCOMP.JAV
AWTERROR.JAV
INSETS.JAV
DIALOG.JAV
MENUCONT.JAV
BUTTONPE.JAV
LABELPEE.JAV
LISTPEER.JAV
MENUPEER.JAV
MENUBARP.JAV
FRAMEPEE.JAV
CHOICEPE.JAV
WINDOWPE.JAV
PANELPEE.JAV
CANVASPE.JAV
DIALOGPE.JAV
TEXTCOMP.JAV
MEDIATRA.JAV
GRIDBAGL.JAV
GRIDBAGC.JAV
VISUALTE.JAV
VISUALTE.HTM
COLORMOD.JAV
DIRECTCO.JAV
IMAGECON.JAV
IMAGEFIL.JAV
IMAGEOBS.JAV
```

```
IMAGEPRO.JAV
INDEXCOL.JAV
RGBIMAGE.JAV
MEMORYIM.JAV
FILTERED.JAV
CROPIMAG.JAV
PIXELGRA.JAV
APPLETCO.JAV
AUDIOCLI.JAV
APPLET.JAV
APPLETST.JAV
TTY.JAV
```

In the example code, listed earlier in this chapter, we made use of the Graphics class. In order to draw on the screen, the **paint()** member function is overridden.

```
public void paint(Graphics graphic)
```

This member function uses an argument, graphics, which is an instance of the Graphics class. The argument name is supplied by the AppExpert for Java. In the next chapter, you'll learn about the member functions provided in the Graphics class for drawing graphics primitives. These simple graphics shapes form the foundation for all graphical drawing done on the screen.

## Java Lingo

*bounding rectangle*—an imaginary rectangular shape used to describe the extents of many Java graphics shapes.

*coordinate system*—defines the capabilities and constraints of the drawing surface for Java member functions.

*default coordinate system*—describes those coordinate system capabilities and constraints initially set in the Java environment.

*reshape()*—is used to size the graphical drawing area on the screen.

# 8

# Graphics Fundamentals

In the previous chapter you have learned how to create a simple Java application while investigating the default Java environment. In this chapter, you will learn more details about the Java Graphics class and specifically the various member functions (methods) available to you for drawing basic graphics shapes. The basic graphics shapes supported by this Java class are called *graphics drawing primitives*. Graphics primitives form the foundation for all drawing done in Java and include arcs, lines, ovals, polygons, rectangles, and so on.

If you have developed Windows applications with the Borland C++ compiler that use Windows graphics drawing primitives, you will feel right at home with the Java graphics drawing primitives. We'll try to point out important similarities and differences between these two groups.

As you examine this chapter notice that each example is code complete. That is, it is wrapped in a complete application. No more guesswork as to how to actually implement these graphics primitives.

## Building Applications

The applications in this chapter can be built with the AppExpert for Java. For a step-by-step approach for developing applications, refer to Chapter 7 for additional details.

Complete coding examples are given for almost all of the drawing primitives discussed in this chapter. This Java code can be entered, compiled, and executed as a standalone application. If you encounter errors during the compile or run process, not related to a typing error, you have probably forgotten one of the steps detailed in Chapter 7.

***Note:*** *Windows programmers will notice that a majority of the graphics primitives are passed a starting x,y coordinate point. This is the point from which the graphics shape will be drawn. Frequently, the next two values are for width and height. The width and height values are measured with respect to the starting point and represent the actual width and height of the object. Windows functions, on the other hand, do not specify the actual width and height. The third and fourth parameters in a similar Windows function represent the end points. Thus width is calculated by subtracting the first parameter from the third parameter and height by subtracting the second parameter from the fourth.*

## clearRect(int x, int y, int width, int height)

This member function clears the specified rectangle by filling it with the current background color. This action takes place on the current drawing surface.

The following example illustrates the **clearRect()** member function by drawing a shape to the screen and then clearing the upper left quarter of the window.

```
//-------------------------------------------------------
// RectClear Illustrates clearRect()
// Copyright 1996, All rights reserved
// Nineveh National Research
// Version: 1.0
// Author: Pappas and Murray
// Created: 3/16/96
//-------------------------------------------------------
```

```
import java.applet.Applet;
import java.awt.*;

public class RectClear extends Applet implements Runnable
{
  // This routine handles the painting
  public void paint(Graphics graphic)
  {
    graphic.fillOval(100,100,439,279);
    graphic.clearRect(0,0,319,239);
  }

  // Implements Runnable Interface
  public void run()
  {
  }

  // For running standalone
  public static void main(String[] argv)
  {
    // Create the frame and launch RectClear
    Frame f = new Frame("RectClearFrame");
    f.reshape(0, 0, 639, 479);
    f.show();

    RectClear x = new RectClear();
    f.add("Center", x);
    x.init();
    x.start();
  }

  // Constructor
  public  RectClear()
  {
  }

} // end class RectClear
```

Figure 8.1 shows the results of this simple application, with the upper left quarter of the screen cleared.

## clipRect(int x, int y, int width, int height)

This member function clips to a rectangle. The clipping area is formed by the intersection of the current clipping area and that

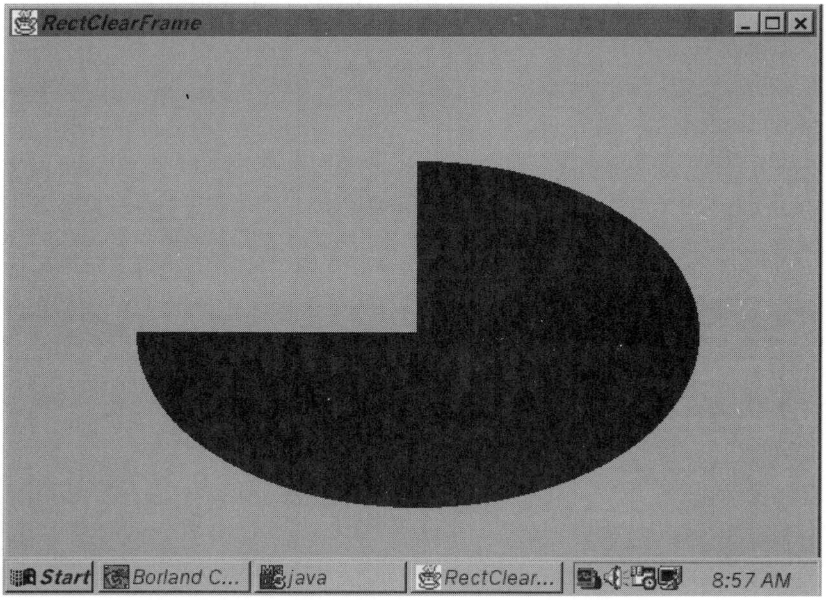


**Figure 8.1:** The clearRect() member function is used to clear the upper left quarter of the screen.

of the given rectangle specified by the member function. Graphic operations have effect only within the clipping area.

Here *x* represents the x screen coordinate and *y* the y screen coordinate for the starting point. *width* represents the width and *height* the height of the clipping rectangle.

In the following listing the **clipRect()** member function is used to clip the graphics image so that only the portion of the image in the upper left quarter of the window is visible.

```
//-------------------------------------------------------
// RectClip Illustrate clipRect()
// Copyright 1996, All rights reserved
// Nineveh National Research
// Version: 1.0
// Author: Pappas and Murray
// Created: 3/16/96
//-------------------------------------------------------

import java.applet.Applet;
import java.awt.*;
```

```
public class RectClip extends Applet implements Runnable
{
  // This routine handles the painting
  public void paint(Graphics graphic)
  {
    graphic.clipRect(0,0,319,239);
    graphic.fillOval(100,100,439,279);
  }

  // Implements Runnable Interface
  public void run()
  {
  }

  // For running standalone
  public static void main(String[] argv)
  {
    // Create the frame and launch RectClip
    Frame f = new Frame("RectClipFrame");
    f.reshape(0, 0, 639, 479);
    f.show();

    RectClip x = new RectClip();
    f.add("Center", x);
    x.init();
    x.start();
  }

  // Constructor
  public  RectClip()
  {
  }

} // end class RectClip
```

Figure 8.2 shows the resulting figure as it is drawn to the screen.

## copyArea(int x, int y, int width, int height, int dx, int dy)

This member function copies a portion of the screen. Here *x* represents the x screen coordinate and *y* the y screen coordinate for the starting point. *width* represents the width and *height* the height of the area to be copied. Here *dx* represents the horizontal distance and *dy* the vertical distance.

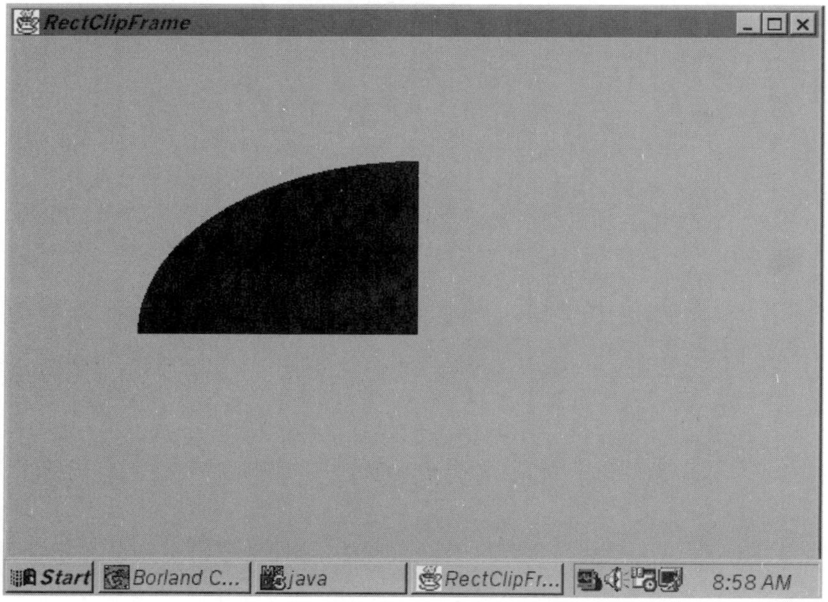


**Figure 8.2:** The clipRect() member function is used to clip a portion of the screen.

The following example shows how the **copyArea()** member function can be used to replicate graphics shapes. One graphics shape is drawn, then copied and drawn again by the **copy-Area()** member function.

```
//---------------------------------------------------------
// AreaCopy Illustrate copyArea()
// Copyright 1996, All rights reserved
// Nineveh National Research
// Version: 1.0
// Author: Pappas and Murray
// Created: 3/16/96
//---------------------------------------------------------

import java.applet.Applet;
import java.awt.*;

public class AreaCopy extends Applet implements Runnable
{
  // This routine handles the painting
  public void paint(Graphics graphic)
  {
    graphic.fillRect(100, 100, 119, 39);
```

```
    graphic.copyArea(0, 0, 319, 239, 320, 240);
  }

  // Implements Runnable Interface
  public void run()
  {
  }

  // For running standalone
  public static void main(String[] argv)
  {
    // Create the frame and launch AreaCopy
    Frame f = new Frame("AreaCopyFrame");
    f.reshape(0, 0, 639, 479);
    f.show();

    AreaCopy x = new AreaCopy();
    f.add("Center", x);
    x.init();
    x.start();
  }

  // Constructor
  public  AreaCopy()
  {
  }

} // end class AreaCopy
```

Figure 8.3 shows the screen after the **copyArea()** function has duplicated the original graphics shape.

## draw3DRect(int x, int y, int width, int height, boolean raised)

This member function draws a highlighted three-dimensional rectangle. Here *x* represents the x screen coordinate and *y* the y screen coordinate for the starting point. *width* represents the width and *height* the height of the three-dimensional rectangle. *raised* is a boolean that specifies whether the rectangle is raised or not raised. The current drawing color is used.

The following listing illustrates the use of the **draw3DRect()** member function. One shape is drawn with the boolean set to **false** and the other shape with the boolean set to **true**.

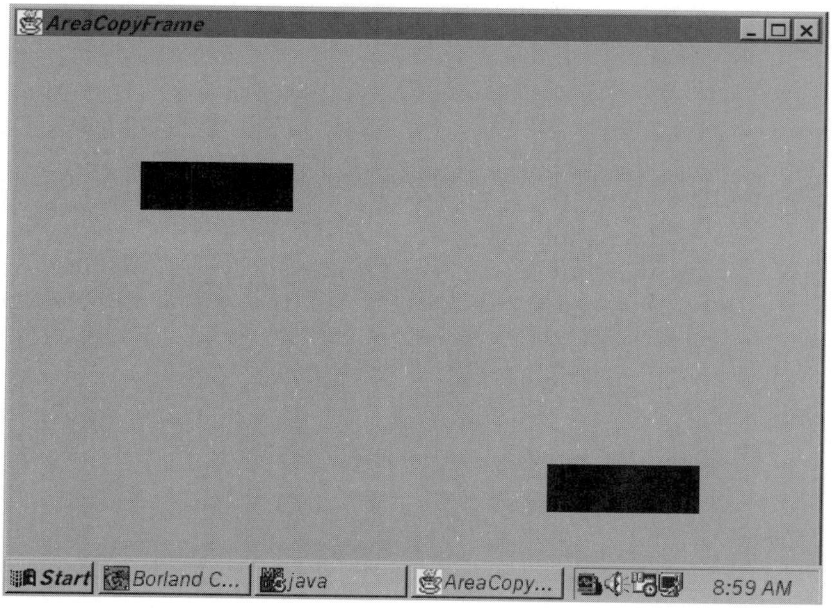


**Figure 8.3:** The copyArea() member function can be used to replicate portions of the screen.

```
//------------------------------------------------------------
// Rect3D Illustrate draw3DRect()
// Copyright 1996, All rights reserved
// Nineveh National Research
// Version: 1.0
// Author: Pappas and Murray
// Created: 3/16/96
//------------------------------------------------------------


import java.applet.Applet;
import java.awt.*;


public class Rect3D extends Applet implements Runnable
{
  // This routine handles the painting
  public void paint(Graphics graphic)
  {
    graphic.setColor(Color.cyan);
    graphic.draw3DRect(50,50,219,139,false);
    graphic.draw3DRect(369,289,219,139,true);
  }
```

```
    // Implements Runnable Interface
    public void run()
    {
    }

    // For running standalone
    public static void main(String[] argv)
    {
      // Create the frame and launch Rect3D
      Frame f = new Frame("Rect3DFrame");
      f.reshape(0, 0, 639, 479);
      f.show();

      Rect3D x = new Rect3D();
      f.add("Center", x);
      x.init();
      x.start();
    }

    // Constructor
    public  Rect3D()
    {
    }

} // end class Rect3D
```

Figure 8.4 shows the screen after the two 3D shapes have been drawn. Notice that the 3D effect is subtle. This is a result of the thin line segments. The effect will also change as you change drawing colors.

## drawArc(int x, int y, int width, int height, int startAngle, int arcAngle)

This member function is used to draw an arc that is bounded by the given rectangle. Drawing starts at *startAngle* and proceeds a total angular distance given by *arcAngle*. Angles start on the positive x-axis. Positive angles are measured counterclockwise. Here *x* represents the x screen coordinate and *y* the y screen coordinate for the starting point. *width* represents the width and *height* the height of the bounding rectangle. *startAngle* marks the start of arc and *arcAngle* the total angular distance of the arc. Angles are measured in degrees. The current drawing color is used.

**Figure 8.4:** The draw3DRect() function can make rectangular shapes appear with a three-dimensional quality.

***Note:*** *Windows programmers will see that angular measurements are specified in degrees. This is an improvement over the convoluted method used for similar Windows API functions.*

The next listing illustrates the use of the **drawArc()** member function by drawing four different arc segments on the screen.

```
//----------------------------------------------------------
// Arc Illustrate drawArc()
// Copyright 1996, All rights reserved
// Nineveh National Research
// Version: 1.0
// Author: Pappas and Murray
// Created: 3/16/96
//----------------------------------------------------------

import java.applet.Applet;
import java.awt.*;

public class Arc extends Applet implements Runnable
{
  // This routine handles the painting
```

```
public void paint(Graphics graphic)
{
  graphic.drawArc(119, 120, 50, 50, 0, 90);
  graphic.drawArc(439, 120, 50, 50, 90, 180);
  graphic.drawArc(119, 339, 50, 100, 180, 270);
  graphic.drawArc(439, 339, 100, 50, 45, 135);
}

// Implements Runnable Interface
public void run()
{
}

// For running standalone
public static void main(String[] argv)
{
  // Create the frame and launch Arc
  Frame f = new Frame("ArcFrame");
  f.reshape(0, 0, 639, 479);
  f.show();

  Arc x = new Arc();
  f.add("Center", x);
  x.init();
  x.start();
}

// Constructor
public  Arc()
{
}

} // end class Arc
```

Figure 8.5 shows the results of this application and the **drawArc()** member function. Remember that the last two parameters passed to **drawArc()** specify the starting angle and the angular span of the arc.

## drawLine(int x1, int y1, int x2, int y2)

This member function is used to draw a line from the coordinate positions *x1,y1* to *x2,y2*. Here *x1* represents the x screen coordinate and *y1* the y screen coordinate for the starting point. Likewise, *x2* represents the x screen coordinate and *y2* the y

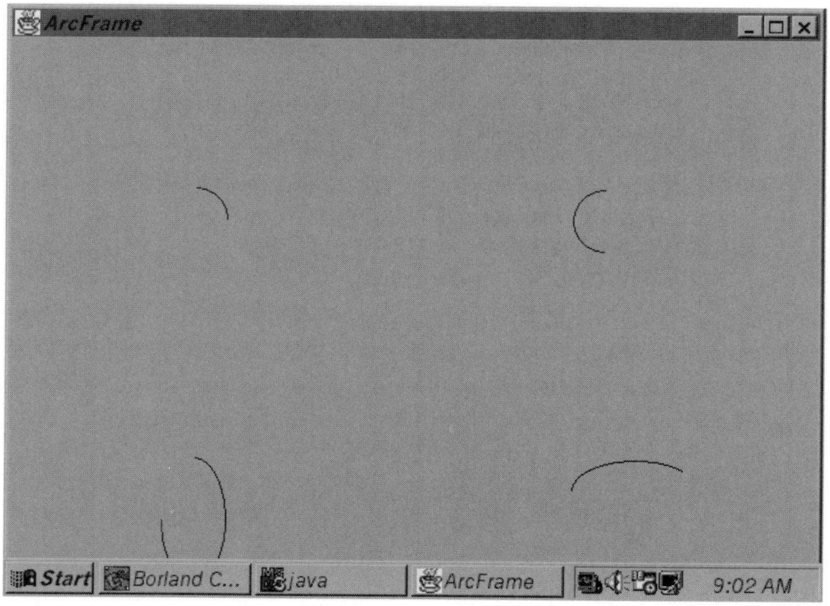


**Figure 8.5:** Several drawArc() member function calls help illustrate the versatility of this member function.

screen coordinate for the ending point. The current drawing color is used.

The following listing illustrates the **drawLine()** member function. Here four separate line segments are drawn to the screen.

```
//-------------------------------------------------------
// Line Illustrate drawLine()
// Copyright 1996, All rights reserved
// Nineveh National Research
// Version: 1.0
// Author: Pappas and Murray
// Created: 3/16/96
//-------------------------------------------------------

import java.applet.Applet;
import java.awt.*;

public class Line extends Applet implements Runnable
{
  // This routine handles the painting
  public void paint(Graphics graphic)
```

```
  {
    graphic.drawLine(50, 120, 220, 120);  // horizontal
    graphic.drawLine(480, 50, 480, 139);  // vertical
    graphic.drawLine(50, 289, 219, 379);  // diagonal
    graphic.drawLine(369, 439, 589, 279); // diagonal
  }

  // Implements Runnable Interface
  public void run()
  {
  }

  // For running standalone
  public static void main(String[] argv)
  {
    // Create the frame and launch Line
    Frame f = new Frame("LineFrame");
    f.reshape(0, 0, 639, 479);
    f.show();

    Line x = new Line();
    f.add("Center", x);
    x.init();
    x.start();
  }

  // Constructor
  public  Line()
  {
  }

} // end class Line
```

Figure 8.6 shows four separate line segments drawn in the quarters of the window.

## drawOval(int x, int y, int width, int height)

This member function is used to draw an oval inside the given bounding rectangle. Here *x* represents the x screen coordinate and *y* the y screen coordinate for the starting point. *width* represents the width and *height* the height of the oval shape. The current drawing color is used.

***Note:*** *The Java **drawOval()** member function is most closely associated with the Windows **Ellipse()** API function.*

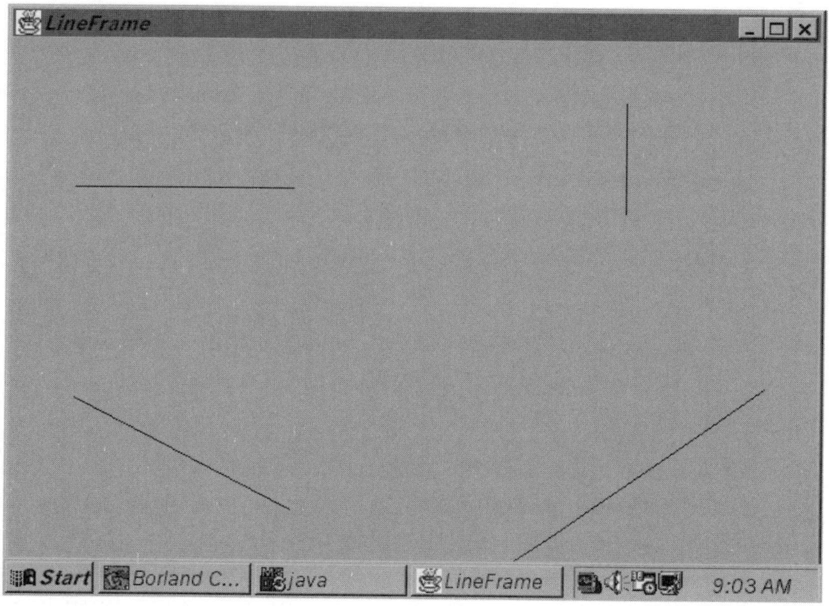


**Figure 8.6:** The drawLine() member function is used to draw four line segments.

This listing illustrates the use of the **drawOval()** member function. This is the member function you'll use to draw ellipses and circles.

```
//---------------------------------------------------------
// Oval Illustrate drawOval()
// Copyright 1996, All rights reserved
// Nineveh National Research
// Version: 1.0
// Author: Pappas and Murray
// Created: 3/16/96
//---------------------------------------------------------

import java.applet.Applet;
import java.awt.*;

public class Oval extends Applet implements Runnable
{
  // This routine handles the painting
  public void paint(Graphics graphic)
  {
    graphic.drawOval(50, 50, 539, 379);
    graphic.drawOval(100, 100, 439, 279);
```

```
    graphic.drawOval(150, 150, 339, 179);
    graphic.drawOval(200, 200, 239, 79);
  }

  // Implements Runnable Interface
  public void run()
  {
  }

  // For running standalone
  public static void main(String[] argv)
  {
    // Create the frame and launch Oval
    Frame f = new Frame("OvalFrame");
    f.reshape(0, 0, 639, 479);
    f.show();

    Oval x = new Oval();
    f.add("Center", x);
    x.init();
    x.start();
  }

  // Constructor
  public  Oval()
  {
  }

} // end class Oval
```

Figure 8.7 shows an interesting pattern of decreasing oval sizes in the window.

## drawPolygon(int xPoints[], int yPoints[], int nPoints)
## drawPolygon(Polygon p)

This member function is used to draw a polygon. The starting and ending points for the polygon's line segments can be described in two arrays. *xPoints[]* holds the x coordinate points and *yPoints[]* the y coordinate points. *nPoints* is the total number of points.

An alternative method is to specify the polygon as an instance of the Polygon class. This is useful if additional points may be added after the polygon is drawn.

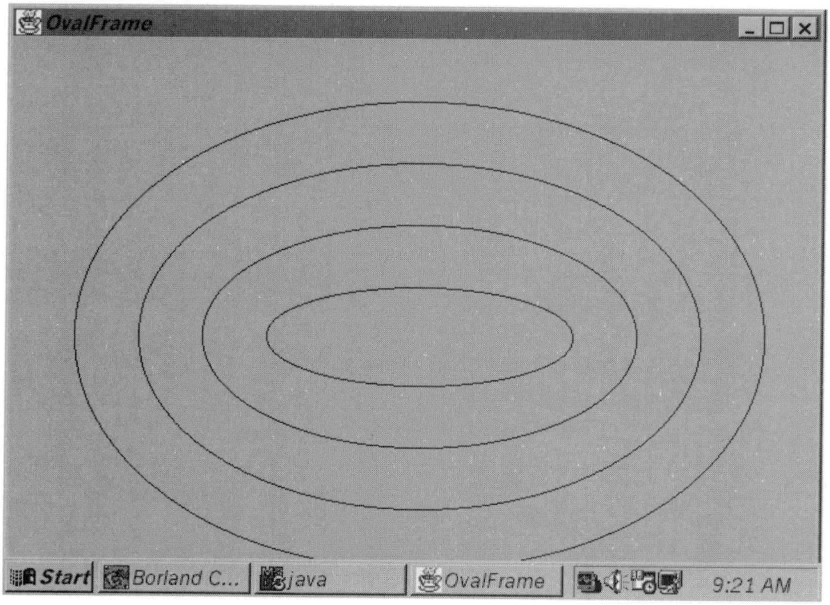


**Figure 8.7:** The drawOval() member function can be used to draw ellipses and circles.

Polygon shapes are not automatically closed by Java. The current drawing color is used.

The following listing illustrates the use of both variations of the **drawPolygon()** member function.

```
//---------------------------------------------------------
// Poly Illustrate drawPolygon()
// Copyright 1996, All rights reserved
// Nineveh National Research
// Version: 1.0
// Author: Pappas and Murray
// Created: 3/16/96
//---------------------------------------------------------

import java.applet.Applet;
import java.awt.*;

public class Poly extends Applet implements Runnable
{
  // This routine handles the painting
  public void paint(Graphics graphic)
  {
```

```
    // technique A (outer polygon)
    int Axpts[] = {319, 400, 600, 200, 25};
    int Aypts[] = {10, 30, 400, 290, 100};
    int Anumpts = Aypts.length;
    graphic.drawPolygon(Axpts, Aypts, Anumpts);

    // technique B (inner polygon)
    int Bxpts[] = {300, 400, 500, 300, 125};
    int Bypts[] = {100, 70, 350, 200, 150};
    int Bnumpts = Bypts.length;
    Polygon mypoly = new Polygon(Bxpts, Bypts, Bnumpts);
    mypoly.addPoint(150, 175);  // add new points
    mypoly.addPoint(175, 150);
    graphic.drawPolygon(mypoly);
  }

  // Implements Runnable Interface
  public void run()
  {
  }

  // For running standalone
  public static void main(String[] argv)
  {
    // Create the frame and launch Poly
    Frame f = new Frame("PolyFrame");
    f.reshape(0, 0, 639, 479);
    f.show();

    Poly x = new Poly();
    f.add("Center", x);
    x.init();
    x.start();
  }

  // Constructor
  public  Poly()
  {
  }

} // end class Poly
```

Figure 8.8 illustrates the use of both versions of the **drawPolygon()** member function. Notice in the figure that two separate shapes are drawn to the screen, one inside the other. Also notice that neither figure is closed.

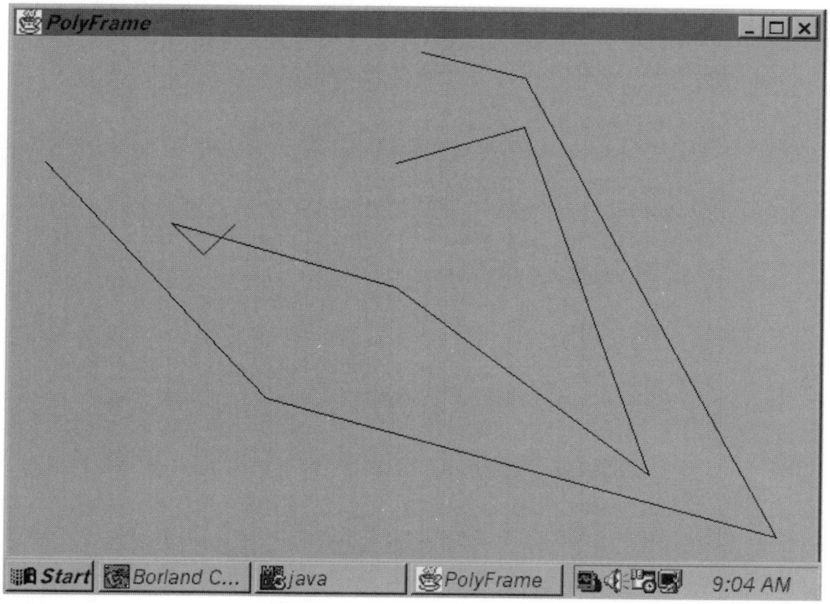


**Figure 8.8:** The drawPolygon() member function can be used to draw multiple-sided shapes to the window.

## drawRect(int x, int y, int width, int height)

This member function is used to draw the outline of a rectangle. Here *x* represents the x screen coordinate and *y* the y screen coordinate for the starting point. *width* represents the width and *height* the height of the rectangular shape. The current drawing color is used.

The following listing illustrates the use of the **drawRect()** member function. In this example four rectangles are drawn to the screen, from largest to smallest.

```
//-------------------------------------------------------
// Rect Illustrate drawRect()
// Copyright 1996, All rights reserved
// Nineveh National Research
// Version: 1.0
// Author: Pappas and Murray
// Created: 3/16/96
//-------------------------------------------------------

import java.applet.Applet;
```

```
import java.awt.*;

public class Rect extends Applet implements Runnable
{
  // This routine handles the painting
  public void paint(Graphics graphic)
  {
    graphic.drawRect(50, 50, 539, 379);
    graphic.drawRect(100, 100, 439, 279);
    graphic.drawRect(150, 150, 339, 179);
    graphic.drawRect(200, 200, 239, 79);
  }

  // Implements Runnable Interface
  public void run()
  {
  }

  // For running standalone
  public static void main(String[] argv)
  {
    // Create the frame and launch Rect
    Frame f = new Frame("RectFrame");
    f.reshape(0, 0, 639, 479);
    f.show();

    Rect x = new Rect();
    f.add("Center", x);
    x.init();
    x.start();
  }

  // Constructor
  public  Rect()
  {
  }

} // end class Rect
```

Figure 8.9 shows the four rectangular shapes drawn to the screen.

## drawRoundRect(int x, int y, int width, int height, int arcWidth, int arcHeight)

This member function is used to draw the outline of a rectangle with rounded corners. Here *x* represents the x screen coordinate and *y* the y screen coordinate for the starting point. *width*

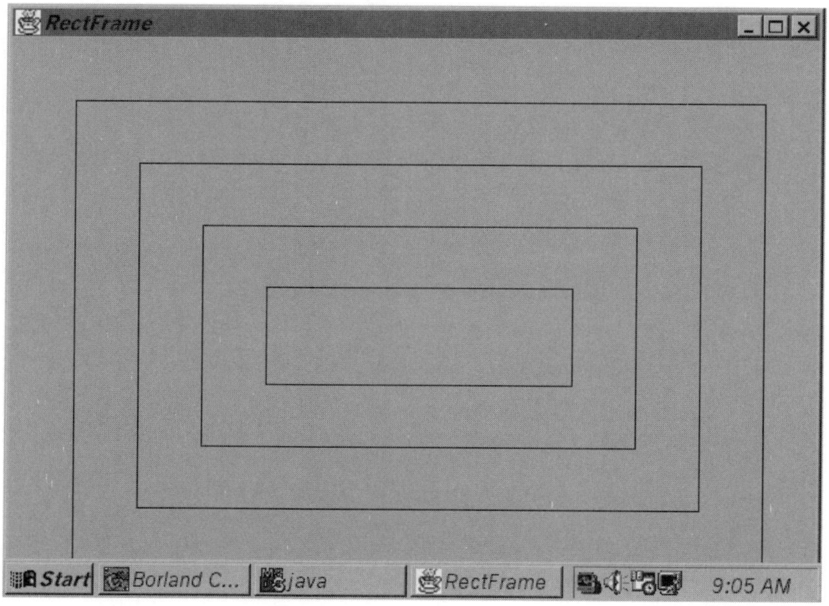


**Figure 8.9:** The drawRect() member function is used to draw these four rectangles to the screen.

represents the width and *height* the height of the rectangular shape. Rounding is specified with the *arcWidth* and *arcHeight* values. The current drawing color is used.

The following listing illustrates the use of the **drawRoundRect()** member function. In this example four rectangles, with various degrees of rounding, are drawn to the screen.

```
//-----------------------------------------------------------
// RectRnd Illustrate drawRoundRect()
// Copyright 1996, All rights reserved
// Nineveh National Research
// Version: 1.0
// Author: Pappas and Murray
// Created: 3/16/96
//-----------------------------------------------------------

import java.applet.Applet;
import java.awt.*;

public class RectRnd extends Applet implements Runnable
{
```

```
  // This routine handles the painting
  public void paint(Graphics graphic)
  {
    graphic.drawRoundRect(50, 50, 539, 379, 0, 0);
    graphic.drawRoundRect(100, 100, 439, 279, 30, 30);
    graphic.drawRoundRect(150, 150, 339, 179, 30, 90);
    graphic.drawRoundRect(200, 200, 239, 79, 90, 30);
  }

  // Implements Runnable Interface
  public void run()
  {
  }

  // For running standalone
  public static void main(String[] argv)
  {
    // Create the frame and launch RectRnd
    Frame f = new Frame("RectRndFrame");
    f.reshape(0, 0, 639, 479);
    f.show();

    RectRnd x = new RectRnd();
    f.add("Center", x);
    x.init();
    x.start();
  }

  // Constructor
  public  RectRnd()
  {
  }

} // end class RectRnd
```

Figure 8.10 shows four rounded rectangles. The largest rectangle has no rounding. The second largest rectangle uses values to symmetrically round the corners. The two smallest rectangles vary the amount of vertical and horizontal rounding.

## fill3DRect(int x, int y, int width, int height, boolean raised)

This member function is used to draw and fill a highlighted three-dimensional rectangle. Here *x* represents the x screen coordinate and *y* the y screen coordinate for the starting point.

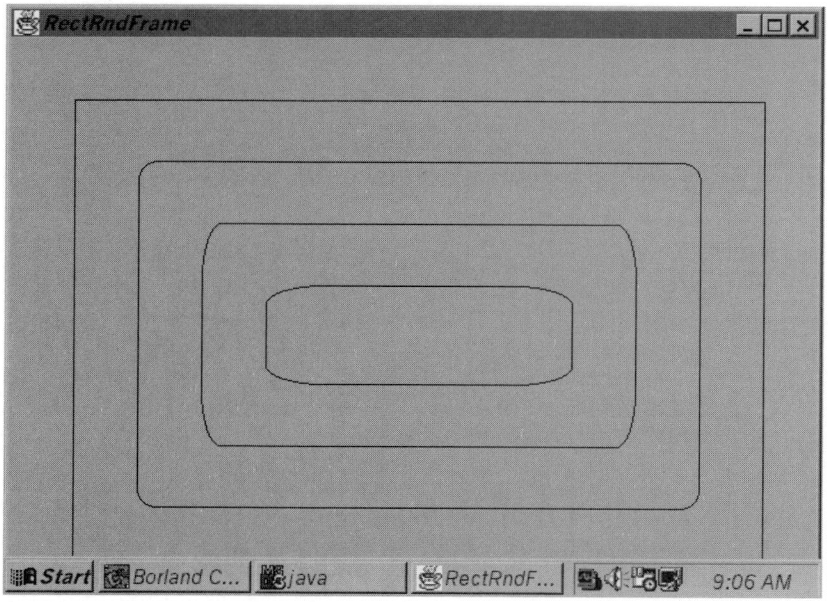


**Figure 8.10:** The drawRoundRect() function rounds the corners of a rectangular shape.

*width* represents the width and *height* the height of the rectangular shape. *raised* is a boolean that specifies whether the three-dimensional rectangle is raised or not raised. The current drawing color is used to draw and fill this shape.

The following listing illustrates the use of the **fill3DRect()** member function. The total 3D effect is dependent on the size of the rectangle and the drawing and fill color selected.

```
//-------------------------------------------------------
// Rect3DFill Illustrate fill3DRect()
// Copyright 1996, All rights reserved
// Nineveh National Research
// Version: 1.0
// Author: Pappas and Murray
// Created: 3/16/96
//-------------------------------------------------------

import java.applet.Applet;
import java.awt.*;

public class Rect3DFill extends Applet implements Runnable
```

```
{
  // This routine handles the painting
  public void paint(Graphics graphic)
  {
    graphic.setColor(Color.cyan);
    graphic.fill3DRect(50,50,219,139,false);
    graphic.fill3DRect(369,289,219,139,true);
  }

  // Implements Runnable Interface
  public void run()
  {
  }

  // For running standalone
  public static void main(String[] argv)
  {
    // Create the frame and launch Rect3DFill
    Frame f = new Frame("Rect3DFillFrame");
    f.reshape(0, 0, 639, 479);
    f.show();

    Rect3DFill x = new Rect3DFill();
    f.add("Center", x);
    x.init();
    x.start();
  }

  // Constructor
  public  Rect3DFill()
  {
  }

} // end class Rect3DFill
```

Figure 8.11 shows the results of two calls to the **fill3DRect()** member function. One call is made with the boolean value set to **true** and the other with this value set to **false**.

## fillArc(int x, int y, int width, int height, int startAngle, int arcAngle)

This member function is used to draw and fill an arc. Drawing starts at *startAngle* and proceeds a total angular distance given by *arcAngle*. Angles start on the positive x-axis. Positive angles are measured counterclockwise. Here *x* represents the x screen

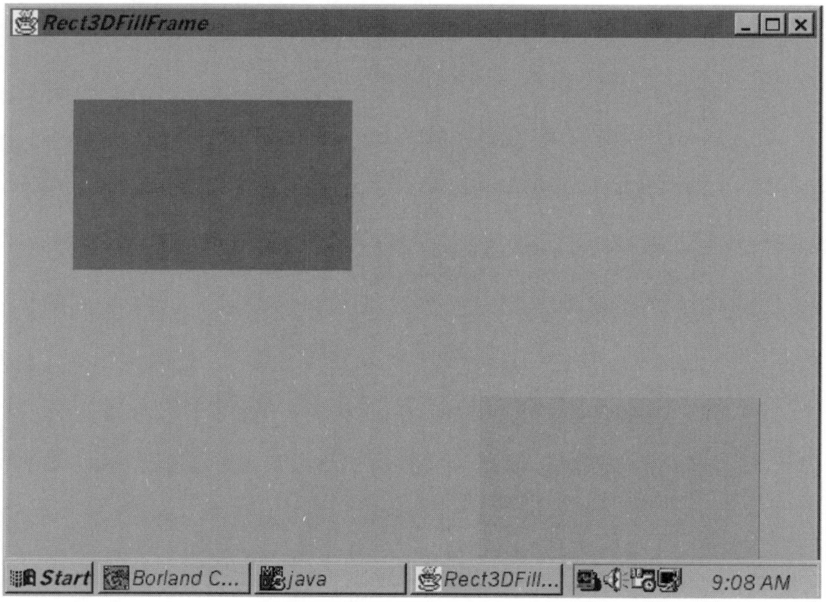


**Figure 8.11:** A filled three-dimensional image results from the fill3DRect() member function.

coordinate and *y* the y screen coordinate for the starting point. *width* represents the width and *height* the height of the bounding rectangle. *startAngle* marks the start of arc and *arcAngle* the total angular distance of the arc. The figure is closed between the starting point and ending point. Angles are measured in degrees. The current drawing color is used to draw and fill the arc segment.

***Note:*** *Windows programmers will see that angular measurements are specified in degrees. This is an improvement over the convoluted method used for similar Windows API functions.*

The following listing illustrates the **fillArc()** member function by drawing and closing four arc segments on the screen.

```
//----------------------------------------------------------
// ArcFill Illustrate fillArc()
// Copyright 1996, All rights reserved
// Nineveh National Research
// Version: 1.0
// Author: Pappas and Murray
```

```
// Created: 3/16/96
//-------------------------------------------------------------

import java.applet.Applet;
import java.awt.*;

public class ArcFill extends Applet implements Runnable
{
  // This routine handles the painting
  public void paint(Graphics graphic)
  {
    graphic.fillArc(119, 120, 50, 50, 0, 90);
    graphic.fillArc(439, 120, 50, 50, 90, 180);
    graphic.fillArc(119, 339, 50, 100, 180, 270);
    graphic.fillArc(439, 339, 100, 50, 45, 135);
  }

  // Implements Runnable Interface
  public void run()
  {
  }

  // For running standalone
  public static void main(String[] argv)
  {
    // Create the frame and launch ArcFill
    Frame f = new Frame("ArcFillFrame");
    f.reshape(0, 0, 639, 479);
    f.show();

    ArcFill x = new ArcFill();
    f.add("Center", x);
    x.init();
    x.start();
  }

  // Constructor
  public  ArcFill()
  {
  }

} // end class ArcFill
```

Figure 8.12 shows four separate filled arc segments. The **fillArc()** member function closes each arc segment before filling it with the current draw and fill color.

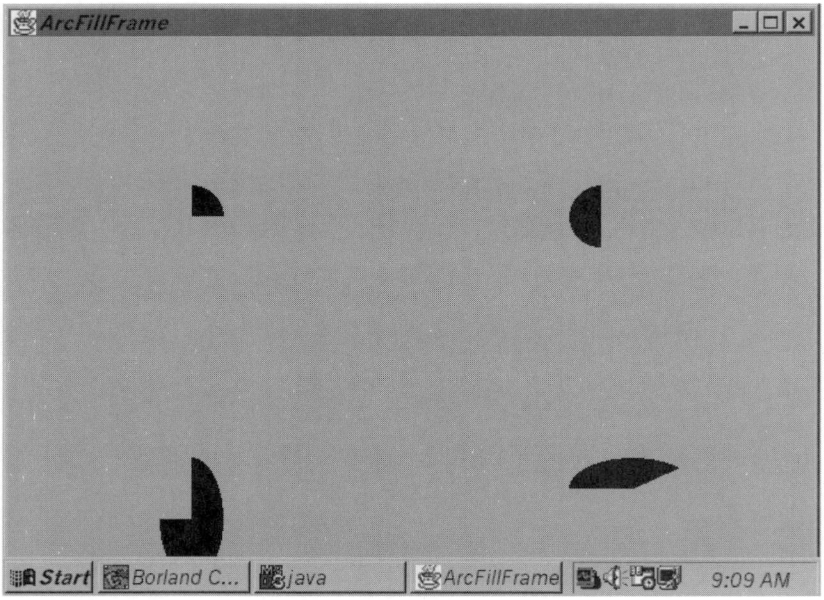


**Figure 8.12:** The fillArc() member function can draw and fill arc segments with the current draw and fill color.

## fillOval(int x, int y, int width, int height)

This member function is used to draw and fill an oval shape bounded by the specified rectangle. Here *x* represents the x screen coordinate and *y* the y screen coordinate for the starting point. *width* represents the width and *height* the height of the oval shape. The current drawing color is used to draw and fill this shape.

***Note:*** *The Java* ***fillOval()*** *member function is most closely associated with the Windows* ***Ellipse()*** *API function.*

The following listing illustrates the use of the **fillOval()** member function to draw four filled oval shapes to the window.

```
//--------------------------------------------------------
// OvalFill Illustrate fillOval()
// Copyright 1996, All rights reserved
// Nineveh National Research
// Version: 1.0
// Author: Pappas and Murray
```

```
// Created: 3/16/96
//--------------------------------------------------------

import java.applet.Applet;
import java.awt.*;

public class OvalFill extends Applet implements Runnable
{
  // This routine handles the painting
  public void paint(Graphics graphic)
  {
    graphic.fillOval(50, 50, 539, 379);
    graphic.setColor(Color.yellow);
    graphic.fillOval(100, 100, 439, 279);
    graphic.setColor(Color.red);
    graphic.fillOval(150, 150, 339, 179);
    graphic.setColor(Color.cyan);
    graphic.fillOval(200, 200, 239, 79);
  }

  // Implements Runnable Interface
  public void run()
  {
  }

  // For running standalone
  public static void main(String[] argv)
  {
    // Create the frame and launch OvalFill
    Frame f = new Frame("OvalFillFrame");
    f.reshape(0, 0, 639, 479);
    f.show();

    OvalFill x = new OvalFill();
    f.add("Center", x);
    x.init();
    x.start();
  }

  // Constructor
  public  OvalFill()
  {
  }

} // end class OvalFill
```

Figure 8.13 shows four separate ovals drawn to the window. The **setColor()** member function, which you'll learn more

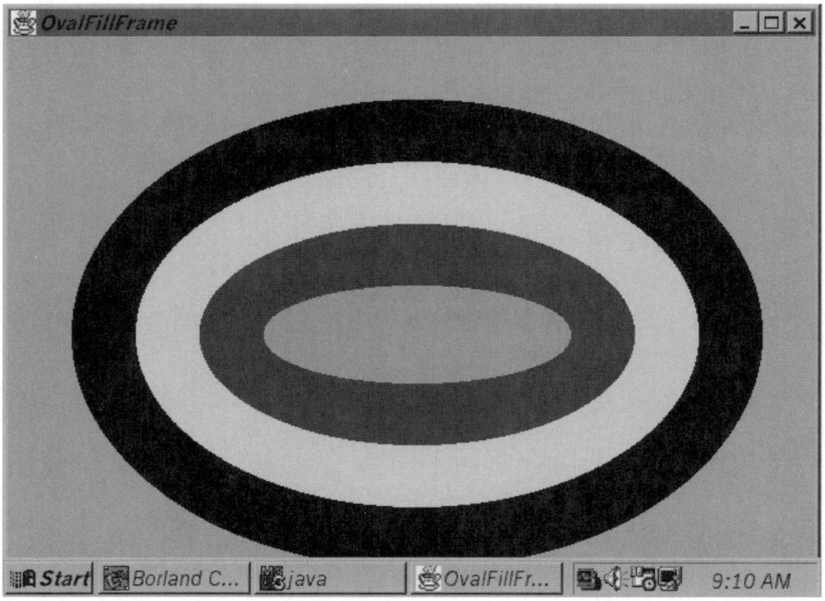


**Figure 8.13:** The fillOval() member function can be used to draw and fill ellipses and circles.

about in the next chapter, changes the draw and fill color before the oval is drawn.

## fillPolygon(int xPoints[], int yPoints[], int nPoints) fillPolygon(Polygon p)

This member function is used to draw and fill a polygon. The starting and ending points for the polygon's line segments can be described in two arrays. *xPoints[]* holds the x coordinate points and *yPoints[]* the y coordinate points. *nPoints* is the total number of points.

An alternative method is to specify the polygon as an instance of the Polygon class. This is useful if additional points may be added after the polygon is drawn.

Filled polygon shapes are automatically closed by Java and filled with the current drawing color.

The following listing illustrates the use of both variations of the **fillPolygon()** member function.

```
//--------------------------------------------------------
// PolyFill Illustrate fillPolygon()
// Copyright 1996, All rights reserved
// Nineveh National Research
// Version: 1.0
// Author: Pappas and Murray
// Created: 3/16/96
//--------------------------------------------------------

import java.applet.Applet;
import java.awt.*;

public class PolyFill extends Applet implements Runnable
{
  // This routine handles the painting
  public void paint(Graphics graphic)
  {
    // technique A (outer polygon)
    int Axpts[] = {319, 400, 600, 200, 25};
    int Aypts[] = {10, 30, 400, 290, 100};
    int Anumpts = Aypts.length;
    graphic.fillPolygon(Axpts, Aypts, Anumpts);

    // technique B (inner polygon)
    graphic.setColor(Color.yellow);
    int Bxpts[] = {300, 400, 500, 300, 125};
    int Bypts[] = {100, 70, 350, 200, 150};
    int Bnumpts = Bypts.length;
    Polygon mypoly = new Polygon(Bxpts, Bypts, Bnumpts);
    mypoly.addPoint(150, 175);  // add new points
    mypoly.addPoint(175, 150);
    graphic.fillPolygon(mypoly);
  }

  // Implements Runnable Interface
  public void run()
  {
  }

  // For running standalone
  public static void main(String[] argv)
  {
    // Create the frame and launch PolyFill
    Frame f = new Frame("PolyFillFrame");
    f.reshape(0, 0, 639, 479);
    f.show();

    PolyFill x = new PolyFill();
```

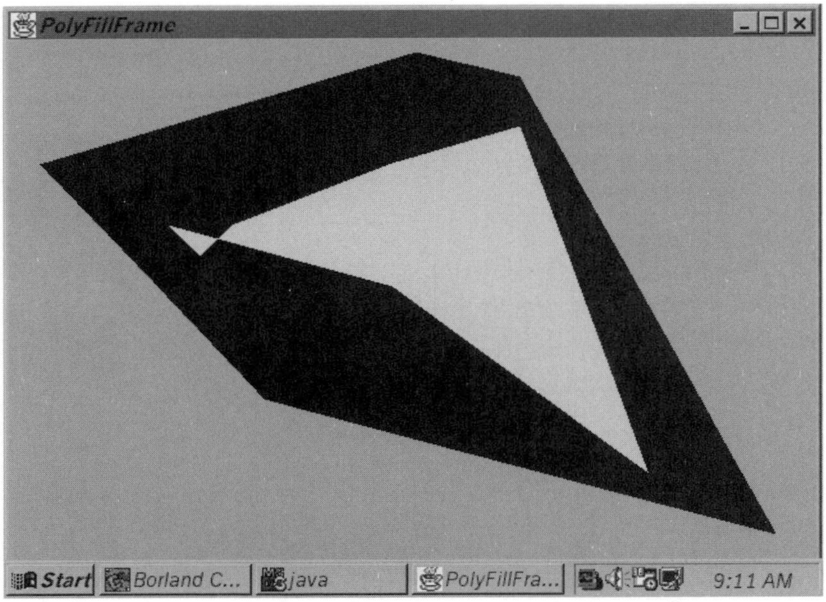


**Figure 8.14:** The fillPolygon() member function can produce dramatic graphics results.

```
      f.add("Center", x);
      x.init();
      x.start();
   }

   // Constructor
   public  PolyFill()
   {
   }

} // end class PolyFill
```

Figure 8.14 illustrates the use of both versions of the **fillPolygon()** member function. Notice in the figure that two separate shapes are drawn to the screen, one inside the other. Also notice the both figures have been closed by the **fillPolygon()** member function.

## fillRect(int x, int y, int width, int height)

This member function is used to draw and fill a rectangular shape. Here *x* represents the x screen coordinate and *y* the y screen coordinate for the starting point. *width* represents the width and *height* the height of the rectangular shape. The current drawing color is used to draw and fill this shape.

The following listing illustrates the use of the **fillRect()** member function to draw four filled rectangular shapes to the window.

```
//-------------------------------------------------------------
// RectFill Illustrate fillRect()
// Copyright 1996, All rights reserved
// Nineveh National Research
// Version: 1.0
// Author: Pappas and Murray
// Created: 3/16/96
//-------------------------------------------------------------

import java.applet.Applet;
import java.awt.*;

public class RectFill extends Applet implements Runnable
{
  // This routine handles the painting
  public void paint(Graphics graphic)
  {
    graphic.fillRect(50, 50, 539, 379);
    graphic.set
    graphic.fillRect(100, 100, 439, 279);
    graphic.setColor(Color.red);
    graphic.fillRect(150, 150, 339, 179);
    graphic.setColor(Color.cyan);
    graphic.fillRect(200, 200, 239, 79);
  }

  // Implements Runnable Interface
  public void run()
  {
  }

  // For running standalone
  public static void main(String[] argv)
  {
    // Create the frame and launch RectFill
    Frame f = new Frame("RectFillFrame");
    f.reshape(0, 0, 639, 479);
    f.show();

    RectFill x = new RectFill();
```

```
    f.add("Center", x);
    x.init();
    x.start();
  }

  // Constructor
  public  RectFill()
  {
  }

} // end class RectFill
```

Figure 8.15 shows four separate rectangles drawn to the window. The **setColor()** member function is again used to change the draw and fill color before each rectangle is drawn.

## fillRoundRect(int x, int y, int width, int height, int arcWidth, int arcHeight)

This member function is used to draw and fill a rectangle with rounded corners. Here *x* represents the x screen coordinate and

**Figure 8.15:** The fillRect() member function is used to draw four rectangles in the window.

*y* the y screen coordinate for the starting point. *width* represents the width and *height* the height of the rectangular shape. Rounding is specified with the *arcWidth* and *arcHeight* values. The current drawing color is used to draw and fill this shape.

The following listing illustrates the use of the **fillRoundRect()** member function to draw four filled rounded rectangular shapes to the window.

```
//--------------------------------------------------------
// RndRectFill Illustrate fillRoundRect()
// Copyright 1996, All rights reserved
// Nineveh National Research
// Version: 1.0
// Author: Pappas and Murray
// Created: 3/16/96
//--------------------------------------------------------

import java.applet.Applet;
import java.awt.*;

public class RndRectFill extends Applet implements Runnable
{
  // This routine handles the painting
  public void paint(Graphics graphic)
  {
    graphic.fillRoundRect(50, 50, 539, 379, 0, 0);
    graphic.setColor(Color.yellow);
    graphic.fillRoundRect(100, 100, 439, 279, 60, 60);
    graphic.setColor(Color.red);
    graphic.fillRoundRect(150, 150, 339, 179, 60, 100);
    graphic.setColor(Color.cyan);
    graphic.fillRoundRect(200, 200, 239, 79, 100, 60);
  }

  // Implements Runnable Interface
  public void run()
  {
  }

  // For running standalone
  public static void main(String[] argv)
  {
    // Create the frame and launch RndRectFill
    Frame f = new Frame("RndRectFillFrame");
    f.reshape(0, 0, 639, 479);
    f.show();
```

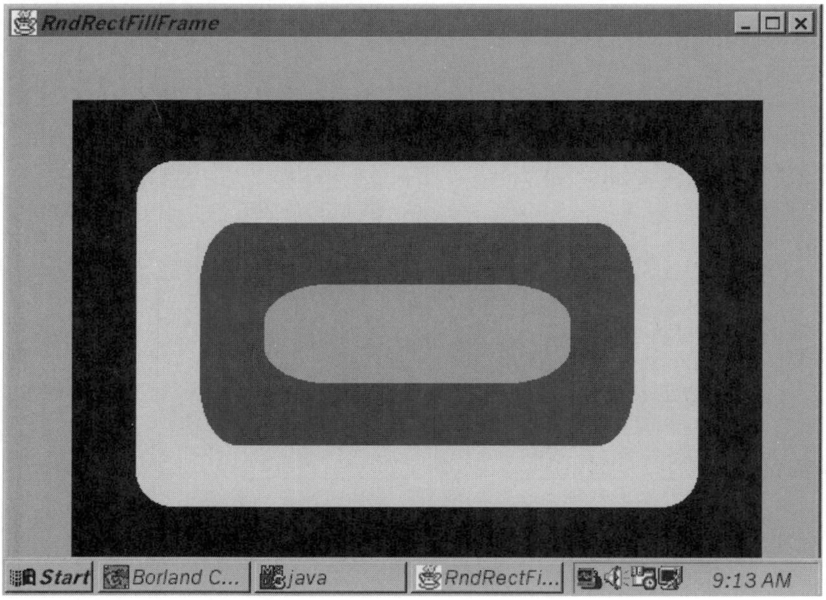


**Figure 8.16:** The fillRoundRect() member function is used to draw four rounded rectangular shapes to the window.

```
        RndRectFill x = new RndRectFill();
        f.add("Center", x);
        x.init();
        x.start();
    }

    // Constructor
    public  RndRectFill()
    {
    }

} // end class RndRectFill
```

Figure 8.16 shows four filled rounded rectangles. The largest rectangle has no rounding. The second largest rectangle uses values to symmetrically round the corners. The two smallest rectangles vary the amount of vertical and horizontal rounding.

## getClipRect()

This member function is used to obtain the bounding rectangle of the current clipping area.

## setPaintMode()

This member function is used to set the paint mode to overwrite the destination with the current color.

## setXORMode(Color c1)

This member function is used to sets the paint mode to alternate between the current color and a new color. The new color is given as *c1*. Pixels using the current color are changed to the new color. Pixels that are the current color are changed to the current color. Other colors are translated in an unpredictable manner.

## Translate(int x, int y)

This member function is used to set the origin of the graphics context. Here *x* represents the new x coordinate and *y* the new y coordinate. Once changed, only subsequent graphics are drawn with respect to this new origin.

The following listing illustrates how the origin can be translated to a new screen position with a call to the **translate()** member function.

```
//-------------------------------------------------------
// Trans Illustrate translate()
// Copyright 1996, All rights reserved
// Nineveh National Research
// Version: 1.0
// Author: Pappas and Murray
// Created: 3/16/96
//-------------------------------------------------------

import java.applet.Applet;
import java.awt.*;

public class Trans extends Applet implements Runnable
{
  // This routine handles the painting
  public void paint(Graphics graphic)
  {
    graphic.drawOval(50,50,100,250);
    graphic.translate(369,0);
    graphic.drawOval(50,50,100,250);
  }
```

```
    // Implements Runnable Interface
    public void run()
    {
    }

    // For running standalone
    public static void main(String[] argv)
    {
      // Create the frame and launch Trans
      Frame f = new Frame("TransFrame");
      f.reshape(0, 0, 639, 479);
      f.show();

      Trans x = new Trans();
      f.add("Center", x);
      x.init();
      x.start();
    }

    // Constructor
    public  Trans()
    {
    }

} // end class Trans
```

Figure 8.17 shows two oval shapes.

If you examine the listing, however, both member function calls use the same parameters. Normally, this would mean that one shape would be drawn on top of the other shape. However, between those two function calls was a call to the **translate()** member function, translating the origin to a new position in the window.

***Note:*** *The Java **translate()** member function is most closely associated with the Windows **SetViewportOrgEx()** API function.*

## Java Lingo

*boolean*—A boolean value can either be **true** or **false**. In this chapter, several member functions use boolean values to indicate whether a 3D images is raised or not.

*drawing primitives*—Drawing primitives are the fundamental drawing shapes, such as lines, rectangles, ovals,

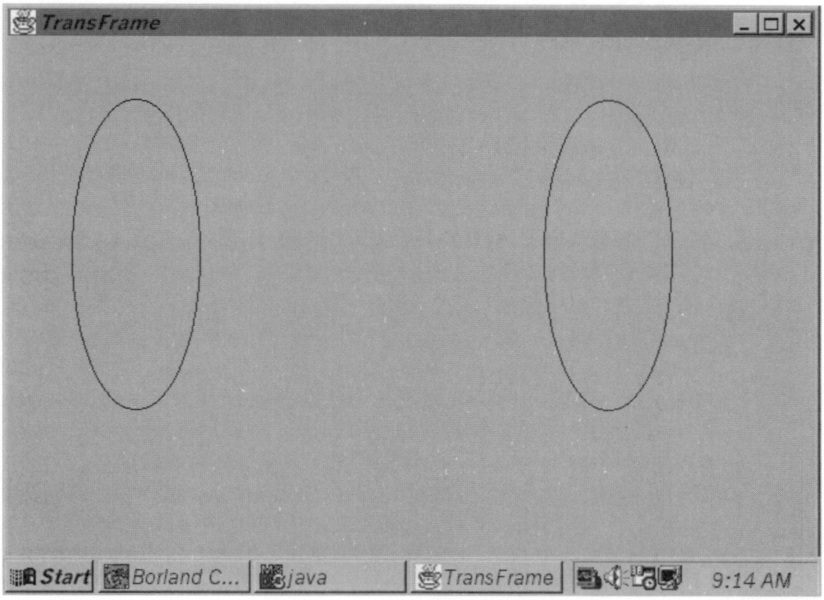


**Figure 8.17:** The translate() member function is used to move the origin on the current drawing surface.

and so on, used to create simple and complicated graphics images.

*origin*—The origin is the starting place (0,0) for the graphics coordinate system. With Java, the origin is, by default, in the upper left corner of the window. The origin can be moved with the **translate()** member function.

# 9

# Color Fundamentals

In Chapter 8 you learned how to use the various graphics drawing primitives described in the Java Graphics base class. In this chapter, you will continue to experiment with those drawing primitives as we investigate the features of the Java Color base class. This class encapsulates RGB colors in a manner very similar to the techniques used in C/C++ Windows applications. Java provides a stock palette of thirteen colors, but also allows programmers to specify any unique combination of red, green, and blue that they desire.

In this chapter we'll also take our first steps toward developing more robust applications by creating simple applications involving graphics and colors. These simple applications, along with those of Chapter 10, will form the basis for the presentation graphics applications discussed and developed in Chapter 15.

## THE STOCK PALETTE

One popular technique for specifying colors allows red, green, and blue colors (RGB) to be specified as integer values ranging from 0 to 255. Black is specified as (0, 0, 0) while white is specified as (255, 255, 255). Java provides a stock palette of thirteen colors specified in this manner.

***Note:*** *C/C++ Windows programmers are familiar with this RGB method, since it is one of the popular ways pen and brush colors can be set.*

Java draws text and lines and does fills with the current brush. To change the current brush to a different color (remember that black is the default color) you can use the **setColor()** member function. For example, if you wanted to draw a fill oval shape in blue, you would use code similar to the following:

```
graphic.setColor(Color.blue);
graphic.fillOval(10, 10, 200, 200);
```

If you want to change the drawing or fill color, simply call the **setColor()** member function once again.

**Table 9.1:** Java's Stock Palette of Colors

| *Color* | *Name* | *RGB Mixture* |
|---|---|---|
| black | Color.black | (0, 0, 0) |
| blue | Color.blue | (0, 0, 255) |
| cyan | Color.cyan | (0, 55, 255) |
| dark gray | Color.darkGray | (64, 64, 64) |
| gray | Color.gray | (128, 128, 128) |
| green | Color.green | (0, 255, 0) |
| light gray | Color.lightGray | (192, 192, 192) |
| magenta | Color.magenta | (255, 0, 255) |
| orange | Color.orange | (255, 200, 0) |
| pink | Color.pink | (255, 175, 175) |
| red | Color.red | (255, 0, 0) |
| white | Color.white | (255, 255, 255) |
| yellow | Color.yellow | (255, 255, 0) |

## A Custom Palette

If one of the stock colors does not suit your needs, there are over 16 million color combinations available with this method of specifying color values.

$$256 \times 256 \times 256 = 16{,}777{,}216 \text{ possible combinations}$$

The only restriction to creating a large custom palette is, of course, your color adapter and monitor. If you hardware can't match your software specifications, Windows will match the best color it is capable of producing to your specifications. This often results in a dithering effect.

To specify a custom color, a new color object needs to be created. The following portion of code illustrates how you might create a vivid light blue brush.

```
Color lightBlue = new Color(85, 170, 255);
graphic.setColor(lightBlue);
graphic.fillOval(10, 10, 200, 200);
```

Java's Color class is overloaded. In addition to passing color values as integers ranging from 0 to 255, it is possible to pass float values ranging from 0.0 to 1.0. In this manner, the previously created light blue brush could have been specified as:

```
Color lightBlue = new Color(0.333, 0.666, 1.0);
```

The float values are converted internally by the class to integer values by simply multiplying the float value by 255. Thus,

$$0.333 \times 255 = 85$$

$$0.666 \times 255 = 170$$

$$1.0 \times 255 = 255$$

The resulting values match the original values used to create the light blue color.

## Member Functions That Manipulate Colors

There are a number of member functions (methods) described in the Color class and additional Java classes for manipulating colors. In this section we'll look at those that are used most frequently. Several short pieces of programming code will enhance your understanding of those member functions' use in this chapter.

## brighter() and darker()

These member functions can be used to quickly increase or decrease the brightness of a specified color. The brightness increases or decreases by a factor of 0.7 when the member function is called. Here is a complete Java application that illustrates the use of both member functions.

```
//--------------------------------------------------------
// BrDk illustrate brighter() and darker()
// Copyright 1996, All rights reserved
// Nineveh National Research
// Version: 1.0
// Author: Pappas and Murray
// Created: 3/22/96
//--------------------------------------------------------

import java.applet.Applet;
import java.awt.*;

public class BrDk extends Applet implements Runnable
{
  // This routine handles the painting
  public void paint(Graphics graphic)
  {
    Color mycolor = new Color(0, 0, 178);

    graphic.setColor(mycolor);
    graphic.fillOval(0, 0, 100, 100);

    graphic.setColor(mycolor.brighter());
    graphic.fillOval(80, 0, 100, 100);

    graphic.setColor(mycolor.darker());
    graphic.fillOval(40, 60, 100, 100);
}

 // Implements Runnable Interface
 public void run()
 {
 }
```

```
  // For running standalone
  public static void main(String[] argv)
  {
    // Create the frame and launch BrDk
    Frame f = new Frame("BrDkFrame");
    f.reshape(0, 0, 639, 479);
    f.show();

    BrDk x = new BrDk();
    f.add("Center", x);
    x.init();
    x.start();
  }

  // Constructor
  public  BrDk()
  {
  }

} // end class BrDk
```

In this example a blue color object is created and named *mycolor*. An oval shape is filled with this color. Next, the brightness of the color is increased by the use of the **brighter()** member function. Another oval shape is fill with the brighter color. Figure 9.1 illustrates these subtle changes in brightness.

Finally, the process is repeated once again with the use of the **darker()** member function.

## getBackground(), getForeground(), setBackground(), and setForeground()

These member functions can be used to get or change the background and foreground colors of an application. When the **setForeground()** member function is called, all graphics will be drawn or filled with the specified foreground color. Likewise, the **setBackground()** member function will change the background color to the specified value. These member functions are described in the Java Component class.

Here is an example that tests the **setForeground()** and **setBackground()** member functions.

```
//-------------------------------------------------------
// ForeBack  Testing setForeground() and setBackground()
```

**Figure 9.1:** The brighter() and darker() member functions can make a color brighter or darker.

```
// Copyright 1996, All rights reserved
// Nineveh National Research
// Version: 1.0
// Author: Pappas and Murray
// Created: 3/20/96
//---------------------------------------------------------

import java.applet.Applet;
import java.awt.*;

public class ForeBack extends Applet implements Runnable
{
  // This routine handles the painting
  public void paint(Graphics graphic)
  {
    graphic.drawOval(10, 10, 100, 100);
    graphic.fillOval(150, 150, 100, 100);
  }

  // Implements Runnable Interface
  public void run()
  {
  }
```

```
    // For running standalone
    public static void main(String[] argv)
    {
      // Create the frame and launch ForeBack
      Frame f = new Frame("ForeBackFrame");
      f.setForeground(Color.blue);
      f.setBackground(Color.white);
      f.reshape(0, 0, 639, 479);
      f.show();

      ForeBack x = new ForeBack();
      f.add("Center", x);
      x.init();
      x.start();
    }

    // Constructor
    public  ForeBack()
    {
    }

} // end class ForeBack
```

Figure 9.2 shows a new background color and two shapes drawn with a new foreground color.

## getColor() and setColor()

These member functions are the backbone of the Color class. The **getColor()** member function can be used to obtain the current drawing or fill color, while the **setColor()** member function is used to set the current drawing or fill color.

Here is a small portion of code that illustrates the use of the **setColor()** member function.

```
Color lightBlue = new Color(85, 170, 255);
graphic.setColor(lightBlue);
graphic.fillOval(10, 10, 200, 200);

graphic.setColor(Color.yellow);
graphic.fillRect(300,300, 200, 200);
```

In the first portion of this example, the **setColor()** member function is used to fill an oval shape with a new light blue custom color. In the final portion of the example, **setColor()** is

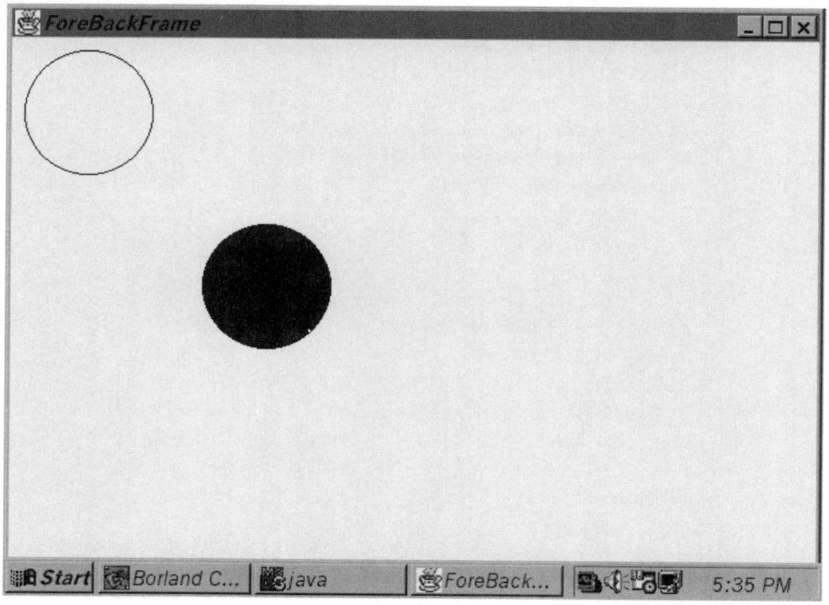


**Figure 9.2:** setForeground() and setBackground() member functions can be used to make global changes in the drawing/fill colors as well as the background color of the drawing surface.

again used to fill a rectangular shape with a stock yellow color. Figure 9.3 illustrates the results of this portion of code.

## getHSBColor()

This member function is used to generate a Color object based on HSB (hue, saturation, and brightness) values. The syntax for this function is:

```
Color getHSBColor(float h, float s, float b);
```

Here *h* represents the hue component, *s* the saturation component and *b* the brightness component. The following portion of code shows how this member function might be called.

```
graphic.setColor(Color.getHSBColor((float) 0.35, (float) 0.7,
                                   (float) 1.0));
graphic.fillRect(100, 100, 200, 200);
```

The color returned, and used to fill the rectangular shape, is a bright green. Figure 9.4 shows the results of calling the **getHSBColor()** member function.

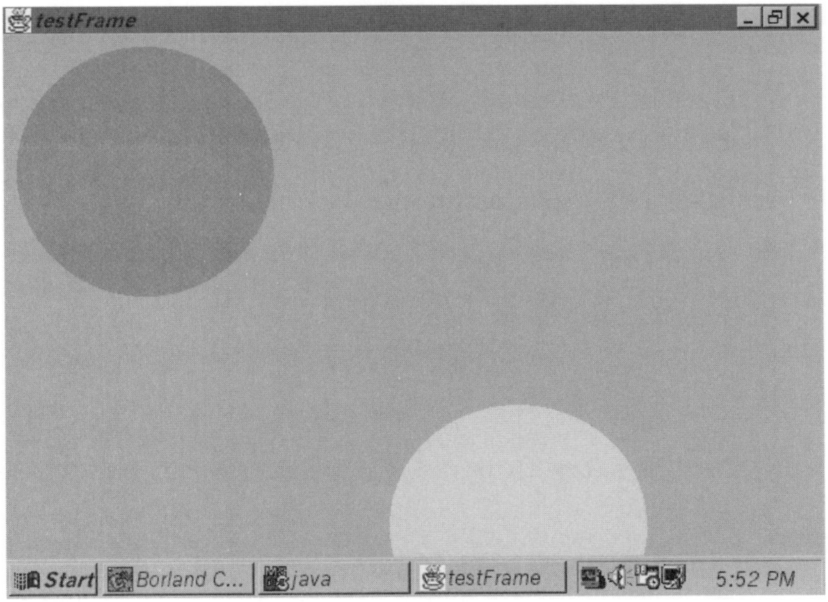


**Figure 9.3:** The setColor() member function allows the drawing and fill colors to be changed.

**Figure 9.4:** The rectangular shape is filled with a color resulting from a call to the getHSBColor() member function.

## getRed(), getGreen(), getBlue()

These member functions return information, as an integer, on specific RGB values of an identified color. In the following portion of code, a lightBlue color object is defined. The green component of the new color is returned to the *mycolor* variable with a call to the **getGreen()** member function.

```
int mycolor;
Color lightBlue = new Color(66, 127, 255);
mycolor = lightBlue.getGreen();
graphic.drawString(String.valueOf(mycolor), 10, 10);
```

In order to draw this value to the graphics area of the window, the integer value is converted to a string, then drawn with the **drawString()** member function.

## getRGB()

This member function gets the RGB value of the specified color. The returned information is represented in the following manner:

bits -> 31–24 are set to $0 \times FF$
23–16 are the red component
15–8 are the green component
7–0 are the blue component

The **getRGB()** member function returns an integer value.

## HSBtoRGB()

This member function returns an RGB value based upon the RGB color model for the HSB (hue, saturation, and brightness) values specified. The syntax for the member function is as follows:

```
int HSBtoRGB(float hue, float saturation, float brightness);
```

This member function returns an integer value. Here is a small portion of code to illustrate this member function.

```
int mycolor;
mycolor = (Color.HSBtoRGB((float) 0.7, (float) 0.35, (float) 1.0));
```

```
graphic.setColor(Color.black);
graphic.drawString(String.valueOf(mycolor), 10, 10);
```

The integer value, because it will be reported as a decimal, will be a complement. In this example the value is -4741633. If you convert to hexadecimal and use the following scheme, you will be able to extract the r,g,b values,

bits -> 31–24 are set to 0 × FF
23–16 are the red component
15–8 are the green component
7–0 are the blue component

The red component is 0 × B7 or 183 decimal. The green component is 0 × A5 or 165 decimal. The blue component is 0×FE or 254 decimal.

## RGBtoHSB()

This member function returns an HSB (hue, saturation, and brightness) value for the RGB values given. The syntax for the member functions is as follows:

```
float[] RGBtoHSB(int r, int g, int b, float[] hsbvals);
```

Here *r*, *g*, and *b* are the integer values for the red, green, and blue values, ranging from 0 to 255 each. The *hsbvals* is an array of type **float** used to return the HSB values.

## toString()

This member function is used to return the specified color's RGB values as a string of formatted values. In the following portion of code a new Color object is created. The lightBlue color information is processed by **toString()** and drawn to the window with the help of the **drawString()** member function.

```
Color lightBlue = new Color(66, 127, 255);
graphic.drawString(lightBlue.toString(), 10, 10);
```

The format for the output will be: r = 66 b = 127 g = 255.

## Building an Application

The applications presented earlier in this chapter and the Rainbow application presented in the next section can be built with the AppExpert for Java as they were in the previous two chapters. For a step-by-step approach for developing Java applications within the Borland IDE, refer to Chapter 7 for additional details.

The code for the Rainbow application, which follows, can be entered, compiled, and executed as a standalone application. If you encounter errors during the compile or run process, not related to a typing error, you have probably forgotten one of the steps detailed in Chapter 7.

## The Rainbow Application

The Rainbow application presented in this section is a straightforward graphics application that illustrates the use of Java's graphics and color capabilities. While this example was kept intentionally simple, there are design considerations that should be taken into account before coding begins. Study the code in the following listing.

```
//-------------------------------------------------------
// Rainbow Demonstrates various Color class  members
// Copyright 1996, All rights reserved
// Nineveh National Research
// Version: 1.0
// Author: Pappas and Murray
// Created: 3/20/96
//-------------------------------------------------------

import java.applet.Applet;
import java.awt.*;

public class Rainbow extends Applet implements Runnable
{
  // This routine handles the painting
  public void paint(Graphics graphic)
  {
    graphic.setColor(Color.red);
    graphic.fillArc(80, 0, 480, 479, 0, 180);
```

```
    graphic.setColor(Color.green);
    graphic.fillArc(140, 60, 360, 359, 0, 180);

    graphic.setColor(Color.blue);
    graphic.fillArc(200, 120, 240, 239, 0, 180);

    graphic.setColor(Color.yellow);
    graphic.fillArc(260, 180, 120, 119, 0, 180);
  }

  // Implements Runnable Interface
  public void run()
  {
  }

  // For running standalone
  public static void main(String[] argv)
  {
    // Create the frame and launch Rainbow
    Frame f = new Frame("RainbowFrame");
    f.reshape(0, 0, 639, 260);
    f.show();

    Rainbow x = new Rainbow();
    f.add("Center", x);
    x.init();
    x.start();
  }

  // Constructor
  public  Rainbow()
  {
  }

} // end class Rainbow
```

This application calls the **fillArc()** member function four times, each time changing the fill color with the **setColor()** member function, to create a rainbow effect on the screen. By this time, you should have a good understanding of how both of these functions work. The challenge here is how the values for the **fillArc()** function are determined. Remember that the Java coordinate system for graphics starts with the origin in the upper left corner of the window. Positive increases proceed to the right and downward.

The rainbow image was designed for a VGA screen that measures 640 × 480 pixels. The **fillArc()** function has four parameters. The first two parameters represent the coordinates of the upper left corner of an imaginary rectangle which bounds the shape. The second two parameters represent the width and height of the bounding rectangle.

To best illustrate how all coordinate values were determined, four separate figures are used. The first figure is for the largest arc. The last figure is for the smallest arc. Examine Figures 9.5, 9.6, 9.7, and 9.8 and make sure you understand how the values used for the **fillArc()** parameters were determined.

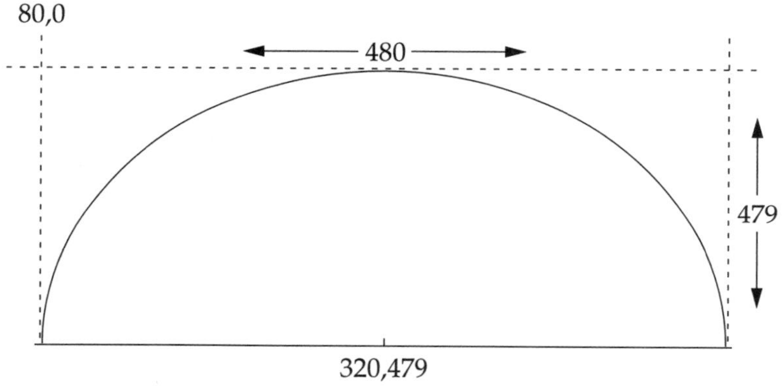


**Figure 9.5:** The red arc uses the following values.

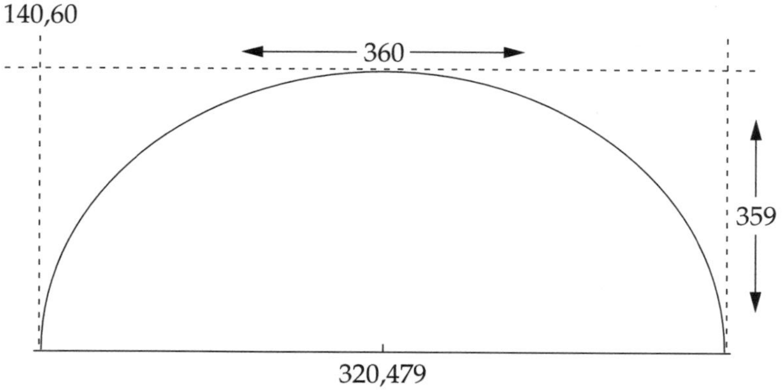


**Figure 9.6:** The green arc uses the following values.

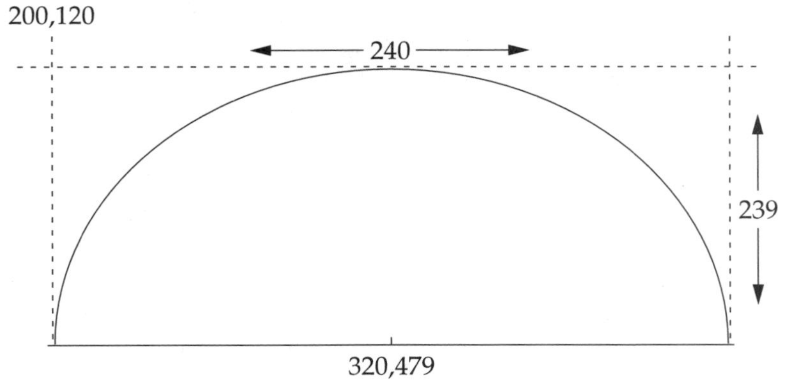


**Figure 9.7:** The blue arc uses the following values.

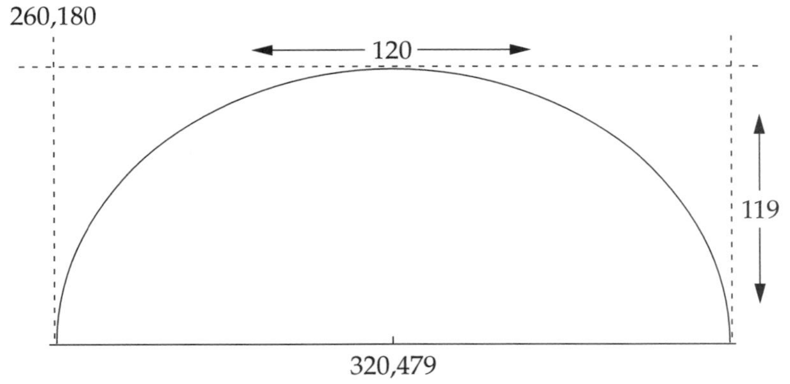


**Figure 9.8:** The yellow arc uses the following values.

If you understand how these values were determined, you are well on your way to creating more complicated graphics applications presented in future chapters. When you execute this application, the rainbow image will be similar to that shown in Figure 9.9.

## JAVA LINGO

*Custom palette*—Java allows the programmer to define a custom palette of colors by mixing color combinations. Over 16 million colors are possible.

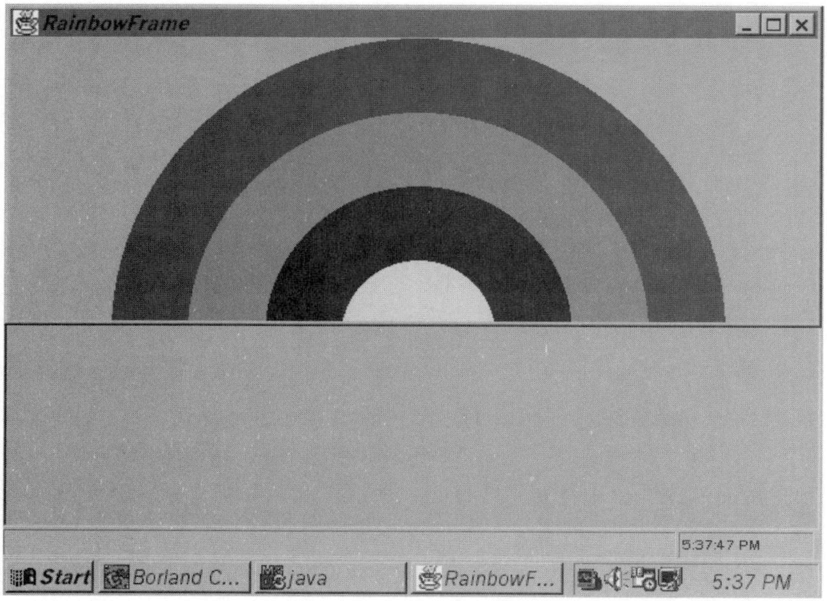


**Figure 9.9:** The Rainbow application draws the following image to a VGA screen.

*HSB*—stands for hue, saturation, and brightness color qualities. In various Java member functions, these quantities are often specified within the range 0.0 to 1.0.

*RGB*—stands for red, green, and blue color components. In various Java member functions, a green color would be specified as (0, 255, 0) or as (0.0, 1.0, 0.0).

*Stock palette*—the stock palette for Java contains thirteen predefined colors that can be used to draw and fill graphics objects.

# 10

# Working with Graphics Resources

In the last two chapters we have been experimenting with various graphics drawing primitives and color palettes. In this chapter, you'll learn how to weave many of these concepts into simple yet impressive Java applications and applets. Additional features included in this chapter are mouse and image control.

The applications are divided into several groups. The bar chart application will teach you how to take an array of integer data points and automatically draw and scale a bar chart. Each bar will be filled with a different color. The pie chart application will show you how to draw and scale a bar chart with similar data. Here you'll learn how to produce a closed pie chart regardless of the pie chart data. You'll learn how to develop a more refined bar and pie chart application in Chapter 15. The sketching application is simple but unique. You'll learn a very simple technique for drawing in the window with your mouse. Push a mouse button, to draw, release the mouse button, and move to a new spot on the canvas. To complete this chapter, two image-manipulating applets are developed. With the first applet, you'll see just how easy it is to incorporate a graphics image with a .jpg or .gif file format. In the second applet, you'll learn how to scale the image to the window. Image manipulations will form the basis of our animation examples in Chapter 16.

## A Simple Bar Chart

The bar chart application is a straightforward adaptation of the charting concepts presented in the previous two chapters. Examine the following listing and identify the various graphics primitives that you've already used.

```
//----------------------------------------------------------
// BarChart A Simple Bar Chart Application
// Copyright 1996, All rights reserved
// Nineveh National Research
// Version: 1.0
// Author: Pappas and Murray
// Created: 3/23/96
//----------------------------------------------------------

import java.applet.Applet;
import java.awt.*;

public class BarChart extends Applet implements Runnable
{
  // This routine handles the painting
  public void paint(Graphics graphic)
  {
    int height[] = {300, 50, 225, 180, 75};
    int numBars = 5;                    // number of bars
                                        // (1 to 11 max)

   int newstart = 2;               // start position
    int width = 400 / numBars;          // width of a bar
    Color barColor[] = {Color.red,      // bar colors
                        Color.blue,
                        Color.yellow,
                        Color.green,
                        Color.cyan,
                        Color.magenta,
                        Color.orange,
                        Color.pink,
                        Color.gray,
```

```
                         Color.darkGray,
                         Color.black};

    // draw coordinate axes
    graphic.translate(99, 379);        // move origin
    graphic.drawLine(0, -329, 0, 0);   // vert. axis
    graphic.drawLine(0, 0, 429, 0);    // horz. axis

    // draw and fill bars
    for (int i = 0; i < numBars; i++) {
      graphic.setColor(barColor[i]);   // set fill color
      graphic.fillRect(newstart,       // draw a bar
                       -height[i],
                       width,
                       height[i] - 1);
      newstart += 2 + width;           // set new position
    }
  }

  // Implements Runnable Interface
  public void run()
  {
  }

  // For running standalone
  public static void main(String[] argv)
  {
    // Create the frame and launch BarChart
    Frame f = new Frame("BarChartFrame");
    f.reshape(0, 0, 639, 479);
    f.show();

    BarChart x = new BarChart();
    f.add("Center", x);
    x.init();
    x.start();
  }

  // Constructor
  public  BarChart()
  {
  }

} // end class BarChart
```

This application charts data in the vertical range from 0 to approximately 329. Data points are entered into the *height[]*

array. No error checking is provided. These values will directly represent the height of each individual bar chart bar. The number of bars is limited to eleven, before the bar chart colors begin to repeat themselves. As the number of bars increases, the width of each individual bar decreases. The bar chart will always be the same total width, regardless of the number of bars plotted. The width of each bar is calculated and stored in the variable *width*. Fill colors are selected sequentially from the *barColor[]* array. This array is filled with eleven Java stock palette colors. Naturally, you could extend the array's size by specifying new color combinations with the techniques learned in the previous chapter.

Three lines of code are all that are required to draw an x and y axis, as you can see from the following partial listing.

```
// draw coordinate axes
graphic.translate(99, 379);       // move origin
graphic.drawLine(0, -329, 0, 0);  // vert. axis
graphic.drawLine(0, 0, 429, 0);   // horz. axis
```

But, wait! What is **translate()** doing here? The **translate()** member function is used to change the bar chart's origin to 99,379. This will mean that the lower left-hand corner of the bar chart will now be represented as 0,0! This spacing provides a margin on the left and bottom edges of the chart.

A **for** loop will help us select color values and plot the individual bars, as you can see in the following portion of code.

```
// draw and fill bars
for (int i = 0; i < numBars; i++) {
  graphic.setColor(barColor[i]);  // set fill color
  graphic.fillRect(newstart,      // draw a bar
                   -height[i],
                   width,
                   height[i] - 1);
  newstart += 2 + width;          // set new position
}
```

As you can see, color values are selected starting with *barColor[0]* and proceeding to *barColor[numBars-1]*. The **fillRect()** member function draws the filled bar in the proper color. The values for **fillRect()** are obtained sequentially from the *height[]* array. The variable *newstart* is used to represent the starting position of each new bar. You might notice that the new start value is actually the accumulated width of all previously plotted bars + 2. This allows a small space between each bar. If you don't want the space, just remove the 2 from the equation. The negative sign is used to flip the positive data value. Remember, even though the origin was moved, the positive y direction is still down.

Well, that's all there is to it. If you enter this application, you should obtain results similar to Figure 10.1.

## A Simple Pie Chart

The bar chart, in the previous application, is a very simple chart to create. The pie chart, discussed in this section, adds a few twists to our programming. First, in the bar chart application, the height of one bar is unrelated to the height of another bar. Second, the heights in the data array could easily be mistyped, sending the plotted bar right off of the screen.

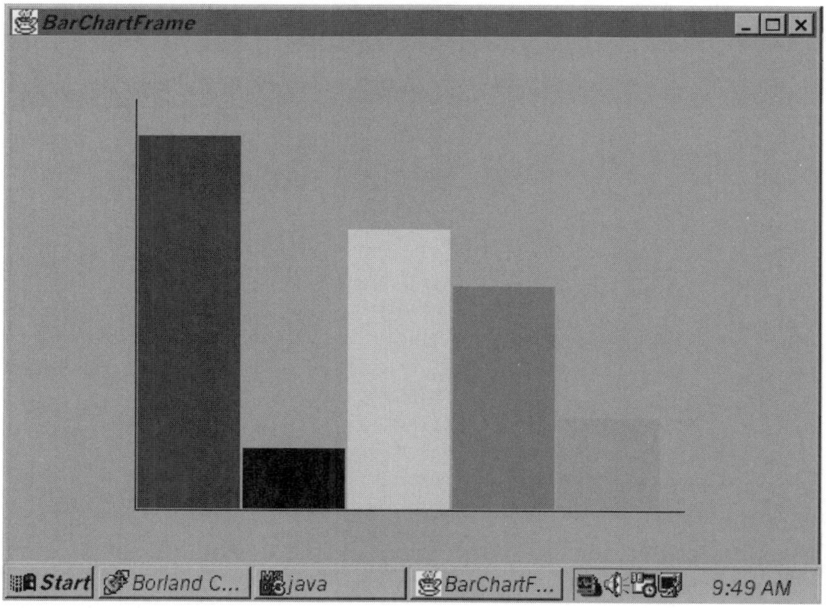


**Figure 10.1:** A simple bar chart produced by the BarChart application.

In the pie chart example, we will always draw a complete pie. Data values will be scaled so that they are proportional to each other and always produce a closed pie chart. This is easier to do than you might initially suspect.

Examine the following listing for the pie chart application and note how many lines of code are similar to those in the bar chart application.

```
//---------------------------------------------------------
// PieChart A Simple Pie Chart Application
// Copyright 1996, All rights reserved
// Nineveh National Research
// Version: 1.0
// Author: Pappas and Murray
// Created: 3/24/96
//---------------------------------------------------------

import java.applet.Applet;
import java.awt.*;

public class PieChart extends Applet implements Runnable
{
  // This routine handles the painting
  public void paint(Graphics graphic)
  {
    int wedgeSize[] = {300, 50, 225, 180, 75};
    int numWedges = 5;                // number of wedges
                                      // (1 to 11 max)
    int wedgeAngle[] = {0, 0, 0, 0, 0};
    int totalWedge = 0;
    int startAngle = 0;
    int sweepAngle = 0;
    Color sliceColor[] = {Color.red,  // pie colors
                          Color.blue,
                          Color.yellow,
                          Color.green,
                          Color.cyan,
                          Color.magenta,
                          Color.orange,
                          Color.pink,
                          Color.gray,
                          Color.darkGray,
                          Color.black};

    graphic.translate(170, 90);       // move origin

    for (int i = 0; i < numWedges; i++)
```

```
        totalWedge += wedgeSize[i];

      for (int i = 0; i < numWedges; i++)
        wedgeAngle[i] = (wedgeSize[i] * 363) / totalWedge;

      sweepAngle = wedgeAngle[0];

      // draw and fill pie slices
      for (int i = 0; i < numWedges; ++i) {
        graphic.setColor(sliceColor[i]); // set fill color
        graphic.fillArc(0, 0, 300, 300,
                        startAngle, sweepAngle);
        startAngle += wedgeAngle[i];
        sweepAngle = wedgeAngle[i+1];
      }
    }

    // Implements Runnable Interface
    public void run()
    {
    }

    // For running standalone
    public static void main(String[] argv)
    {
      // Create the frame and launch PieChart
      Frame f = new Frame("PieChartFrame");
      f.reshape(0, 0, 639, 479);
      f.show();

      PieChart x = new PieChart();
      f.add("Center", x);
      x.init();
      x.start();
    }

    // Constructor
    public  PieChart()
    {
    }

  } // end class PieChart
```

The data array, *wedgeSize[]*, contains the identical data used in the bar chart. While we're at it, notice that the array of colors for the pie slices is similar to the bar chart's array. Here, *slice-Color[]* contains the same eleven colors from Java's stock palette. The *wedgeAngle[]* array will be used to hold angle values for each pie slice's angular sweep.

The game plan is simple: Add up all individual data values in *wedgeSize[]*, obtain a total, and save it in a variable named *totalWedge*. To calculate individual *wedgeAngle[]* values, divide each *wedgeSize[]* value by *totalWedge* and multiply by 363 degrees. (Yes, we know there are 360 degrees in a complete circle. We cheated a little and we'll tell you why shortly.) These individual values being stored in *wedgeSize[]* represent the original data values scaled to make them fit into a complete circle (pie).

The origin is moved to 170,90 in order to approximately center our pie chart on a VGA screen. The charting begins with the use of a **for** loop, once again.

```
// draw and fill pie slices
for (int i = 0; i < numWedges; ++i) {
  graphic.setColor(sliceColor[i]); // set fill color
  graphic.fillArc(0, 0, 300, 300,
                  startAngle, sweepAngle);
  startAngle += wedgeAngle[i];
  sweepAngle = wedgeAngle[i+1];
}
```

You'll recall from Chapter 8 that the first two parameters in the **fillArc()** member function represent the coordinates for the center point of the arc. The values used here are 0,0 because the origin was moved. The next two parameters represent the width and height of the bounding rectangle for this member function. The values are identical in order to produce a round pie chart. The final two parameters are used to specify the start angle for the arc and how many degrees are actually transversed. Remember, unlike Windows GDI graphics functions, these values are expressed in degrees.

The variable, *startAngle*, is initialized to 0. Plotting takes place in the counterclockwise direction. The extent of the sweep, *sweepAngle*, is obtained for the first slice from the first value stored in the *wedgeAngle[]* array. Then notice what happened; *startAngle* is increased by the value first *wedgeAngle[]* value, which represents the finishing position for the first pie slice.

The process repeats itself until all slices have been drawn. The last slice touches the first slice, closing the pie shape. Well, not exactly. Here is the problem and the answer to why we used 363 instead of 360 degrees. There is a problem with round-off error in making calculations. You see, we're saving integer values when we make that calculation, but the results are not always integer values. The results are rounded up or down. This round-off error tends to make the pie chart just miss closing if 360 is used in the equation. By using 363, we take the chance of distorting the figure just a bit, but the technique works fine for this simple example.

If you execute this application, you should see a pie chart similar to that shown in Figure 10.2.

## Adding Mouse Capabilities

In the next application, we'll use the mouse in a sketching application that will allow you to doodle on the screen. Mouse events are handled by a half-dozen methods or member functions. Before continuing, let's look at the syntax for using each of these mouse member functions.

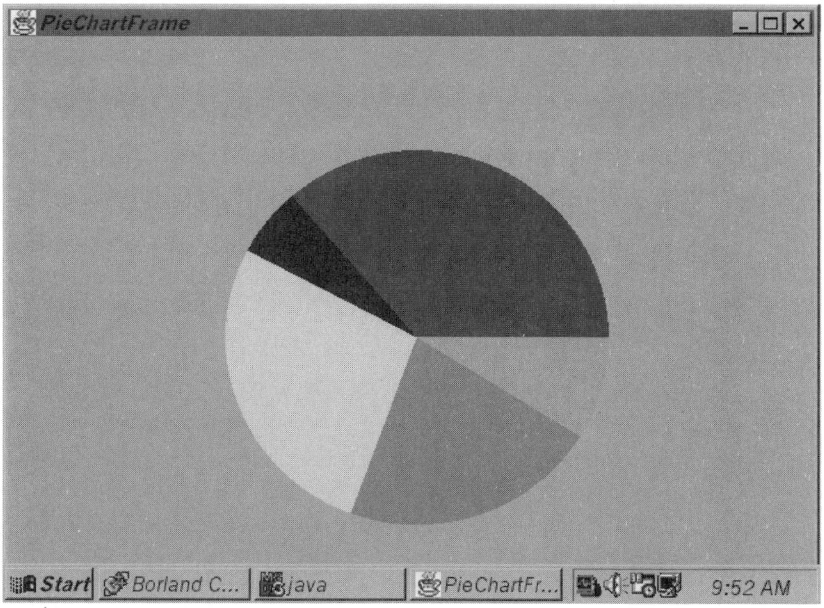


**Figure 10.2:** The pie chart drawn with the PieChart application.

## Handling Mouse Events

As you study the member functions listed below, you will notice that all six use similar arguments. The parameter *evt* is an instance of **Event.** The **Event** class provides information on an event's occurrence. This log information tells where and when the event took place. The *x* and *y* parameters provide coordinate information on the mouse's current location.

The **mouseDown()** member function signals a mouse button event when any mouse button is depressed. The syntax is:

```
mouseDown(Event evt, int x, int y);
```

The **mouseDrag()** member function signals an event when the mouse is dragged while a mouse button is depressed. The syntax is:

```
mouseDrag(Event evt, int x, int y);
```

The **mouseEnter()** member function signals an event when the mouse pointer is moved into an application or applet. The syntax is:

```
mouseEnter(Event evt, int x, int y);
```

The **mouseExit()** member function signals an event when the mouse pointer is moved outside an application or applet. The syntax is:

```
mouseExit(Event evt, int x, int y);
```

The **mouseMove()** member function signals an event when the mouse is moved. The syntax is:

```
mouseMove(Event evt, int x, int y);
```

The **mouseUp()** member function signals an event when a depressed mouse button is released. The syntax is:

```
mouseUp(Event evt, int x, int y)
```

Now, we'll look at a simple application that uses several of these member functions.

## Mouse-A-Sketch

The Mouse-A-Sketch application is a simple sketching application that allows the user to draw in the window with the mouse. The drawing color and window size are set before drawing starts. Examine the following listing and find where the **mouseDown()** and **mouseDrag()** member functions are used.

```
//-------------------------------------------------------
// Sketch Mouse-A-Sketch
// Copyright 1996, All rights reserved
// Nineveh National Research
// Version: 1.0
// Author: Pappas and Murray
// Created: 3/24/96
//-------------------------------------------------------

import java.applet.Applet;
import java.awt.*;

public class Sketch extends Applet implements Runnable
{
  Point newPoint, oldPoint;

  // Mouse button pressed handling code
  public boolean mouseDown(Event event, int x, int y)
  {
    newPoint = new Point(x, y);
    return true;
  }

  public void update(Graphics graphic)
  {
    paint(graphic);
  }

  public boolean mouseDrag(Event event, int x, int y)
  {
    oldPoint = newPoint;
    newPoint = new Point(x, y);
    repaint();
    return true;
  }

  // This routine handles the painting
  public void paint(Graphics graphic)
```

```
  {
    graphic.setColor(Color.blue);
    graphic.drawLine(oldPoint.x, oldPoint.y, newPoint.x,
                     newPoint.y);
  }

  // Implements Runnable Interface
  public void run()
  {
  }

  // For running standalone
  public static void main(String[] argv)
  {
    // Create the frame and launch Sketch
    Frame f = new Frame("SketchFrame");
    f.reshape(0, 0, 639, 479);
    f.show();

    Sketch x = new Sketch();
    f.add("Center", x);
    x.init();
    x.start();
  }

  // Constructor
  public  Sketch()
  {
  }

} // end class Sketch
```

The **mouseDown()** method is used in this application to signal when a mouse button is depressed. This marks the beginning point of a doodle on the screen. This member function is used to return a **Point()** value, the x and y coordinates, to variable *newPoint*.

As the mouse is moved, with a mouse button depressed, new x and y coordinate values must be returned. The **mouseDrag()** method will allow us to obtain this information. A previously obtained coordinate value, currently held in *newPoint*, is saved in *oldPoint*.

```
oldPoint = newPoint;
```

Now, a new current point is obtained with the following line of code.

```
newPoint = new Point(x, y);
```

Together, *oldPoint* and *newPoint* give us the information needed to draw a line segment. The line segment will be short because the application is continuously checking mouse movement, so even small changes in the mouse's position will generate new values for *oldPoint* and *newPoint*.

Each time a new pair of points is generated, it will be necessary to use the **paint()** method to draw the new line segment in the window. This is as simple as calling **repaint()** from within **mouseDrag()**. Now, it is possible to draw the line in any color you choose.

```
graphic.setColor(Color.blue);
graphic.drawLine(oldPoint.x, oldPoint.y, newPoint.x,
                 newPoint.y);
```

If we stopped here, the results would not be very satisfactory. Each new line segment would request a **repaint()**, which in turn would use the **update()** method to erase and draw on a cleared screen. You would see a series of flashing short line segments as you moved the mouse across the screen. What we need to do, to complete this application, is to override the **update()** method so that it does not clear the screen when handling a request for a screen update. This is done, simply, with the following method.

```
public void update(Graphics graphic)
{
  paint(graphic);
}
```

Now, you can sketch to your heart's content, as you can see in Figure 10.3.

***Note:*** *Unlike Windows API functions that allow the pen width to be set, Java currently allows a one-pixel-width pen.*

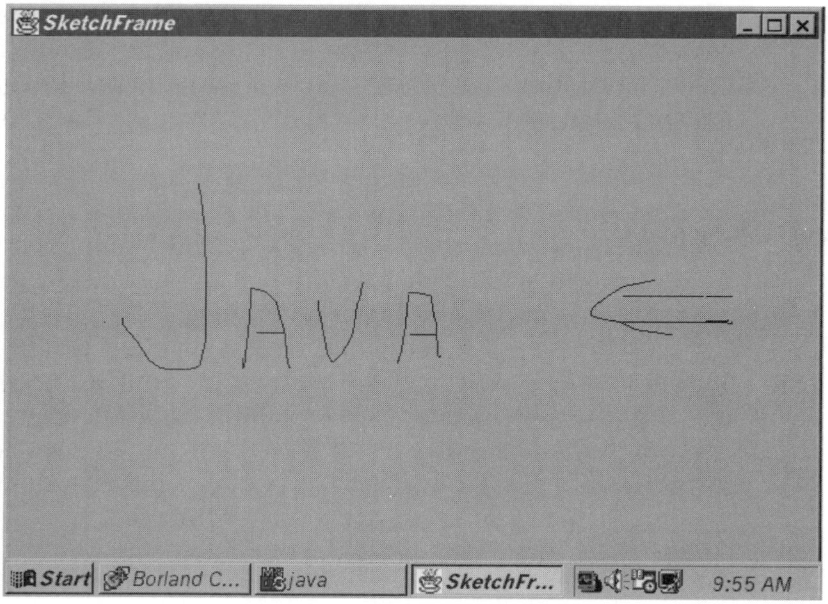


**Figure 10.3:** Doodling in a window is now possible with the Mouse-A-Sketch sketching application.

*Note: Unlike Windows API functions that allow the user to detect which mouse button triggered an event, Java cannot currently distinguish between mouse buttons.*

In Chapters 13 and 14 you will learn how to provide menu and dialog box selections. You might want to return to this application, armed with that information, and provide the user with a choice of pen colors.

## Adding Image Capabilities

In Windows, information is often placed in the client area of a window by issuing a series of Windows GDI graphics function calls or moving a bitmapped image from memory to a specific screen area. Java allows the same type of action. Under Windows, the native image format is a bitmapped file with a .bmp file extension. As you know, other types of image formats exist. Currently, Java will allow graphics formats with .jpg and .gif file extensions.

In this section, we'll take a look a two applets, Image1 and Image2, that will allow you to experiment with previously saved image files.

## Getting Images

In Java, there are basically two key member functions for getting and drawing images. Traditional coding techniques are then applied to manipulate these images. For example, to add animation to an application or applet to move an image uses essentially the same code whether you are programming in Windows, OS/2, or Java. In this section we'll look at how images are obtained.

Images are obtained with the use of the **getImage()** member function. There are two variations of **getImage()**.

Let's look at the syntax for the first one:

```
public abstract Image getImage(URL url);
```

This version returns an image which obtains pixel data from the given Universal Resource Locator or URL.

The syntax for the second variation is:

```
public abstract Image getImage(String filename);
```

This version returns an image which obtains pixel data from the given file. Currently, the file format must be a file saved as a .jpg or .gif file.

The URL is typically an address, such as:

```
"http://www.thelocation.com/image/car.jpg"
```

If a program uses the URL, it might appear in this format:

```
Image output;

output = getImage("http://www.thelocation.com/image/car.jpg");
```

Hardwiring addresses sometimes makes an application or applet inflexible. Java provides two methods for obtaining URL information, without the need for a specific string. If **getDocumentBase()** is used, a URL is returned with the directory containing the HTML file, for this applet. If **getCodeBase()** is used, directory information will also be returned. In this case, however, the applet and the HTML can be in different directories.

For example, if the image and applet files are located in the same directory as the HTML files, the following syntax can be used:

```
Image output;

output = getImage(getDocumentBase(), "car.jpg");
```

It is possible that you might save images in a subdirectory separate from your applet and HTML file. This seems to be a standard practice for Java programmers and one used in many Borland examples. In this case, you might prefer this method:

```
Image output;

output = getImage(getBaseCode(), "image/car.jpg");
```

If Java cannot load the given file, a null will be returned. You will be looking at a blank screen, with no other error messages, unless your application signals you when this condition occurs.

## Drawing Images

Once an image is obtained with **getImage()**, it can be drawn on the screen. There are four variations of the **drawImage()** member function. Here is the syntax for the first variation:

```
public abstract boolean drawImage(Image img, int x, int y,
                                  ImageObserver observer);
```

Here, the image, specified by *img*, will be drawn starting at the given *x,y* coordinate location. The *observer* parameter will return information regarding whether the image is complete.

The second variation expands the capabilities of the previous member function.

```
public abstract boolean drawImage(Image img, int x, int y,
                                  int width, int height,
                                  ImageObserver observer);
```

This member function allows the image to be scaled to fit within the given rectangle. Here *x,y* mark the beginning of the rectangle and *width* and *height* the breadth of the rectangle. All other parameters are similar to the first variation.

**Note:** *The width and height parameters are not the end points of the rectangle, as they are when specifying rectangles in Windows. If your application needs end points, for some reason, they will have to be calculated by algebraically adding the x,y starting point values to the appropriate width or height values.*

The remaining two variations are similar to the first two variations already discussed. These member functions allow a solid background color to be specified during the call to **drawImage()**. Here is the syntax for the third variation.

```
public abstract boolean drawImage(Image img, int x, int y,
                                  Color bgcolor,
                                  ImageObserver observer);
```

Here is the syntax for the fourth variation:

```
public abstract boolean drawImage(Image img, int x, int y,
                                  int width, int height,
                                  Color bgcolor,
                                  ImageObserver observer);
```

All parameters except the color parameter are similar to those in the first two variations. In both of these member functions, *bgcolor* is of type **Color**. Stock or custom colors can be specified.

Let's see how simple images can be manipulated, in the following sections, with two simple applets.

## The Image 1 Applet

The first applet, Image1, will load a small JPEG image of a GG-1 engine to the window. The code is straightforward, as you can see in the following listing.

```
//-------------------------------------------------------
// Image1 Getting An Image In The Window
// Copyright 1996, All rights reserved
// Nineveh National Research
```

```
// Version: 1.0
// Author: Pappas and Murray
// Created: 3/29/96
//---------------------------------------------------------

import java.awt.*;
import java.applet.Applet;

public class Image1 extends Applet implements Runnable
{
  Image output;

  // Class initialization code
  public void init()
  {
    output = getImage(getCodeBase(), "Train.jpg");
  }

  // This routine handles the painting
  public void paint(Graphics graphic)
  {
    graphic.drawImage(output, 10, 10, this);
  }

  // Implements Runnable Interface
  public void run()
  {
  }

  // For running standalone
  public static void main(String[] argv)
  {
    // Create the frame and launch Image1
    Frame f = new Frame("Image1Frame");
    f.reshape(0, 0, 639, 479);
    f.show();

    Image1 x = new Image1();
    f.add("Center", x);
    x.init();
    x.start();
  }

  // Constructor
  public  Image1()
  {
  }

} // end class Image1
```

The image is drawn, starting at a coordinate position of 10,10 in the window.

The size of the initial applet screen is actually controlled by the HTML file. We modified the width and height values in the Borland default HTML file, which follows, to fit a standard VGA screen.

```
<title>The Image1 Applet</title>
<hr>
<applet code=Image1.class width=639 height=479>

</applet>

<hr>
<hr>
<a href="Image1.java">The source.</a>
```

The version of the **drawImage()** member function used here will draw the portion of the image that fits within the window. In this case, the window is large enough to accommodate the whole image of the train, as you can see in Figure 10.4.

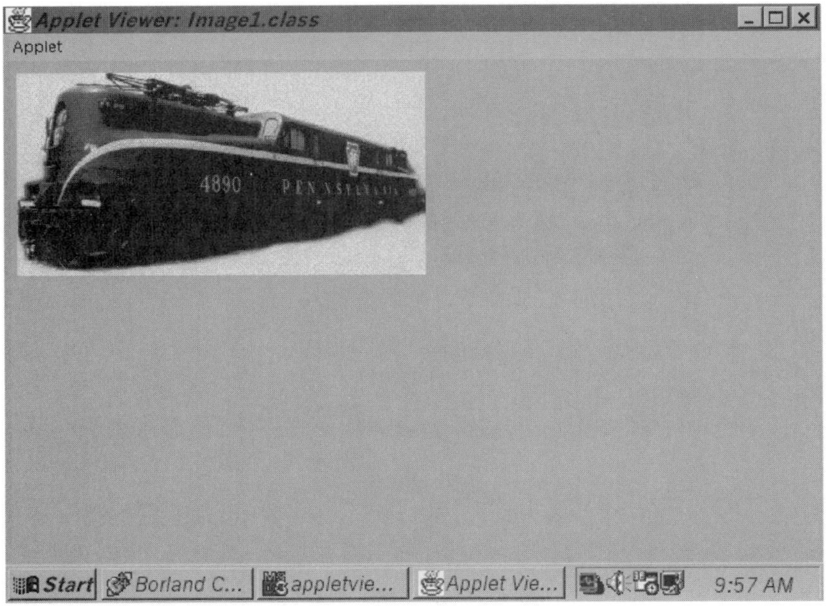


**Figure 10.4:** The mighty GG-1 thunders out of the clouds in this Java applet.

*Note: The GG-1 was an electric engine used by the Pennsylvania Railroad. It saw peak service in the 1940s pulling passenger trains from Washington D.C. to New York City.*

## The Image2 Applet

The second applet, Image2, will load a GIF image to the window. This applet used the second variation of the **drawImage()** member function. The code is similar to the previous listing.

```
//-------------------------------------------------------
// Image2 Manipulating An Image
// Copyright 1996, All rights reserved
// Nineveh National Research
// Version: 1.0
// Author: Pappas and Murray
// Created: 3/29/96
//-------------------------------------------------------

import java.awt.*;
import java.applet.Applet;

public class Image2 extends Applet implements Runnable
{
  Image output;

  // Class initialization code
  public void init()
  {
    output = getImage(getCodeBase(), "Object.gif");
  }

  // This routine handles the painting
  public void paint(Graphics graphic)
  {
    int objwidth = output.getWidth(this);
    int objheight = output.getHeight(this);
    graphic.drawImage(output, 0, 0, objwidth,
                      objheight, this);
  }

  // Implements Runnable Interface
  public void run()
  {
  }
```

```
  // For running standalone
  public static void main(String[] argv)
  {
    // Create the frame and launch Image2
    Frame f = new Frame("Image2Frame");
    f.reshape(0, 0, 639, 479);
    f.show();

    Image2 x = new Image2();
    f.add("Center", x);
    x.init();
    x.start();
  }

  // Constructor
  public  Image2()
  {
  }

} // end class Image2
```

The trick used here stretches or shrinks the image to fit the window. The width and height of the image are obtained with **getWidth()** and **getHeight()**. They are then used as the *width* and *height* parameters in the **drawImage()** member function.

The image is drawn, starting at a coordinate position of 0,0 in the window. Again, since the initial applet screen is controlled by the HTML file, it is modified to produce VGA screen dimensions.

```
<title>The Image2 Applet</title>
<hr>
<applet code=Image2.class width=640 height=480>

</applet>

<hr>
<hr>
<a href="Image2.java">The source.</a>
```

Run this applet, and you'll see a screen similar to Figure 10.5. Have you seen this screen before? Did you register your Borland C++ Compiler?

**Figure 10.5:** A reminder screen is borrowed for this Java applet.

## JAVA LINGO

*AWT*—Abstract Windowing Toolkit forms the communications pathway for communicating events to you or the applet. Mouse events use the AWT.

*GUI*—The Graphics User Interface forms the basis of communications between graphics elements and the user. Windows, for example, like Java, has its own collection of GUI functions and member functions.

*images*—A wide variety of image formats are available. For example, bitmap and JPEG images are very popular. Java currently supports JPEG and GIF image formats. These have .jpg and .gif file extensions.

*UI*—The User Interface forms the basis of communications between programming elements and the user. Mouse and keyboard events might be considered UI components.

*URL*—The Universal Resource Locator helps identify the path to files.

# 11

# Working with Sound Resources

Java provides the capability to add sound to your applets through the **play()** and **getAudioClip()** methods. Currently, only Sun's formatted audio clips can be played. These are files ending with the .au file extension.

A large number of audio samples are available on the Web. Use the Yahoo search engine and search for **sound au.** You'll find everything from simple sound effects to complete speeches and music scores.

In this chapter we'll investigate three simple applets and how they make use of Java's sound capabilities. You'll find other examples that incorporate sound capabilities throughout the remainder of this book.

## Sound Methods

We'll make use of two methods in our sound applets. The first member function or method is **getAudioClip()**. This function is available in two versions:

```
AudioClip getAudioClip(URL url);
```

Here the URL (Universal Resource Locator) locates and loads the audio clip.

```
AudioClip getAudioClip(URL url, String name);
```

In this version, the URL functions as it did in the first version. A string can now be used to specify a path name and file name. These two formats should look familiar. They are identical to the formats used to locate and obtain images. These were discussed in the previous chapter.

The **getDocumentBase()** or **getCodeBase()** member functions can be used to obtain the URL information, as they were in the previous chapter. Typically, sound information will be obtained with code similar to the following sequence:

```
AudioClip soundclip;
      .
      .
      .
soundclip = getAudioClip(getCodeBase(), "audio/testclip.au");
```

Here the sound clip is loaded into an instance of the AudioClip class, *soundclip*. The file, testclip.au, is located in the audio subdirectory located off the parent directory containing the applet. If the sound clip isn't located a **null** will be returned.

The sound clip can be played, stopped, and repeated. To play the sound clip, use the **play()** method.

If you are using the previous sequence of code to locate the sound clip, the **play()** method can be called without passing any parameters.

```
soundclip.play();
```

If the sound clip is long and you want to stop playing it at any time, the **stop()** method can be used. Again, no parameters are needed.

```
soundclip.stop();
```

Likewise, a sound clip can be played repeatedly with the use of the **loop()** method.

```
soundclip.loop();
```

Let's investigate the use of these member functions in three simple applets. You'll find that sound gives your Java applets a new dimension—a dimension that adds a professional touch to your work.

## A Simple Sound Example

The following applet, Sound1, illustrates just how easy it is to add sound to an applet. The Borland's Java AppExpert generated the basic code. We've bolded the additional lines required to add a sound clip to the applet.

```
//-----------------------------------------------------------
// Sound1 Test an audio clip
// Copyright 1996, All rights reserved
// Nineveh National Research
// Version: 1.0
// Author: Pappas and Murray
// Created: 4/2/96
//-----------------------------------------------------------

import java.awt.*;
import java.applet.Applet;
import java.applet.AudioClip;

public class Sound1 extends Applet implements Runnable
{
  AudioClip soundclip;

  // Class initialization code
  public void init()
  {
    soundclip = getAudioClip(getCodeBase(),
                             "audio/testclip.au");

  }

  // This routine handles the painting
  public void paint(Graphics graphic)
  {
    graphic.drawString("Listen to the sound clip...",
                       20, 20);
```

```
    soundclip.play();
  }

  // Implements Runnable Interface
  public void run()
  {
  }

  // For running standalone
  public static void main(String[] argv)
  {
    // Create the frame and launch Sound1
    Frame f = new Frame("Sound1Frame");
    f.reshape(0, 0, 639, 479);
    f.show();

    Sound1 x = new Sound1();
    f.add("Center", x);
    x.init();
    x.start();
  }

  // Constructor
  public  Sound1()
  {
  }

} // end class Sound1
```

Execute this example as an applet in the applet viewer provided by Borland. The following HTML file was generated by Borland's Java AppExpert, too.

```
<title>The Sound1 Applet</title>
<hr>
<applet code=Sound1.class width=200 height=200>

</applet>

<hr>
<hr>
<a href="Sound1.java">The source.</a>
```

This is really a very simple applet. Start the applet, hear the sound. If you're using the applet and sound resource from the diskette, you might be surprised when you hear the audio clip. Give it a try!

## Starting and Stopping Sounds

The previous applet was rather limited. It played a sound clip when the applet was started, but that was it. We can expand the sound capabilities of an applet by adding some techniques learned in the previous chapter.

In the following applet, a sound clip will be played any time a mouse button is depressed. The sound clip will continue to play until the mouse button is released. Want to hear the sound clip again? Just depress the mouse button to start the sound clip at the beginning. The code that relates directly to producing sound is boldface in the following applet.

```
//-----------------------------------------------------------
// MouseSnd Mouse button activates sound
// Copyright 1996, All rights reserved
// Nineveh National Research
// Version: 1.0
// Author: Pappas and Murray
// Created: 4/2/96
//-----------------------------------------------------------

import java.awt.*;
import java.applet.Applet;
import java.applet.AudioClip;

public class MouseSnd extends Applet implements Runnable
{
  AudioClip mouseclip;

  // Class initialization code
  public void init()
  {
    mouseclip = getAudioClip(getCodeBase(),
                             "audio/mouseclip.au");
  }

  // Mouse button pressed handling code
  public boolean mouseDown(Event event, int x, int y)
  {
    mouseclip.play();
    return true;
  }
```

```
  // Mouse button released handling code
  public boolean mouseUp(Event event, int x, int y)
  {
    mouseclip.stop();
    return true;
  }

  // This routine handles the painting
  public void paint(Graphics graphic)
  {
    graphic.drawString("Click button to play...", 20, 20);
    graphic.drawString("Release to stop play...", 20, 40);
  }

  // Implements Runnable Interface
  public void run()
  {
  }

  // For running standalone
  public static void main(String[] argv)
  {
    // Create the frame and launch MouseSnd
    Frame f = new Frame("MouseSndFrame");
    f.reshape(100, 100, 200, 100);
    f.show();

    MouseSnd x = new MouseSnd();
    f.add("Center", x);
    x.init();
    x.start();
  }

  // Constructor
  public  MouseSnd()
  {
  }

} // end class MouseSnd
```

That's all there is to it. Borland's Java AppExpert created the following HTML file for this application.

```
<title>The MouseSnd Applet</title>
<hr>
<applet code=MouseSnd.class width=200 height=200>

</applet>
```

```
<hr>
<hr>
<a href="MouseSnd.java">The source.</a>
```

This applet illustrates how the user can control sound resources with just a click of a mouse button. In the final example, we'll use the mouse once again and expand our control of sound resources even more.

## A Sketching Applet with Sound Prompts

In the previous chapter, we created a sketching application that allows the user to doodle in the window. Lines are drawn when a mouse button is depressed.

In the following applet, the sketching application has been modified to include to audio prompts. One audio prompt sounds when the mouse button is depressed, signaling the user that drawing is about to commence. Another audio prompt sounds when the mouse button is released, signaling the user that that line segment is complete. Only the code related to the sound resource is boldface in the following listing.

```
//------------------------------------------------------
// SketSnd Sketching with audio prompts
// Copyright 1996, All rights reserved
// Nineveh National Research
// Version: 1.0
// Author: Pappas and Murray
// Created: 4/2/96
//------------------------------------------------------

import java.awt.*;
import java.applet.Applet;
import java.applet.AudioClip;

public class SketSnd extends Applet implements Runnable
{
  AudioClip sketclip1;
  AudioClip sketclip2;
  Point newPoint, oldPoint;

  // Class initialization code
```

```
public void init()
{
  sketclip1 = getAudioClip(getCodeBase(),
                           "audio/sndclip1.au");
  sketclip2 = getAudioClip(getCodeBase(),
                           "audio/sndclip2.au");
}

// Mouse button pressed handling code
public boolean mouseDown(Event event, int x, int y)
{
  newPoint = new Point(x, y);
  sketclip1.play();
  return true;
}

// Mouse button released handling code
public boolean mouseUp(Event event, int x, int y)
{
  sketclip2.play();
  return true;
}

// Mouse drag handling code
public boolean mouseDrag(Event event, int x, int y)
{
  oldPoint = newPoint;
  newPoint = new Point(x, y);
  repaint();
  return true;
}

public void update(Graphics graphic)
{
  paint(graphic);
}

// This routine handles the painting
public void paint(Graphics graphic)
{
  graphic.setColor(Color.blue);
  graphic.drawLine(oldPoint.x, oldPoint.y,
                   newPoint.x, newPoint.y);
}

// Implements Runnable Interface
public void run()
{
}
```

```
  // For running standalone
  public static void main(String[] argv)
  {
    // Create the frame and launch SketSnd
    Frame f = new Frame("SketSndFrame");
    f.reshape(0, 0, 639, 479);
    f.show();

    SketSnd x = new SketSnd();
    f.add("Center", x);
    x.init();
    x.start();
  }

  // Constructor
  public  SketSnd()
  {
  }

} // end class SketSnd
```

Now, the sketching application is complete with audio prompts. In order to size the initial drawing screen to VGA size, modify the HTML file returned by Borland's Java AppExpert to match the following listing.

```
<title>The SketSnd Applet</title>
<hr>
<applet code=SketSnd.class width=640 height=480>

</applet>

<hr>
<hr>
<a href="SketSnd.java">The source.</a>
```

As you have learned, sound resources are easy to add to your applet. As you develop more involved applications, keep in mind that too much of a good thing can get a little boring. Use resources wisely.

## JAVA LINGO

*AU*—Sun's audio format for sound resources. Literally thousands of these sound resource files can be found on the Web.

# 12

# Working with Font Resources

Having the ability to create different fonts with various properties can greatly enhance your applications and applets. Font properties include the ability to size characters and turn bold and italic characteristics on or off. Strings can then be drawn to the screen with the new fonts in any color you desire. Color selections were discussed in Chapter 9.

If you are an experienced Windows programmer, your will find that you don't have quite as much flexibility as Windows GDI functions allow. For example, you have no control over orientation or escapement. These two characteristics allow Windows programmers to rotate characters or whole strings. This ability is great for printing vertical axis labels. Also missing is the ability to use Windows TrueType fonts.

With all of that aside, there are a great number of things you can do with font resources to enhance your projects. We'll look at a number of these features in this chapter and continue using font resources in the remaining chapters of the book.

## Font Methods

In this section, we'll concentrate our discussion on the member functions (methods) described in Java's Font class. However, throughout out this chapter we'll also make reference to the Toolkit and FontMetrics classes. Member functions from the previous two classes will be explained as they are used. Table 12.1 shows an abbreviated list of the member functions that appear in the Font class.

The Font class allows you to create font objects. These objects are specified by a name, style, and point size. Font names currently include Helvetica, Dialog, TimesRoman, Symbol, and Courier. As we mentioned earlier, you do not have access to Windows TrueType fonts. Font styles include PLAIN, BOLD, and ITALIC. A bold italic font can be created, too, by logically oring the BOLD and ITALIC styles together. Point size

**Table 12.1:** Font Class Methods

| *Method* | *Return Type* | *Parameters* | *Description* |
|---|---|---|---|
| Font() | Font | String name,<br>int style,<br>int size | Creates a new font. |
| getFamily() | String | | Gets platform family name of font. |
| getName() | String | | Gets logical name of font. |
| getStyle() | int | | Gets the style of the font. |
| getSize() | int | | Gets the size of the font. |
| isPlain() | boolean | | true when font is plain. |
| isBold() | boolean | | true when font is bold. |
| isItalic() | boolean | | true when font is italic. |
| getFont() | static | string nm<br>or<br>String nm,<br>Font font | Gets a font from the system properties list. |
| hashcode() | int | | Returns a hash code for the font. |
| equals() | boolean | Object obj | Compares this object to given object. true when both are the same. |
| toString() | String | | Converts object to a string. |

is a number. An 8 point font is very small, a 12 point font is very common for applications and applets. A 72 point font is very large. An application that might use a very large font would be a countdown timer that would show only a few digits on the whole screen.

Creating a new font is easy. The following sequence of code is required:

```
Font newfont;
   .
   .
   .
newfont = new Font("Courier", Font.PLAIN, 12);
graphic.setFont(newfont);
   .
   .
   .
```

As you can clearly see, a 12 point plain Courier font will be requested. Java will supply the closest font possible to your specifications. If a 12 point font isn't available, the closest point size, for example, will be provided.

**Note:** *Remember that while it is possible to manipulate a lot of Java's font characteristics it is not possible to directly rotate characters or strings in Java as it is with Windows. If you need to print a vertical label, for example, you will have to parse a string of characters, printing them one at a time in a vertical column.*

## Getting a List of Fonts

Many projects require a variety of fonts. These projects include graphics applications such as the bar and pie chart applications in Chapter 10. If you do not know which fonts are available on your system, the **getFontList()** member function can be used to obtain the information. The **getFontList()** member function is described in the Toolkit class.

The syntax for this member function is:

```
String[] getFontList();
```

When calling **getFontList()**, the following sequence of code should be used:

```
import java.awt.Toolkit
   .
   .
   .
Toolkit tk;
   .
   .
   .
tk = getToolkit();
mystring = tk.getFontList();
```

Other than that, the use of the member function is quite simple. In the following application, created with the Borland AppExpert, those lines of code are bold.

```
//---------------------------------------------------------
// Font1 Finding new fonts
// Copyright 1996, All rights reserved
// Nineveh National Research
// Version: 1.0
// Author: Pappas and Murray
// Created: 4/4/96
//---------------------------------------------------------

import java.awt.*;
import java.applet.Applet;

public class Font1 extends Applet implements Runnable
{
  Toolkit tk;
  String[] mystring;

  // This routine handles the painting
  public void paint(Graphics graphic)
  {
    tk = getToolkit();
    mystring = tk.getFontList();

    for (int i = 0; i < 6; i++) {
      graphic.drawString(mystring[i], 0, 30 * (i + 1));
    }
  }
  // Implements Runnable Interface
```

```
  public void run()
  {
  }

  // For running standalone
  public static void main(String[] argv)
  {
    // Create the frame and launch Font1
    Frame f = new Frame("Font1Frame");
    f.reshape(0, 0, 639, 479);
    f.show();
    Font1 x = new Font1();
    f.add("Center", x);
    x.init();
    x.start();
  }

  // Constructor
  public  Font1()
  {
  }

} // end class Font1
```

For our installation, the **getFontList()** member function returns a font list which includes Courier, Dialog, Helvetica, TimesRoman, and Symbol fonts. Figure 12.1 shows the output sent to the screen.

## Font Sizes

Many projects require different size fonts from the same font family. For example, a project might need a 28 point Courier font for a title and a 12 point font for labels. Font size is a property that is very easy to alter.

In the following application, a string is drawn in the window, several times, as the point size is increased. As you study the listing, notice that the font's point size is set with the use of the **Font()** member function. This member function, described earlier in this chapter, is part of Java's Font class.

```
//-------------------------------------------------------
// Font2 Font Sizes
```

**Figure 12.1:** The getFontList() member function returns a list of available fonts.

```
// Copyright 1996, All rights reserved
// Nineveh National Research
// Version: 1.0
// Author: Pappas and Murray
// Created: 4/6/96
//-----------------------------------------------------------

import java.awt.*;
import java.applet.Applet;

public class Font2 extends Applet implements Runnable
{
  Font newfont;

  // This routine handles the painting
  public void paint(Graphics graphic)
  {
    // A Courier font is sized
    for (int i = 1; i < 11; i++) {
    newfont = new Font("Courier", Font.PLAIN, (i * 5));
    graphic.setFont(newfont);
    graphic.drawString("Sizing a Courier font",
                       0, 10 + (i * 40));
    }
  }
```

```
  // Implements Runnable Interface
  public void run()
  {
  }

  // For running standalone
  public static void main(String[] argv)
  {
    // Create the frame and launch Font2
    Frame f = new Frame("Font2Frame");
    f.reshape(0, 0, 639, 479);
    f.show();

    Font2 x = new Font2();
    f.add("Center", x);
    x.init();
    x.start();
  }

  // Constructor
  public  Font2()
  {
  }

} // end class Font2
```

The **Font()** member function is included in a loop. Each pass through the loop requests a larger font. The size varies from 5 points to 50 points. Figure 12.2 illustrates these various font sizes.

When a font size is requested, the closest match to the requested size will be returned. For example, if you request a 14 point and a 15 point font size, it is possible that only a 14 point size is available. If that is the case, both requests will be filled with a 14 point font size.

***Note:*** *Windows programmers are making use of a very scalable font type called TrueType fonts. These are not available for Java programmers at this time.*

## Font Properties

Font families are often made up of a plain, bold, italic, and bold-italic components. These terms, along with point size, are considered font properties. In the following example you'll see

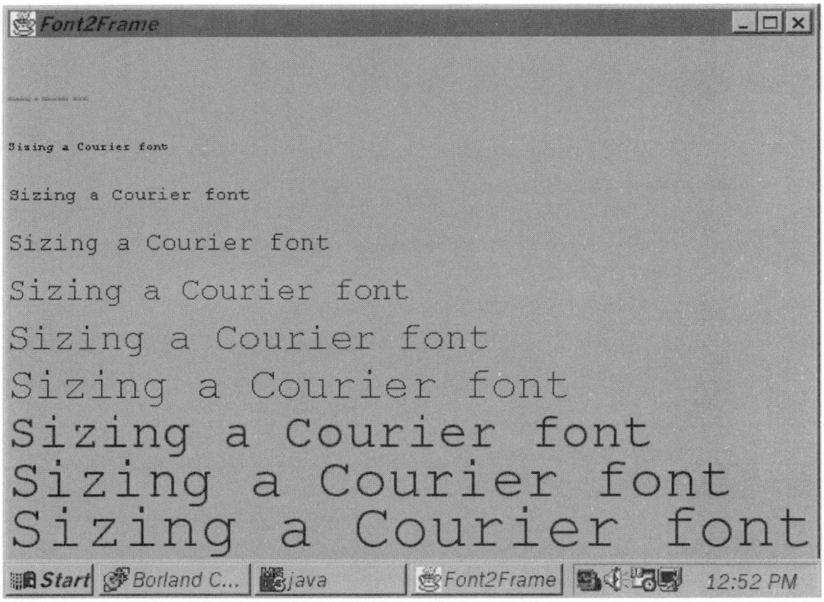


**Figure 12.2:** Using the Font() member function to experiment with font sizes.

how font properties can be changed. Font properties were described earlier in this chapter.

Study the following listing and find the properties PLAIN, ITALIC, BOLD, and ITALIC + BOLD.

```
//-------------------------------------------------------
// Font3 Font Properties
// Copyright 1996, All rights reserved
// Nineveh National Research
// Version: 1.0
// Author: Pappas and Murray
// Created: 4/6/96
//-------------------------------------------------------

import java.awt.*;
import java.applet.Applet;

public class Font3 extends Applet implements Runnable
{
  Font newfont;
  // This routine handles the painting
  public void paint(Graphics graphic)
```

```
    {
      // Helvetica Font Properties
      newfont = new Font("Helvetica", Font.PLAIN, 30);
      graphic.setFont(newfont);
      graphic.drawString("Helvetica 30pt", 0, 50);

      newfont = new Font("Helvetica", Font.ITALIC, 30);
      graphic.setFont(newfont);
      graphic.drawString("Helvetica 30pt italic", 0, 150);

      newfont = new Font("Helvetica", Font.BOLD, 30);
      graphic.setFont(newfont);
      graphic.drawString("Helvetica 30pt BOLD", 0, 250);

      newfont = new Font("Helvetica",
                         Font.ITALIC + Font.BOLD, 30);
      graphic.setFont(newfont);
      graphic.drawString("Helvetica 30pt BOLD italic",
                         0, 350);
    }

    // Implements Runnable Interface
    public void run()
    {
    }

    // For running standalone
    public static void main(String[] argv)
    {
      // Create the frame and launch Font3
      Frame f = new Frame("Font3Frame");
      f.reshape(0, 0, 639, 479);
      f.show();

      Font3 x = new Font3();
      f.add("Center", x);
      x.init();
      x.start();
    }

    // Constructor
    public  Font3()
    {
    }

  } // end class Font3
```

This application makes continued use of the **Font()** member function described earlier in this chapter. All of the strings are printed with a 30 point Helvetica font. As you can see from Figure 12.3, the application sequences from plain to italic plus bold.

## Using FontMetrics()

The FontMetrics class provides a number of member functions (methods) for obtaining detailed information about a font family. Table 12.2 lists the individual member functions for this class.

The font information returned by these various methods can be obtained individually, or in a string format by using the **toString()** member function. The **toString()** member function is overridden in FontMetrics to provide this information.

The following application illustrates the use of the **toString()** member function to obtain information about a bold italic Hel-

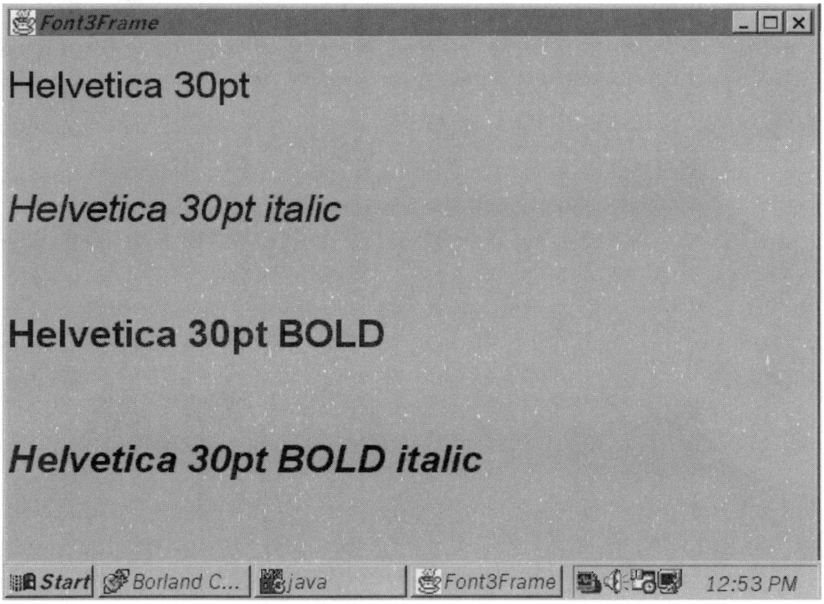


**Figure 12.3:** Font properties such as PLAIN, ITALIC, and BOLD can be used to create fonts for every purpose.

**Table 12.2:** FontMetrics Class Methods

| *Method* | *Return Type* | *Parameters* | *Description* |
|---|---|---|---|
| getFont() | Font | | Obtains the current font. |
| getLeading() | int | | Obtains leading or line space. |
| getAscent() | int | | Obtains ascent—distance from font's base line to top of char. |
| getDescent() | int | | Obtains descent—distance from font's base line to bottom of char. |
| getHeight() | int | | Obtains ascent + descent + leading. |
| getMaxAscent() | int | | Obtains the max ascent in the font. |
| getMaxDescent() | int | | Obtains the max descent in the font. |
| getMaxAdvance() | int | | Obtains max advance width in the font. |
| charWidth() | int | int ch | Obtains the width of the given char. or char ch |
| stringWidth() | int | String str | Obtains the width of the given string. |
| charsWidth() | int | char data[], int off, int len | Obtains the width of the given char array |
| bytesWidth() | int | byte data[], int off, int len | Obtains width of given array of bytes. |
| getWidths() | int[] | | Obtains widths for first 256 char. |
| toString() | String | | FontMetric values for font returned as string. |

vetica 14 point font. If you are not prepared to parse the string of information, set your screen parameters so that you can display a large number of horizontal characters.

```
//--------------------------------------------------------
// Font4 Using FontMetrics()
```

```
// Copyright 1996, All rights reserved
// Nineveh National Research
// Version: 1.0
// Author: Pappas and Murray
// Created: 4/6/96
//-----------------------------------------------------------

import java.awt.*;
import java.applet.Applet;

public class Font4 extends Applet implements Runnable
{
  Font newfont;
  FontMetrics fm;

  // This routine handles the painting
  public void paint(Graphics graphic)
  {
    String mystring;

    newfont = new Font("Helvetica",
                       Font.ITALIC + Font.BOLD, 14);
    graphic.setFont(newfont);

    fm = graphic.getFontMetrics();
    mystring = fm.toString();
    graphic.drawString(mystring, 0, 300);
  }

  // Implements Runnable Interface
  public void run()
  {
  }

  // For running standalone
  public static void main(String[] argv)
  {
    // Create the frame and launch Font4
    Frame f = new Frame("Font4Frame");
    f.reshape(0, 0, 1023, 479);
    f.show();

    Font4 x = new Font4();
    f.add("Center", x);
    x.init();
    x.start();
  }
  // Constructor
```

```
    public  Font4()
    {
    }

} // end class Font4
```

You can see that the use of the function is very straightforward. FontMetric information is very useful when you are designing applications that, for example, center strings of characters in a line.

Figure 12.4 shows the results of the information returned in this application.

## A Bar Chart with Labels

In Chapter 10, a bar chart application was developed. This application taught you several concepts used in making a chart application. However, the chart application did not

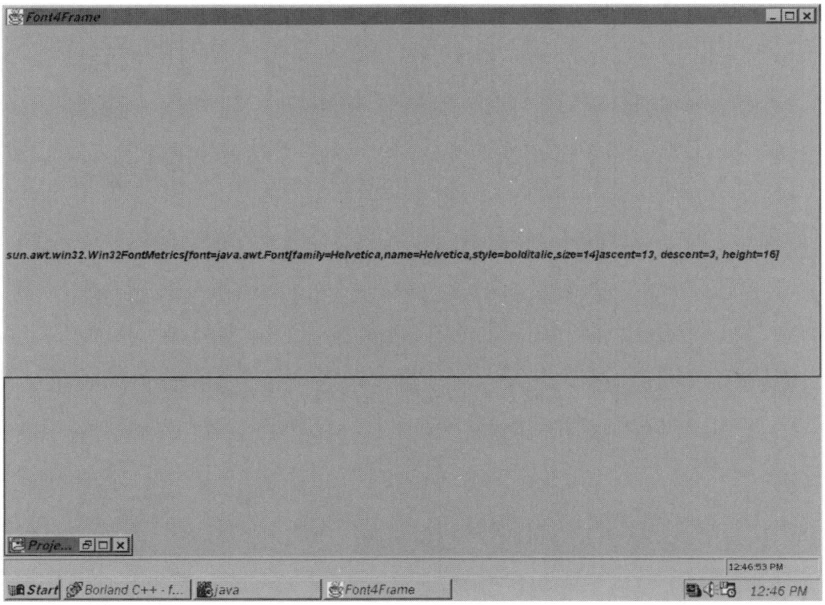


**Figure 12.4:** FontMetric information can be returned by member functions in the FontMetrics class.

have any labels! In this section, we'll show you how to put the information you've learned about fonts to a practical use.

The following listing is a modified version of the bar chart application presented in Chapter 10. The bold lines represent the portions of code added to allow a title, vertical and horizontal axis labels, and the creation of a legend.

Examine the following listing. You might want to compare it with the application developed and explained in Chapter 10.

```
//----------------------------------------------------------
// Font5 A Simple Bar Chart Application
// Copyright 1996, All rights reserved
// Nineveh National Research
// Version: 1.0
// Author: Pappas and Murray
// Created: 3/23/96
//----------------------------------------------------------

import java.applet.Applet;
import java.awt.*;

public class Font5 extends Applet implements Runnable
{
  Font titlefont, labelfont, legendfont;
  FontMetrics fm;

  // This routine handles the painting
  public void paint(Graphics graphic)
  {
    int height[] = {300, 50, 225, 180, 75};
    int numBars = 5;                    // number of bars
                                        // (1 to 11 max)
    String charttitle = "Profit Margin"; // title
    String vertlabel = "$$$";           // vertical label
    String horzlabel = "Months";        // horizontal label
    String[] legend = { "January",      // legend labels
                        "February",
                        "March",
                        "April",
                        "May",
                        "June",
                        "July",
                        "August",
                        "September",
```

```
                    "October",
                    "November",
                    "December" };

int newstart = 2;                   // start position
int width = 300 / numBars;          // width of a bar
Color barColor[] = {Color.red,      // bar colors
                    Color.blue,
                    Color.yellow,
                    Color.green,
                    Color.cyan,
                    Color.magenta,
                    Color.orange,
                    Color.pink,
                    Color.gray,
                    Color.darkGray,
                    Color.black};

// create fonts
titlefont = new Font("TimesRoman", Font.BOLD, 36);
labelfont = new Font("TimesRoman", Font.PLAIN, 14);
legendfont = new Font("TimesRoman", Font.ITALIC, 10);

// draw coordinate axes
graphic.translate(99, 379);         // move origin
graphic.drawLine(0, -329, 0, 0);    // vert. axis
graphic.drawLine(0, 0, 329, 0);     // horz. axis

// draw and center chart title
graphic.setFont(titlefont);
fm = getFontMetrics(titlefont);
graphic.drawString(charttitle,
                   165 - (fm.stringWidth(charttitle)/2),
                   -340);

// draw vertical label and center horizontal label
graphic.setFont(labelfont);
fm = getFontMetrics(labelfont);
graphic.drawString(vertlabel,
                   -10 - fm.stringWidth(vertlabel),
                   -150);
graphic.drawString(horzlabel,
                   165 - (fm.stringWidth(horzlabel)/2),
                   40);

// draw and fill bars
for (int i = 0; i < numBars; i++) {
```

```
      graphic.setColor(barColor[i]);  // set fill color
      graphic.fillRect(newstart,      // draw a bar
                       -height[i],
                       width,
                       height[i] - 1);
      newstart += 2 + width;          // set new position
    }

    // draw, fill and label chart legend
    graphic.setFont(legendfont);
    for (int i = 0; i < numBars; i++) {
      graphic.setColor(barColor[i]);  // set fill color
      graphic.fillRect(360, -300 + (i * 30), 15, 15);

      // first bar will be for March
      graphic.setColor(Color.black);  // set font color
      graphic.drawString(legend[i + 2], 380,
                         -290 + (i * 30));
    }
  }

  // Implements Runnable Interface
  public void run()
  {
  }

  // For running standalone
  public static void main(String[] argv)
  {
    // Create the frame and launch Font5
    Frame f = new Frame("Font5Frame");
    f.reshape(0, 0, 639, 479);
    f.show();

    Font5 x = new Font5();
    f.add("Center", x);
    x.init();
    x.start();
  }

  // Constructor
  public  Font5()
  {
  }

} // end class Font5
```

Examine the second portion of bold code in the previous listing. The chart label, axis labels, and legend labels are included in this portion of code. For this application, each bar value will represent data on a particular month. The months can be accessed sequentially, as is done in this application, or one at a time.

Next, three TimesRoman fonts are created with the following portion of code.

```
// create fonts
titlefont = new Font("TimesRoman", Font.BOLD, 36);
labelfont = new Font("TimesRoman", Font.PLAIN, 14);
legendfont = new Font("TimesRoman", Font.ITALIC, 10);
```

The chart title and axis labels are drawn next. For example, the title can be drawn and centered in the window with the following portion of code.

```
// draw and center chart title
graphic.setFont(titlefont);
fm = getFontMetrics(titlefont);
graphic.drawString(charttitle,
                   165 - (fm.stringWidth(charttitle)/2),
                   -340);
```

The value 165 represents the center of the bar chart proper. To center a line of text, the application needs to move to the left of this center by one-half the width of the string being used for the chart title. Ah, FontMetrics to the rescue. Here the **stringWidth()** member function is used to obtain information on the width of the string. This process must be used because proportional fonts, such as TimesRoman, will not produce equal string widths for strings made up of various characters. This is because an "i" in TimesRoman is not as wide as a "w," for example.

A good bar chart application will allow you to identify individual bar values. Here the developer has a choice. The bar value can be drawn within the bar proper, under the bar, above the bar, or in a legend. The first option is not a good choice since the bar can be very small, not allowing the bar value to be drawn. If drawn under the bar, the label can interfere with the horizontal axis label or, if long enough, run into a neighboring label. Drawing above the bar presents its own set of programming problems as the bar heights vary up and down. The best choice is to draw a legend to the right of the bar chart itself.

The user can identify which legend label goes with a bar because a small rectangle of the proper bar's color is drawn in the legend table, too.

Here is the portion of code that creates the legend for this application.

```
// draw, fill and label chart legend
graphic.setFont(legendfont);
for (int i = 0; i < numBars; i++) {
  graphic.setColor(barColor[i]);  // set fill color
  graphic.fillRect(360, -300 + (i * 30), 15, 15);

  // first bar will be for March
  graphic.setColor(Color.black);  // set font color
  graphic.drawString(legend[i + 2], 380,
                     -290 + (i * 30));
}
```

As you can see, there is no secret to creating a legend. The rectangle is drawn in the proper color and the legend label is drawn to its right. A new location is selected, and the next group is drawn.

Examine Figure 12.5, however, and see what a legend adds to the value of a bar chart application.

## Java Lingo

*fixed*—a fixed font, like Courier, means that all characters occupy the same cell width. An "i" takes up just as much space as a "w." The earliest versions of Windows used fixed fonts.

*name*—a font name refers to the name associated with the font. Currently, Helvetica, Dialog, TimesRoman, Symbol, and Courier are available with the resources provided by Borland.

*point* size— font size is measured in points. A 12 point font is very common. The larger the point size the larger the font.

*proportional*—a proportional font, like Helvetica and TimesRoman, provides a proportional amount of space

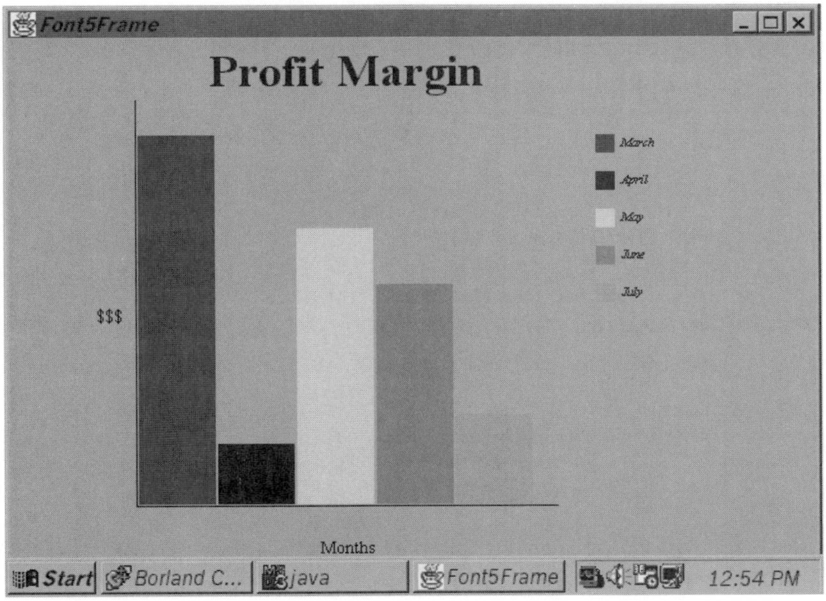


**Figure 12.5:** Adding a title, axis labels, and labels to a bar chart application.

for each character. Thus an "i" requires less horizontal width than a "w". Windows now uses proportional fonts.

*style*—font style refers to whether the font is normal, bold, italic, or a combination of the three.

# 13

# Abstract Window Toolkit and Menu Design

Microsoft Windows Graphical User Interface (GUI) provides a consistent appearance to all Windows applications. You are familiar with the design of a standard window that includes a title bar, client area, borders, and various system buttons. A window can also include a menu bar, scroll bars, a variety of different window styles, and so on. Users have come to depend on the use of the familiar Windows GUI.

The Abstract Window Toolkit (AWT) gives Java's programmers the ability to create applets and applications within a graphical user interface which provides programming components similar to those provided to Microsoft Windows programmers. A Java programmer can create canvases, panels, frames, menus, and even objects that look like standard Windows dialog boxes. Additionally, controls such as scroll bars, check boxes, radio buttons, and text fields can be used in any Java project.

In this chapter you will learn about the many aspects of the AWT, how to use it to control the Java environment and then build several applets and applications with various layout features and menus to demonstrate AWT features.

## From the Beginning

You have been working with various pieces of the AWT since the beginning of this book. Have you noticed that the following line of code is added to each applet or application you developed with the Borland Java AppExpert?

```
import java.awt.*;
```

This line of code allowed you to access all of the classes provided in the AWT package. These classes hold all of the graphical functions and procedures needed when working in the GUI. For example, you have already used the Color.class, Font.class, Frame.class, Graphics.class, and Image.class in earlier programming examples. If you were certain that your applet or application needed access to only a few specific classes, code size could be reduced by using statements such as the following:

```
import java.awt.Font;
import java.awt.Graphics;
```

You can examine the contents of these classes by unzipping the SRC.ZIP file provided by Borland. If you performed a default installation of your Borland C++ compiler and added the Java option, this file can probably be found at:

```
C:BC5JAVASCR.ZIP
```

We recommend that you unzip a copy of this file in a separate subdirectory since the unzipped contents comprise many individual files. The individual unzipped files will have a .JAV file extension. These ASCII files can be examined with almost any editor. For example, if you wanted to examine the contents of the Font class, you would bring the FONT.JAV file into the editor.

## Why Now?

You might very well be asking the question, "If we've already done so much work with the AWT, why have the authors waited until now to explain the details of the AWT as it relates to a windowing environment"? That's a good question that has a fairly simple answer. The Borland Java AppExpert created a default applet or application that was simple enough to allow us to experiment with many Java components. All GUI environments provide font, graphics functions, text capabilities, and so on. By keeping the AWT overhead as simple as possible, the Java AppExpert allowed you to focus on those aspects of the Java language.

Now, as we begin to approach the task of creating interactive Java applets and applications, more horsepower will be required from the AWT.

## What Is Seen and Used in Java

The Borland AppExpert has provided a launching ground for each applet or application developed in this book. This has helped us keep each project consistent in appearance and, hopefully, made your task of learning the Java language that much simpler. If you have built your applets and applications with the techniques we have suggested throughout this book, your Java code can be used as either an applet or a standalone Java application.

Standalone Java applications require the creation of a frame. A frame is required if the application is to draw text or graphics on the screen. The Java AppExpert provides the following code to aid in the creation of a simple drawing surface.

```
// For running standalone
  public static void main(String[] argv)
  {
    // Create the frame and launch Menu2
    Frame f = new Frame("Menu2Frame");
    f.reshape(100, 100, 200, 100);
    f.show();

    Menu2 x = new Menu2();
    f.add("Center", x);
    x.init();
    x.start();
  }
```

The previous code is not required if you are building just an applet. The Applet Viewer provides the default drawing surface and is specified in the HTML file, also produced by the Java AppExpert. Thus, if the parameters in the **reshape()** member function are changed, in the previous listing, the new parameters will affect only standalone Java applications. If you want to achieve the same results with an applet, you will have to change the values given in the HTML file. At least, that's the way it has been to this point, working with the basic Borland Java AppExpert code.

In the following sections, you'll learn the Java concepts that will allow you to gain more control over the environment you are working in. Once you have mastered these concepts, you will be able to build applications and applets that can take on the appearance of a regular Microsoft Windows program, if you desire, and give your project true interactive capabilities.

## Component

The Component class is an abstract class that encapsulates all of the components of the visual interface. On a smaller scale, this Java class is nearly the equivalent of the Borland Object Windows Library (OWL) for C++ Windows programmers. All other classes for the visual interface are derived from the abstract Component class.

```
Hierarchy:
Abstract Component Class -
```

***Note:*** *The term component is used frequently in Java to refer to user interface (UI) components such as buttons, and check boxes. While these UI components are part of the hierarchy of the Component class, they are not abstract Component classes in their own right. We prefer to call them controls, as is done in Windows.*

## Container

The Container class is an abstract class derived from the Component class. Other classes are, in turn, derived from the Container class, such as the Panel class, Frame class and Dialog class.

```
Hierarchy:
Abstract Component Class -
  Abstract Container Class
```

## Panel

The Panel class is derived from the Container class and is used to produce a generic container. An applet, for example, may use several panels, created with the Panel class. These panels can then contain several canvases, additional panels, and so on. Panels typically contain multiple UI components or controls.

```
Hierarchy:

Abstract Component Class -
  Abstract Container Class
    Panel Class
```

Panels can contain additional panels. Frames, too, can contain multiple panels. The following portion of code illustrates how two panels can be added to a frame.

```
Class MyFrame extends Frame

MyFrame(String title) {
  super("Multiple panels in a frame");

  setLayout(new BorderLayout());
  Panel PanelEast = new Panel();
  Panel PanelWest = new Panel();
  add("East", PanelEast);
  add("West", PanelWest);
    .
    .
    .
}
```

The created panels are placed on the right-hand edge (East) and left-hand edge (West) of the frame by the layout manager. The use of the layout manager will be discussed in this chapter.

## Frame

A Frame class is derived from the Window class, which is in turn derived from the abstract Container Class. Frames are similar to panels but are Windows in their own right. A frame is considered a top-level window containing, as a minimum, a title. Frames are provided with a default layout. This layout is a BorderLayout. The concept of layouts will be explained shortly. Frames can be created moved, and resized and have menu bars just like Windows programs. Frames, like panels, can hold UI components such as buttons, check boxes, and so on.

```
Hierarchy:

Abstract Component Class -
  Abstract Container Class
    Window Class
      Frame Class
```

New or additional frames can be created easily. Here is a small portion of code that adds a new frame to an applet or application.

```
// initialize upon entry
Public void init()
{
    .
    .
    .
  Frame myframe = new Frame("An additional frame");
  myframe.resize(100, 200);
  myframe.show();
    .
    .
    .
}
```

This portion of code would create a new frame, identified as *myframe*, sized to 100 by 200 pixels. The **show()** member function is used to make the frame visible.

## Canvas

The Canvas class is derived from the abstract Component class and provides a drawing surface for other UI components or controls. Panels and frames can contain multiple canvases.

```
Hierarchy:
```

```
Abstract Component Class -
  Canvas Class
```

New or additional canvases are easy to create and add to an applet or application. Here is a small portion of code that creates a new canvas.

```
NewCanvas newcanvas;
    .
    .
    .
class NewCanvas extends Canvas {
  public void paint(Graphics graphic) {
    graphic.fillOval(50, 50, 100, 100);
  }
}
```

This portion of code extends the Canvas class to create a new canvas. The new canvas uses **paint()** to draw a filled oval on the canvas.

## UI Components

User Interface (UI) components include check boxes, buttons, menus, dialog boxes, and so on. Note: Under Microsoft Windows, the same types of items are called controls.

```
Hierarchy:

Abstract Component Class -
  Button, Check Box, Choice Menu Classes, and so on.
```

The following portion of code illustrates how a two buttons can be added and modified slightly.

```
// initialize upon entry
Public void init()
{
    .
    .
    .
  Button On = new Button("Turn machinery on");
  Button Off = new Button("Turn machinery off");
  add(On);
  add(Off);
```

```
    On.reshape(20, 20, 40, 40);
     .
     .
     .
}
```

Most UI components, with the exception of menus, which are covered in this chapter, will be discussed in detail in Chapter 14.

## Layout

Java was designed to create applets and applications that operate across many platforms. Java applets and applications are unlike Microsoft Windows applications. Windows applications operate with the benefit of a whole operating system designed to specific specifications. Java applets and applications must exist across many operating systems and platforms. That leads to an immediate problem. For example, Windows handles the hardware interfacing that resolves differences between EGA, VGA, and SVGA screen resolutions. Therefore, if you draw a round oval in the upper corner of an SVGA screen it will still be a round circle on an EGA screen. Java doesn't have that total degree of luxury.

It would be possible to design full screen Java applets or applications on an SVGA screen that would be a total disaster if run on a VGA screen. The Java solution to the problem is to employ a *layout manager* to aid in the resolution of these types of problems. The layout manager does not resolve problems in the manner in which you probably think it might. It resolves problems by constraining the types of layouts you are permitted. Initially, this will sound like a design nightmare, especially if you are a Windows programmer. You'll find, however, that things will work rather smoothly.

A layout manager manages the placement of components within a panel. Since multiple panels are permissible in a Java applet or application, so are multiple layout managers. Since multiple panels and layout managers are possible, it is almost always possible to design your screens exactly the way you wish them to appear. There are five basic styles used as layout managers. These are BorderLayout, CardLayout, FlowLayout, GridLayout, and GridBagLayout. Insets, while not a style of layout manager, are often discussed here because they provide component spacing within the panel.

## BorderLayout

The BorderLayout class provides four fixed areas, around the edges of a panel. These fixed areas are labeled North, West, South, and East. A fifth central area varies in size with the panel and is designated as Center. Figure 13.1 shows a border layout, with all five areas marked.

The following code shows an example of how the BorderLayout can be used to position four buttons. The four buttons are located on the top, bottom, and side borders of the screen.

```
//-----------------------------------------------------------
// Border Demo of BorderLayout
// Copyright 1996, All rights reserved
// Nineveh National Research
// Version: 1.0
// Author: Pappas and Murray
// Created: 4/16/96
//-----------------------------------------------------------
```

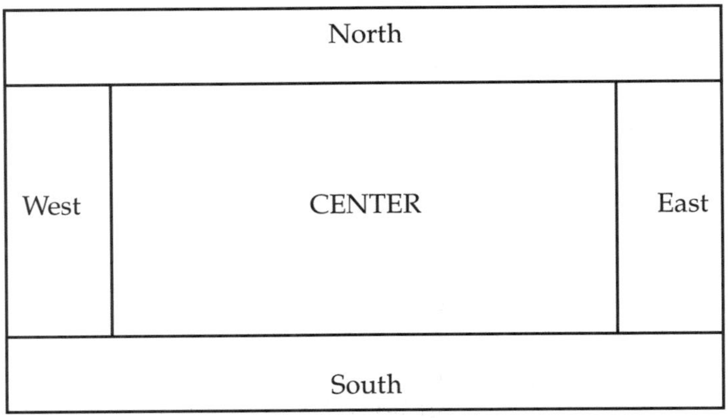


**Figure 13.1:** The BorderLayout class provides four fixed and one variable area for designating the layout of a panel.

```
import java.awt.*;
import java.applet.Applet;

public class Border extends Applet implements Runnable
{

  // initialize
  public void init()
  {
    setLayout(new BorderLayout());
    add("West", new Button("Left Button"));
    add("East", new Button("Right Button"));
    add("North", new Button("Top Button"));
    add("South", new Button("Bottom Button"));

  }

  public boolean action(Event event, Object object)
  {
    if (event.target instanceof Button) {
      newColor();
      return true;
    } else
    return false;
  }

  void newColor()
  {
    setBackground(Color.yellow);
    this.repaint();
  }

  // Implements Runnable Interface
  public void run()
  {
  }

  // For running standalone
  public static void main(String[] argv)
  {
    // Create the frame and launch Border
    Frame f = new Frame("BorderFrame");
    f.reshape(0, 0, 639, 479);
    f.show();

    Border x = new Border();
    x.init();
    f.add("Center", x);
```

```
    x.start();
  }

  // Constructor
  public  Border()
  {
  }

} // end class Border
```

The application or applet is functional. Push on any of the four buttons and the central portion of the window will turn yellow. There is only a small portion of code required to implement the border layout, as you can see in the following partial listing:

```
setLayout(new BorderLayout());
add("West", new Button("Left Button"));
add("East", new Button("Right Button"));
add("North", new Button("Top Button"));
add("South", new Button("Bottom Button"));
```

The layout is set with a call to the **setLayout()** member function, and then each button is added with a call to the **add()** member function. Figure 13.2 shows the output from this application.

In order to make the buttons functional, a technique for interfacing with them is required. In this, and the remaining examples in this section, a very simple event handler is used. Later in this chapter, event handling will be discussed in detail.

If you desire to have a gap placed between buttons, simply specify the gap in pixels, as shown next:

```
setLayout(new BorderLayout(20, 15));
```

In this case, a gap of 20 pixels would be placed between horizontal boundaries and 15 pixels between vertical boundaries.

## CardLayout

The CardLayout class is unique in the sense that not all areas are visible to the user at the same time. Card layouts usually involve the use of multiple panels that are displayed one at a time, like the top card in a deck of cards. Figure 13.3 shows the concept of a card layout. Only the top area is visible to the user.

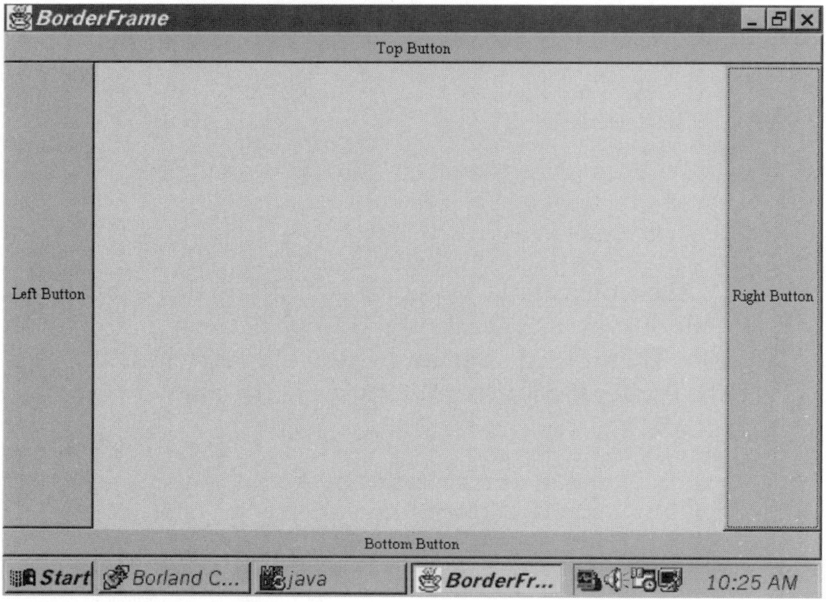


**Figure 13.2:** The BorderLayout class is used to place four buttons.

The following code shows an example of how the CardLayout can be used to position a new button on each of three panels. The buttons are placed on the top center portion of each panel.

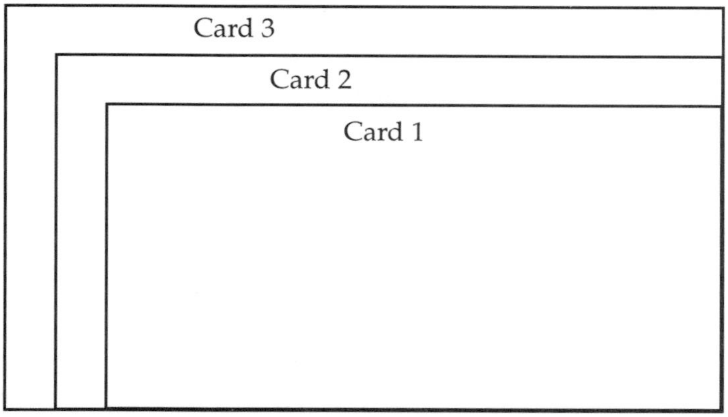


**Figure 13.3:** The CardLayout class makes only the top area visible.

```
//-----------------------------------------------------------
// Card Demo of CardLayout
// Copyright 1996, All rights reserved
// Nineveh National Research
// Version: 1.0
// Author: Pappas and Murray
// Created: 4/16/96
//-----------------------------------------------------------

import java.awt.*;
import java.applet.Applet;

public class Card extends Applet implements Runnable
{

  // initialize
  public void init()
  {
    CardLayout mycard = new CardLayout();
    setLayout(mycard);

    Panel one = new Panel();
    add("1", one);
    Panel two = new Panel();
    add("2", two);
    Panel three = new Panel();
    add("3", three);

    one.add(new Button("First Button"));
    two.add(new Button("Second Button"));
    three.add(new Button("Third Button"));

    // shows third panel
    mycard.show(this, "3");
  }

  // Implements Runnable Interface
  public void run()
  {
  }

  // For running standalone
  public static void main(String[] argv)
  {
    // Create the frame and launch Card
```

```
    Frame f = new Frame("CardFrame");
    f.reshape(0, 0, 639, 479);
    f.show();

    Card x = new Card();
    x.init();
    f.add("Center", x);
    x.start();
  }

  // Constructor
  public  Card()
  {
  }

} // end class Card
```

One new button is installed at the top center of each of three panels. There is only a small portion of code required to implement the card layout, as you can see in the following partial listing:

```
CardLayout mycard = new CardLayout();
setLayout(mycard);
```

The layout is set with a call to the **setLayout()** member function. It is then necessary to create each of the three panels, as shown in the following partial listing:

```
Panel one = new Panel();
add("1", one);
Panel two = new Panel();
add("2", two);
Panel three = new Panel();
add("3", three);
```

The panels are added with a call to the **add()** member function. Finally, the three buttons are created and added to the named panel with the following code:

```
one.add(new Button("First Button"));
two.add(new Button("Second Button"));
three.add(new Button("Third Button"));
```

Only one "card" or panel is visible at a time. The following portion of code makes the third panel visible:

```
// shows third panel
mycard.show(this, "3");
```

Figure 13.4 shows the output from this application.

Other panels can be viewed with the **show()** member function or other member functions, such as **last()**, provided in the CardLayout class.

## FlowLayout

The FlowLayout class adds UI components (controls) to a panel in consecutive order. UI components are added to the first row, until it is filled. Additional UI components are then added to the second row, and so on. Alignment can be designated as LEFT, CENTER, or RIGHT. Gaps can also be set vertically or horizontally between UI components by specifying the number of pixels in the gap. Figure 13.5 shows a flow layout with three buttons centered in the first row.

The following code shows an example of how the FlowLayout can be used to position three buttons. The three buttons are centered along the top portion of the window, by default.

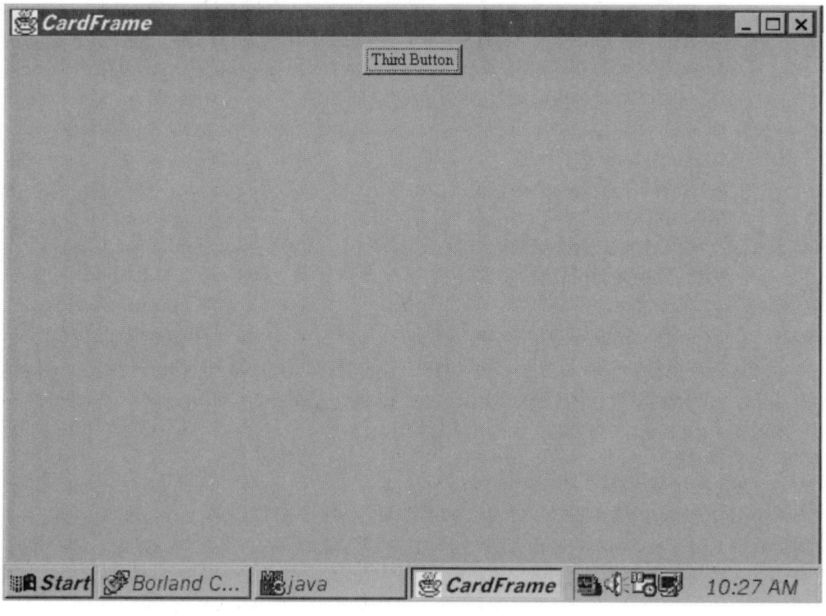


**Figure 13.4:** The CardLayout class places three buttons, each on a separate panel.

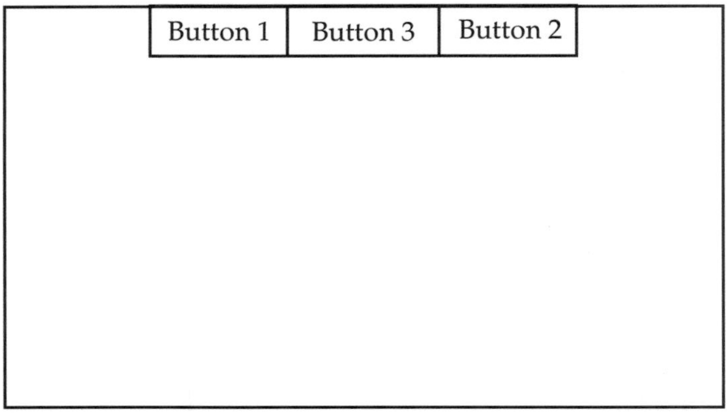


**Figure 13.5:** The FlowLayout class allows UI components to be added row by row.

```
//----------------------------------------------------------
// Flow Demo of FlowLayout
// Copyright 1996, All rights reserved
// Nineveh National Research
// Version: 1.0
// Author: Pappas and Murray
// Created: 4/16/96
//----------------------------------------------------------

import java.awt.*;
import java.applet.Applet;

public class Flow extends Applet implements Runnable
{

  // initialize
  public void init()
  {
    setLayout(new FlowLayout());
    add(new Button("First Button"));
    add(new Button("Second Button"));
    add(new Button("Third Button"));
  }

  public boolean action(Event event, Object object)
  {
    if (event.target instanceof Button) {
      newColor();
```

```
      return true;
    } else
    return false;
  }

  void newColor()
  {
    setBackground(Color.yellow);
    this.repaint();
  }

  // Implements Runnable Interface
  public void run()
  {
  }

  // For running standalone
  public static void main(String[] argv)
  {
    // Create the frame and launch Flow
    Frame f = new Frame("FlowFrame");
    f.reshape(0, 0, 639, 479);
    f.show();

    Flow x = new Flow();
    x.init();
    f.add("Center", x);
    x.start();
  }

  // Constructor
  public  Flow()
  {
  }

} // end class Flow
```

The application or applet is functional. Push on any of the three buttons and the remaining portion of the window will turn yellow. Only a small portion of code is required to implement the flow layout.

```
// initialize
public void init()
{
  setLayout(new FlowLayout());
```

```
  add(new Button("First Button"));
  add(new Button("Second Button"));
  add(new Button("Third Button"));
}
```

The layout is set with a call to the **setLayout()** member function, and then each button is added with a call to the **add()** member function. Figure 13.6 shows the output from this application.

The simple event handler, used earlier, is used to intercept the button events.

If you desire to change text alignment or place a gap between buttons any of the following variations are acceptable for the flow layout.

```
setLayout(new FlowLayout());                  // Centered
setLayout(new FlowLayout(FlowLayout.LEFT));  // Left Just.
setLayout(new FlowLayout(FlowLayout.RIGHT)); // Right Just.
setLayout(new FlowLayout(FlowLayout.LEFT), 20, 15); // Gap
```

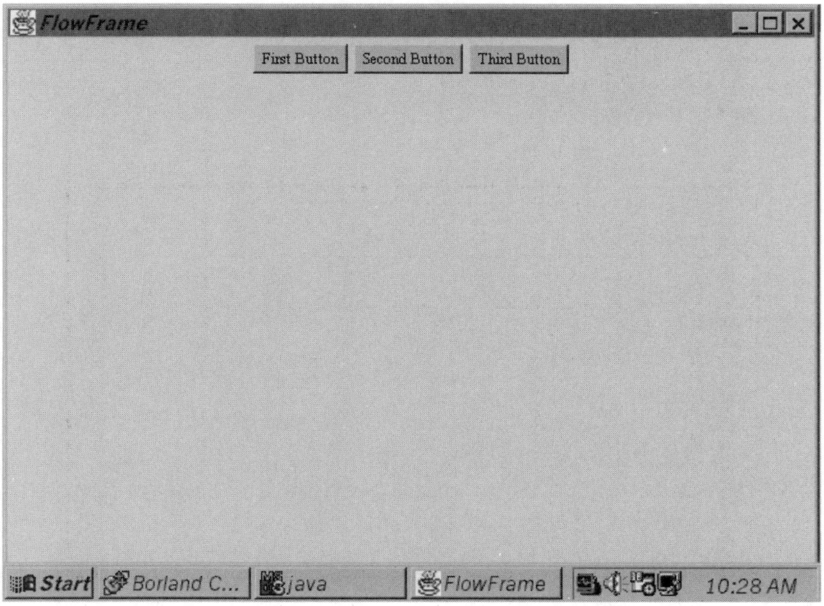


**Figure 13.6:** The FlowLayout class is used to place and center three buttons.

In the final case, a gap of 20 pixels would be placed between horizontal boundaries and 15 pixels between vertical boundaries of any UI components.

## GridLayout

The GridLayout class allows a portion of a panel to be partitioned into cells, designated by rows and columns. UI components are added to a cell, sequentially from left to right and then top to bottom, each time the **add()** member function (method) is invoked. Gaps between cells can be specified in pixels. Figure 13.7 shows a grid layout with a small gap between row and column components.

The following code shows an example of how the GridLayout can be used to position three buttons. The grid is designated as having four rows and one column. Thus, the three buttons will be placed in this grid starting at the top of the window. The fourth grid position will not have a button.

```
//--------------------------------------------------------
// Grid Demo GridLayout
// Copyright 1996, All rights reserved
// Nineveh National Research
// Version: 1.0
```

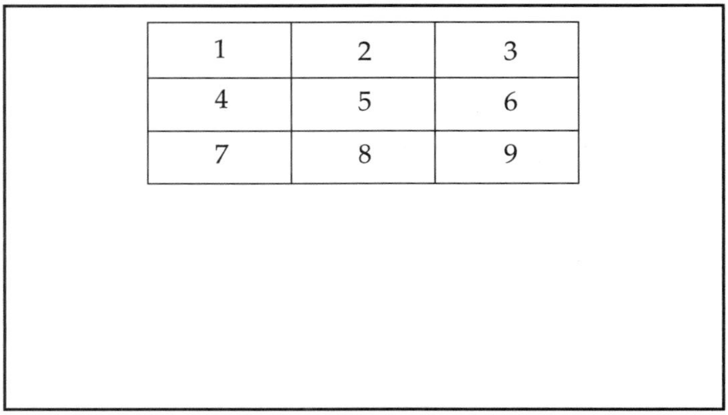


**Figure 13.7:** The GridLayout class allows UI components to be added to cells specified by row and column.

```
// Author: Pappas and Murray
// Created: 4/16/96
//-----------------------------------------------------------

import java.awt.*;
import java.applet.Applet;

public class Grid extends Applet implements Runnable
{

  // initialize
  public void init()
  {
    setLayout(new GridLayout(4, 1, 20, 20));
    add(new Button("Top Button"));
    add(new Button("Middle Button"));
    add(new Button("Bottom Button"));
  }

  public boolean action(Event event, Object object)
  {
    if (event.target instanceof Button) {
      newColor();
      return true;
    } else
    return false;
  }

  void newColor()
  {
    setBackground(Color.yellow);
    this.repaint();
  }

  // Implements Runnable Interface
  public void run()
  {
  }

  // For running standalone
  public static void main(String[] argv)
  {
    // Create the frame and launch Grid
    Frame f = new Frame("GridFrame");
    f.reshape(0, 0, 639, 479);
    f.show();
```

```
    Grid x = new Grid();
    x.init();
    f.add("Center", x);
    x.start();
  }

  // Constructor
  public  Grid()
  {
  }

} // end class Grid
```

The application or applet is functional. Push on any of the three buttons and the bottom portion of the window will turn yellow. Only a small portion of code is required to implement the grid layout.

```
// initialize
public void init()
{
  setLayout(new GridLayout(4, 1, 20, 20));
  add(new Button("Top Button"));
  add(new Button("Middle Button"));
  add(new Button("Bottom Button"));
}
```

The layout is set with a call to the **setLayout()** member function, and then each button is added with a call to the **add()** member function. Again, the first parameter specified in the **GridLayout()** call represents the number of rows in the grid. The second number represents the number of columns. The remaining two numbers are optional and represent the gap between UI components. Figure 13.8 shows the output from this application.

The event handler used in earlier examples is used to intercept the button events.

## GridBagLayout

The GridBagLayout class is actually a variation on the GridLayout class. The GridBagLayout class operates in a similar manner to the GridLayout class, but offers the additional capability of specifying the format used in each cell. Formatting for

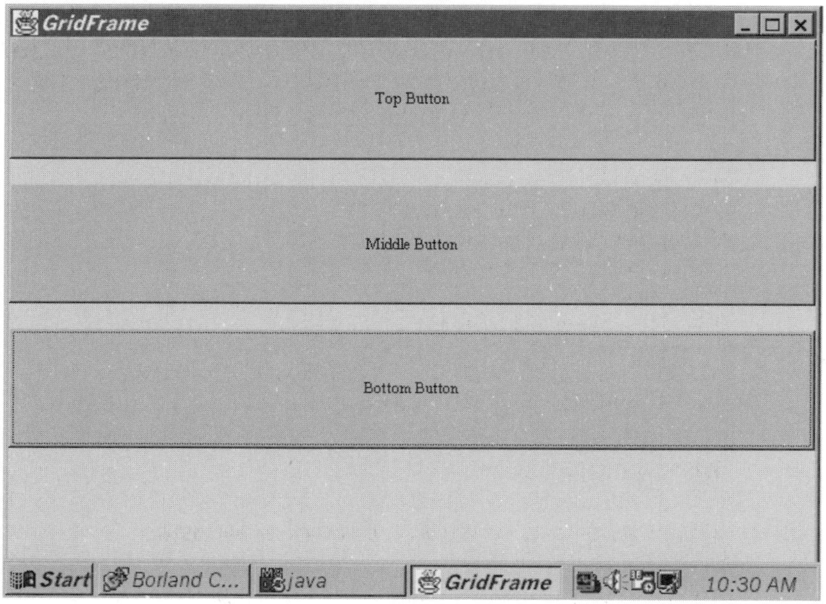


**Figure 13.8:** The GridLayout class is used to place three buttons, one on top of the other.

this class is achieved with the help of the GridBagConstraints class.

Figure 13.9 shows a grid bag layout with each cell formatted differently.

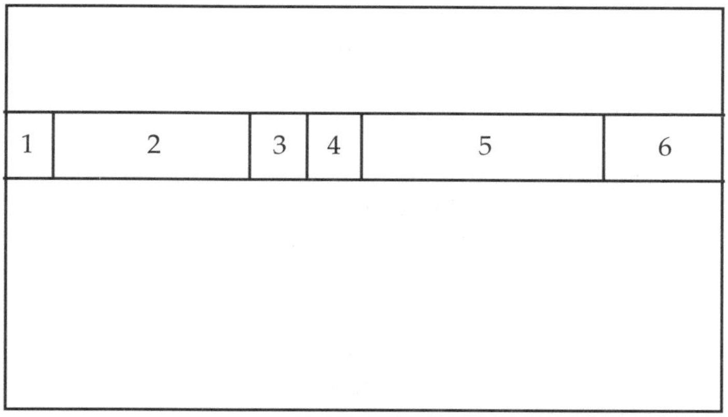


**Figure 13.9:** The GridBagLayout class in conjunction with the GridBagConstraints class allows individual cells to be formatted differently.

The following code shows an example of how the GridBag-Layout can be used to format and position three buttons. The buttons will be placed horizontally. The width of the buttons will vary since each is assigned a different weight.

```
//-----------------------------------------------------------
// GridBag Demo of GridbagLayout
// Copyright 1996, All rights reserved
// Nineveh National Research
// Version: 1.0
// Author: Pappas and Murray
// Created: 4/16/96
//-----------------------------------------------------------

import java.awt.*;
import java.applet.Applet;

public class GridBag extends Applet implements Runnable
{
  Button But1, But2, But3;

  // initialize
  public void init()
  {
    GridBagLayout gridbag = new GridBagLayout();
    GridBagConstraints cts = new GridBagConstraints();

    setLayout(gridbag);
    cts.fill = GridBagConstraints.BOTH;

    cts.weightx = 0.0;
    But1 = new Button("Button #1");
    gridbag.setConstraints(But1, cts);
    add(But1);

    cts.weightx = 1.0;
    But2 = new Button("Button #2");
    gridbag.setConstraints(But2, cts);
    add(But2);

    cts.weightx = 2.0;
    But3 = new Button("Button #3");
    gridbag.setConstraints(But3, cts);
    add(But3);
    resize(639, 479);
  }
```

```
  public boolean action(Event event, Object object)
  {
    if (event.target instanceof Button) {
      newColor();
      return true;
    } else
    return false;
  }

  void newColor()
  {
    setBackground(Color.yellow);
    this.repaint();
  }

  // Implements Runnable Interface
  public void run()
  {
  }

  // For running standalone
  public static void main(String[] argv)
  {
    // Create the frame and launch GridBag
    Frame f = new Frame("GridBagFrame");
    f.reshape(0, 0, 639, 479);
    f.show();

    GridBag x = new GridBag();
    x.init();
    f.add("Center", x);
    x.start();
  }

  // Constructor
  public  GridBag()
  {
  }

} // end class GridBag
```

The application or applet is functional. Push on any of the three buttons and the remaining portion of the window will turn yellow. The new layout and required constraints are implemented with the following code.

```
// initialize
public void init()
```

```
{
  GridBagLayout gridbag = new GridBagLayout();
  GridBagConstraints cts = new GridBagConstraints();

  setLayout(gridbag);
  cts.fill = GridBagConstraints.BOTH;
```

The GridBagConstraints class *fill* parameter, *cts.fill* in this example, is used to determine how a component will fill a display area when the component's display area is larger than the component's requested size. Valid values include NONE, BOTH, HORIZONTAL, and VERTICAL.

The *anchor* parameter, not used in this example, is used to determine how a component will be placed in a display area when the component is smaller than the display area. Valid values include CENTER, NORTH, NORTHEAST, EAST, SOUTHEAST, SOUTH, SOUTHWEST, WEST, and NORTHWEST.

As the buttons are added horizontally, the weight constraint for each button is varied. This changes the horizontal cell width so that each button is proportionally larger.

```
  cts.weightx = 0.0;
  But1 = new Button("Button #1");
  gridbag.setConstraints(But1, cts);
  add(But1);
   .
   .
   .
  cts.weightx = 1.0;
   .
   .
   .
  cts.weightx = 2.0;
```

The *weight* parameter, *cts.weightx* in this example, is used to specify a resizing weight. Default values of zero are used for unspecified values of weightx and weighty. If either value is unspecified, components are centered. determine how a component will fill a display area when the component's display area is larger than the component's requested size. Valid values include NONE, BOTH, HORIZONTAL, and VERTICAL.

Additional parameters can be studied by close examination of the GridBagLayout and GridBagConstraints classes. Figure

13.10 shows how the *fill* and *weight* parameters affect this example, when placing buttons.

The event handler used in earlier examples is used to intercept the button events and color the window when any of the buttons is pushed.

## Insets

Insets can be used to provide a borderlike effect around a group of controls. First, select the layout desired, then override the **insets()** method. Figure 13.11 shows three buttons with insets and gaps included.

The height and width of the inset are specified in pixels. For example, the following portion of code will provide a left and right inset of 20 pixels and a top and bottom inset of 15 pixels.

```
Public Insets insets()
{
```

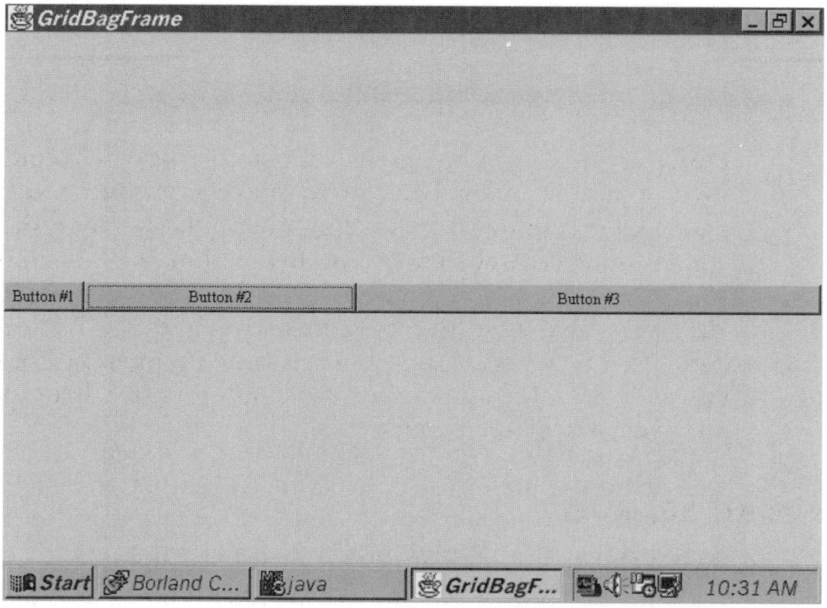


**Figure 13.10:** The GridBagLayout() is used to add three different-width buttons to the window.

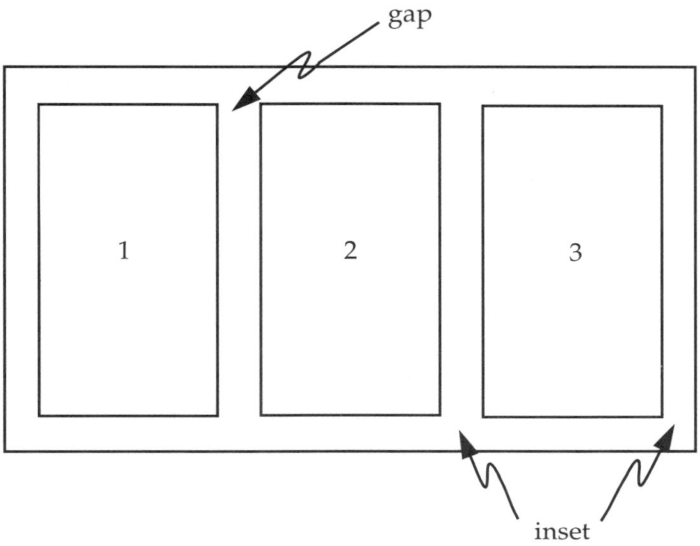


**Figure 13.11:** Insets can provide a border effect around a group of UI components.

```
  return new Insets(20, 15, 20, 15);
}
```

## Events

Many of the examples used to illustrate various layouts have used a simple event handler to process button information. Every UI component, or control, must interface with the application or applet to be useful. In this section, we'll examine two techniques for processing returned by UI components. The examples in this section will focus on buttons, but other UI components can be handled in the same manner. In Chapter 14 you will see additional examples dealing with UI components and their associated events.

### The action() Method

The **action()** member function provides one of the simplest techniques for interfacing an application or applet to UI component events. One form for the **action()** member function is:

```
public boolean action(Event event, Object object)
{
  if(event.target instanceof UI_component)
  {
    .
    .
    .
    return true;
  } else
  return false;
}
```

The **if()** statement will test the event against the object that generated the event by examining the instance variable. For example, if the *UI_component* was BUTTON, and a button had been pushed, the **if()** statement would have been true. Additional UI components will be examined in the next chapter.

Thus, for our simple layout examples that simply tested to see if any button had been pushed, the **action()** member function's code took the following form:

```
public boolean action(Event event, Object object)
{
  if (event.target instanceof Button) {
    newColor();
    return true;
  } else
  return false;
}
```

Here, our only concern was whether a button had been pushed, but not which button. How could we determine whether a particular button had been pushed?

That could have been done by casting the *object* to a String and comparing it to the actual button name. For example, in the flow layout application:

```
if((String)object.equals("First Button"))
{
   .
   .
   .
} else
if((String)object.equals("Second Button"))
```

.
.
.

You'll see a variation of this technique in the menu bar example which follows shortly.

## The handleEvent() Method

The **handleEvent()** member function provides another simple technique for interfacing an application or applet to UI component events. The most popular form for the **handleEvent()** member function involves the use of a switch-case statement. Windows programmers are very familiar with switch-case statements because they are used frequently when processing menu and dialog box information. The flow layout example could process the first two buttons in the following manner.

```
public boolean handleEvent(Event event)
{
  switch(event.id)
  {
    case Event.ACTION_EVENT:
    {
      if (event.object == "First Button") {
        .
        .
        .
        return true;
      } else
      if (event.object == "Second Button") {
        .
        .
        .
        return true;
      } else
        return false;
    }
    default:
      return false;
  }
}
```

You will, no doubt, choose one style to use when writing event handlers. There is no major advantage of one over the other. We prefer the use of the **action()** member function, because of the simplicity of the coding.

## A Simple Menu

The GUI Windows interface has become very popular because correctly written applications take on a consistent look and feel. We all know, for example, what to expect when we click the mouse on the File menu in a word processing, spreadsheet, or database application.

One of the important reasons for developing a good understanding of Java's AWT is so that our Java applications and applets can have the same consistent look and feel. In the previous sections, you have learned about panels, frames, layouts, and placement of UI components (controls). You have even learned how to interact with these components. What's the point? You are now on the verge of being able to create applications and applets that are interactive. The first step toward creating interactive applications and applets is to provide menu capabilities similar to those of Microsoft Windows.

The Menu1 project, shown in the next listing, is one of the simplest menu techniques possible. Here a menu will allow the user to select one of three shape sizes. When the shape size is selected, the new shape will be drawn in the window.

Examine the following listing. Notice, too, that an event handler has been included to process the information returned when a menu selection is made.

```
//-------------------------------------------------------
// Menu1 Experimenting with menus
// Copyright 1996, All rights reserved
// Nineveh National Research
// Version: 1.0
// Author: Pappas and Murray
// Created: 4/9/96
//-------------------------------------------------------

import java.awt.*;
import java.applet.Applet;
```

```
public class Menu1 extends Applet implements Runnable
{

  int index;

  // initialize upon entry
  public void init()
  {
    Choice menuchoice = new Choice();

    menuchoice.addItem("small");
    menuchoice.addItem("Medium");
    menuchoice.addItem("LARGE");
    add(menuchoice);
  }

  // prepare to intercept menu item
  public boolean action(Event event, Object arg)
  {
    switch (event.id)
    {
      case Event.ACTION_EVENT: {
        if (event.arg == "small") {
          index = 0;
        } else
        if (event.arg == "Medium") {
          index = 1;
        } else
        if (event.arg == "LARGE") {
          index = 2;
        } else {
          repaint();
          return false;
        }
      }
      default:
        repaint();
        return true;
    }
  }

  // This routine handles the painting
  public void paint(Graphics graphic)
  {
    if (index == 0) {
      graphic.fillOval(50, 50, 100, 100);
    } else
```

```
    if (index == 1) {
      graphic.fillOval(50, 50, 200, 200);
    } else
    if (index == 2) {
      graphic.fillOval(50, 50, 300, 300);
    } else
      graphic.drawString("This event never happened",
                         10, 10);
  }

  // Implements Runnable Interface
  public void run()
  {
  }

  // For running standalone
  public static void main(String[] argv)
  {
    // Create the frame and launch Menu1
    Frame f = new Frame("Menu1Frame");
    f.reshape(0, 0, 639, 479);
    f.show();

    Menu1 x = new Menu1();
    f.add("Center", x);
    x.init();
    x.start();
  }

  // Constructor
  public  Menu1()
  {
  }

} // end class Menu1
```

If you have been following the examples in this chapter, you have probably realized that the component that adds the menu is contained in the following portion of code.

```
// initialize upon entry
public void init()
{
  Choice menuchoice = new Choice();

  menuchoice.addItem("small");
  menuchoice.addItem("Medium");
```

```
    menuchoice.addItem("LARGE");
    add(menuchoice);
}
```

This portion of code implements a choice list. A choice list is created by using the Choice class. A choice list consists of a number of menu items. The currently selected item appears in a small window. When that window is clicked upon with the mouse, all of the remaining choices become visible. New items, from the list, can be selected just as in Microsoft Windows.

In the previous listing, the choice list is named *menuchoice*. Menu items are added to the menu with the **addItem()** member function. Figure 13.12 shows the default choice list and the figure corresponding to that menu item.

Figure 13.13 shows the whole choice list for this example.

The menu was placed without the use of a layout. If the grid layout from an earlier example is used, the choice list will be added in the fourth row, as specified in the following partial listing.

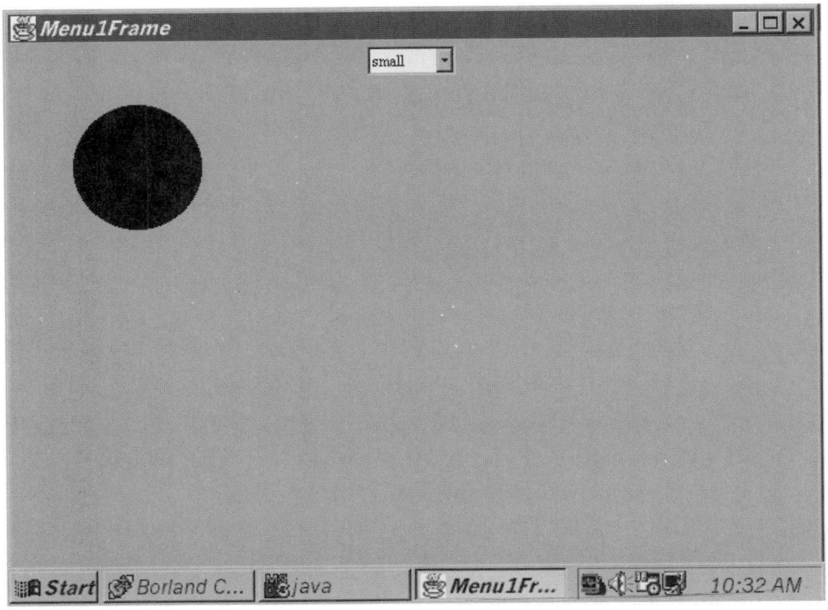


**Figure 13.12:** The first item in the choice list serves as the initial menu value.

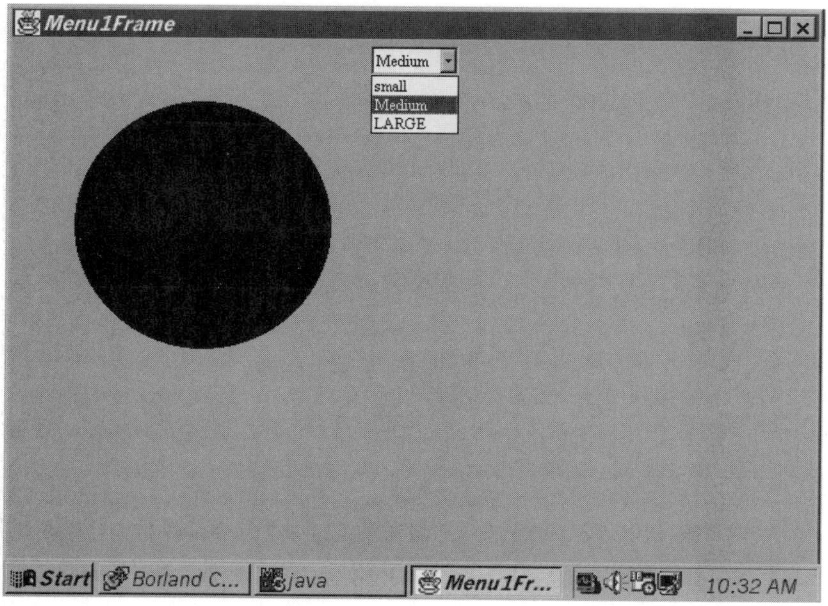


**Figure 13.13:** The whole choice list for this example includes three size options.

```
// initialize
public void init()
{
  setLayout(new GridLayout(4, 1, 20, 20));
  add(new Button("Top Button"));
  add(new Button("Middle Button"));
  add(new Button("Bottom Button"));

  Choice menuchoice = new Choice();
  menuchoice.addItem("small");
  menuchoice.addItem("Medium");
  menuchoice.addItem("LARGE");
  add(menuchoice);
}
```

Compare Figure 13.14 to Figure 13.8, shown earlier. With layouts, you will have control over the placement of all UI components, even choice lists!

But wait! The menus you are most familiar with, from Microsoft Windows, have a menu contained in a menu bar. When the menu name is clicked, the menu pops up. You'll see how to add a menu bar in the next example.

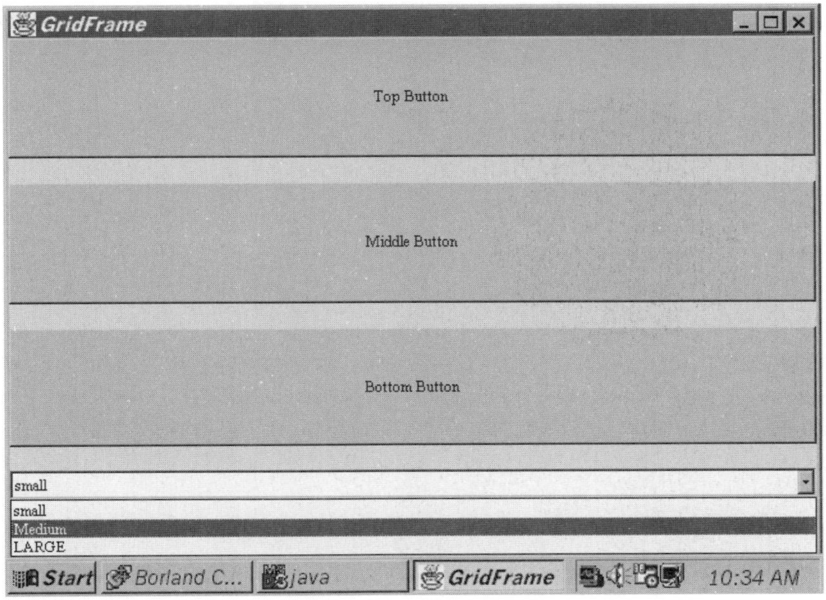


**Figure 13.14:** The choice list (menu) is added on the fourth row of the grid as specified in the gridLayout class.

## A MENU BAR

Menu bars give your application or applet an appearance that closely matches Microsoft Windows applications.

As you learned earlier, the Frame class produces a window most closely associated with a Microsoft Windows window. The Window class, which is similar to a panel, can also produce a top-level window. Both of these classes serve as the base for adding menu bars to applications and applets. To add a menu bar, it is necessary to create a frame.

In the following listing, three classes help add the menu bar to this application. Each is shown in a bold font. You know from earlier work in this chapter that the **action()** member function is responsible for processing the menu item selection events. A new canvas, *newcanvas*, is created from the Canvas class to allow drawing to occur in the new frame. That leaves the class *MyFrame* as the class that actually implements the menu bar. Examine the complete listing below, and note each of these portions of code.

```
//----------------------------------------------------------
// Menu2 A Simple Menu Bar
// Copyright 1996, All rights reserved
// Nineveh National Research
// Version: 1.0
// Author: Pappas and Murray
// Created: 4/12/96
//----------------------------------------------------------

import java.awt.*;
import java.applet.Applet;

public class Menu2 extends Applet implements Runnable
{
  static int index;

  // initialize upon entry
  public void init()
  {
    new MyFrame("");
  }

  // Implements Runnable Interface
  public void run()
  {
  }

  // For running standalone
  public static void main(String[] argv)
  {
    // Create the frame and launch Menu2
    Frame f = new Frame("Menu2Frame");
    f.reshape(100, 100, 200, 100);
    f.show();

    Menu2 x = new Menu2();
    f.add("Center", x);
    x.init();
    x.start();
  }

  // Constructor
  public  Menu2()
  {
```

```
  }

} // end class Menu2

class MyFrame extends Frame
{
  NewCanvas newcanvas;
  MyFrame(String title) {
    super("Simple Menu Bar");
    add("Center", newcanvas = new NewCanvas());
    reshape(0, 0, 639, 479);
    MenuBar menubar = new MenuBar();
    setMenuBar(menubar);
    Menu size = new Menu("Size");
    size.add(new MenuItem("small"));
    size.add(new MenuItem("Medium"));
    size.add(new MenuItem("LARGE"));
    size.add(new MenuItem("-"));
    size.add(new MenuItem("Close"));
    menubar.add(size);
    show();
  }

  public boolean action(Event event, Object object) {
    String tag = (String)object;
    if(tag == "small") {
      Menu2.index = 0;
      newcanvas.repaint();
      return true;
    } else
    if(tag == "Medium") {
      Menu2.index = 1;
      newcanvas.repaint();
      return true;
    } else
    if(tag == "LARGE") {
      Menu2.index = 2;
      newcanvas.repaint();
      return true;
    } else
    if(tag == "Close") {
      System.exit(0);
    } else
      return false;
    return true;
  }
}
class NewCanvas extends Canvas {
```

```
  public void paint(Graphics graphic) {
    if (Menu2.index == 0) {
      graphic.fillOval(50, 50, 100, 100);
    } else
    if (Menu2.index == 1) {
      graphic.fillOval(50, 50, 200, 200);
    } else
    if (Menu2.index == 2) {
      graphic.fillOval(50, 50, 300, 300);
    } else
      graphic.drawString("This event never happened",
                         10, 10);
  }
}
```

The code used in the *MyFrame* class establishes a new canvas, new frame, new menu bar, and adds several menu items to the menu bar.

```
class MyFrame extends Frame
{
  NewCanvas newcanvas;
  MyFrame(String title) {
    super("Simple Menu Bar");
    add("Center", newcanvas = new NewCanvas());
    reshape(0, 0, 639, 479);
    MenuBar menubar = new MenuBar();
    setMenuBar(menubar);
    Menu size = new Menu("Size");
    size.add(new MenuItem("small"));
    size.add(new MenuItem("Medium"));
    size.add(new MenuItem("LARGE"));
    size.add(new MenuItem("-"));
    size.add(new MenuItem("Close"));
    menubar.add(size);
    show();

  }
```

The new canvas is created with the *NewCanvas* class. The new frame, *MyFrame*, uses **super()** to allow this class to communicate with the constructor of the parent class. This statement allows the objects we wish to draw to be drawn on the new canvas. A **MenuBar()** member function is used to create a new menu bar named *menubar*. The **setMenuBar()** member function places the menu bar in the new frame. A menu, named *size*, is placed on the menu bar with the **Menu()** member function. Individual menu items are identified with the **MenuItem()** member function and added to the menu bar with the **add()** member function. Once all of the items are created, the menu bar is added with a call to the **add()** member function. The **show()** member function makes the menu bar and menu visible.

The remainder of the code, used in this application, is similar to code discussed in previous example in this chapter. Because of the techniques we used in developing this code, the project can be used as either a standalone application or applet. Figure 13.15 shows a sample screen show with the pop-up menu extended.

Chapter 14 will extend the concepts you have learned here by introducing you to additional UI components (controls), menus, and dialog boxes.

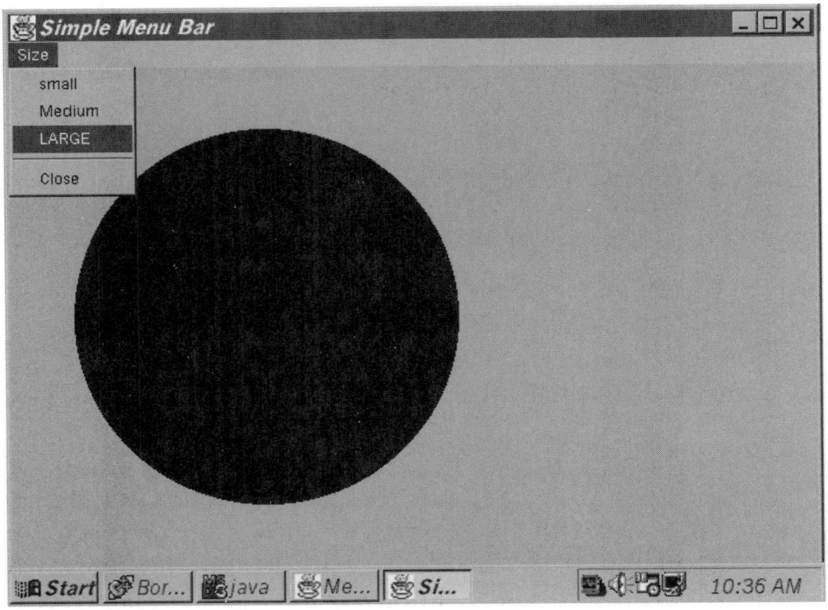


**Figure 13.15:** A simple menu bar and menu are created in this Java project.

## JAVA LINGO

*AWT*—the Abstract Window Toolkit gives Java's programmers the ability to create applets and applications within a graphical user interface.

*canvas*—a canvas provides a drawing surface for other UI components or controls. Panels and frames can contain multiple canvases.

*component*—in the strictest sense, the Component class is an abstract class that encapsulates all of the components of the GUI visual interface.

*container*— another abstract class from which other classes are derived. These include the Panel class, Frame class, Dialog class, and so on.

*event*—in the context of this chapter, an event is a notification by a UI component that some action has taken place. Applications and applets must provide event handlers in order to process information between applications, applets, and UI components.

*frame*—frames are considered windows in their own right. A frame typically has a title, sizing buttons, and very frequently a menu bar.

*gap*—refers to the space provided between UI components in various layout configurations. Usually specified in pixels.

*GUI*—a Graphical User Interface provides an environment that supports graphical elements such as font, graphics functions, text capabilities, and so on.

*inset*— refers to the space that can be used for a border around a group of UI components in a specific layout situation.

*layout*—how UI components are placed within a panel or frame. Predefined layouts prevent problems with screen configurations when moving from one hardware platform to another.

*panel*—the Panel class is used to produce a generic container for an application or applet. Panels can then contain several canvases, additional panels, UI components, and so on.

*UI component*—these items include buttons, check boxes, and so on. They are called controls by Windows programmers.

*window*—similar to a panel, but with the added ability of creating a top-level window.

# 14

# UI Components and Dialog Boxes

In the previous chapter, we studied the Abstract Window Toolkit (AWT) from a macro perspective. This perspective allows us to view the components of the AWT in terms of large-scale components such as panels, frames, layouts, and menus. In this chapter, we'll concentrate on items such as buttons, check boxes, labels, and dialog boxes.

The individual UI components, described in this chapter, are called *controls* by Windows programmers. We'll use that name exclusively from this point on, to avoid confusion with Java's abstract Component class, which was also discussed in the previous chapter.

Much of the work in the last chapter focused on how to control the Java screen and produce menus similar to those used in Windows applications. Recall that it is Windows' consistent appearance and operation that have made it so successful. In this chapter, we'll continue our study of controls with that thought in mind. In Windows programs, controls are most frequently found in dialog boxes. We'll study individual controls and then investigate how they can be used to create effective dialog boxes for data entry.

By the conclusion of this chapter, you will have learned the techniques for creating truly interactive applications and applets. Dialog boxes will give those projects a consistent look and operation, similar to their Windows counterparts.

## Buttons

Buttons were the only control discussed in Chapter 13. As a matter of fact, they were used in most of the examples. Why? Buttons are one of the easiest controls to implement. A control similar to this is often referred to as a pushbutton by Windows programmers. The following portion of code was extracted from an application discussed in the previous chapter.

```
// initialize
  public void init()
  {
    setLayout(new FlowLayout());
    add(new Button("First Button"));
    add(new Button("Second Button"));
    add(new Button("Third Button"));
  }
```

In this listing three buttons are added by using the Button class, as you can see from the bold text. When a user pushes (clicks the mouse on) a button, the button is activated and generates an event. You learned how to intercept these events in the previous chapter, too. The **getLabel()** and **setLabel()** member functions are available in this class for manipulating button labels. Figure 14.1 shows the placement of several buttons.

The **reshape()** method can be used to change the size of the button control once it is created.

## Check Boxes and Radio Buttons

In Windows, there are two closely associated controls; Checkboxes and Radio Buttons. Under Windows, multiple items in a group can be checked. Radio buttons, however, permit only one item in a group to be selected.

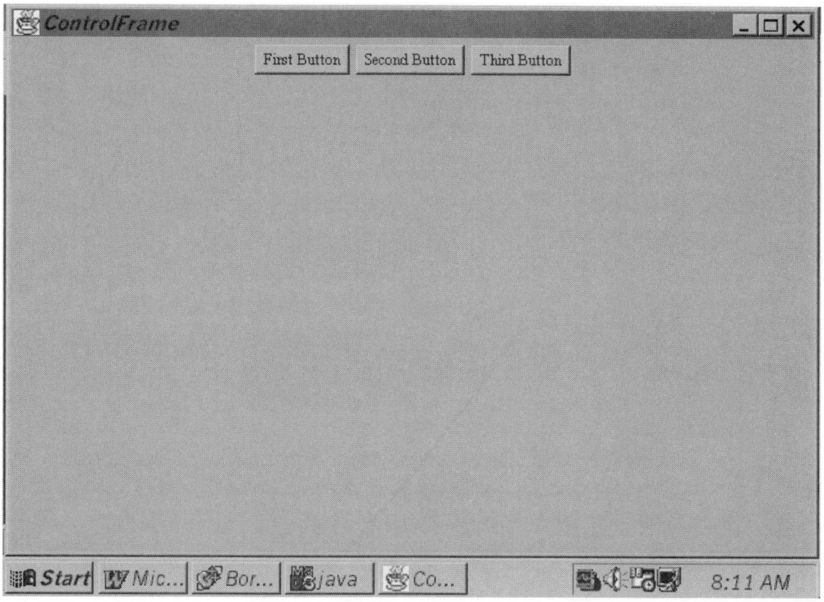


**Figure 14.1:** Buttons are easy to implement. Layout managers can determine a button's placement.

Java uses two forms of Checkboxes. One form behaves like a Windows Checkbox and the other like a Windows Radio button. Java uses a small rectangle symbol for the true check box form. However, instead of an "x," a small check symbol is used within the rectangle to indicate selected items. When being used as a Radio button, a small circle symbol is used with a central dot to indicated a selected item. These appear just like Windows check boxes and radio buttons, otherwise. In the first check box form, called a nonexclusive Checkbox, the check box functions like a normal Windows Checkbox where multiple items can be selected at the same time. The other form of Java Checkbox, called an exclusive Checkbox, function more like Windows Radio buttons where only a single selection is permitted.

Several nonexclusive check box items are added with the following code. Here multiple items can be checked.

```
// initialize
  public void init()
  {
    setLayout(new FlowLayout());
```

```
    add(new Checkbox("Background"));
    add(new Checkbox("Foreground"));
    add(new Checkbox("New Font"));
  }
```

Figure 14.2 shows the placement of several check boxes.

An exclusive check box list can be created with the following portion of code. Here only one item in the group can be selected.

```
// initialize
public void init()
{
  setLayout(new GridLayout(4, 1, 20, 20));
  CheckboxGroup cbgroup = new CheckboxGroup();

  add(new Checkbox("Times Roman Font", cbgroup, false));
  add(new Checkbox("Courier Font", cbgroup, true));
  add(new Checkbox("System Font", cbgroup, false));
}
```

Figure 14.3 shows several exclusive check box items which form radio controls.

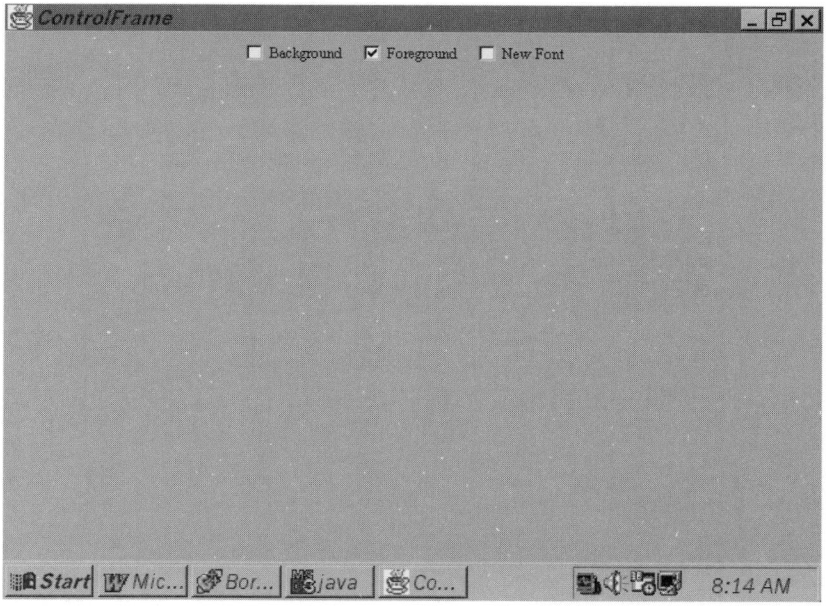

**Figure 14.2:** Multiple selections can be checked with the nonexclusive form of Checkbox control.

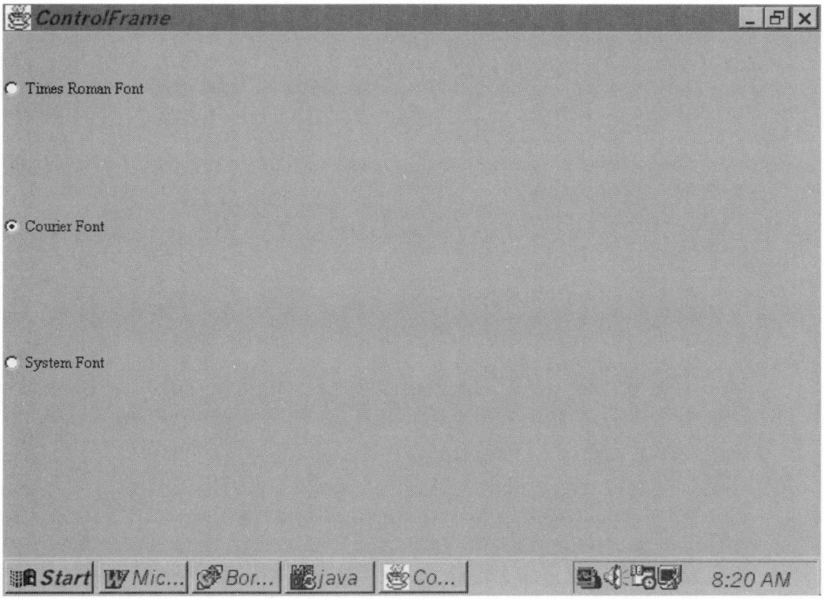


**Figure 14.3:** Only single selections can be selected with the exclusive form of Checkbox control.

In the previous example, the second item will appear checked when the check box group is drawn.

The **getLabel()**, **getState()**, **setState(boolean)**, **setCheckbox-Group(),** and **setLabel(String)** member functions are available for this class. The **getState()** and **setState()** member functions allow you to get or toggle whether a check box item is selected.

Checkbox controls usually do not generate events on their own, so you will not normally use an event handler with check boxes. They are typically used to set features for some other event, such as a color or font selection. When used in a dialog box, for example, they set features that are intercepted when an Okay button is pushed to close the dialog box.

## Scroll Bars

The Scrollbar class allows individual scroll bars to be drawn and managed easily in a Java application or applet. It is also possible to simulate the action of a slide control with the Scroll-bar class. Scroll bars and slide controls have up-down or left-right arrows, a slider (thumb), and a range of motion which the slider can be moved through. Figure 14.4 shows a vertical scroll bar and a simulated horizontal slide control.

The syntax for creating a scroll bar can taken on any of the following three forms. These constructors are described as follows:

```
Scrollbar();
Scrollbar(int orientation);
Scrollbar(int orientation, int initial_value, int thumb_size,
        int minimum, int maximum);
```

The first form will create a vertical scroll bar with a default thumb size. The initial minimum and maximum values will be set to 0. The second form allows the orientation to be set. HORIZONTAL or VERTICAL can be used. The third form gives the greatest control over the appearance of a scroll bar. Orientation is specified in the same manner as it is for the second form. The second parameter gives the initial thumb position. The third parameter gives the thumb size. Larger value are used to represent the need for less overall scrolling. Small values are used to

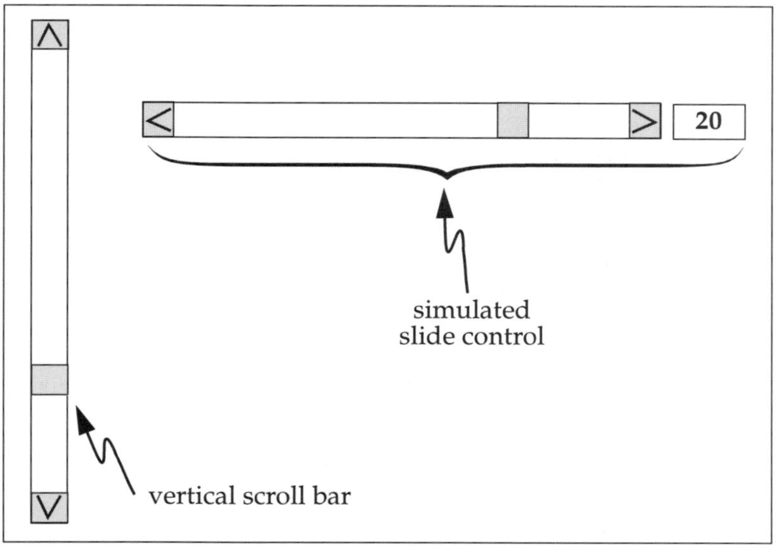


**Figure 14.4:** Scroll bars can be vertical or horizontal. When used in conjunction with a label control, their combined action simulates a slide control.

indicate a large amount of scrolling. The final two parameters specify the minimum and maximum extents of the scroll as the thumb position is moved from top to bottom or left to right.

The placement of scroll bar controls and slide controls is dependent upon the layout manager selected. Various layout managers were discussed in Chapter 13.

In the following application, a vertical and a horizontal scroll bar are created. They are placed with the border layout manager. The vertical scroll bar simulates a slide control, reporting the current scroll position to the screen. Examine the bold portions of code in the following listing.

```
//-------------------------------------------------------
// Scroll Scroll bar and slide control demo
// Copyright 1996, All rights reserved
// Nineveh National Research
// Version: 1.0
// Author: Pappas and Murray
// Created: 4/21/96
//-------------------------------------------------------
import java.awt.*;
import java.applet.Applet;

public class Scroll extends Applet implements Runnable
{
  Label myinit;
  Scrollbar VScroll, HScroll;
  int vert, horz;

  // initialize
  public void init()
  {
    setLayout(new BorderLayout());
    myinit = new Label("20");
    add("North", myinit);

    VScroll = new Scrollbar(Scrollbar.VERTICAL, 20,
                            1, 0, 400);
    add("West", VScroll);

    HScroll = new Scrollbar(Scrollbar.HORIZONTAL, 20,
                            1, 0, 400);
    add("South", HScroll);

    show();
  }
```

```
  public boolean handleEvent(Event event)
  {
    String newVvalue, newHvalue;
    if (event.target == VScroll ||
        event.target == HScroll) {
      vert = VScroll.getValue();
      horz = HScroll.getValue();
      newVvalue = String.valueOf(vert);
      myinit.setText(newVvalue);

      repaint();
      return true;
    } else
    return false;
  }

  public void paint(Graphics graphic)
  {

    graphic.fillOval(160 - horz, 120 - vert, 200, 300);
  }
  // Implements Runnable Interface
  public void run()
  {
  }

  // For running standalone
  public static void main(String[] argv)
  {
    // Create the frame and launch Scroll
    Frame f = new Frame("ScrollFrame");
    f.reshape(0, 0, 639, 480);
    f.show();

    Scroll x = new Scroll();
    f.add("Center", x);
    x.init();
    x.start();
  }

  // Constructor
  public  Scroll()
  {
  }

} // end class Scroll
```

A slide control is simulated with a combination of a label control and a scroll bar control. Examine the following portion of code and note where both are created. Remember, too, that with a border layout, controls can be placed on any border of the screen.

```
// initialize
public void init()
{
  setLayout(new BorderLayout());
  myinit = new Label("20");
  add("North", myinit);

  VScroll = new Scrollbar(Scrollbar.VERTICAL, 20,
                          1, 0, 400);
  add("West", VScroll);

  HScroll = new Scrollbar(Scrollbar.HORIZONTAL, 20,
                          1, 0, 400);
  add("South", HScroll);

  show();
}
```

The message handler is similar to examples discussed in Chapter 13. Note, however, in the following portion of code that the current thumb position for the vertical scroll bar is retrieved with a call to **getValue()** and then used to set the value shown in the label control with the **setText()** member function.

```
public boolean handleEvent(Event event)
{
  String newVvalue, newHvalue;
  if (event.target == VScroll ||
      event.target == HScroll) {
    vert = VScroll.getValue();
    horz = HScroll.getValue();
    newVvalue = String.valueOf(vert);
    myinit.setText(newVvalue);

    repaint();
    return true;
  } else
  return false;
}
```

The scroll bars can now be used to scroll a text document, an image retrieved from a file, or a simple graphics shape. In our

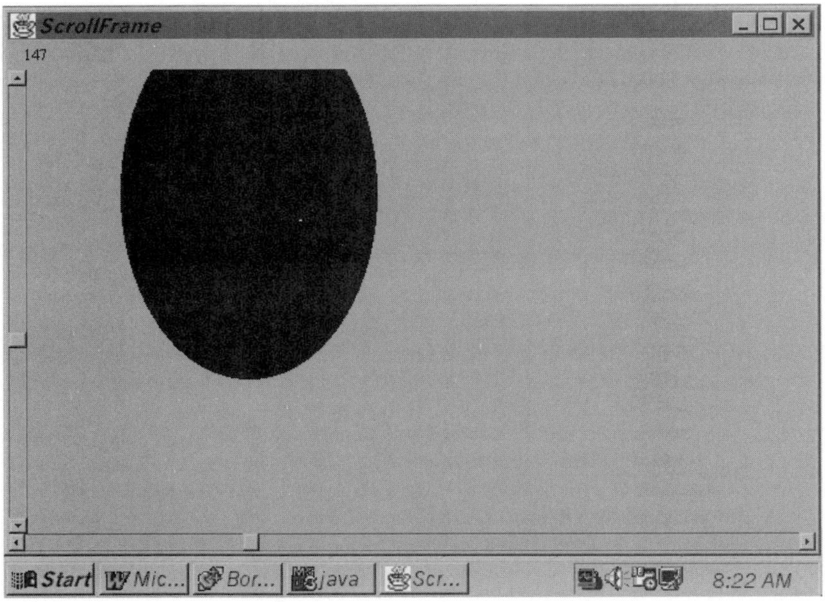


**Figure 14.5:** Two scroll bars are used to scroll about a graphics figure. The vertical scroll bar simulates a slide control.

example, we'll use the scroll bar information to allow scrolling an oval shape.

```
public void paint(Graphics graphic)
{
  graphic.fillOval(160 - horz, 120 - vert, 200, 300);
}
```

Figure 14.5 shows the scroll bar code during execution.

One final interesting note: if you resize the window, Java will resize both scroll bars accordingly.

## Lists

A list control will manage a list of items added by the programmer. If the list control is created in an exclusive form, the user will be able to select only one item from the list. If the list control is created in an nonexclusive form, multiple items in the list can be selected. Recall that check box controls provided similar forms.

If the number of items in a list control exceeds the size of the list control, Java will automatically add and manage a vertical scroll bar for the list control. The List class provides two forms via the following constructors:

```
List();
List(int number, boolean value);
```

The first constructor creates a list control that operates in the exclusive form, allowing only one selection from the list. The second constructor allows the number of items to be displayed to be specified as the first parameter, and whether the list control will operate in exclusive or nonexclusive form by the second parameter. If the second parameter is false, the list control operates in exclusive form. If true, multiple items can be selected from the list.

Here is a small portion of code that will implement two list controls. The first list control will display two items in the list and allow the user to select one item at a time. The second list control will display three items in the list and allow the user to make multiple selections at the same time. Remember that the layout manager selected will often determine the limits of what is visible on the screen.

```
public void init()
{
  setLayout(new FlowLayout(FlowLayout.CENTER, 20, 20));

  List res_list = new List(2, false);
  res_list.addItem("640 x 480");
  res_list.addItem("800 x 600");
  res_list.addItem("1024 x 768");
  res_list.addItem("1024 x 1024");

  List font_char = new List(3, true);
  font_char.addItem("bold");
  font_char.addItem("italic");
  font_char.addItem("redline");
  font_char.addItem("underscore the whole line");

  add(res_list);
  add(font_char);
}
```

Figure 14.6 shows the two list controls created in this example.

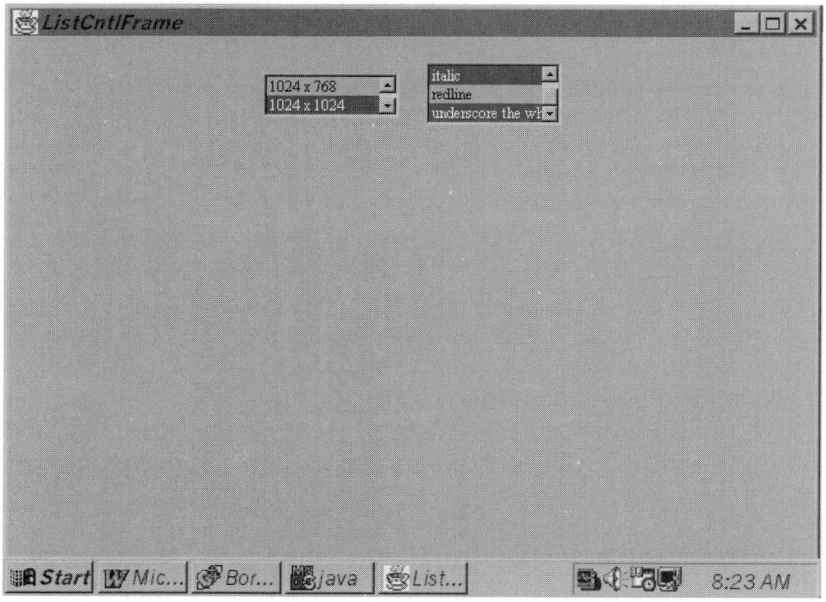


**Figure 14.6:** List controls allow single and/or multiple selection of list items.

Additional member functions such as **countItems()**, **getItem()**, **getSelectedItem()**, **select()**, and so on give this control added flexibility. For example, **countItems()** can be used to return the number of items in a list. Examine this class to investigate other member functions.

## TEXT AREAS

A text area control will manage text in an area of the screen. A text area control is created by the TextArea class. This class manages the text area and will provide and activate scroll bars when needed.

```
// initialize
public void init()
{
  String mystring = "     Text can be entered in a "+
                    "text area from a simple string, "+
                    "like this example or from a "+
                    "file.n"+
```

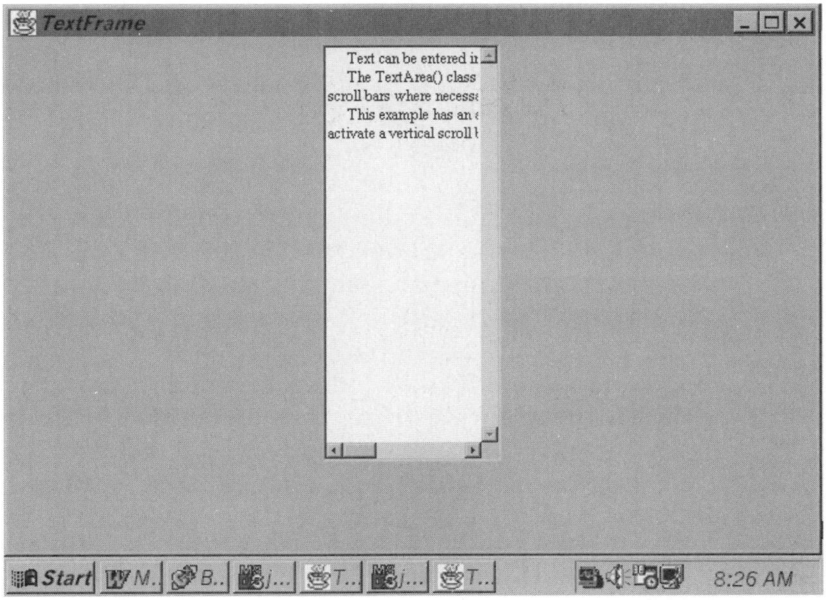


**Figure 14.7:** The TextArea class provides and activates scroll bars to help manage text on the screen.

```
                    "     The TextArea() class will "+
                    "automatically add and managen"+
                    "scroll bars where necessary.n"+
                    "     This example has an active "+
                    "horizontal scroll bar. There is "+
                    "not sufficient text ton"+
                    "activate a vertical scroll bar.n";

  TextArea text = new TextArea(mystring, 20, 20);
  add(text);
}
```

In this code, the TextArea class will create a text area 20 characters wide and 20 characters high within the frame. Figure 14.7 shows an example output for this code.

There are actually four variations for creating text areas with this class, based upon the supplied constructors.

```
TextArea();
TextArea(String mystring);
TextArea(int width, int height);
TextArea(String mystring, int width, int height);
```

The first form creates a text area without text with no width or height. This information, it is assumed, will be supplied at a later time. The second form creates a text area with the supplied string information, but still with no preset width or height. The third form creates a text area with a predefined size, but with no initial string information. The final form creates a text area with initial string information and a predefined size.

When the TextArea class is used in conjunction with a layout manager, the layout manager will affect what you see in the layout area.

The TextArea class provides additional methods, such as **getColumns()**, **getRows()**, **insertText(String mystring)**, and **replaceText(String mystring, int newwidth, int newheight)**. These member functions provide additional flexibility and make this control ideal for managing and displaying large amounts of text on the screen.

## Labels and Text Fields

Labels and text fields are frequently used together. The Label class allows you to draw single line string labels anywhere in the panel. It is one of the simplest controls available to the Java programmer because an event handler is never required in its implementation. Labels are frequently used to tag other controls, such as those produced by the TextField class. When labels are used in conjunction with text fields, the basic data entry component used in most dialog boxes is created.

Text fields are very similar to Windows Edit controls. They allow the user to enter string information from the keyboard. This information is usually limited to one line. The string information can be converted by the programmer to other data types. For example, 34.14 can be accepted and used as a string of characters or converted to the real number 34.14 with the appropriate routines.

### Labels

The Label class provides three forms of constructors which allow the programmer more flexibility in label entry and alignment.

```
Label();
Label(String mystring);
Label(String mystring, int myalignment);
```

By default, labels are aligned on the left. The first form simply creates an empty label. The second form creates a label with an initial string. This default string can be changed at a later date with the **setText()** method. The third form adds an alignment option. Label alignments include CENTER, LEFT, and RIGHT. RIGHT justification is often used when a label is placed to the left of a text field.

The Label class also provides additional member functions that provide additional flexibility for this class. These member functions include **getAlignment()**, **getText()**, **setAlignment()** and **setText(String newstring)**. Additionally, labels are printed in the current font and current color. The **reshape()** method can also be used to change the size of the label control.

## Text Fields

The TextField class provides four forms of constructors which allow variations in the manner in which these controls are created.

```
TextField();
TextField(int newwidth);
TextField(String mystring);
TextField(String mystring, int newwidth);
```

If no additional parameters are specified, an empty text field will be created. The *newwidth* parameter allows the number of characters, for the text field, to be set. The *mystring* parameter allows an initial string to be specified as the default.

The **getText()** and **setText(String newstring)** member functions give this class additional flexibility.

Additionally, in situations where you do not want the typed information to appear in the text field, the **setEchoCharacter()** member function can be used. For example:

```
textfield.setEchoCharacter(" ");
```

In this case, each character which appears in the text field will be a blank. If used for password entry, an asterisk (*) could be substituted for the blank character.

## A Label and Text Field Example

In the following portion of code, several Label and TextField controls are placed in the panel. As you examine the code, notice the order in which the controls are added with the **add()** member function.

```
// Initialize
public void init()
{
  Label name = new Label("User Name:",
                         Label.RIGHT);
  Label ss = new Label("Social Security Number:",
                       Label.RIGHT);
  Label id = new Label("Password:", Label.RIGHT);

  TextField namedata = new TextField(20);
  TextField ssdata = new TextField(10);
  TextField iddata = new TextField("********", 20);
  iddata.setEchoCharacter('*');

  add(name);
  add(namedata);
  add(ss);
  add(ssdata);
  add(id);
  add(iddata);
}
```

The order in which controls are added is important, as well as the initial size of the frame, since no layout method is used. This piece of code will correctly draw and place the various controls. However, since no event handler is provided, there is no way to process the information entered by the user. This example is useful because it forms the foundation for the most important data entry control available—the dialog box. Dialog boxes are covered in detail in the next section. Figure 14.8 shows our panel of label and text field controls.

## DIALOG BOXES

You learned in the previous chapter that menus are simple ways to interact with a Java application or applet. In this section you will explore a more significant means of data entry, the dialog box. You have also learned, in earlier sections of this chapter, that it is possible to place Java controls directly into an application's main panel or frame. While this is a common practice, dialog boxes are a preferable data entry technique for maintaining consistency among all Java platforms.

Dialog boxes designed for Java can contain the same types of controls Windows dialog boxes contain. This includes buttons, check boxes, radio buttons, labels, scroll bars, text fields, text areas, and so on. The dialog box gives the Java user true interactive communications with an application or applet while maintaining the consistent look and operation of the familiar Windows interface.

A dialog box is usually accessed as a menu item, in a normal Java menu. When selected as a menu item, the dialog box will appear as pop-up windows to the user. To distinguish a dialog box entry from ordinary menu items, three dots or an ellipsis (...) follow the dialog box menu item. Thus, when you view a menu and see three dots after a menu item, you know that a dialog box will follow that menu item selection.

Dialog boxes range in complexity from very simple to very complicated. About boxes are simple dialog boxes that require very little programming effort. They are used to inform the user about the application and usually contain the developer's name(s) and a copyright notice. On the other hand, dialog boxes used for data entry can be very complicated, take days to design properly, and require an extensive programming interface.

The remaining examples in this chapter will illustrate simple About and data entry dialog boxes. The Dialog1 example shows how to create an About box. The Dialog2 example shows how to use a dialog box, in conjunction with several

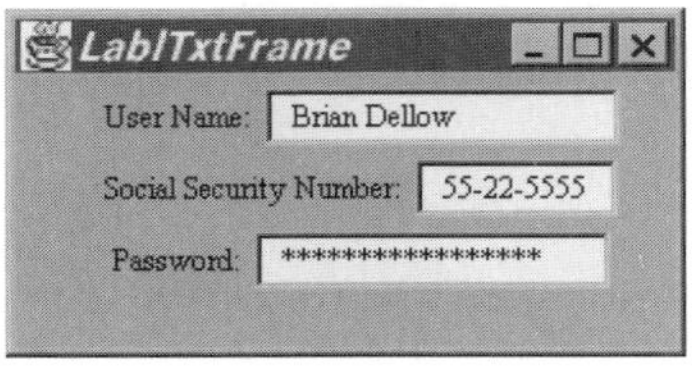


**Figure 14.8:** Careful alignment allows label controls and text field controls to form a data entry box that is the precursor to a dialog box.

controls, to retrieve a title for some simple screen graphics. Dialog3 is used to show how numeric data can be entered in a dialog box and used directly in the application or applet.

The dialog box concepts you learn in the following sections will really be put to work in the next chapter, Chapter 15, as you develop several professional quality Java applications and applets.

## Dialog 1

An About dialog box is the simplest style of dialog box possible. They consist of several lines of text, usually created with a Label control. They usually contain a single Button control, labeled "Okay." Their sole purpose is not to collect data but to inform the user regarding the application or applet they are using.

As you examine the following listing, you will notice many of the components that were present in the menu bar example from the previous chapter. This should not surprise you, as you have already learned that dialog boxes are typically accessed through a normal menu.

```
//-------------------------------------------------------
// Dialog1 Dialog About Box Demo
// Copyright 1996, All rights reserved
// Nineveh National Research
// Version: 1.0
// Author: Pappas and Murray
// Created: 4/24/96
//-------------------------------------------------------

import java.awt.*;
import java.applet.Applet;

public class Dialog1 extends Applet implements Runnable
{
  // initialize upon entry
  public void init()
  {
    new MyFrame("");
  }

  // Implements Runnable Interface
  public void run()
  {
  }
```

```
  // For running standalone
  public static void main(String[] argv)
  {
    // Create the frame and launch Dialog1
    Frame f = new Frame("Dialog1Frame");
    f.reshape(100, 100, 200, 100);
    //f.show();

    Dialog1 x = new Dialog1();
    f.add("Center", x);
    x.init();
    x.start();
  }

  // Constructor
  public  Dialog1()
  {
  }

} // end class Dialog1
class MyFrame extends Frame
{
  NewCanvas newcanvas;
  Dialog AboutDialog;

  MyFrame(String title) {
    // Add a menu bar
    super("Simple Menu Bar");
    add("Center", newcanvas = new NewCanvas());
    reshape(0, 0, 639, 479);
    MenuBar menubar = new MenuBar();
    setMenuBar(menubar);

    // Add a menu and menu items
    Menu help = new Menu("Information");
    help.add(new MenuItem("About..."));
    help.add(new MenuItem("-"));
    help.add(new MenuItem("Close"));
    menubar.add(help);

    // Add an About DialogBox
    AboutDialog = new Dialog(this, "About", true);
    AboutDialog.setLayout(new GridLayout(4, 1, 10, 10));
    AboutDialog.add(new Label("About Box Demo",
                              Label.CENTER));
    AboutDialog.add(new Label("C. Pappas and W. Murray",
                              Label.CENTER));
    AboutDialog.add(new Label("Copyright (c) 1996",
                              Label.CENTER));
```

```
      AboutDialog.add(new Button("Okay"));
      AboutDialog.reshape(200, 200, 300, 200);

      show();
    }

    public boolean action(Event event, Object object) {
      String label = (String)object;
      if (event.target instanceof Button) {
        if(label.equals("Okay")) {
          AboutDialog.hide();
        }
        return true;
      } else
      if (event.target instanceof MenuItem) {
        if(label.equals("About...")) {
          AboutDialog.show();
        } else
        if(label.equals("Close")) {
          System.exit(0);
        }
        return true;
      }
      else
        return false;
    }
  }

  class NewCanvas extends Canvas {
    public void paint(Graphics graphic) {
      // Draw a couple of shapes on canvas
      graphic.drawRect(50, 50, 100, 100);
      graphic.drawOval(200, 200, 200, 200);
    }
  }
```

A menu bar requires a separate frame, so for this application or applet a new frame is created and displayed.

A new canvas is created for the drawing surface and resized to a VGA screen size. The menu bar is then added as you can see in the following portion of code.

```
// Add a menu bar
super("Simple Menu Bar");
add("Center", newcanvas = new NewCanvas());
reshape(0, 0, 639, 479);
MenuBar menubar = new MenuBar();
setMenuBar(menubar);
```

The menu contains three menu items. These are an About..., menu bar break, and Close option. The About... option will pop-up an About dialog box when selected. The Close option will simply close the application or applet.

```
// Add a menu and menu items
Menu help = new Menu("Information");
help.add(new MenuItem("About..."));
help.add(new MenuItem("-"));
help.add(new MenuItem("Close"));
menubar.add(help);
```

The Dialog class is used to create a new dialog box. There are two versions of constructors used by the Dialog class.

```
Dialog(Frame, boolean modal);
Dialog(Frame, String title, boolean modal);
```

The Frame parameter refers to the newly created frame for the application or applet. The *title*, if used, represents the string displayed within the title bar of the dialog box. The boolean *modal* value is used to determine whether the dialog box must be closed before other screen action can take place. Modal dialog boxes are the most common dialog boxes used in both Java and Windows applications. A Modeless dialog box is typically used when the user must constantly change a value or select a particular control while the application is actually in operation. For example, a CD player application would permit you to start, stop, and pause a playback. The user would not be required to open a menu and make a dialog box selection for each choice. A boolean true marks the dialog box as a modal dialog box.

```
// Add an About DialogBox
AboutDialog = new Dialog(this, "About", true);
```

Designing a good-looking and functional dialog box can require a large investment in time. Windows programmers have the advantage of a Dialog Box editor that allows the graphical placement of controls. Java programmers do not have the advantage of such a tool—yet. Java programmers must rely on the use of a layout manager when placing Java controls. In this example, the GridLayout() class is used to place three labels and one button.

```
AboutDialog.setLayout(new GridLayout(4, 1, 10, 10));
AboutDialog.add(new Label("About Box Demo",
                          Label.CENTER));
AboutDialog.add(new Label("C. Pappas and W. Murray",
                          Label.CENTER));
AboutDialog.add(new Label("Copyright (c) 1996",
                          Label.CENTER));
AboutDialog.add(new Button("Okay"));
AboutDialog.reshape(200, 200, 300, 200);

show();
```

Those four controls are added in a vertical fashion, with each label being centered on its given grid position. As the dialog box becomes more complicated, the designer must make careful use of various layout managers.

Making a menu item selection or clicking on the button in the dialog box will trigger an event that can be intercepted and processed by the application. The dialog box is placed on the screen, when the user selects the About... menu item. Examine the following portion of code.

```
if (event.target instanceof MenuItem) {
  if(label.equals("About...")) {
    AboutDialog.show();
  } else
   .
   .
   .
```

When the user selects About..., the **show()** member function will display the dialog box. This gives the effect of popping up a dialog box. The focus is now on the dialog box, and the user can make use of any controls placed within the dialog box area. When the user has made the proper selections within the dialog box, the dialog box must be hidden. This is done with the following portion of code.

```
if (event.target instanceof Button) {
  if(label.equals("Okay")) {
    AboutDialog.hide();
  }
   .
   .
   .
```

The dialog box is hidden with a call to the **hide()** member function. If the dialog box is a modal dialog box, this is also the point where dialog box information is transferred to the application or applet. If the dialog box is modeless, another technique must be used to continuously transfer dialog box information to the application while the dialog box remains open.

To make this application or applet fully functional, some simple graphics are drawn on the canvas. Figure 14.9 shows the dialog box and the canvas for this application.

As we continue to investigate dialog boxes in the remaining two examples, we will keep our code as consistent as possible with this example. The code changes you will see for the dialog box are those required to add new functionality to the application or applet.

## Dialog 2

Dialog boxes are often used to allow the user to enter strings of text. These strings are then used as labels for charts, graphs, and other graphics presentations. The following dialog box

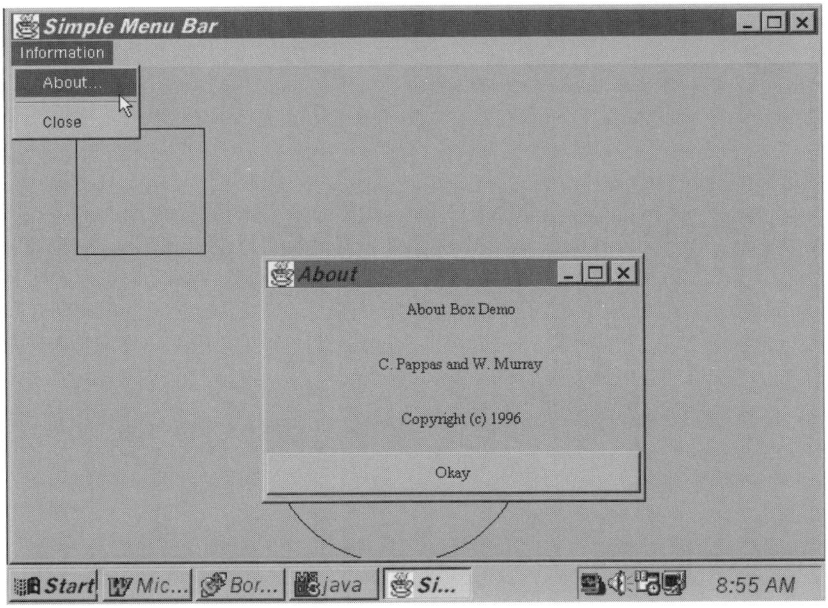


**Figure 14.9:** An About dialog box created for the Dialog1 example.

example is patterned after the previous About box example. In this case, however, the dialog box has been expanded to include a label, text field control, and two buttons. The text field control will allow the user to enter a string which will later be used on the canvas as a label for the graphics image. Two buttons are included. One functions as a normal "Okay" button, while the other is a "Cancel" button. Cancel buttons allow users to back out of a dialog box change they have decided not to use.

Examine the following code listing. The items shown in a boldface are the portions of the example you should focus on. You'll notice that this code is patterned after the menu bar example in the previous chapter. All we've added is the new dialog box.

```
//-----------------------------------------------------------
// Dialog2 Dialog Text Entry Demo
// Copyright 1996, All rights reserved
// Nineveh National Research
// Version: 1.0
// Author: Pappas and Murray
// Created: 4/26/96
//-----------------------------------------------------------

import java.awt.*;
import java.applet.Applet;

public class Dialog2 extends Applet implements Runnable
{
  // initialize upon entry
  public void init()
  {
    new MyFrame("");
  }

  // Implements Runnable Interface
  public void run()
  {
  }

  // For running standalone
  public static void main(String[] argv)
  {
    // Create the frame and launch Dialog2
    Frame f = new Frame("Dialog2Frame");
```

```
    f.reshape(100, 100, 200, 100);
    //f.show();

    Dialog2 x = new Dialog2();
    f.add("Center", x);
    x.init();
    x.start();
  }

  // Constructor
  public  Dialog2()
  {
  }

} // end class Dialog2

class MyFrame extends Frame
{
  NewCanvas newcanvas;
  Dialog TextDialog;
  TextField NewText;
  static int index;
  static String mystring;

  MyFrame(String title) {
    // Add menu bar
    super("Simple Menu Bar");
    add("Center", newcanvas = new NewCanvas());
    reshape(0, 0, 639, 479);
    MenuBar menubar = new MenuBar();
    setMenuBar(menubar);

    // Add Menu and Menu Items
    Menu size = new Menu("Size");
    size.add(new MenuItem("small"));
    size.add(new MenuItem("Medium"));
    size.add(new MenuItem("LARGE"));
    size.add(new MenuItem("-"));
    size.add(new MenuItem("Close"));
    menubar.add(size);

    Menu info = new Menu("Information");
    info.add(new MenuItem("Text..."));
    menubar.add(info);

    // Add Label, TextField and Buttons
    TextDialog = new Dialog(this, "Text", true);
    TextDialog.setLayout(new GridLayout(2, 2, 10, 10));
```

```
      TextDialog.add(new Label("Enter Title:", Label.RIGHT));
      NewText = new TextField(20);
      TextDialog.add(NewText);
      TextDialog.add(new Button("Okay"));
      TextDialog.add(new Button("Cancel"));
      TextDialog.reshape(200, 200, 200, 100);

      show();
    }

    public boolean action(Event event, Object object) {
      String label = (String)object;

      if (event.target instanceof Button) {
        if(label.equals("Okay")) {
          mystring = NewText.getText();
          TextDialog.hide();
          newcanvas.repaint();
        } else
        if(label.equals("Cancel")) {
          TextDialog.hide();
        }
        return true;
      } else
      if (event.target instanceof MenuItem) {
        if(label.equals("small")) {
          index = 0;
        } else
        if(label.equals("Medium")) {
          index = 1;
        } else
        if(label.equals("LARGE")) {
          index = 2;
        } else
        if(label.equals("Text...")) {
          TextDialog.show();
        } else
        if(label.equals("Close")) {
          System.exit(0);
        }
        newcanvas.repaint();
        return true;
      }
      else
        return false;
    }
  }
  class NewCanvas extends Canvas {
```

```
  public void paint(Graphics graphic) {
    // Draw graphics, draw entered string
    if (MyFrame.index == 0) {
      graphic.fillOval(50, 50, 100, 100);
    } else
    if (MyFrame.index == 1) {
      graphic.fillOval(50, 50, 200, 200);
    } else
    if (MyFrame.index == 2) {
      graphic.fillOval(50, 50, 300, 300);
    }
    graphic.drawString(MyFrame.mystring, 100, 400);
  }
}
```

The new dialog box is designed to draw a label and text field on one grid line, then place both buttons on the next grid line. As you design dialog boxes, you will probably have to experiment with layout managers and reshape the dialog box until it suits your design.

```
// Add Label, TextField and Buttons
TextDialog = new Dialog(this, "Text", true);
TextDialog.setLayout(new GridLayout(2, 2, 10, 10));
TextDialog.add(new Label("Enter Title:", Label.RIGHT));
NewText = new TextField(20);
TextDialog.add(NewText);
TextDialog.add(new Button("Okay"));
TextDialog.add(new Button("Cancel"));
TextDialog.reshape(200, 200, 200, 100);
```

Apart from the fact that this dialog box contains more controls, the layout is not that much different from the About dialog box of the previous example. This dialog box does differ from the previous example in that it returns a string of text to the application or applet. Can you see where this takes place in the following portion of code?

```
if (event.target instanceof Button) {
  if(label.equals("Okay")) {
    mystring = NewText.getText();
    TextDialog.hide();
    newcanvas.repaint();
   .
   .
   .
```

The *mystring* variable was declared **static** so that its information could be shared with the graphics functions used in the new canvas. Here is the portion of code that draws the string of text on the new canvas.

```
.
.
.
graphic.drawString(MyFrame.mystring, 100, 400);
```

Figure 14.10 shows the dialog box which allows text entry and the graphics on the canvas.

## Dialog 3

Many times you'll want to use dialog boxes to enter numeric information. This information can then be used to make numeric calculations or draw pie, bar, and line charts. In the following example, two text fields are used to allow the user to enter integer values as strings. These string values are converted to integers and used to define the size of the graphics

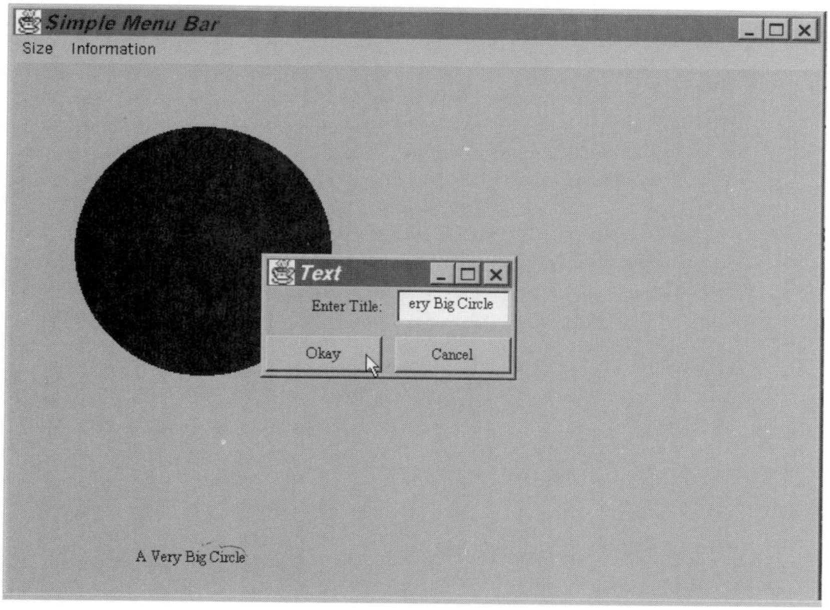


**Figure 14.10:** A dialog box that allows text entry is used in the Dialog2 example.

drawn to the canvas. Once again, pay particular attention to the bold text, since it represents the significant changes from the previous example.

```
//------------------------------------------------------------
// Dialog3 Dialog Integer/Float Demo
// Copyright 1996, All rights reserved
// Nineveh National Research
// Version: 1.0
// Author: Pappas and Murray
// Created: 4/26/96
//------------------------------------------------------------

import java.awt.*;
import java.applet.Applet;

public class Dialog3 extends Applet implements Runnable
{
  // initialize upon entry
  public void init()
  {
    new MyFrame("");
  }

  // Implements Runnable Interface
  public void run()
  {
  }

  // For running standalone
  public static void main(String[] argv)
  {
    // Create the frame and launch Dialog3
    Frame f = new Frame("Dialog3Frame");
    f.reshape(100, 100, 200, 100);

    //f.show();

    Dialog3 x = new Dialog3();
    f.add("Center", x);
    x.init();
    x.start();
  }
  // Constructor
  public  Dialog3()
  {
  }
```

```
} // end class Dialog3

class MyFrame extends Frame
{
  NewCanvas newcanvas;
  Dialog NumDialog;
  TextField NewNum1, NewNum2;
  static String mystring1, mystring2;

  MyFrame(String title) {
    // Add menu bar
    super("Simple Menu Bar");
    add("Center", newcanvas = new NewCanvas());
    reshape(0, 0, 639, 479);
    MenuBar menubar = new MenuBar();
    setMenuBar(menubar);

    Menu info = new Menu("Numbers");
    info.add(new MenuItem("Data..."));
    info.add(new MenuItem("-"));
    info.add(new MenuItem("Exit"));
    menubar.add(info);

    // Add Label, TextField and Buttons
    NumDialog = new Dialog(this, "Data", true);
    NumDialog.setLayout(new GridLayout(3, 2, 10, 10));
    NumDialog.add(new Label("Integer #1:", Label.RIGHT));
    NewNum1 = new TextField(20);
    NumDialog.add(NewNum1);
    NumDialog.add(new Label("Integer #2:", Label.RIGHT));
    NewNum2 = new TextField(20);
    NumDialog.add(NewNum2);

    NumDialog.add(new Button("Okay"));
    NumDialog.add(new Button("Cancel"));
    NumDialog.reshape(200, 200, 300, 150);

    show();
  }

  public boolean action(Event event, Object object) {
    String label = (String)object;
    if (event.target instanceof Button) {
      if(label.equals("Okay")) {
        mystring1 = NewNum1.getText();
        mystring2 = NewNum2.getText();
        NumDialog.hide();
        newcanvas.repaint();
```

```
      } else
      if(label.equals("Cancel")) {
        NumDialog.hide();
      }
      return true;
    } else
    if (event.target instanceof MenuItem) {
      if(label.equals("Data...")) {
        NumDialog.show();
      } else
      if(label.equals("Exit")) {
        System.exit(0);
      }
      newcanvas.repaint();
      return true;
    }
    else
      return false;
  }
}

class NewCanvas extends Canvas {
  public void paint(Graphics graphic) {
    int intx, inty;

    intx = Integer.parseInt(MyFrame.mystring1);
    inty = Integer.parseInt(MyFrame.mystring2);
    graphic.drawOval(50, 50, intx, inty);
  }
}
```

The first job is, of course, to design a properly laid out dialog box capable of accepting the two integer values. This is done in a manner similar to that in the previous example, since the integer values are entered as strings in a text field. You can see this in the following portion of code.

```
// Add Label, TextField and Buttons
NumDialog = new Dialog(this, "Data", true);
NumDialog.setLayout(new GridLayout(3, 2, 10, 10));
NumDialog.add(new Label("Integer #1:", Label.RIGHT));
NewNum1 = new TextField(20);
NumDialog.add(NewNum1);
NumDialog.add(new Label("Integer #2:", Label.RIGHT));
NewNum2 = new TextField(20);
NumDialog.add(NewNum2);
```

```
    .
    .
    .
```

When the "Okay" button is clicked, the string information is returned to *mystring1* and *mystring2*. Remember, this is how modal dialog box information is processed.

```
    .
    .
    .
mystring1 = NewNum1.getText();
mystring2 = NewNum2.getText();
    .
    .
    .
```

Before the graphics are drawn on the canvas, the string must be converted to actual integer data. This is fairly easy to do, as you can see in the following portion of code.

```
int intx, inty;

intx = Integer.parseInt(MyFrame.mystring1);
inty = Integer.parseInt(MyFrame.mystring2);
graphic.drawOval(50, 50, intx, inty);
```

Figure 14.11 shows this dialog box along with a corresponding graphics shape on the screen.

This dialog box and the dialog boxes in the previous examples will form the foundation for collecting data for the presentation graphics examples in the next chapter. You now have all of the tools for creating completely interactive applications and applets.

## Java Lingo

*About dialog box*—A special dialog box used to inform the user about the application, developer, and any copyright information.

*dialog box*—A dialog box allows your application or applet to take on a Windows appearance and provide a familiar and consistent interface to the user. Dialog boxes can by a major form for data entry.

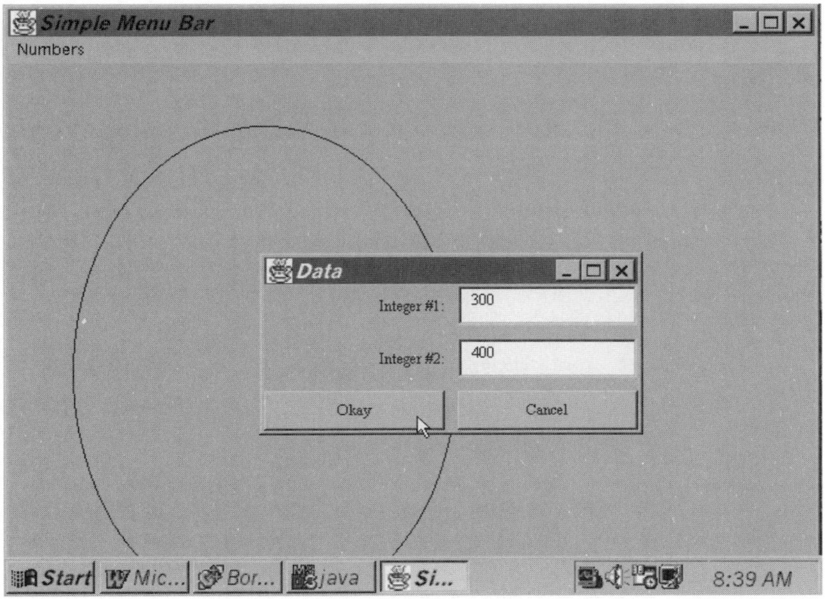


**Figure 14.11:** The numeric entry dialog box for the Dialog3 example.

*modal*—When referring to a dialog box, means that the dialog box will capture the focus of the application. Normal screen operation will not be returned until the dialog box is closed. This is the most frequently encountered mode of dialog box operation.

*modeless*—When referring to a dialog box, it means that the dialog box does not capture the complete focus. Normal screen operations can continue with the dialog box present on the screen. This mode is preferred when frequent changes are made to an applications operation.

*UI component*—These Java components are often called controls by the Windows programmer. We prefer the term controls to prevent confusion with the Abstract Component class. Controls include buttons, check boxes, radio buttons, labels, text fields, text areas, and so on.

# 15

# Presentation Graphics

This chapter will introduce two presentation graphics applications or applets that are the culmination of the graphical techniques taught across several past chapters. The bar chart and pie chart applications are robust examples using the graphical, color, font, menu, and dialog taught in Chapters 8 through 14.

In this chapter, you'll learn how to use all of the power of the Java language to build applications that function like professionally developed graphics applications used by Windows 95 or NT.

## A Presentation Quality Bar Chart

In Chapter 12, you studied the development of a simple bar chart program. That bar chart program generated a simple bar chart using fixed data. This was necessary because you did not learn how to include menu and dialog resources until the previous two chapters. That simple bar chart application can now be expanded to include both menu and dialog resources.

You might want to take a minute to return to Chapter 12 to study the bar chart components of that simple program. In this section, we'll concentrate on the efforts required to add the menu and dialog resources.

The base code for the bar chart application, BarCht, is created by the Borland Java AppExpert. All other code is then added to complete the application. If you have written Windows programs with the Borland C++ compiler, you know that these applications usually contain separate header, resource, and C++ source code files. They are compiled and linked together to form a final executable. Java applications and applets, such as the following example, are usually written in one file with a .java file extension. Since this is the case, listings tend to get quite long. If you are entering the following code from the text, take your time to do it carefully. Here is the complete listing for the BarCht example. As you examine the listing, notice that several areas have been set in a bold font for later discussion.

```
//--------------------------------------------------------
// BarCht Quality Bar Chart Application
// Copyright 1996, All rights reserved
// Nineveh National Research
// Version: 1.0
// Author: Pappas and Murray
// Created: 4/28/96
//--------------------------------------------------------

import java.awt.*;
import java.applet.Applet;

public class BarCht extends Applet implements Runnable
{
  // initialize upon entry
  public void init()
  {
    new MyFrame("");
  }

  // Implements Runnable Interface
  public void run()
  {
  }

  // For running standalone
```

```
  public static void main(String[] argv)
  {
    // Create the frame and launch BarCht
    Frame f = new Frame("BarChtFrame");
    f.reshape(100, 100, 200, 100);
    //f.show();

    BarCht x = new BarCht();
    f.add("Center", x);
    x.init();
    x.start();
  }

  // Constructor
  public  BarCht()
  {
  }

} // end class BarCht

class MyFrame extends Frame
{
  NewCanvas newcanvas;
  Dialog AboutDialog, LabelDialog,
         DataDialog, LegendDialog;
  TextField TitleText, VertText, HorzText;
  TextField Num1, Num2, Num3, Num4,
            Num5, Num6, Num7, Num8,
            Num9, Num10, Num11, Num12;
  TextField Leg1, Leg2, Leg3, Leg4, Leg5, Leg6,
            Leg7, Leg8, Leg9, Leg10, Leg11, Leg12;

  static String charttitle, vertlabel, horzlabel;
  static String[] legend = new String[12];
  static String[] height = {"1", "4", "2", "3", "0", "0",
                            "0", "0", "0", "0", "0", "0"};

  MyFrame(String title) {
    // Add menu bar
    super("Presentation Quality Bar Chart");
    add("Center", newcanvas = new NewCanvas());
    reshape(0, 0, 639, 479);
    MenuBar menubar = new MenuBar();
    setMenuBar(menubar);

    // Information menu and menu items
    Menu chtinfo = new Menu("Information");
    chtinfo.add(new MenuItem("About..."));
```

```
chtinfo.add(new MenuItem("-"));
chtinfo.add(new MenuItem("Exit"));
menubar.add(chtinfo);

// Data menu and menu items
Menu chtdata = new Menu("Data");
chtdata.add(new MenuItem("Labels..."));
chtdata.add(new MenuItem("Bar Heights..."));
chtdata.add(new MenuItem("Legend..."));
menubar.add(chtdata);

// About dialog box
AboutDialog = new Dialog(this, "About", true);
AboutDialog.setLayout(new GridLayout(4, 1, 5, 5));
AboutDialog.add(new Label("Bar Chart Application",
                          Label.CENTER));
AboutDialog.add(new Label("C. Pappas and W. Murray",
                          Label.CENTER));
AboutDialog.add(new Label("Copyright (c) 1996",
                          Label.CENTER));

AboutDialog.add(new Button("Okay"));
AboutDialog.reshape(200, 200, 300, 200);

// Label dialog box
LabelDialog = new Dialog(this, "Labels", true);
LabelDialog.setLayout(new GridLayout(4, 2, 5, 5));
LabelDialog.add(new Label("Title:", Label.RIGHT));
TitleText = new TextField("Title", 15);
LabelDialog.add(TitleText);
LabelDialog.add(new Label("Vert Axis Label:",
                          Label.RIGHT));
VertText = new TextField("Vert. Label", 15);
LabelDialog.add(VertText);
LabelDialog.add(new Label("Horz Axis Label:",
                          Label.RIGHT));
HorzText = new TextField("Horz. Label", 15);
LabelDialog.add(HorzText);

LabelDialog.add(new Button("Okay"));
LabelDialog.add(new Button("Cancel"));
LabelDialog.reshape(200, 200, 300, 175);

// Bar Heights dialog box
DataDialog = new Dialog(this, "Bar Data", true);
DataDialog.setLayout(new GridLayout(13, 2, 5, 5));
DataDialog.add(new Label("Height Bar #1:",
                         Label.RIGHT));
```

```
Num1 = new TextField("1", 10);
DataDialog.add(Num1);
DataDialog.add(new Label("Height Bar #2:",
                         Label.RIGHT));
Num2 = new TextField("4", 10);
DataDialog.add(Num2);
DataDialog.add(new Label("Height Bar #3:",
                         Label.RIGHT));
Num3 = new TextField("2", 10);
DataDialog.add(Num3);
DataDialog.add(new Label("Height Bar #4:",
                         Label.RIGHT));
Num4 = new TextField("3", 10);
DataDialog.add(Num4);
DataDialog.add(new Label("Height Bar #5:",
                         Label.RIGHT));
Num5 = new TextField("0", 10);
DataDialog.add(Num5);
DataDialog.add(new Label("Height Bar #6:",
                         Label.RIGHT));
Num6 = new TextField("0", 10);
DataDialog.add(Num6);
DataDialog.add(new Label("Height Bar #7:",
                         Label.RIGHT));
Num7 = new TextField("0", 10);
DataDialog.add(Num7);
DataDialog.add(new Label("Height Bar #8:",
                         Label.RIGHT));
Num8 = new TextField("0", 10);
DataDialog.add(Num8);
DataDialog.add(new Label("Height Bar #9:",
                         Label.RIGHT));
Num9 = new TextField("0", 10);
DataDialog.add(Num9);
DataDialog.add(new Label("Height Bar #10:",
                         Label.RIGHT));
Num10 = new TextField("0", 10);
DataDialog.add(Num10);
DataDialog.add(new Label("Height Bar #11:",
                         Label.RIGHT));
Num11 = new TextField("0", 10);
DataDialog.add(Num11);
DataDialog.add(new Label("Height Bar #12:",
                         Label.RIGHT));
Num12 = new TextField("0", 10);
DataDialog.add(Num12);

DataDialog.add(new Button("Okay"));
```

```
DataDialog.add(new Button("Cancel"));
DataDialog.reshape(200, 50, 200, 400);

// Legend dialog box
LegendDialog = new Dialog(this, "Legend", true);
LegendDialog.setLayout(new GridLayout(13, 2, 5, 5));
LegendDialog.add(new Label("Label Bar #1:",
                           Label.RIGHT));
Leg1 = new TextField("red", 10);
LegendDialog.add(Leg1);
LegendDialog.add(new Label("Label Bar #2:",
                           Label.RIGHT));
Leg2 = new TextField("blue", 10);
LegendDialog.add(Leg2);
LegendDialog.add(new Label("Label Bar #3:",
                           Label.RIGHT));
Leg3 = new TextField("yellow", 10);
LegendDialog.add(Leg3);
LegendDialog.add(new Label("Label Bar #4:",
                           Label.RIGHT));
Leg4 = new TextField("green", 10);
LegendDialog.add(Leg4);
LegendDialog.add(new Label("Label Bar #5:",
                           Label.RIGHT));
Leg5 = new TextField(10);
LegendDialog.add(Leg5);
LegendDialog.add(new Label("Label Bar #6:",
                           Label.RIGHT));
Leg6 = new TextField(10);
LegendDialog.add(Leg6);
LegendDialog.add(new Label("Label Bar #7:",
                           Label.RIGHT));
Leg7 = new TextField(10);
LegendDialog.add(Leg7);
LegendDialog.add(new Label("Label Bar #8:",
                           Label.RIGHT));
Leg8 = new TextField(10);
LegendDialog.add(Leg8);
LegendDialog.add(new Label("Label Bar #9:",
                           Label.RIGHT));
Leg9 = new TextField(10);
LegendDialog.add(Leg9);
LegendDialog.add(new Label("Label Bar #10:",
                           Label.RIGHT));
Leg10 = new TextField(10);
LegendDialog.add(Leg10);
LegendDialog.add(new Label("Label Bar #11:",
                           Label.RIGHT));
```

```
    Leg11 = new TextField(10);
    LegendDialog.add(Leg11);
    LegendDialog.add(new Label("Label Bar #12:",
                               Label.RIGHT));
    Leg12 = new TextField(10);
    LegendDialog.add(Leg12);

    LegendDialog.add(new Button("Okay"));
    LegendDialog.add(new Button("Cancel"));
    LegendDialog.reshape(200, 50, 200, 400);

    show();
  }

  public boolean action(Event event, Object object) {
    String label = (String)object;

    if (event.target instanceof Button) {
      if(label.equals("Okay")) {
        charttitle = TitleText.getText();
        vertlabel = VertText.getText();
        horzlabel = HorzText.getText();

        height[0] = Num1.getText();
        height[1] = Num2.getText();
        height[2] = Num3.getText();
        height[3] = Num4.getText();
        height[4] = Num5.getText();
        height[5] = Num6.getText();
        height[6] = Num7.getText();
        height[7] = Num8.getText();
        height[8] = Num9.getText();
        height[9] = Num10.getText();
        height[10] = Num11.getText();
        height[11] = Num12.getText();

        legend[0] = Leg1.getText();
        legend[1] = Leg2.getText();
        legend[2] = Leg3.getText();
        legend[3] = Leg4.getText();
        legend[4] = Leg5.getText();
        legend[5] = Leg6.getText();
        legend[6] = Leg7.getText();
        legend[7] = Leg8.getText();
        legend[8] = Leg9.getText();
        legend[9] = Leg10.getText();
        legend[10] = Leg11.getText();
        legend[11] = Leg12.getText();
```

```
          AboutDialog.hide();
          LabelDialog.hide();
          DataDialog.hide();
          LegendDialog.hide();
          newcanvas.repaint();
        } else
        if(label.equals("Cancel")) {
          AboutDialog.hide();
          LabelDialog.hide();
          DataDialog.hide();
          LegendDialog.hide();
        }
        return true;
      } else
      if (event.target instanceof MenuItem) {
        if(label.equals("About...")) {
          AboutDialog.show();
        } else
        if(label.equals("Labels...")) {
          LabelDialog.show();
        } else
        if(label.equals("Bar Heights...")) {
          DataDialog.show();
        } else
        if(label.equals("Legend...")) {
          LegendDialog.show();
        } else
        if(label.equals("Exit")) {
          System.exit(0);
        }
        newcanvas.repaint();
        return true;
      }
      else
        return false;
    }
  }

class NewCanvas extends Canvas {

  Font titlefont, labelfont, legendfont;
  FontMetrics fm;

  public void paint(Graphics graphic) {

    Color barColor[] = {Color.red,    // bar colors
                        Color.blue,
```

```
                    Color.yellow,
                    Color.green,
                    Color.cyan,
                    Color.white,
                    Color.magenta,
                    Color.orange,
                    Color.pink,
                    Color.gray,
                    Color.darkGray,
                    Color.black};
int iBarMax;
int oldBar[] = new int[12];
int newBar[] = new int[12];
int numBars = 0;
int maxBars = 12;
int newstart = 2;                // start position

// convert string to integer find # of bars
for(int i = 0; i < maxBars; i++) {
  oldBar[i] = Integer.parseInt(MyFrame.height[i]);
  if(oldBar[i] > 0) numBars++;
}

int width = 300 / numBars;       // width of a bar

// Find bar with highest value
iBarMax = oldBar[0];
for(int i = 0; i < numBars; i++)
  if (iBarMax < oldBar[i]) iBarMax = oldBar[i];

// Scale data values
for (int i = 0; i < numBars; i++)
  newBar[i] = oldBar[i] * 270 / iBarMax;

// create fonts
titlefont = new Font("TimesRoman", Font.BOLD, 36);
labelfont = new Font("TimesRoman", Font.PLAIN, 14);
legendfont = new Font("TimesRoman", Font.ITALIC, 10);

// draw coordinate axes
graphic.translate(99, 379);        // move origin
graphic.drawLine(0, -329, 0, 0);   // vert. axis
graphic.drawLine(0, 0, 329, 0);    // horz. axis

// draw and center chart title
graphic.setFont(titlefont);
fm = getFontMetrics(titlefont);
graphic.drawString(MyFrame.charttitle,
```

```
                        165 -
                        (fm.stringWidth(MyFrame.charttitle)/2),
                        -340);

    // draw vertical label and center horizontal label
    graphic.setFont(labelfont);
    fm = getFontMetrics(labelfont);
    graphic.drawString(MyFrame.vertlabel,
                        -10 -
                        fm.stringWidth(MyFrame.vertlabel),
                        -150);
    graphic.drawString(MyFrame.horzlabel,
                        165 -
                        (fm.stringWidth(MyFrame.horzlabel)/2),
                        40);

    // draw and fill bars
    for (int i = 0; i < numBars; i++) {
      graphic.setColor(barColor[i]);  // set fill color
      graphic.fillRect(newstart,      // draw a bar
                        -newBar[i],
                        width,
                        newBar[i] - 1);
      newstart += 2 + width;          // set new position
    }

    // draw, fill and label chart legend
    graphic.setFont(legendfont);
    for (int i = 0; i < numBars; i++) {
      graphic.setColor(barColor[i]);  // set fill color
      graphic.fillRect(360, -330 + (i * 30), 15, 15);

      // bar labels
      graphic.setColor(Color.black);  // set font color
      graphic.drawString(MyFrame.legend[i], 380,
                         -320 + (i * 30));
    }
  }
}
```

In the following sections we'll discuss the key aspects of this application's code and then examine several sample executions.

## Bar Chart Menus and Dialog Boxes

The techniques used to build the menu and dialog boxes for this application are the same as those discussed in Chapters 13 and 14. Let's look at several sections of the program code, each preceded by a comment.

// **Add menu bar**—the code under this comment is responsible for adding a new menu bar. Recall, from Chapter 13, that a new frame is created and that drawing will take place on a new canvas created on this frame. Two menus will be added to the menu bar. The first menu is the Information menu and the second is the Data menu.

// **Information menu and menu items**—the code under this comment adds a pop-up menu with two menu items and a separator bar. The user will use this menu to bring up an About... dialog box or Exit the application. Figure 15.1 shows the Information menu.

// **Data menu and menu items**—this code produces several data entry dialog boxes: Labels..., Bar Heights..., and Legends. Figure 15.2 shows this pop-up menu.

// **About dialog box**—this code describes the look and layout of the About dialog box. This code is patterned after the about dialog box code discussed in Chapter 14. The About dialog box uses a single Okay button. Figure 15.3 shows the About dialog box for this example.

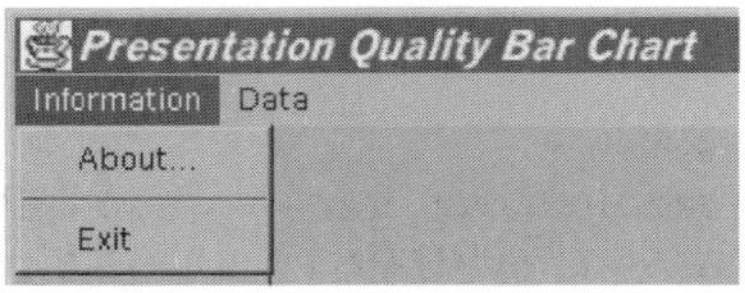


**Figure 15.1:** The Information menu allows the user to view an About dialog box or exit the application.

**Figure 15.2:** The Data menu allows the user to select any of three data entry dialog boxes.

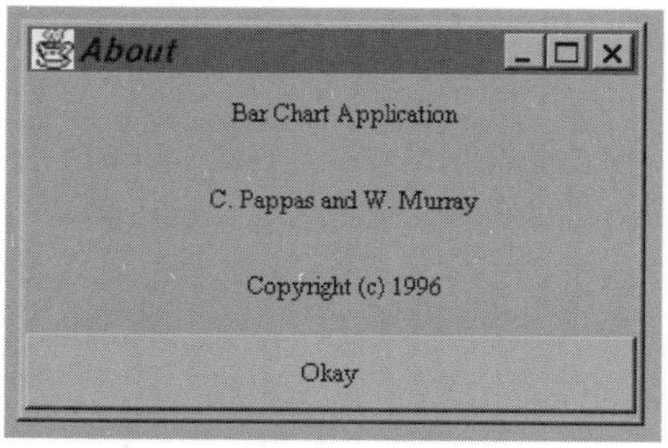


**Figure 15.3:** The About dialog box for the bar chart application.

// **Label dialog box**—this code is used to generate three labels and three text fields for various bar chart labels. Figure 15.4 shows the label data entry dialog box for this example.

Notice that this data entry dialog box supplies default labels and uses both an Okay and a Cancel button.

// **Bar Heights dialog box**—this code produces a data entry dialog box that allows the user to enter the height of each bar on the bar chart. Figure 15.5 shows an example of this dialog box.

Twelve bars are permitted on this bar chart, so twelve text fields and twelve labels are used in the dialog box's layout. Notice that this dialog box provides default values. The text information entered in the text entry controls will eventually be converted to integer values for plotting.

// **Legends dialog box**—this code produces a data entry dialog box that allows the user to enter twelve legend values. These legend values are then used to identify each

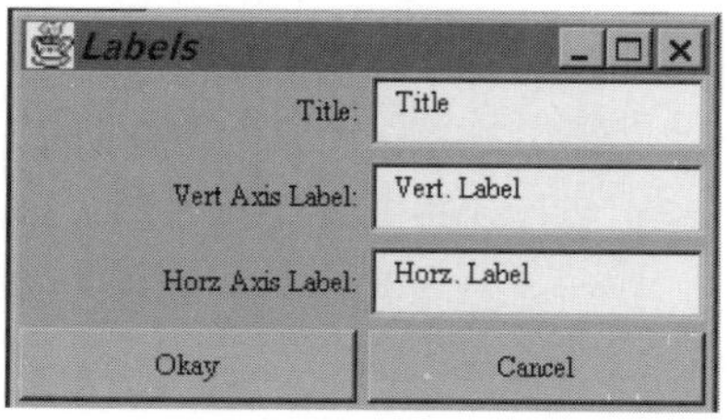


**Figure 15.4:** The label dialog box allows a chart title and axes labels to be entered by the user.

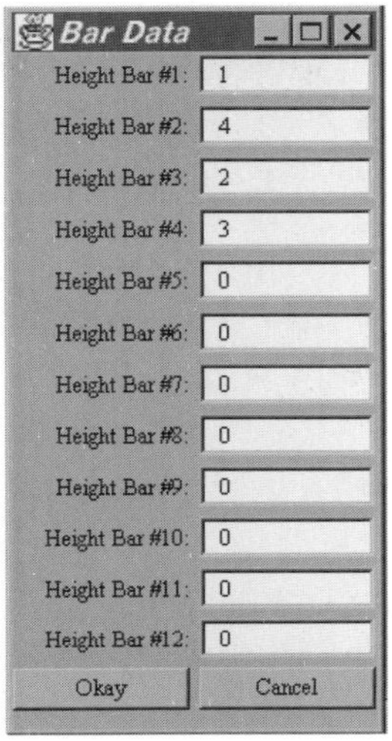


**Figure 15.5:** The Bar Data dialog box allows the user to enter each bar's relative height for the bar chart.

bar on the bar chart. Figure 15.6 shows an example of this dialog box.

Notice that this dialog box also provides default labels.

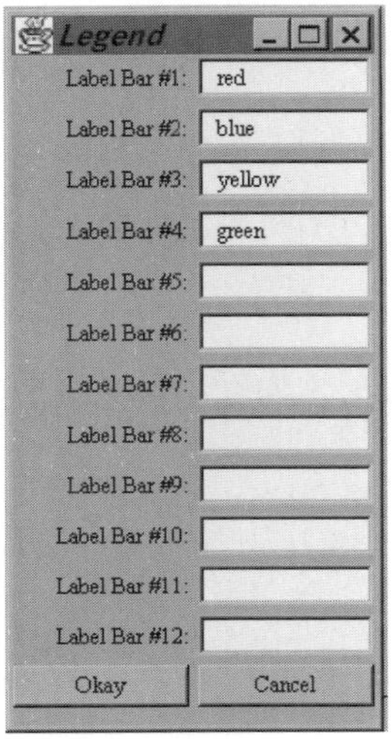


**Figure 15.6:** Twelve legend labels can be entered using the Legend dialog box.

As you have studied the code in the original listing, we're sure you have noticed that the techniques from Chapters 13 and 14 have been used without much modification. The main difference here is that this application uses two pop-up menus and four dialog boxes. As the number of menus and dialog boxes grows, so do the size and complexity of the listing. If you view each new addition as a building block, you will not become overwhelmed with the increased code size.

## Bar Chart Action Events

All of the dialog boxes are modal dialog boxes whose information is processed when a button control event occurs. In this example, an Okay button is used to intercept new information from any of the dialog boxes. Here is a small portion of the code used in the application.

```
    .
    .
    .
if (event.target instanceof Button) {
  if(label.equals("Okay")) {
    charttitle = TitleText.getText();
    vertlabel = VertText.getText();
    horzlabel = HorzText.getText();

    height[0] = Num1.getText();
    height[1] = Num2.getText();
      .
      .
      .
    legend[0] = Leg1.getText();
    legend[1] = Leg2.getText();
      .
      .
      .
    legend[11] = Leg12.getText();

    AboutDialog.hide();
    LabelDialog.hide();
    DataDialog.hide();
    LegendDialog.hide();
    newcanvas.repaint();
      .
      .
      .
```

This code uses the **getText()** member function to return three chart labels, up to twelve data values for bar heights, and up to twelve legend descriptions. The important thing to notice is that all of this information is returned in essentially the same manner. Once the information has been collected, the dialog boxes are hidden, the canvas is repainted, and the application awaits any further changes requested by the user.

In this application, there are four dialog boxes each with its own Okay button. No distinction is made between Okay button events; thus the application processes all dialog box information and attempts to hide all dialog boxes when any button event occurs.

Again, this code is built on the models developed in Chapters 13 and 14 for handling and processing menu and dialog box information—it's just bigger.

## Bar Chart Code

This section discusses the code responsible for creating the bar graph itself. Recall that much of this code has already been developed and discussed in Chapters 10 and 12. We'll concentrate our discussion on blocks of important code preceded by a comment. All comments refer to the complete listing shown earlier in this chapter.

> // **convert string to integer find number of bars**—converts the information returned to the *height[]* array as a string to integer information stored in the *oldBar[]* array. A parser, **Integer.parseInt()**, is used to make the conversion. Up to twelve bars can be used on the bar chart, but the actual number is determined by scanning each entry looking for the first "0" value. The first zero value marks the end of the bar data. And, yes, that means for this example there can be no bar heights of zero! Each time a nonzero entry is found, the counter, *numBars*, is incremented.

Bar widths are determined by taking the horizontal drawing area used for bars and dividing it by the number of bars.

> // **Find bar with highest value**—Bar data is scaled to fit the parameters of the charting surface. The bar with the largest value will always be drawn to the maximum drawing height. All bars are adjusted proportionally to

this height. So the first job is to find the bar, in the array, with the greatest height. This is done with a simple **for** loop and **if** statement.

// **Scale data values**—this section of code takes the maximum bar value, just found, scales it to 270 pixels, and adjusts all other values proportionally. Again, a **for** loop is used.

Next, the chart's fonts are created. Then the coordinate axes are drawn along with the chart title and axis labels. See Chapter 12 for more details on the creation and use of fonts.

// **draw and fill bars**—this section of code selects a bar color from the *barColor[]* array, then draws the bar using the **fillRect()** member function. Values in the *newBar[]* array are used to denote the new horizontal positions and widths for each bar.

// **draw, fill, and label chart legend**—this code is used to draw a small rectangular icon, of the same color as the present bar, and then plot a bar legend label to the right of the icon. In this manner, each bar on the chart can be identified.

Applications that reach this size are best developed incrementally. You have seen this process at work as you have studied Chapters 10, 12, and 15. While the code has grown quite large, it has not become conceptually more difficult.

### Running the Bar Chart Application

Let's look at a few examples generated by this application. Figure 15.7 shows the default bar chart, with the default labels, bars, and legend.

Next, we'll experiment by changing the bar chart labels, increasing the number of bars, and writing meaningful legend labels. As you view Figure 15.8, remember that everything you read might not necessarily be true.

## A Presentation Quality Pie Chart

In Chapter 12, you studied the development of a simple pie chart program. That simple pie chart application can now be

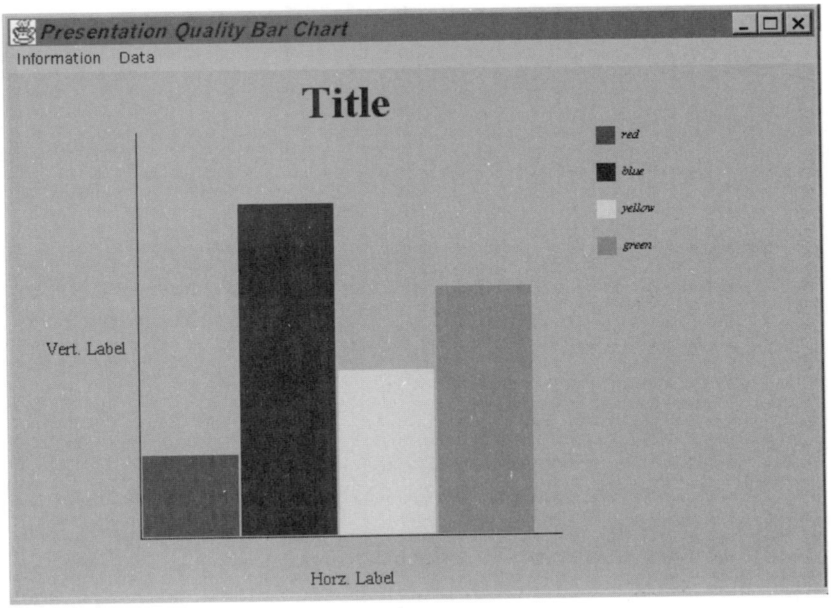


**Figure 15.7:** The default bar chart produced by the bar chart application.

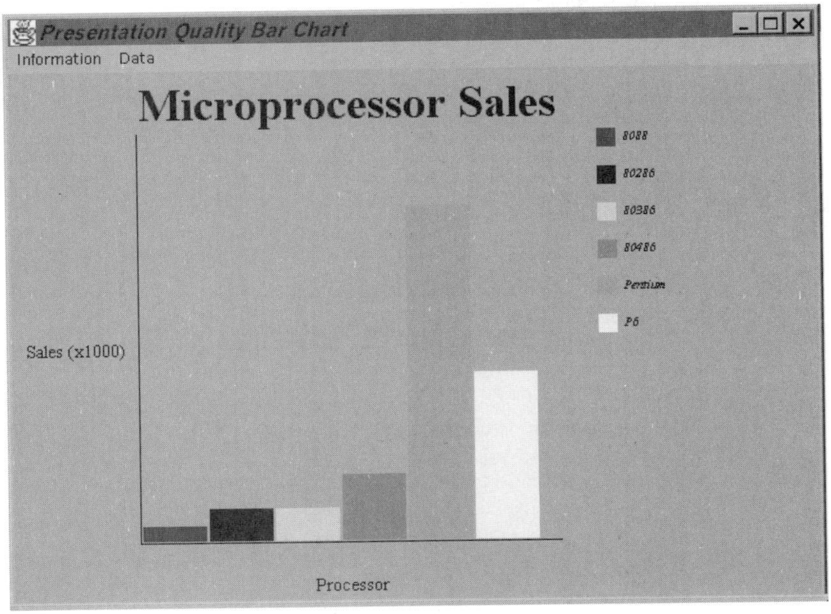


**Figure 15.8:** A unique bar chart demonstrates the range of values that can be used when plotting bar chart data.

expanded to include both menu and dialog resources. In this section, we'll concentrate on the efforts required to add the menu and dialog resources to the base code developed in Chapter 12.

The base code for the pie chart application, PieCht, is created by the Borland Java AppExpert. If you are entering the pie chart application from the following listing, take your time to do it carefully. Here is the complete listing for the PieCht example. As you examine the listing, notice that several areas have been set in a bold font for later discussion, as we did with the bar chart example.

```
//-------------------------------------------------------
// PieCht Quality Pie Chart App
// Copyright 1996, All rights reserved
// Nineveh National Research
// Version: 1.0
// Author: Pappas and Murray
// Created: 4/28/96
//-------------------------------------------------------

import java.awt.*;
import java.applet.Applet;

public class PieCht extends Applet implements Runnable
{
    // initialize upon entry
  public void init()
  {
    new MyFrame("");
  }

  // Implements Runnable Interface
  public void run()
  {
  }

  // For running standalone
  public static void main(String[] argv)
  {
    // Create the frame and launch PieCht
    Frame f = new Frame("PieChtFrame");
    f.reshape(100, 100, 200, 100);
    //f.show();

    PieCht x = new PieCht();
```

```
    f.add("Center", x);
    x.init();
    x.start();
  }

  // Constructor
  public  PieCht()
  {
  }

} // end class PieCht

class MyFrame extends Frame
{
  NewCanvas newcanvas;
  Dialog AboutDialog, LabelDialog,
         DataDialog, LegendDialog;
  TextField TitleText;
  TextField Num1, Num2, Num3, Num4,
            Num5, Num6, Num7, Num8,
            Num9, Num10, Num11, Num12;
  TextField Leg1, Leg2, Leg3, Leg4,
            Leg5, Leg6, Leg7, Leg8,
            Leg9, Leg10, Leg11, Leg12;

  static String charttitle = "Title";
  static String[] legend = new String[12];
  static String[] wedge = {"1", "2", "3", "4",
                           "0", "0", "0", "0",
                           "0", "0", "0", "0"};

  MyFrame(String title) {

    // Add menu bar
    super("Presentation Quality Pie Chart");
    add("Center", newcanvas = new NewCanvas());
    reshape(0, 0, 639, 479);
    MenuBar menubar = new MenuBar();
    setMenuBar(menubar);

    // Information menu and menu items
    Menu chtinfo = new Menu("Information");
    chtinfo.add(new MenuItem("About..."));
    chtinfo.add(new MenuItem("-"));
    chtinfo.add(new MenuItem("Exit"));
    menubar.add(chtinfo);
```

```
// Data menu and menu items
Menu chtdata = new Menu("Data");
chtdata.add(new MenuItem("Label..."));
chtdata.add(new MenuItem("Pie Wedges..."));
chtdata.add(new MenuItem("Legend..."));
menubar.add(chtdata);

// About dialog box
AboutDialog = new Dialog(this, "About", true);
AboutDialog.setLayout(new GridLayout(4, 1, 5, 5));
AboutDialog.add(new Label("Pie Chart Application",
                          Label.CENTER));
AboutDialog.add(new Label("C. Pappas and W. Murray",
                          Label.CENTER));
AboutDialog.add(new Label("Copyright (c) 1996",
                          Label.CENTER));

AboutDialog.add(new Button("Okay"));
AboutDialog.reshape(200, 200, 300, 200);

// Label dialog box
LabelDialog = new Dialog(this, "Label", true);
LabelDialog.setLayout(new GridLayout(2, 2, 5, 5));
LabelDialog.add(new Label("Title:", Label.RIGHT));
TitleText = new TextField("Title", 15);
LabelDialog.add(TitleText);

LabelDialog.add(new Button("Okay"));
LabelDialog.add(new Button("Cancel"));
LabelDialog.reshape(200, 200, 300, 100);

// Pie Wedge dialog box
DataDialog = new Dialog(this, "Pie Data", true);
DataDialog.setLayout(new GridLayout(13, 2, 5, 5));
DataDialog.add(new Label("Wedge #1:",
                         Label.RIGHT));
Num1 = new TextField("1", 10);
DataDialog.add(Num1);
DataDialog.add(new Label("Wedge #2:",
                         Label.RIGHT));
Num2 = new TextField("2", 10);
DataDialog.add(Num2);
DataDialog.add(new Label("Wedge #3:",
                         Label.RIGHT));
Num3 = new TextField("3", 10);
DataDialog.add(Num3);
DataDialog.add(new Label("Wedge #4:",
                         Label.RIGHT));
```

```
Num4 = new TextField("4", 10);
DataDialog.add(Num4);
DataDialog.add(new Label("Wedge #5:",
                         Label.RIGHT));
Num5 = new TextField("0", 10);
DataDialog.add(Num5);
DataDialog.add(new Label("Wedge #6:",
                         Label.RIGHT));
Num6 = new TextField("0", 10);
DataDialog.add(Num6);
DataDialog.add(new Label("Wedge #7:",
                         Label.RIGHT));
Num7 = new TextField("0", 10);
DataDialog.add(Num7);
DataDialog.add(new Label("Wedge #8:",
                         Label.RIGHT));
Num8 = new TextField("0", 10);
DataDialog.add(Num8);
DataDialog.add(new Label("Wedge #9:",
                         Label.RIGHT));
Num9 = new TextField("0", 10);
DataDialog.add(Num9);
DataDialog.add(new Label("Wedge #10:",
                         Label.RIGHT));
Num10 = new TextField("0", 10);
DataDialog.add(Num10);
DataDialog.add(new Label("Wedge #11:",
                         Label.RIGHT));
Num11 = new TextField("0", 10);
DataDialog.add(Num11);
DataDialog.add(new Label("Wedge #12:",
                         Label.RIGHT));
Num12 = new TextField("0", 10);
DataDialog.add(Num12);

DataDialog.add(new Button("Okay"));
DataDialog.add(new Button("Cancel"));
DataDialog.reshape(200, 50, 200, 400);

// Legend dialog box
LegendDialog = new Dialog(this, "Legend", true);
LegendDialog.setLayout(new GridLayout(13, 2, 5, 5));
LegendDialog.add(new Label("Wedge Label #1:",
                           Label.RIGHT));
Leg1 = new TextField("red", 10);
LegendDialog.add(Leg1);
LegendDialog.add(new Label("Wedge Label #2:",
                           Label.RIGHT));
```

```
Leg2 = new TextField("blue", 10);
LegendDialog.add(Leg2);
LegendDialog.add(new Label("Wedge Label #3:",
                           Label.RIGHT));
Leg3 = new TextField("yellow", 10);
LegendDialog.add(Leg3);
LegendDialog.add(new Label("Wedge Label #4:",
                           Label.RIGHT));
Leg4 = new TextField("green", 10);
LegendDialog.add(Leg4);
LegendDialog.add(new Label("Wedge Label #5:",
                           Label.RIGHT));
Leg5 = new TextField(10);
LegendDialog.add(Leg5);
LegendDialog.add(new Label("Wedge Label #6:",
                           Label.RIGHT));
Leg6 = new TextField(10);
LegendDialog.add(Leg6);
LegendDialog.add(new Label("Wedge Label #7:",
                           Label.RIGHT));
Leg7 = new TextField(10);
LegendDialog.add(Leg7);
LegendDialog.add(new Label("Wedge Label #8:",
                           Label.RIGHT));
Leg8 = new TextField(10);
LegendDialog.add(Leg8);
LegendDialog.add(new Label("Wedge Label #9:",
                           Label.RIGHT));
Leg9 = new TextField(10);
LegendDialog.add(Leg9);
LegendDialog.add(new Label("Wedge Label #10:",
                           Label.RIGHT));
Leg10 = new TextField(10);
LegendDialog.add(Leg10);
LegendDialog.add(new Label("Wedge Label #11:",
                           Label.RIGHT));
Leg11 = new TextField(10);
LegendDialog.add(Leg11);
LegendDialog.add(new Label("Wedge Label #12:",
                           Label.RIGHT));
Leg12 = new TextField(10);
LegendDialog.add(Leg12);

LegendDialog.add(new Button("Okay"));
LegendDialog.add(new Button("Cancel"));
LegendDialog.reshape(200, 50, 200, 400);

show();
```

```
}
public boolean action(Event event, Object object) {
  String label = (String)object;

  if (event.target instanceof Button) {
    if(label.equals("Okay")) {
      charttitle = TitleText.getText();

      wedge[0] = Num1.getText();
      wedge[1] = Num2.getText();
      wedge[2] = Num3.getText();
      wedge[3] = Num4.getText();
      wedge[4] = Num5.getText();
      wedge[5] = Num6.getText();
      wedge[6] = Num7.getText();
      wedge[7] = Num8.getText();
      wedge[8] = Num9.getText();
      wedge[9] = Num10.getText();
      wedge[10] = Num11.getText();
      wedge[11] = Num12.getText();

      legend[0] = Leg1.getText();
      legend[1] = Leg2.getText();
      legend[2] = Leg3.getText();
      legend[3] = Leg4.getText();
      legend[4] = Leg5.getText();
      legend[5] = Leg6.getText();
      legend[6] = Leg7.getText();
      legend[7] = Leg8.getText();
      legend[8] = Leg9.getText();
      legend[9] = Leg10.getText();
      legend[10] = Leg11.getText();
      legend[11] = Leg12.getText();

      AboutDialog.hide();
      LabelDialog.hide();
      DataDialog.hide();
      LegendDialog.hide();
      newcanvas.repaint();
    } else
    if(label.equals("Cancel")) {
      AboutDialog.hide();
      LabelDialog.hide();
      DataDialog.hide();
      LegendDialog.hide();
    }
    return true;
  } else
```

```
    if (event.target instanceof MenuItem) {
      if(label.equals("About...")) {
        AboutDialog.show();
      } else
      if(label.equals("Label...")) {
        LabelDialog.show();
      } else
      if(label.equals("Pie Wedges...")) {
        DataDialog.show();
      } else
      if(label.equals("Legend...")) {
        LegendDialog.show();
      } else
      if(label.equals("Exit")) {
        System.exit(0);
      }
      newcanvas.repaint();
      return true;
    }
    else
      return false;
  }
}

class NewCanvas extends Canvas {

  Font titlefont, legendfont;
  FontMetrics fm;

  public void paint(Graphics graphic) {

    Color sliceColor[] = {Color.red,   // pie colors
                          Color.blue,
                          Color.yellow,
                          Color.green,
                          Color.cyan,
                          Color.white,
                          Color.magenta,
                          Color.orange,
                          Color.pink,
                          Color.gray,
                          Color.darkGray,
                          Color.black};
    int numWedges = 0;
    int oWeg[] = new int[12];
    int nWeg[] = new int[13];

    int maxWedge = 12;
```

```
int tWeg = 0;
int startAngle = 0;
int sweepAngle = 0;

graphic.translate(100, 90);         // move origin

// convert string to integer find # of wedges
for(int i = 0; i < maxWedge; i++) {
  oWeg[i] = Integer.parseInt(MyFrame.wedge[i]);
  if (oWeg[i] > 0) numWedges++;
}

for (int i = 0; i < numWedges; i++)
  tWeg += oWeg[i];

for (int i = 0; i < numWedges; i++)
  nWeg[i] = (int)Math.round((double)(oWeg[i]*360)/tWeg);

sweepAngle = nWeg[0];

// create fonts
titlefont = new Font("TimesRoman", Font.BOLD, 36);
legendfont = new Font("TimesRoman", Font.ITALIC, 10);

// draw and center chart title
graphic.setFont(titlefont);
fm = getFontMetrics(titlefont);

graphic.drawString(MyFrame.charttitle,
                   165 -
                   (fm.stringWidth(MyFrame.charttitle)/2),
                   -25);

// draw and fill pie slices
for (int i = 0; i < numWedges; ++i) {
  graphic.setColor(sliceColor[i]); // set fill color
  graphic.fillArc(0, 0, 300, 300,
                 startAngle, sweepAngle);
  startAngle += nWeg[i];
  sweepAngle = nWeg[i+1];
}

// draw, fill and label chart legend
graphic.setFont(legendfont);
for (int i = 0; i < numWedges; i++) {
  graphic.setColor(sliceColor[i]); // set fill color

  graphic.fillRect(360, -20 + (i * 30), 15, 15);

  // wedge labels
```

```
            graphic.setColor(Color.black);    // set font color
            graphic.drawString(MyFrame.legend[i], 380,
                               -10 + (i * 30));
         }
      }
   }
```

In the following sections we'll discuss the key aspects of this application's code and then examine several sample executions. You'll also discover that much of the work done in the previous bar chart example can be used again in the pie chart application.

## Pie Chart Menus and Dialog Boxes

The techniques used to build the menu and dialog boxes for this application are the same as those discussed in the bar chart example. Let's look as several sections of the program code, each preceded by a comment.

// **Add menu bar**—the code under this comment is responsible for adding a new menu bar. Remember that a new frame must be created and that drawing will take place on a new canvas created on this frame. Two menus will be added to the menu bar. The first menu is the Information menu and the second is the Data menu.

// **Information menu and menu items**—pop-up menus are added with this code. The user will use this menu to bring up an About... dialog box or Exit the application. Figure 15.9 shows the Information menu.

// **Data menu and menu items**—this code produces several data entry dialog boxes: Labels..., Pie Wedges..., and Legends. Figure 15.10 shows this pop-up menu.

// **About dialog box**—this code is used to describe the About dialog box. The About dialog box uses a single Okay button. Figure 15.11 shows the About dialog box for this example.

// **Label dialog box**—this code is used to generate one label and one text field for the pie chart title. Figure 15.12 shows the label data entry dialog box for this example.

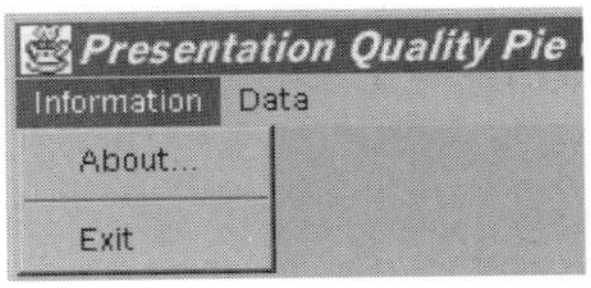


**Figure 15.9:** The Information menu allows the user to view an About dialog box or exit the application.

**Figure 15.10:** The Data menu allows the user to select any of three data entry dialog boxes.

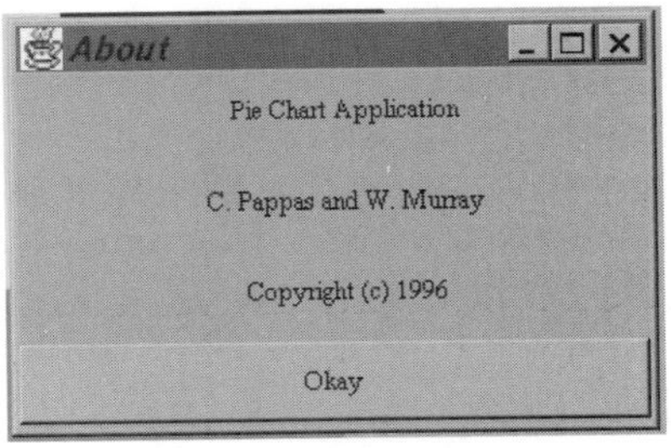


**Figure 15.11:** The About dialog box for the Pie chart application.

**Figure 15.12:** The label dialog box allows a chart title to be entered by the user.

Notice that this data entry dialog box supplies a default title and uses both an Okay and a Cancel button.

// **Pie Wedge dialog box**—this code produces a data entry dialog box that allows the user to enter the relative width of each pie slice on the Pie chart. Figure 15.13 shows an example of this dialog box.

Twelve slices are permitted on this pie chart, so twelve text fields and twelve labels are used in the dialog box's layout. Notice that this dialog box provides default values. The text information entered in the text entry controls will eventually be converted to integer values for plotting.

> // **Legend dialog box**—this code produces a data entry dialog box that allows the user to enter twelve legend values. These legend values are then used to identify each slice on the pie chart. Figure 15.14 shows an example of this dialog box.

This dialog box also provides default legend labels.

## Pie Chart Action Events

As in the bar chart example, all of the dialog boxes are modal dialog boxes. Their information is processed when a button control event occurs. The Okay button is used to fire an event for this processing. See the bar chart example for more details of this process.

In this section of code, notice that the **getText()** member function is used to return the chart title, up to twelve data val-

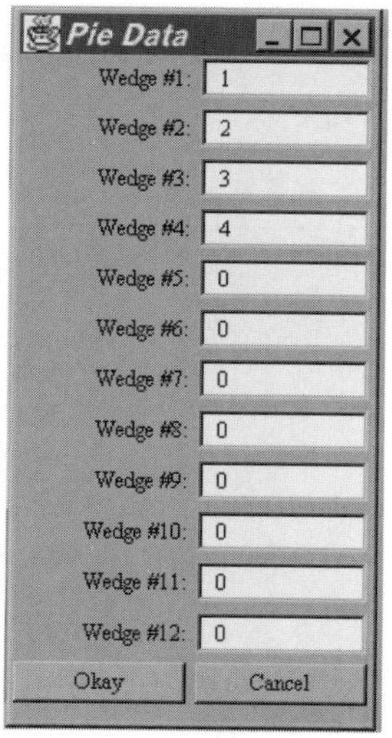


**Figure 15.13:** The Pie Data dialog box allows the user to enter each pie's relative width for the pie chart.

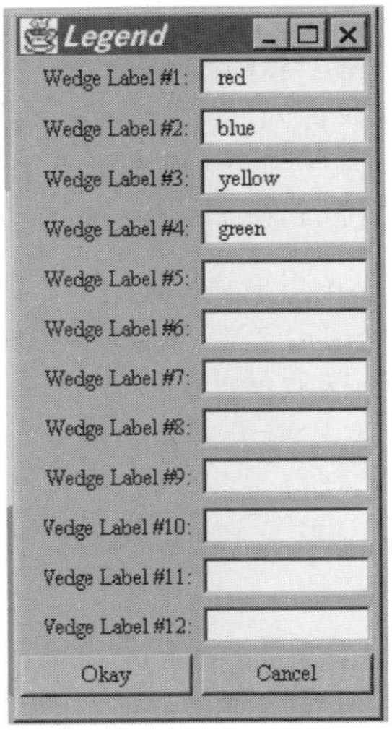


**Figure 15.14:** Twelve legend labels can be entered using the Legend dialog box.

ues for Pie wedges, and up to twelve legend descriptions. Once the information has been collected the dialog boxes are hidden and the canvas repainted.

As in the bar chart example, this application used four dialog boxes each with its own Okay button. No distinction is made between Okay button events from any of the dialog boxes. This means that the application processes all dialog box information and attempts to hide all dialog boxes when any Okay button event occurs.

## Pie Chart Code

The code for generating the pie graph, itself, will be discussed in this section. The pie graph discussed here has been under construction since Chapter 10. Many of the programming details have already been explained. We'll concentrate our discussion on blocks of important code that are preceded by a comment. All comments refer to the complete listing for the pie chart code shown earlier.

// **convert string to integer find # of wedges**—converts the information returned to the *wedge[]* array as a string to integer information stored in the *oWeg[]* array. A parser, **Integer.parseInt()**, is used to make the conversion. Up to twelve pie slices can be used on the pie chart, but the actual number is determined by scanning each entry looking for the first "0" value. The first zero value marks the end of the pie data. Each time a nonzero entry is found, the counter, *numWedges*, is incremented.

Pie widths are determined by first calculating the total number of individual width values, then dividing each slice by the number to form a proportional slice value. This is done with the use of two separate **for** loops, as you can see by examining the code.

Next, the chart's fonts are created, then the chart title is drawn.

// **draw and fill pies slices**—this section of code selects a slice color from the *sliceColor[]* array, then draws the slice using the **fillArc()** member function. Values in the *startAngle* and *sweepAngle* variables are used to denote the new starting positions and ending positions for each slice.

// **draw, fill and label chart legend**—this code is used to draw a small rectangular icon, of the same color as the present pie slice. A legend label is drawn to the right of the icon. In this manner, each pie slice on the chart can be identified.

## Running the Pie Chart Application

Let's look at a few examples generated by this application. Figure 15.15 shows the default pie chart, with the default labels, pies, and legend.

Next, we'll experiment by changing the pie chart title, increasing the number of slices, and writing meaningful legend labels. As you view Figure 15.16, remember that everything you read might not necessarily be true.

## What's Next

First, notice that this chapter doesn't have a Java Lingo section! There are no new concepts presented in this chapter. Each application that you have studied, even though quite large, is built upon the concepts presented in earlier chapters.

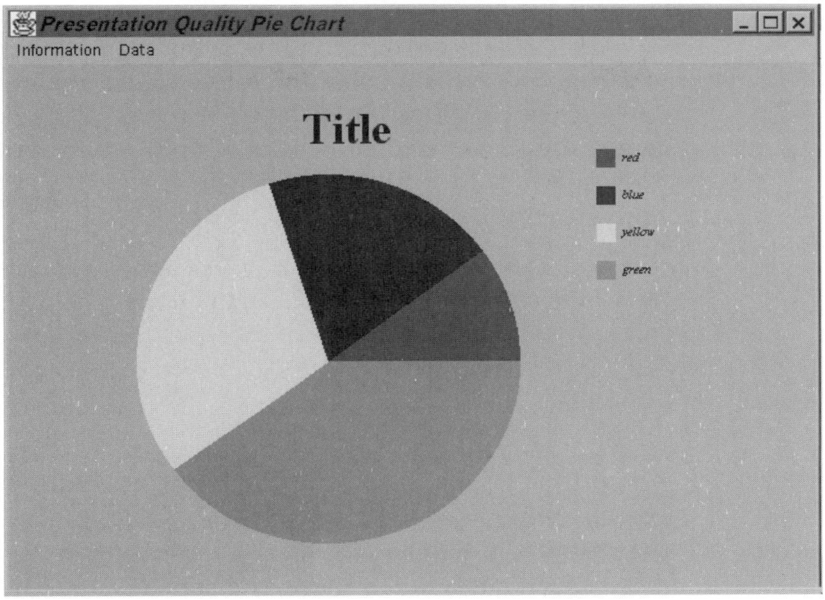


**Figure 15.15:** The default pie chart produced by the PieCht application.

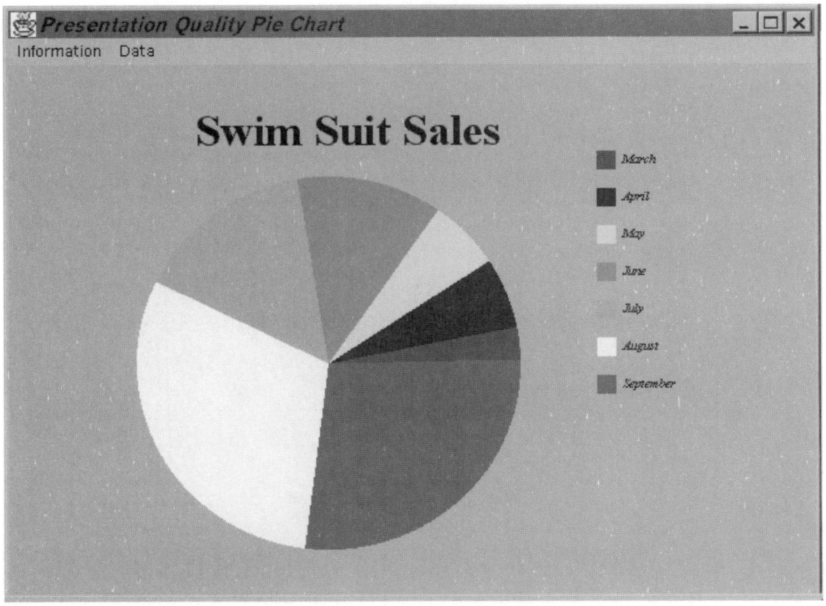


**Figure 15.16:** A unique pie chart demonstrates the unique values that can be used when plotting pie chart data.

So, what's next? It's up to you. You have studied all of the fundamental tools necessary to write robust Java applications. Use the examples in this chapter as a guide for developing your own unique applications.

There is only one topic left—animation. If your application demands motion during execution, you'll want to study the animation techniques presented in the next chapter.

# 16

# Threads and Animation

This chapter, like Chapter 15, combines the knowledge you have learned in earlier chapters with a few new programming concepts to create applets with animation. For example, in Chapter 4 you learned the concepts related to single and multiple threaded programs. In Chapter 10 you learned techniques for retrieving graphics files and then drawing those objects in an applet. In Chapter 11 you learned how to incorporate sound resource files into your project. We'll use these key concepts and a little programming knowledge to draw a few different images on the screen, then move them about with a timing method. Instant animation!

Specifically, this applet will use four images of a flying saucer with a little creature inside. As the saucer bounces off each edge of the screen, the creature will emit a yell (after all—it hurts). Four images are used to give the saucer and creature movement, within the larger context of moving the saucer about on the screen. All saucer movement is done with classical animation code, for this type of action.

## WHY THREADS?

In Chapter 4 you learned that threads can be used to allow multiple applets to run independently on the same screen. Threads are easy to add with the Borland Java AppExpert. If thread support is requested during the applet specification process, the AppExpert will add all necessary code.

Here is the Java AppExpert's template code, named NewThread, with thread support requested. We've boldfaced that portion of the listing that deals directly with threads and which was added by the AppExpert.

```
//-------------------------------------------------------------
// NewThread Template with Thread Capabilities
// Copyright 1996, All rights reserved
// Nineveh National Research
// Version: 1.0
// Author: Pappas and Murray
// Created: 5/9/96
//-------------------------------------------------------------

import java.awt.*;
import java.applet.Applet;

public class NewThread extends Applet implements Runnable
{

  // Variables for thread guards
  Thread thread = null;
  int count = 0;

  // Class initialization code
  public void init()
  {
    startThread();

  }

  void startThread()
  {
    if (thread == null)
    {
      // Start another thread on this object);
      thread = new Thread(this);
      // Will ultimately cause a separate thread to call
```

```
      // the run method
      thread.start();
    }
  }

  void stopThread()
  {

   if (thread != null)
    {
      thread.stop();
      thread = null;
    }
  }

  // Implements Runnable Interface
  public void run()
  {

    // This method is called when a new thread is
    // started (care of Runnable interface)
    // This is a waste of CPU resources
    while (true)
    {
      try
        Thread.sleep(1000);
      catch (InterruptedException e)
        ;
      repaint();
    }
  }

  // For running standalone
  public static void main(String[] argv)
  {
    // Create the frame and launch NewThread
    Frame f = new Frame("NewThreadFrame");
    f.reshape(100, 100, 200, 100);
    f.show();

    NewThread x = new NewThread();
    f.add("Center", x);
    x.init();
    x.start();
  }

  // Constructor
  public  NewThread()
```

```
  {
  }

} // end class NewThread
```

This applet contains the necessary code and methods for initializing (**init()**), starting (**startThread()**), and stopping (**stopThread()**) a thread. As you examine the previous listing, you'll also notice a **try/catch** block of code. This code is used to set a timer interval between moves of the saucer. When **Thread.sleep()** throws an exception, the exception will be caught by the catch portion of the code. In this case, an effective timer is created for each thread.

The previous portion really doesn't do much. However, if this base code is now integrated into our animation example, we'll be able to run multiple instances of the same applet independently of one another.

## THE SAUCER ANIMATION EXAMPLE

This applet uses code that you should be very familiar with. Examine the following listing carefully.

```
//-------------------------------------------------------
// Saucer Animation Demonstration
// Copyright 1996, All rights reserved
// Nineveh National Research
// Version: 1.0
// Author: Pappas and Murray
// Created: 5/7/96
//-------------------------------------------------------

import java.awt.*;
import java.applet.Applet;
import java.applet.AudioClip;

public class Saucer extends Applet implements Runnable
{
  Image saucer1, saucer2, saucer3, saucer4;
  AudioClip soundclip;
  Thread myThread;
  static int xPosInit, yPosInit, xStep, yStep;
  static int xPos, yPos;
  // Class initialization code
```

```
public void init()
{
  startThread();

  saucer1 = getImage(getCodeBase(), "images/BMP1.gif");
  saucer2 = getImage(getCodeBase(), "images/BMP2.gif");
  saucer3 = getImage(getCodeBase(), "images/BMP3.gif");
  saucer4 = getImage(getCodeBase(), "images/BMP4.gif");
  soundclip = getAudioClip(getCodeBase(),
                           "audio/sound.au");

  int xPosInit = 100;
  int yPosInit = 100;
  xStep = 2;
  yStep = 2;
  xPos = xPosInit;
  yPos = yPosInit;
}

// Mouse button pressed handling code
public boolean mouseDown(Event event, int x, int y)
{
  System.exit(0);
  return true;
}

// Key pressed
public boolean keyDown(Event event, int key)
{
  System.exit(0);
  return true;
}

public void startThread()
{
  if (myThread == null) {
  myThread = new Thread(this);
  myThread.start();
  }
}

public void stopThread()
{
  if (myThread != null) {
  myThread.stop();
  myThread = null;
  }
}
```

```
// This routine handles the painting
public void paint(Graphics graphic)
{
  xPos+=xStep;
  yPos+=yStep;

  // draw image 1
  int objwidth = saucer1.getWidth(this);
  int objheight = saucer1.getHeight(this);
  graphic.drawImage(saucer1, xPos, yPos, this);
  timedelay(50);

  // draw image 2
  objwidth = saucer2.getWidth(this);
  objheight = saucer2.getHeight(this);
  graphic.drawImage(saucer2, xPos, yPos, this);
  timedelay(50);

  // draw image 3
  objwidth = saucer3.getWidth(this);
  objheight = saucer3.getHeight(this);
  graphic.drawImage(saucer3, xPos, yPos, this);
  timedelay(50);

   // draw image 4
  objwidth = saucer4.getWidth(this);
  objheight = saucer4.getHeight(this);
  graphic.drawImage(saucer4, xPos, yPos, this);
  timedelay(50);

  // check left and right window edges
  if((xPos+objwidth > 640) ||
     (xPos < 0)) {
      xStep=-xStep;
      soundclip.play();
  }

  // check top and bottom window edges
  if((yPos+objheight > 480) ||
     (yPos < 0)) {
      yStep=-yStep;
      soundclip.play();
  }
}

void timedelay(int time) {
  try
    Thread.sleep(time);
```

```
    catch (InterruptedException e) {};
  }

  // Implements Runnable Interface
  public void run()
  {
    setBackground(Color.white);

    for (;;) {
      repaint();
      timedelay(100);
      xPos+=xStep;
      yPos+=yStep;
    }
  }

  // For running standalone
  public static void main(String[] argv)
  {
    // Create the frame and launch Saucer
    Frame f = new Frame("SaucerFrame");
    f.reshape(100, 100, 200, 100);
    f.show();

    Saucer x = new Saucer();
    f.add("Center", x);
    x.init();
    x.start();
  }

  // Constructor
  public  Saucer()
  {
  }

} // end class Saucer
```

In the **init()** method, the **startThread()** method is called and then several graphical resources and a sound resource are brought into the thread. Additionally, several variables are initialized for starting the saucer's movement.

The **mouseDown()** and **keyDown()** member functions are added to allow the user to terminate the applet by striking a key or pushing a mouse button.

The real programming action takes place under the paint() method, starting with the following portion of code.

```
xPos+=xStep;
yPos+=yStep;

// draw image 1
int objwidth = saucer1.getWidth(this);
int objheight = saucer1.getHeight(this);
graphic.drawImage(saucer1, xPos, yPos, this);
timedelay(50);
```

Each time the saucer is moved to a new screen location, a series of four saucer images is drawn with a 50 millisecond delay between images. Each of the four images moves an arm and changes a saucer light color. This gives the illusion that the creature within the saucer is having a panic attack at the thought of another collision with a screen edge. As you examine the listing, you'll notice four similar portions of code.

After the four images have been properly displayed, the xPos and yPos are checked against the screen boundaries. In this example, we hardwired the dimensions of a VGA screen into our code. You may choose to change these values to a smaller number, or determine them automatically for the screen size you are currently using. Hardwiring the values kept the coding much simpler. It is necessary to make two checks: one for the top and bottom collisions and one for the right and left collisions. Here is the portion of code that accomplishes that task.

```
// check left and right window edges
    if((xPos+objwidth > 640) ||
       (xPos < 0)) {
        xStep=-xStep;
        soundclip.play();
    }

    // check top and bottom window edges
    if((yPos+objheight > 480) ||
       (yPos < 0)) {
        yStep=-yStep;
        soundclip.play();
    }
```

The strategy is simply to change the direction of movement once a boundary is hit. The sound clip is played when any boundary is hit, making the user aware that the little creature has just suffered another rough encounter.

Each movement of the saucer requires that the old image be erased. In the following portion of code, this is done with **repaint()** without too much flicker on the screen. The time delay for the saucer movement, in addition to the delay inserted by drawing four different objects, is 100 milliseconds. The endless for() loop ensures that the saucer will continue to fly until the user terminates the application.

```
setBackground(Color.white);

for (;;) {
  repaint();
  timedelay(100);
  xPos+=xStep;
  yPos+=yStep;
}
```

The background color must be set to white in order to match the background color of each small graphic image.

A small HTML file is generated by the AppWizard since we plan to run this as an applet. Here is that code.

**Figure 16.1:** The creature and saucer moving about in a classical animation example written in Java.

```
<title>The Saucer Applet</title>
<hr>
<applet code=Saucer.class width=640 height=480>

</applet>

<hr>
<hr>
<a href="Saucer.java">The source.</a>
```

The width and height values have been changed to match the dimensions of a VGA screen.

Figure 16.1 shows our helpless creature flying about on the screen.

## What's Next

Well, this it! This is the last chapter. You are now ready to launch your creative efforts to build standalone applications or applets that you might use on your own home page. The potential for programs is limitless—it's all up to you.

# Index

## A

## D

## E



## F

## H



## I

## J

## K



## L

# W

## A 3.5-inch High-density Disk Offer

A 3.5-inch high-density floppy disk is available containing all of the program listings in this book. To use the disk, you need a computer capable of using a 3.5-inch high-density (1.44MB) disk, with the proper version of Windows properly installed and running. You must also be using the latest version of the Borland C/C++ compiler with the Java component installed.

To order the disk, send a bank check, money order, or personal check for $20.00 in U.S. currency to the address below. Please allow three weeks for personal checks to clear. No purchase orders can be accepted. For all foreign orders, outside North America, please include a check drawn on a U.S. bank (U.S. currency) for $25.00. Foreign orders will be sent via Air Mail.

*Please send me the program listings for this Java programming book by Pappas and Murray. Enclosed is a money order, bank check, or personal check for $20.00 ($25.00 for foreign orders) in U.S. funds, which covers the cost of the disk and all handling and postage. Sorry, no purchase orders can be accepted! This coupon may be copied. Note: Only 3.5-inch high-density (1.44MB) disks are available.

Mail to: **Nineveh National Research**
**Borland Java Disk Offer**
**P.O. Box 2943**
**Binghamton, NY 13902**

---

Name: ______________________________

Address: ______________________________

City: ______________________________

State: ____________________ ZIP: ______________

Country: ______________________________

---

This is solely the offer of the authors. Academic Press takes no responsibility for the fulfillment of this offer.